Spiritual Turning Points
of North American History

SPIRITUAL TURNING POINTS
OF NORTH AMERICAN HISTORY

Luigi Morelli

2010
LINDISFARNE BOOKS

Lindisfarne Books
An imprint of SteinerBooks/Anthroposophic Press, Inc.
610 Main Street, Great Barrington, MA 01230

Illustrated by Mira Fraser
Edited by Kristine Hunt
Cover Artwork by Angi Shearstone
Designed by Luigi Morelli

Library of Congress Cataloging-in-Publication data is available.

ISBN: 978-1-58420-097-0

CONTENTS

APPENDICES

Appendix 1

Appendix 2

Acknowledgments

I want to thank Joya Birns for her pre-editing, input, and constant support; Timothy Cox for his comprehensive overlook and courageous suggestions; Veronica Oliva-Clour for her encouragement and for inviting me to offer lectures before this manuscript was finished. Thanks to Stephen Clarke, Colin McEwan, Emory Michael for input, references, and bouncing off ideas on the topic.

INTRODUCTION

T HIS WORK will look at cardinal events—the spiritual turning points—of North American history. Classic historic research often points to these events without being able to substantiate their nature, their importance, and their far-reaching consequences. We will be concerned with two such turning points. The first one occurred in Central America some two thousand years ago. The second is a set of events that occurred in two places in the continent at a time preceding European colonization. These turning points set the stage for North American modern times.

For most Americans of the Northern and Southern continents the name Vitzliputzli—the initiate of the Americas at the time of Christ—is completely unfamiliar. Those who have heard the name may know just the few things that Rudolf Steiner mentioned in two lectures given in 1916.[1] There, Steiner surveys facts and events said to have occurred two thousand years ago. At the time of Christ an initiate fought against the practices of black magic that had reached an apogee in certain forms of human sacrifice. His life and deeds carried consequences for the whole of the Americas. Even if history did not record his name, an individual of such alleged importance as Vitzliputzli would have left many traces. This work will gather the strands that point toward the existence of this legendary-historical individuality. We will do so by first following the indications of native legends throughout the Americas. Different myths and legends in North, Central, and South America seem to point to the same individual. How is it possible that his presence is recorded throughout these continents? And where did this individuality live?

The lack of specific records of Vitzliputzli seems to leave us with no answers to these questions. Fortunately, we will see that the continent has preserved an invaluable document, the Popol Vuh, undoubtedly the most important esoteric writing of the Americas. The Popol Vuh retraces in mythical language the stages of civilization that all of America has undergone to some degree or another. These stages are known as the Four Ages by the Maya and Inca, and as the Four Worlds by the Hopi. The Aztecs added to these a Fifth Sun.

The Popol Vuh is a very important historical record that can help us retrace American mythology and history. In addition, this research would not have been possible without the work of Rafael Girard, who penetrated Mayan culture with an interest going beyond the academic. He could discern that tradition has preserved to this day much of the ancient knowledge within Mayan rituals, because his understanding could rise from the factual-scientific to the imaginative level where Mayan and Native American consciousness lives. In his work he confirmed mythology through an interdisciplinary use of archaeology, anthropology and linguistics. His discoveries indirectly confirm Steiner's indications that an event of central importance once occurred in Central America. With the help of Girard's work as a starting point we can have a very precise idea of the roots of Mayan and Native American spirituality and their common sources. Recognizing the origins of much of Native American spirituality will paradoxically help us understand how various religions at the same point in time or the religion of the same people over the course of time can be so diametrically opposed. These oppositions in fact are the greatest source of confusion in the study of American religions and history. Similar names can refer to different beings, justifying very different, or even diametrically opposed kinds of religious practices.

Through Girard's little-known contribution to Mesoamerican archaeology, and what Steiner's spiritual science can add to the interpretation of the facts that he and others have unearthed, it is now possible to lay the foundation for the history of the spiritual forces that have stirred the American continent from the time of Christ to the arrival of the conquistadors and beyond. Girard's knowledge of the interconnections between religion and myth is an invaluable documentary source. Even though in various instances spiritual science offers us different insights than the ones he reaches, he nevertheless remains the best source of data and esoteric material.

In a first step we will attempt to penetrate the different layers of Mayan esotericism and compare them with what Steiner has to say. Taking this step in the understanding of Mesoamerican spirituality will allow us to locate with a great degree of certainty the central ceremonial center of the Americas from which Vitzliputzli operated.

After reviewing myth and before entering history proper, we will attempt to reach a deeper understanding of the nature of the being that Steiner calls Vitzliputzli. This is a great undertaking, one that can only be definitely resolved with the help of clairvoyant consciousness. Nothing else could provide "proof." Therefore, everything we will bring forth will have the value of supporting evidence. In the process it will appear that spiritual science and Mayan esotericism speak two parallel languages.

It is the scope of the second part of the work to research the rise of new spiritual influences around the time preceding the discovery of America by Columbus. We will see that the decadent Mexican Mysteries re-emerged just like they had before the time of Christ. They did so in a new way, in what became the Aztec Empire. Other forces opposed them, particularly in the north through the Iroquois League. Both political systems had many obvious links with the esoteric knowledge of the Popol Vuh. The Iroquois Mysteries have been analyzed in my previous book, *Hidden America*. Whereas there they were examined in relation to their interactions with and influence over the colonial experience, here their meaning is deepened from the perspective of the contrast between Iroquois and Aztecs.

It is not my claim to be in any way exhaustive on the theme of the American Mysteries. More will appear in the future about this topic, of which this work is a mere beginning. From the time of the original Mexican Mysteries and the time of the conquest our gaze will point to the present. How does the legacy of these Mysteries affect us all at a global level? How do they continue in a modified way in our modern world?

The Mexican Mysteries are as much a legacy of the past as an important source of knowledge for the future. The American continent has undergone a very unique historical development that differentiates it from the rest of the world for a very simple reason. Europe, and to a certain degree Africa and Asia, knew of the deed of the Christ simply because of geographical proximity that facilitated the spread of this knowledge. America may certainly have heard about it to a very limited extent through the migrations coming from Europe. However, most of American mythology points not to the Christ Jesus, but to the initiate that lived in this continent at the time of Christ. The Mexican Mysteries seem to acquire a larger importance through time. They were primarily Mexican Mysteries at the time of Christ. Their influence spread much further fifteen centuries later, justifying our calling them American Mysteries. Finally, as we will see in the third part of this work, the Mexican and American Mysteries foreshadow the developments that humanity is undergoing at the present time.

Contrary to European history, where events have been recorded and understood in chronological fashion in the last three thousand years,

American history lives in the twilight between fact and imagination. Therefore, we invite our reader to take a step into the world of the Native American. Facts of historical importance occurred at unspecified times and acquired what seems to have magical qualities. This in fact corresponded to the outlook and concrete perception of the Native American, a perception that encompassed facts together with their spiritual imprints. Central to the understanding of this book is knowledge of the Popol Vuh. A summary of the book is offered here, at the beginning of every new topic in order to invite the reader to see America's past through the eyes of its original inhabitants.

A word of caution is added here for those who may have read this book when it was first published by Trafford. A minor change appears in chapter 7, under the heading titled "Individuality of the Initiate: a Hypothesis." The hypothesis there presented followed the arguments presented by Lievegoed in *The Battle for the Soul*. I had not pursued in depth research myself on this matter. A couple of individuals who read the book in the early days alerted me to research they had conducted on the matter, pointing to the separate destinies of the eternal individualities of those known as Manu on one hand and Mani on the other. The latter incarnated historically in the second century AD. Having followed their arguments, and agreed with their conclusions, I have omitted the hypothesis previously formulated. What appears under that heading remains nevertheless hypothetical.

PART I

AMERICAN PREHISTORY

CHAPTER 1

Prophet Legends
across the Americas

ALL ACROSS the Americas legends exist of a being with a mixture of attributes, which make him both mortal and immortal. His birth, when mentioned, almost always has a miraculous character. The mother is impregnated by a spiritual being in the form of a North or West wind, or other spiritual entity. Often she dies at birth and a grandmother raises the boy.

Our central character is very often called "the Prophet" for his ability to see both past and future. Likewise, numerous traditions call him "the Healer" and relate that he can cure the sick, give sight to the blind and restore the crippled by his word alone. In all myths he converses with the elements and animals and has power over them. Although endowed with super-earthly attributes, he definitely walks the earth as a man. Quite universally he is recognized as the civilizing hero who introduces many arts such as writing, farming and animal domestication, and astronomy. Some of his recurrent names are the Pale God or the Dawn God. Dawn God meaning in this case the god of the dawning of humankind, as we will see later. In many Native American cultures he either fights against monsters and beasts to bring peace, or does so by vanquishing the priesthood that practices human sacrifice.

Although his feats are most well known in Central America, echoes of them linger in all mythologies from Canada down to the southern Andes. A significant collection of his stories has been gathered by H. T. Taylor.[1] In the following section we will differentiate between North, South and Mesoamerica in a slightly different way than the geographical fashion of distinguishing northern, southern and central parts of the continent.

Mesoamerica in this section corresponds to the area that covers all of Mexico and most of Central America. This characterization reflects the common history that these two regions share.

NORTH AMERICA: GLOOSKAP, MANABOZHO AND "HIAWATHA"

Many of us may remember the verses:

> There he sang of Hiawatha,
> Sang the song of Hiawatha,
> Sang his wondrous birth and being,
> How he prayed and how he fasted,
> How he lived, and toiled, and suffered,
> That the tribes of men might prosper,
> That he might advance his people.

It may cause some surprise that an example of the mythology of the Prophet is actually quite familiar to Americans: the famous Hiawatha of Longfellow. There are many reasons why we might not immediately recognize the being of Hiawatha. Longfellow drew his inspiration from H. R. Schoolcraft's *Indian Stories*.[2] We know from his diaries that he wove the story of Hiawatha together with many other native legends.[3] Finally, the name of Hiawatha itself is another source of confusion. The stories of Schoolcraft refer to the Algonquian hero Manabozho, whom Longfellow mistakenly associates with the Iroquois name Hiawatha. We will see later that Hiawatha is an individual living fifteen centuries after Manabozho. There are good reasons to confuse the two figures. Hiawatha's legend of the White Roots of Peace does in effect echo the figure of the Prophet, as we will see in chapter 3, Part II.

Schoolcraft calls Manabozho the "great incarnation of the north" (north of the US). He recognizes that this myth is the most widespread among the Indian nations. The rest of his odyssey is told through Longfellow's poem. From here onwards whenever Longfellow's Hiawatha is mentioned the reader should understand that we are actually referring to Manabozho.

Hiawatha's mother is said to be a virgin, his grandmother the daughter of the moon. The West Wind (Mudjekeevis), who impregnates the mother, causes her death at childbirth. The child grows up developing great gifts of observation and communion with animals and elemental beings. After reaching manhood Hiawatha wants to fight Mudjekeevis for causing his mother's death. Mudjekeevis, who cannot be killed, puts him to a test and gives him the mission of delivering his people from monsters and beasts (Chapter 3: Hiawatha's Childhood).

Hiawatha sets out on his new mission and fights against the great king fish Mishe-Nahma. The fish swallows him, but the hero kills the fish and is freed with the help of the squirrel and the seagull (Chapter 8: Hiawatha's Fishing). The next challenge comes through the encounter with the magician Megissogwon, the great Pearl-Feather, living across the Great Lake. Hiawatha is first challenged by the fiery serpents, which he shoots with his arrows. Then he oils the sides of his canoe to get through an area of pitch-water. After landing, Hiawatha finally overtakes the magician by striking an arrow at the tuft of hair upon his head, the only place where the Pearl-Feather is vulnerable. He can then strip him of his magic shirt of wampum shells (Chapter 9: Hiawatha and the Pearl-Feather). As the civilizing hero, Hiawatha is the one who introduces picture writing (Chapter 14: Picture-Writing).

With poetic feeling Longfellow also describes the hero as a prophet to his nation:

> I beheld, too, in that vision
> All the secrets of the future,
> Of the distant days that shall be…
> Then a darker, drearier vision
> Passed before me, vague and cloud-like;
> I beheld our nation scattered,
> All forgetful of my counsels,
> Weakened, warring with each other….
> (Chapter 21: The White Man's Foot)

Another staple of American lore is Glooskap. He too is an equivalent of Manabozho. In Micmac tradition Glooskap is said to have come from a country from the east, across the sea. He is a divine being in the form of a man. The North Wind impregnates the mother, and Glooskap lives with his mother and grandmother. Upon growing up, Glooskap teaches the Micmacs agriculture and animal husbandry. He is said to ride a granite canoe, a recurrent theme in many North American legends, indicating the ability to travel to the realm of the dead. The Micmacs in effect believe that Glooskap awaits them at their death.[4]

Other names for the being of Manabozho according to Schoolcraft are Inigorio and Micabo, according to different Indian tribes.[5] In the extensive research of L. T. Hansen, the prophet is called E-See-Co-Wah (Lord of Wind and Water) in Georgia, and Chee-Zoos (the Dawn God), in West Virginia. The Pawnees call him Paruxti; Wacona or Waicomah by the Dakotah; the Chippewa, Wis-Ah-Co; the Choctaw (Oklahoma), Ee-Me-Shee; the Yakima (Washington), Tacoma (the highest mountain is named after him); the Seri (Gulf of California), Tlazoma.[6]

A special mention should be made of Pueblo mythology. As the Pueblo have deep bonds with the Uto-Aztecan populations of Mexico, so they also share many common elements in their mythology. A theme that frequently reappears is of the boy who doesn't know his father and goes out seeking for him. Such is the story "Arrow to the Sun," here retold in full.

Long ago the Lord of the Sun sent the spark of life to earth. It traveled down the rays of the sun, through the heavens and it came to the pueblo. There it entered the house of a young maiden. In this way the Boy came into the world of men. He lived and grew and played in the pueblo. But the other boys would not let him join their games. "Where is your father?" they asked. "You have no father!" They mocked him and chased him away. The Boy and his mother were sad.

"Mother," he said one day, "I must look for my father. No matter where he is, I must find him." So the Boy left home. He traveled through the world of men and came to Corn Planter. "Can you lead me to my father?" he asked. Corn Planter said nothing, but continued to tend his crops. The Boy went to Pot Maker. "Can you lead me to my father?" asked the Boy. Pot Maker said nothing, but continued to make her clay pots. Then the Boy went to Arrow Maker, who was a wise man. "Can you lead me to my father?" he asked. Arrow Maker did not answer, but, because he was wise, he saw that the Boy had come from the Sun. So he created a special arrow. The Boy became the arrow. Arrow Maker fitted the Boy to his bow and drew it. The Boy flew into the heavens. In this way the Boy traveled to the Sun.

When the Boy saw the mighty Lord, he cried, "Father, it is I, your son!"

"Perhaps you are my son," the Lord replied, "perhaps you are not. You must prove yourself. You must pass through the four chambers of ceremony: the kiva of Lions, the kiva of Serpents, the kiva of Bees and the kiva of Lightning."

The Boy was not afraid. "Father," he said, "I will endure these trials." And so he endured these trials. When the Boy came from the kiva of Lightning, he was transformed. He was filled with the power of the sun. The father and his son rejoiced. The father said, "Now you must return to earth, my son, and bring the spirit to the world of men."

Once again the Boy became the arrow. When the arrow reached the earth the Boy emerged and went to the pueblo. The people celebrated his return in the dance of life.[7]

Similar to this legend is the story "The Twins Visit Tawa." Here we are told of the twin grandsons of Spider Woman, called respectively Puukonhoya, the Youth, and Palunhoya, the Echo. They too go in search of their father whom they don't know. Their first trial is an encounter with beings that guard the threshold: an old man, two angry bears and Gatoya, guardian of all snakes. Behind them the Closing Canyon bars the way. Having overcome all the obstacles they arrive at the abode of Tawa. The Sun God is angry at the intrusion and throws them into a flint oven where a fire rages. When he opens the door to the oven, the Twins leap out unscathed. By this Tawa knows that they are his sons.[8]

The element of the kivas where the initiation trials occur reappears in the tests undergone by the Twins in the realm of Xibalba—the Mayan underworld—as we will see from the retelling of the Popol Vuh. The theme of the oven where the Twins are thrown also reappears. Another element similar to Mayan mythology is the role of the Twins. The same archetypal story can be the feat of one or two youths. That there is no difference between the one or the two is elucidated by the fact that the single hero is often called the Youth or Puukonhoya. Even when the two appear together, it is the Youth who performs the active role throughout most or all of the story. The second Twin seems to be faithful to his name, the Echo.[9] It is too soon to elucidate this mystery. We will see that the Twins appear in the Popol Vuh in a similar fashion.

SOUTH AMERICA: THE TWO CREATIONS

Some of the best preserved Andean legends come from the Bolivian Altiplano called the Collao. Here was situated one of the most sacred cities of the time preceding the Incan civilization: Tiwanaku. It was probably the largest ceremonial center of South America. The chronicler Juan Betanzos took down the following legend:

> They say that in ancient times the land of Peru was dark and there was no light or day in it. In those times there dwelt there a certain people who owed allegiance to an overlord whose name they no longer remember. And they say that in those times when all was night in the land there came forth from a lake in the district called Collasuyu, a lord named Con Ticci Viracocha, bringing with him a certain number of people, though they don't remember how many. And after emerging from the lake he went to a place nearby, where is now the village they call Tiahuanaco in the Collao. And while he was there with his followers they say that he suddenly made the sun and the day and commanded the sun to follow the course that it does follow. Then he made the stars and the moon. They say that this Con Ticci Viracocha had emerged on an earlier occasion and that on this first appearance he made the heaven and the earth and left everything dark. It was then that he created this race of men who lived during the times of darkness. And this race did something which angered Viracocha, so he came forth the second time as has been said and turned that race and the overlord to stone as a punishment for the anger they had caused him.[10]

Although Con Ticci Viracocha performs a "creation," this is not a repetition of the first creation; rather it is a quickening or a "re-enlivening of creation" marked by the appearance of the sun, moon, and stars in the heavens. We can hear an account similar to the above from Cieza de Leon:

> Before the Incas ruled or had even been heard of in these kingdoms these Indians relate a thing more noteworthy than anything else that they say. They assert that they were a long time without seeing the sun and, suffering much hardship from this, they offered prayers and vows to those whom they held for gods, beseeching of them the

light they lacked. At this the sun very brilliant rose from the island of Titicaca in the great lake of the Collao, and all rejoiced. After this had happened they say that there suddenly appeared, coming from the south, a white man of large stature and authoritative demeanor. This man had such great power that he changed the hills into valleys and from the valleys made great hills, causing streams to flow from the living stone. When they saw his power they called him Maker of all things created and Prince of all things, Father of the sun. They say that this man traveled along the highland route to the north, working marvels as he went and that they never saw him again. They say that in many places he gave men instructions how they should live, be good and to do no damage or injury one to another, but to love one another and show charity to all. In most places they name him Ticci Viracocha, but in the province of Collao he is called Tuapaca or in some parts of it Arunaua. In many places they built temples to him and in them they set up statues in his likeness and offered sacrifices before them. The huge statues in the village of Tiahuanaco are held to be from those times....

They have it from their forebears that wherever he passed he healed all that were sick and restored sight to the blind by words alone....[11]

The native chronicler Juan de Santa Cruz Pachacuti confirms the two previous accounts. He too talks about a bearded man with long hair, dressed with a long cloak. The ability to make springs burst from the ground is related in the legend of the Waters of Cacha, told by H. T. Hansen. Cacha is a city situated between Cuzco and Titicaca. There, during a drought, the prophet appeared to his people and set forth a spring thrusting his staff into the lava. The spring is known as the Fountain of Viracocha.[12]

A final point of interest comes from Calancha's *Cronica moralizada del orden de San Agustin en el Peru*. Here, apart from the previous recurring themes, we are also told that the hero, called Thunupa, came to fight against drunkenness, war and polygamy. He in fact opposed the black magician Makuri.[13] Juan de Santa Cruz Pachacuti mentions that, before their banishment by Viracocha, the idols that were worshipped required human sacrifice by their followers.[14] Mention of the fact that the prophet overcame the tradition of human sacrifice is made in legends from the city of Cacha, and from the coastal city of Pachacamac.[15]

The old Inca empire was not the only one to preserve the lore of the knowledge of the prophet. L. T. Hansen found memory of this being among the Amazon tribe of the Waikanoes. They call themselves with the name of the being, Waikano, whom they say was bearded, taught them the use of plants, and left them the ceremonies that they continued to practice.[16] Even more indicative are the legends of the Amuesha—an Amazonian tribe of Central Peru—who were in contact with the conquistadors from the very early stages of the conquest. It is among them that we find preserved a myth that gathers many of the motifs found in the central part of the Popol Vuh, one that is related to the deeds of the prophet. The Amuesha myth is of added interest because they belong to a completely different cultural group than the Inca. The myth is given in full in Appendix 1; here we will mention the main themes. The story is called "Yompor Ror and Yachor Arror," or "The Origin of the Sun and the Moon."[17] It is set at a time when "the world almost came to an end." Physical reproduction was threatened because the people had forgotten the will of the creator. A priest decided to raise a boy and a girl according to ritual procedure. Upon turning adult, the woman found two beautiful flowers, picked them up and became pregnant. The priest realized that this had been the work of the Grandfather Yos, the supreme deity. Soon after, the woman was killed by Patonell, the mother of jaguars. Before dying she managed to give birth to Twins, a boy and a girl. The armored catfish, Meshet, suckled the babies. The priest asked Sha'rep, the lizard, to fetch the Twins, and the lizard did this successfully. Nevertheless they would not grow, and one day they were entrusted to Patonell's care. The text specifies at this point that "they looked like children but were already adults." One day Patonell was going to cook them because she had no other meat. The Twins managed to deceive her and give her the beer that had been prepared for them by their "sister bee." In turn they slew the mother jaguar and buried some parts of her body in different places. The rest they cooked. When the other jaguars returned the Twins tricked them into eating the body of Patonell that they had cooked. The jaguars realized the deceit and went after the Twins. Finally, the Twins fled across a river through a bridge they had formed with their slings, and twisted its ropes when the jaguars ran across it. This spelled the end of the jaguars, which fell into the boiling waters of the lake. The Twins finally became adults, although in reality they had only pretended not to be able to grow. Afterward the two ascended to the heavens, where the girl became the moon and the boy the sun.

What is interesting about the above myth is the mention of a period of uncertainty and danger preceding the appearance of the Twins. The women were threatened with biological sterility. The ascension of the Twins marks the beginning of a new epoch of culture. The theme of the legend is also mirrored in a Carib myth of Guiana, and in a Chiriguano myth. A similar, shorter, Amazonian myth mentions a wondrous child instead of the Twins.[18] Alfred Metraux has compiled all the Twin myths of South America. The Twin theme, he says, occurs from Panama to the southernmost tip of the continent (e. g., myths of the Ona, Yaghan, Alakaluf) and from Brazil to Peru.[19] These myths can be broadly distinguished in two categories. In one of these the Twins are antithetical entities, a sort of brother-enemies. In others they play complementary roles. Only the second ones concern us here. Various elements often reappear as a common theme. The Twins' apotheosis is their transformation into sun and moon. Additionally they are culture heroes to which the tribes owe the most important step of their cultural development. The myths just mentioned give us a foretaste of the text of the Popol Vuh, and the imagery there contained. Since the Popol Vuh is a much more elaborate myth, we will explore the above imagery through the Mayan text in the following chapters.

Mesoamerica: One or Two? The Prophet and the Twins

It would not be possible to do justice to the wealth of material from Mesoamerican sources. We will enter into the analysis of the deepest Mayan esoteric document, the Popol Vuh. Other such documents exist, for example the Chilam Balam or "Book of Prophecies." In this part we will deal with the most "exoteric" material, Mexican and Guatemalan legends pointing to an individual who lived in Mesoamerica. Although Steiner never mentioned the exact site of the Mexican Mysteries initiated by Vitzliputzli, he did point toward this area of the Americas. It should come as no surprise that we find here the most abundant material about this initiate.

We will give an example of a retelling of a legend, where the prophet appears as a healer. The powers of prophecy and healing stand here in an interesting, mutual relationship. I have taken the liberty to weave together three very similar legends. Most of the plot belongs to the *Legend of the Pass of the Popocatepetl*. The general content of the legend has been preserved and amplified with two other legends that propose the same themes: the *Prophecy at Cholula* and the *Legend of the Lightning Tree*.[20]

At that time the visions increasingly came to haunt the Prophet Kate-Zahl. He had seen far into the future into a time when human sacrifice would resurface and the people would forget his teachings; everything he had lived and fought for would be of no use.

Weary and heart-rended the Prophet sought loneliness to commune with the Great Spirit on the top of the volcano Popocatepetl. There, he sought strength to renew his teachings or ask God to take him to His bosom. On the ascent Kate-Zahl noticed that the jesters were following him at a distance. These were the dwarves and hunchbacks whom he had healed. They were united to him by a deep bond of love. Vainly did he try to dissuade them from attempting the perilous journey.

Now the heavens rumbled and the lightning struck; soon the mountain was wrapped in a snow blizzard. After a time Kate-Zahl turned to the jesters that were following him. Retracing his steps, he found them huddled together, frozen and lifeless. He tried to bring them warmth but realized he had lost the gift of healing.

On the pass of the Popocatepetl, the lightning struck again, the thunder roared. Looking down on the valley, Kate-Zahl beheld a vision of the destruction of Tula. Now he felt that he had lost the favor of the Almighty and renewed his prayer to be taken up to Him. His life felt useless and useless his teachings; he doubted there would be any real future in store for the earth.

The lightning struck again and the mountain shook. Only now it was as if heaven and earth were swept away. A golden sun shone over a new earth and a new heaven, and down in the valley he beheld Tula, the city of his love, but now a far more resplendent Tula than the one he knew. Restored were all its former glories. New temples of unsurpassed beauty rivaled with each other. Everywhere were gardens, sculptures of precious stones and frescoes. He admired the inscriptions telling of times of old. Now he noticed that everybody could read them. Humanity had outgrown its infancy of war and destruction and entered a Golden Age of Learning.

Returning down to the valley, Kate-Zahl told his people of the visions. When they brought him the sick and deformed, the Prophet realized he had recovered the gift of healing. But even more marvelous to behold was his countenance. His lineaments and white hair showed him as much older. A new wisdom lit up in his deep peaceful eyes.

In Central America as in Peru legends re-propose the theme of the initiate who helped overcome human sacrifice. An example is the *Legend of The Priests of Ek Balaam*, the priesthood of the tiger. This legend shows in essence how the presence of the initiate was more than the sacrificing priesthood could bear. They were overwhelmed by his power.[21]

Quite different from any of the previous legends is the *Legend of the Woman*, preserved in Yucatan. In Yucatan reigned a lovely, cruel and heartless queen, with skin the color of old ivory and hair as blue as the wings of the raven. Knowing that the prophet could not be hurt or poisoned, she decided to entrap him in a dungeon. On the evening of his arrival the volcano started to belch dark smoke from its summit. At the queen's signal the prophet fell into the dungeon. Then the mountain exploded and the palace crumbled. In the palace, only the queen and a guard survived. After escaping from captivity the prophet healed the people who had been wounded and burned.[22]

Most, if not all, of the elements that have been introduced above reappear in the esoteric content of the Popol Vuh. A few additional elements appear in other sources, particularly the Chilam Balam or Book of Prophecies.

CHAPTER 2

Popol Vuh:
The Cosmic Ages

ALTHOUGH THIS WORK is concerned primarily with the time between the Mystery of Golgotha and the present, pre-historical influences dating back to Lemurian and Atlantean times have a continued influence on the events that we will explore. A basic overview of both the indigenous presence during Lemurian and Atlantean times and the movements of populations from Atlantis to Northern and Central America is therefore essential for this work. In order to understand these ancient influences and cosmic history from the first chapters of the Popol Vuh, we will refer to what we know from spiritual science:
  – Earth evolution from Lemuria to post-Atlantean time and its relation to the course of the Platonic Year.
  – Cultural innovations: evolution of the Mysteries and the important breakthroughs that resulted from them.
The first line of analysis follows the evolution of the earth through the stages that lead to the present. For all practical purposes we need only go as far as Lemuria to cover our areas of concern. To this key of understanding we will add the notion of the rhythms of the Platonic Year of about 26,000 years. This added consideration will allow us to anchor the evolution of consciousness with a modern chronological timeline. It will additionally shed light on the nature of Mesoamerican cosmology. The second key of reference follows the major cultural innovations. The most important of these is the evolution of the Mysteries that connect the human beings with the divine. These evolved in a way that Steiner summarized thus: Ancient Mysteries, Semi-Ancient Mysteries, Semi-New Mysteries, and New Mysteries. Finally, we will refer to the major cultural

breakthroughs, primarily writing and the forms of calendar that emerged from the historical record.

I: EARTH EVOLUTION

As the indigenous mind recognizes, evolution does not proceed in a linear fashion, but rather in cycles of alternating expansion and contraction, ascent and descent, evolution and decline. Such a view, familiar to ancient civilizations, can be reconciled with the scientific method through the work of Rudolf Steiner. Thus, the distance between the indigenous mind and the scientific outlook can be bridged, and this will allow us access to the legends and documents of ancient Mesoamerica. Mesoamerican civilizations spoke of cycles of time ending in natural catastrophes and ever-new beginnings following them. The destruction and the period of emptiness—the cosmic night that precedes a new beginning—is called *pralaya* in ancient Indian cosmology. The indigenous Mesoamericans compared the cosmic cycles to the daily course of the sun; this is why we hear as much of Ages as of Suns. In the Bible this notion of cycles appears for example in the "seven days of creation." Each new cycle introduces new elements after repeating the preceding cycle in a new way through a process of metamorphosis and intensification.

The earth went through four cycles before attaining the present one. These are Polaris, Hyperborea, Lemuria, and Atlantis, leading to the present post-Atlantean age. In Polaris began a densification process out of the fire element in conditions of primeval darkness. In Hyperborea, the air densified and lit up as a sun. At this stage the sun separated from the earth. Earth development had its center in the far north of our hemisphere; this is what is indicated by the Greek name Hyperborea. Human development however, did not occur on the earth but in the sphere surrounding it.

The progressing densification of the earth was resolved at the Lemurian stage with the expulsion of the sun first and of the moon later. Lemuria was a continent in the regions now covered by the Indian Ocean, although we could not think of it in terms of landmasses. It was destroyed by great volcanic catastrophes. In Atlantis the world came to a still denser state with an atmosphere impregnated with water. Atlantis was the first continent to resemble those of today. It was destroyed by the mythical flood, whose memory is preserved in practically all world mythologies.

Let us now circumscribe our interest to the last three rounds of earth evolution. In effect in the early part of Lemuria there was no time as we know it, because there were no sun and moon to regulate those cycles. Nor was there a process of incarnation marked by death and rebirth, rather a continuous breathing in and out, a process of penetrating in the denser matter and withdrawing from it.

Lemuria

In Lemuria the solid earth minerals did not yet exist. The inner fire of the earth could only eject boiling water and steam, and later boiling mud. The plants and animals only existed in the archetypal realm, hovering above the corporeal. This is what the Bible refers to in telling us that they were created each according to its own kind and later specifying: "When no plant of the field was yet in the earth and no herb of the field had yet sprung up" (Gen. 2:5). There were species but no single individual physical forms yet.

The human being was only present in the ethereal realm, in a form that had not condensed yet into the physical. Physical eyes could not have perceived the human being yet. The Bible indicates the above by saying: "there was no man to till the ground" (Gen 2:5). The primordial human form of Adam was hermaphroditic. "Male-female they created him" (Gen 1:27). He could produce his kin from within, given the power and presence of the soul-spirit over the etheric form. In the early stages of Lemuria human beings hovered in a vitalized atmosphere in which no permanent forms condensed. Forms arose and dissolved, but they had no permanence and hence could not be preserved in the geological strata.

While these processes were going on, the tendency toward rigidifying of the earth reached a stage in which the process of incarnation was hindered, and most souls remained in the etheric sphere near to the earth or the cosmic planetary spheres. If what later became the moon had remained united with the earth, both earth and humankind would have attained a stage of mummification. The earth would have become what Steiner called "a great cosmic graveyard." Only those bodies that preserved the strongest forces could survive in these harsh conditions. In fact only a handful of such bodies persisted.[1] The moon took with itself the coarsest substances. Steiner describes this process as air and water being purified of their dense matter. What was previously dissolved now precipitated. Air and water came into existence. On the earth, after the separation of the moon, substances returned to a more malleable state. The process of incarnation and excarnation, indicating a further descent into earth, was established in the middle and later parts of Lemuria.

After the expulsion of the moon the area of the Pacific Ocean remained disturbed for a time, and development first occurred on the African continent as modern research has confirmed. Later, further development occurred in the Lemurian continent located between Asia, Africa and Australia in the region of present-day Indian Ocean. However, these were not landmasses as we are accustomed of thinking of in present terms. There were no clear boundaries between earth and oceans. Even the most solid parts were continuously under the sway of volcanic processes. Since the surface of the earth underwent continuous changes, there were no permanent settlements. What materials were used were taken from the plant world.

It is said that the "second man" was made of the "dust of the earth." Adamah means "earthly matter." This was then the first stage of an individual life. Human beings at that stage did not possess the upright form, or hands. Only gradually did they become warm-blooded. Hearing was the first of the senses to open. Physical sight did not appear until Atlantis. The inner life was inhabited by images that informed humans about their environment.

Human beings, constituted of an almost gelatin-like substance, had gigantic dimensions. The crown of the head was open and rays of light could enter this opening, giving the human being the appearance of having a lantern on top of a body. The fontanelles on top of the skull are the last modern remnant of this ancient bodily constitution. The above peculiarities endowed our forebears with the ability to perceive with the soul. A flower was perceived through inner organs as a shining astral configuration. There was as yet no outer sight providing color, form or external qualities. In fact the human being of those times could only act out of the inspiration of the spiritual forces that surrounded him.

Human beings were developing the instincts that drove them. The capacities of thinking and memory did not yet exist. Not having developed memory meant not being able to articulate language. The first rudiments of speech only evolved at the end of Lemuria. The formative forces and the will forces still exerted a strong influence over a body that was much more plastic and subject to change. This manifested with the appearances of giants and dwarves. The etheric body was more independent from the physical body, particularly in the region of the head, and this allowed humanity to perceive cosmic and atmospheric events. The human and the environment had mutual effects and influences upon each other. Through the rise of gravity following the expulsion of the moon, the human being acquired the erect position and developed the function and use of hands in the later part of Lemuria.

The separation of earth and moon was reflected with the differentiation of the sexes that the Bible indicates with the creation of Eve. This stage, which the Bible calls the Fall, is characterized by the growing consciousness of separation from the bosom of the divine. The separation of the sexes brought about the specialization of part of the organism for the purpose of reproduction and freed part of the remaining forces for the development of an incipient individual soul life. The male developed in the direction of the will forces, through which he could still influence the natural realms with which he was much more vitally interconnected. Nature was still pliable and able to be affected by human consciousness. Women developed the seeds of an imaginative and conceptual life linked to the realm of feelings; this life created the germs of memory that further developed upon Atlantis and there replaced in importance the life of instincts. Due to this differentiation and to their future-oriented role the women became the natural leaders—the origin of matriarchy. Where elements of this matriarchy survive, we see the remnants of Lemurian civilizations on earth.

At the end of Lemuria, an exodus took place in the direction of the northwest, diagonally across Africa toward the place in the Atlantic where Atlantis stood. Part of the populations migrating remained in Africa, particularly north and central Africa.[2] Surviving Lemurian consciousness is found in many of the things associated with matriarchy, such as the clan system, marriage rules and the division of villages in moieties (from the French word *moitié* for half). Totemism, which is the arrangement of the tribe, originally according to zodiac signs, is also a surviving practice from these original times.

Before humanity entered Lemurian incarnation the human being was a purely etheric form. "... the human gradually solidified out of that shadow-form." This shadow-form is what Steiner calls also Phantom. This phantom hovered in the periphery of the earth. When humans were not yet physically condensed, they were was developed in a manner that is revealed by clairvoyant imagination as four group-souls: they had something of the image of the bull on one hand, of the lion for the second, of the eagle for the third, and something similar to man on the fourth.[3] These are the same forces that work upon the group-souls of animals and are responsible for their physical form. In order to become human our ancestors had to pass through four animal group-souls in succession. Human beings felt that they belonged to the group-souls, just as we feel that our fingers belong to our body and ego. When humans were among spiritual beings they heard the name of what they were. "One group heard the word which in the original language was the word for that group; another group heard a different word. Man could not name himself from within; his name sounded into him from without."[4]

The group-souls acted as archetype or prototypes from the region of the sun upon the physical replicas present on earth. In speaking about the physical human beings and the spiritual beings, Steiner compares the latter to the astrality that comes down to meet the plant in the spring and summer. The same occurred with the human being. The astral principle at some times approached and at others retreated (i.e., during the rigidification stage, it retreated). The relationship between human beings on earth and their archetypal counterparts evolved in stages, particularly at the turning points of the expulsion of the sun and moon. When the sun split off, the higher beings departed there, separating with the finer substances. The most advanced had integrated the three natures and could be called "Spirit Humans," the true human prototypes. When the earth started to rigidify, the Bull, Lion and Eagle spirits lost the ability to influence the replicas below on earth. After the separation of the moon they regained the ability to influence the human replicas below. The souls returned from the planetary spheres and started occupying the rejuvenated bodies, but only gradually. The first to regain their life and develop their forms were the plants, then the animals. The later the souls incarnated, the more developed were the bodies that they found. Those that waited the least were those that acquired an animal form. Those that came soon after formed the most primitive human races.

The first forces that worked during the Lemurian time were those that emanated from the Bull spirits. If no other forces had worked upon human beings but the Bull forces, they would have physically resembled a bull. But the forces of the Bull were countered by the forces of the Lion. With these forces the same could be said. If they alone had worked humans would have resembled the lion form. The forces of the Lion also worked from the center of the earth toward the surface but added their effects only later at the approach of Atlantean time.

Both Bull and Lion forces worked from the depths of the earth. Other forces worked from the periphery, from the expanses of the universe downward. These are the forces streaming from the Eagle spirits. When the three forces work together, they are harmonized in the formation of the human body. Thus human beings were able to integrate various forces in such a way that one would neutralize the other, and in so doing bring about a higher harmony. Humanity gives a new direction and manifestation to the stream of forces that work through it. Human beings harmonize them in the form of their physical body. To the clairvoyant gaze the archetypal phantom appears today in physical form because humanity has harmonized the Eagle, the Bull and the Lion influences. This perception is what is present in the description of the sphinx as the ancient Egyptian initiates saw it. "The features that stand out separately in the Sphinx are in human nature inwardly interwoven...If one allows such a Sphinx, made up of a lion and a bull form, together with the wings of a bird, to work upon the clairvoyant vision, and if one completes it by adding the human Phantom which underlies it, if one weaves these elements together, the human form as we have it today comes into being before us."[5]

While humanity was becoming ever more human—differentiating in worlds of spirit—animal beings remained at the above stages. If they had been able to wait to incarnate, to develop their love for the physical world only later, they would have become human beings. The humans who descended earliest to earth had especially strong-formed bodies with crude and brutal countenances. This esoteric knowledge is preserved in some American myths throughout the continent; suffice to think of the already mentioned Amwesha myth (See Appendix 1).

Another important aspect of Lemurian development is summarized in the Biblical event called the Fall, coinciding with the time of crisis occurring at the separation of the moon and the differentiation of the sexes. After man began to return to inhabit earthly bodies, he started to receive the influence of the Luciferic beings. These acted in his astral body instilling passions, desires, instincts, and drives. Thus, instead of preserving the old dim clairvoyance and adding to it an object consciousness, the human being lost more and more the original clairvoyance while starting to develop ego-consciousness. Interest in the physical world set in a solidification process, earlier than was meant to happen. The Luciferic spirits worked to individuate and separate human beings, whereas the divine-spiritual beings counteracted these forces by bringing human beings together. Together with the Luciferic beings, the Ahrimanic beings started affecting human's perception of the outer world, so that gradually over time they could only see the outer physical forms, but no longer the spiritual reality that animated them.

The First Half of the Atlantean Epoch

The continent of Atlantis should not be imagined in the way modern continents are configured. The continent was in a semi-fluid, viscous state. The plants were not solidly anchored to a soil; rather they glided and hovered above the fluid substance of the earth. Sea and land did not form clear boundaries. The waters all around Atlantis were perceived as the land of the gods. The air was saturated with moisture and the mists were denser toward the north. Over the whole of Atlantean evolution the air progressively clarified.

As for human beings, they were still able—as they had been in Lemuria—to change their shape, to grow larger or smaller in reflection of the inner soul state. They felt that it was only God who had real being and essence, not themselves. The feeling of individuality was stimulated from the outside during the first half of Atlantis, particularly through the way the sun worked upon the human being. Sleeping and waking states were consequently markedly different from the present. During the first half of Atlantean civilization the human being lived in sleep in the companionship of spiritual beings. There was no feeling of fatigue or needing to rest before going to sleep. The reverse was true; the need for rest was felt when entering the physical body during the day. This state of consciousness was a reflection of the way in which the etheric body extended beyond the physical head. During the initial part of Atlantis, the human being still saw objects as if surrounded by an aura with colored edges. To offer an analogy Steiner indicates that objects looked a little like things would on an evening with thick fog under street lamp illumination. The sun appeared like a circle formed of color through a mist.

The "I" did not shine in the single individual. The tribe represented a single organism, one ego-soul held in common. The group-ego memory linked the individual with parents and grandparents; events of previous generations were just as real to the ego that reached beyond the individual. The blood of the ancestors flowed down the line of generations and the person did not feel limited by death and birth. This situation continued to a certain degree even until the time of the Hebrew patriarchs. Thus, even at the time of the old Hebrews they would say: "I and Father Abraham are one." Whoever was related by blood was included in one "I". The individual at that time felt that one's immortal part found refuge in the group-soul of the race and of its primeval ancestors. The Israelites saw Jahve as the spiritual group-soul of the people—the "I am." Even in the time of the patriarchs a man remembered not only his own experiences but also those of his father, grandfather, etc. Thus, names such as Adam, Abel, Cain, and Noah signified the memories that passed through the generations.

The above was the result of the continued influence of the group-souls, of the Bull, Lion, and Eagle spirits. Their influence also constituted an element of differentiation in the Mysteries. Those who perceived the Bull spirits—the Bull initiates—acquired insights over the working of the etheric principle and everything connected to the glandular system, and everything of the nature of a human being that is firmly connected and attached to the earth. A second group received the influences of the Eagle spirits. This group was more independent from their vital functions and more open to the spiritual/cosmic element. They experienced more strongly those forces that acted upon the formation of the head. Through the influence of the Bull spirits a tendency to over-incarnate arose; through the Eagle spirits the contrary tendency not to incarnate deeply. Through the Lion spirits an intermediate situation developed. Through them the initiates received insight of the working of everything connected to the rhythmic system of lung and heart. The above influences continued even in post-Atlantean times: examples of it are the Mysteries of the Apis Bull in Egypt or of Mythras in Ancient Persia for the Bull spirits. The initiates who saw one of these types of spirits portrayed it with the body of the animal and a human head.[6]

To the influence of the group souls was added that of the planets, which further characterized the so-called "Atlantean oracles." In effect, after the expulsion of the moon, souls returning to earth were still united with the spirits of the planets from which they descended. Thus in the Jupiter oracles the souls that had descended from Jupiter communed with the higher spiritual beings from the region from which they themselves had descended. They were learning to see the Jupiter beings. The same was true for the Saturn, Mars, and other planetary oracles. The most advanced were those who were able to apprehend the Sun beings.

The first Mysteries preserved the teachings of the Mysteries of the cosmos, connected to the outer planets: Saturn, Jupiter, and Mars. The Planetary Mysteries spread out in different regions. The oracles of the south were Saturn oracles concerned with the Mysteries of warmth. To the north were the Jupiter oracles more concerned with the Mysteries of light. To the center developed the Mars and Sun oracles. The Mars Mysteries were teachings about the formative forces acting particularly in the watery element. The Sun Mysteries formed a unity of all the other teachings brought to a higher level; they carried all impulses for the future.

The people of the south were the first to feel the need to develop social forms centered on the notion of the state. In the west this later manifested through the Toltecs; in the east this was initiated by Egyptians and Babylonians. Leadership was assumed by the priest-king who united in himself the male function of rulership with the female quality of revelation. From the south originated the forerunners of Toltecs (henceforth called Ancient Toltecs to distinguish them from the later historical Toltecs) and other American Indians. Later on (particularly from the fourth period) were added the oracles connected to the inner planets—Mercury, Venus and Vulcan—leading to the development of inner faculties.

Instruction in the Atlantean Mystery centers markedly differed from anything that followed in post-Atlantean time. It was imparted through the sheer presence of the initiate teachers, through the powerful impression exercised by their conduct and presence. Learning was awakened through the imitative capacity, which was then very developed. Those who had reached a certain maturity had to be exposed over a considerable length of time to the beneficent influence of the teacher. Eventually such a bond was created between the teacher and the pupil that everything the teacher possessed in the form of wisdom was poured into the soul of the disciple. At that time, although etheric and physical bodies were coming to coincide more and more—especially in the later part of Atlantis—their union was not that strong, so that the teacher could still facilitate the withdrawal of the etheric body from the physical body for the sake of initiation. At that moment the pupil could share what the teacher held in spiritual vision.

The Second Half of Atlantis: Development of Ego Consciousness

The fourth period of Atlantis was primarily the time of the development of the Mars and Sun Mysteries. The Mars Mysteries explored the formative forces of the water element. This was also the time of differentiation toward the future Turanian races. The Sun Mysteries were the most exalted mysteries holding a central place between the mysteries we have seen and the mysteries of the following periods. Both Sun and Mars Mysteries occupied an intermediate geographical position, in between the Saturn and Jupiter Mysteries. The latter two and Mars are the so-called "outer planets." Their Mysteries conveyed the forces of the cosmos and bestowed the revelation of the gods.

Only in the places of the Sun Mysteries was found the mastery of earthly forces necessary for the construction of temples. Manu was the initiate who led the Sun Mysteries in the center of Atlantis. He is the one that the Bible calls Noah. His name meant "the bringer of stillness." He brought stillness through the power of thought, initiating important changes for the whole of Atlantean evolution.

The fourth period marked an important turning point. Gradually, over the second half of Atlantean development, humans started to feel themselves as an ego, immersed in a physical body, while at the same time losing consciousness of the spiritual world. Physical reality started to appear more clearly—to emerge from the fog as it were. At that point the individual started to grow away from the four group souls. Thus, in the fifth Atlantean Age the impulse of the ego-soul was first implanted. At that time it was Manu who said: "Until now you have seen those who have led you; but there are higher leaders whom you do not see. It is these leaders to whom you are subject. You shall carry the orders of the god whom you do not see; and you shall obey one of whom you can make no image to yourselves."[7]

The mysteries that followed from the fifth period onwards enabled human beings to gain independence from the cosmos and imbued themselves with inner faculties, particularly the ability for abstract thinking—a further stage of separation from cosmic revelation. These were the Mercury, Venus, Moon, and Vulcan Mysteries existing both in the north and the south of Atlantis. The last one represented a particular intensification of the other three. In the last stages of Atlantis the cults celebrating the ancestors originated. In these rituals the soul, having lost connection with the divine, sought knowledge of immortality in the continuation of the line of generations.

The fifth period saw the first differentiation toward what would later be the Semitic type. The sixth and seventh periods have little bearing on the fate of the Ancient Toltecs and Amerindians. These epochs gave rise to the primeval Sumerian and the primeval Mongolian populations. The seventh period sowed the first seeds of the differentiation between white and black magic. White magic was practiced primarily within the Sun Mysteries. The misuse of the life force, initiating the practice of black magic, was undertaken primarily within the Mars Mysteries. From this misuse resulted the final catastrophe that caused the flood and disappearance of Atlantis.

At the end of Atlantean time air and water further separated. As the mists dissipated the sun, moon, and stars became visible. The dispersal of the water also made possible the new phenomenon of the rainbow, another central image of myths relating to this epoch such as the biblical flood.

In the later stages of Atlantis more and more human beings developed the inklings of intellectual thinking. Their loss of clairvoyant faculties was a reason for derision on the part of those who clung to the earlier endowment of natural clairvoyance. Nevertheless it was these new "thinkers" who could devise how to elaborate a navigation technology that would assure their survival and emigration out of Atlantis.

To recapitulate, the groups that migrated from Atlantis to the Americas had their origin in southern Atlantis, and corresponded to what we have characterized as the eagle-type. They were part of the Saturn Mysteries. Later, the Venus and Mercury Mysteries added their effects. The parallels detectable between the Mayan/Toltec and the ancient Babylonian civilizations derive more from their exposure to the Saturn, Venus, and Mercury Mysteries than from any later and possible historical contact. The Venus and Mercury Mysteries would acquire great importance in the Toltec worldview.

According to Wachsmuth's research three groups reached the Americas from Atlantis.[8] The migrations began around 15,000 BC, during the fifth period of Atlantean civilization. An earlier group spread through the area of Florida and directed itself toward the northeast of the continent. These were the forerunners of the Algonquian tribes. This group preserved mostly the eagle signature and they retained a nomadic lifestyle. A second group populated Central America. Among those were the forerunners of the Maya and Toltecs. These populations gave great importance to the calendar and the computation of time. Their legends speak of the original "water paradise." This is the stream that will concern us most of all in the present study. The third stream directed itself toward South America. The ancient Aymara of the high plateau of Bolivia and Peru are most likely the descendents of this group in South America. They preserved a very complex social differentiation and flourished mostly around the Lake Titi-caca basin, where the famous Tiwanaku civilization developed.

To the first three groups emigrating from Atlantis was added the Mongolian type that crossed the Bering Strait and descended from the north. This type is clearly recognizable in the Inuit and populations of the northwest of North America. They mixed in the northeast with the Algonquians and reached much further south in the American West. Their influence touched Central America through the Chichimecs and Aztecs. This is the only source of migrations recognized by most modem histori-cal sources.

Post-Atlantean Time

In olden times tribal law often required that individuals marry their kinfolk—the so-called "endogamic marriage." That was still the case with the Hebrews. The result of this practice was the ability to generate magical forces, which worked from one soul to another. Steiner offers an example of this in the changing of the water into wine at the marriage of Cana, indicating that it was the force that flowed between Mary and Jesus that allowed the performance of the miracle. The water was not changed into wine: it was experienced and sensed completely as wine, through the result of the forces of consanguinity. Not only did it taste like wine; it also had the same effect upon the organism.[9] Through consanguinity, inheritance was preserved in the etheric body. The wisdom of the etheric body preserved the old clairvoyance.

Coming closer to the time of Christ, endogamic marriage gave way to more and more exogamic marriage—outside of the kinfolk—with the resulting dilution of the faculties carried in the blood. The dimming of old atavistic faculties eventually led individuals to seek truth through their feelings, will, and their own ego. This led to increasing anti-social tenden-cies, separating people from each other. The blood became progressively unable to carry the old wisdom and became more and more the bearer of egotism. It was no longer fit to lead people upward, when they relied on the old vision. The etheric body, as it were, retained a certain capital of wisdom from the far past, but nothing came to renew that wisdom. There was just a process of continuous dying away of what little the etheric body could carry of the old wisdom. This "erosion of wisdom" came about through the increasing role of the Luciferic and Ahrimanic beings. The Luciferic beings directed people toward the physical world. Through Ahriman, people became unable to see past what the senses revealed to them; they relied solely on the world of maya. Thus, it was through the combined action of the Luciferic and Ahrimanic beings that the heritage of wisdom progressively dwindled down. After each death, the "capital of wisdom" progressively waned, due to the reality of life in the conditions of the physical body. This state of affairs was reversed by the deed of Christ in Golgotha.[10] In our time the etheric body is no longer so closely tied to the physical body. However, when the etheric body starts to expand again, it cannot draw anything from the physical body. Thus, if things had continued unchanged, this etheric body would have been unable to preserve the wisdom of old or acquire new wisdom. The etheric body would have been devitalized and the physical body dried up. This would spell out the end of the mission of the earth. However, through the deed of Christ, two choices are now available to humanity. Without the Christ the etheric body has nothing to give to the drying up physical body. The deed of Christ occurred in such a way to replenish the old dwindling store of wisdom. When we take up the Christ impulse it pervades the etheric body with new life.

Rhythms of the Platonic Year: The Place of Mesoamerican Mythology

The phases that we have outlined in the succession from Lemuria to Atlantis and in the succession of the seven periods of Atlantis up to the present are influenced by many cosmic rhythms, the primary being the rhythm of the so-called Platonic Year. This is measured by the movement of the precession of the equinoxes, which can be assessed by the position of the earth in relation to the fixed stars. Every year at the spring equinox the sun rises in a different part of the horizon of the zodiac. This movement, while at first imperceptible, measures 1° every 72 years. Every 72 x 30 or 2160 years the sun moves from one sign of the zodiac to the next. We are presently in the sign of Pisces and we are moving toward the sign of Aquarius. This is why we are talking about the coming Age of Aquarius. It takes 2160 x 12 or 25,920 years for the sun to return to its original position in the world-clock and rise from the same place in the zodiac. The cosmos imprints its influences on the earth in a rhythmic way that becomes visible in the movement of the Platonic Year. Each of the signs of the zodiac imparts its unique qualitative influence in turn. Humanity receives these impulses in freedom and in turn imprints the results of its choices over the course of the universe. There is no ironbound necessity in the expression of this interplay.

At the end of the Lemurian Age the sun stood in Pisces at the spring equinox. There have been seven Atlantean ages following and we are now in the fifth post-Atlantean age. There have been twelve ages following the end of Lemuria—a whole Platonic Year—and we stand in the same position in the cosmic clock as we stood then, 26,000 years ago.

We measure the year, as did the Mesoamerican ancestors, through the four seasons. For our ancestors the quartering of the year was indicated by the intersolstitial cross, marking the position of the sun at sunrise and sunset at the summer and winter solstices—the positions of the sun's farthest elongation over the horizon. At the summer solstice the sun at sunrise and sunset marks the farthest southeastern and southwestern elongations in the northern hemisphere. In winter, it marks the farthest northeastern and northwestern elongations. The four positions form the intersolstitial cross. This cross points to four signs of the zodiac. Thus, during the course of a cosmic year there are three basic variations of 3 x 4 groups of zodiac constellations. These are the following:

- — Pisces, Gemini, Virgo, Sagittarius
- — Aquarius, Taurus, Leo, Scorpio
- — Capricorn, Aries, Cancer, Libra

Guenther Wachsmuth calls these sets of constellations respectively Prototype I, Prototype II, and Prototype III, each prototype having 4 possible variations.[11] The world's mythological traditions give us indications about the time of their formation because of their emphasis on one of the groups of four constellations. Steiner points out an example of this: the ancient Persians (Prototype I) projected what emanates from the constellation of the Twins onto the constellation of the Virgo. They represented the latter not only with the ears of corn but also with the child that is represented by the Twins. Likewise in the ancient Egypto-Chaldean epoch (Prototype II) Leo was looked upon in the same way as Virgo was by the Persians. Now, upon the Lion they projected what came from the Bull and so arose the Mythras religion. The same was done for the constellation of Cancer upon which was projected what came from the Ram by the Romans (Prototype III) at the beginning of the time of Aries.[12]

Mesoamerican mythology is strongly centered on the constellations of Prototype II. At the beginning of the Atlantean epoch Taurus stood at the highest point—the summer solstice—and Scorpio at the lowest. This was the time when man was starting to develop his physical body through the forces of the earth. The pair Taurus-Scorpio reflects the strength that the forces of the earth acquire in the bodily organization. The pair Leo-Aquarius formed the complement, which indicates the possibility of resurrection and reconnection to the spiritual world through the forces of the heart. Scorpio stood as the image of the reproductive organs; the eagle often took the place of the scorpion, and it is most often under this form that it is known in Mesoamerican cosmology. The eagle, so significant of all Mesoamerican civilization, also stands for the hardening of the forces of the head. At the beginning of Atlantis the sun descended over the horizon in the sign of Leo, the position of the autumn equinox. This gave rise to the image of the sun swallowed by the jaguar or of the night sun as a jaguar.

Evolution of the Mysteries

Steiner characterized four successive stages in the evolution of the basic forms of the sacred Mysteries in which human beings received the revelations of the gods. These are: the Ancient Mysteries, Semi-Ancient, Semi-New and New Mysteries.[13] Only the first three concern us here.

Ancient Mysteries

Of these Mysteries nothing historical is preserved. The gods descended from the spirit world and came down to dwell among human beings, albeit only in an etheric body. They bore the priestly office within the Mysteries and imparted their teachings to human beings. The ceremonies were planned in accordance with certain astrological configurations; the movements of the planets determined conditions favorable to an exchange between worlds. The priests were the living human form of the gods. The members of the congregation were expected to perceive no difference between them and the gods.

This first stage of Mysteries led to the elaboration of the first very simple calendars of 364–365 days that only very loosely corresponded to the solar year. After the end of the lunar months, in order to complete the year, the priest had to insert days that were considered holy. These times were special because they underscored that the thinking of humanity differed from the thinking of the gods. These were also those special windows of time that allowed communication between the worlds. "It was in such times that the priests of old sought to preserve the effective forces of sun and moon in the substances with which they celebrated the sacred ceremonies, so that what they received in the holy times could be spread out over all the other parts of the year when they would need to celebrate."[14] These ceremonies were the means for carrying out transubstantiation, during which the substantiality of earthly matter is transformed, spiritualized.

The initiated priests had to submit completely to the influences of the cosmos in order to achieve transubstantiation. The substances thus generated were preserved in order to carry out the transubstantiation at other times of the year. Within the Ancient Mysteries, and particularly when transubstantiation was carried out, an understanding of apocalyptic future was granted to the priests. The ceremonies were carried out under the ground, in caves in the cliffs, because there, during the act of transubstantiation, the priest experienced how his physical organism became one with the whole earth.

Semi-Ancient Mysteries

Of these Mysteries we have at least a few records historically preserved. The Gods did not descend anymore but they sent their forces to work in the precinct of the Mysteries. To achieve transubstantiation the priests had now to make recourse to "leavens." These worked just like bread dough leaven, when a part of the previous dough is preserved for the next batches of bread. The leavens facilitated transubstantiation in other substances while preserving their own substance. They were stored in ancient holy vessels that had been long preserved in the Mysteries. This is what Steiner says about them: "The initiated priest understands the transformation, the transubstantiation taking place through the forces preserved in the substances; he knows that they send forth sun-radiance in the holy quartz-crystal vessels. What was looked for in them, the reason they were needed, was that they were seen to be the celebrant's organ of perception for apocalypse, for revelation." And further: "The moment when [the priest] saw the sun-radiance of the Host was the moment in which he became a priest in his inner being."[15]

The temples were no longer built underground. They rose to the surface of the earth and a great importance was given to water, through ablution and later with baptism. The cultus worked with the forces of the etheric body. The priest inwardly felt the transformed substances merging with his etheric body. The beings that worked at that time among humanity were the ancient "Teachers of Wisdom" who have withdrawn in the Sphere of the Moon. They worked among humans only in etheric bodies.[16] The Semi-Ancient Mysteries were inaugurated after the end of Atlantis.

Semi-New Mysteries

The Eucharistic Mass is the most well known survivor of the Semi-New Mysteries in modern times. The Semi-New Mysteries were created when human beings could perceive the Word, the magical Word in themselves. Now human speech was added to the speech of the cultus. A last remnant of this is present in the different religious creeds. The new element of these cults was the central place of the rhythmic element of the sacred word.

Of such nature were the Mysteries of the Cabeiri, when Greek consciousness started to emancipate itself from the old Mysteries of the East. On the altars of the Cabeiri instead of leavens, substances themselves were offered. Sacrificial substances preserved in special jars were set alight and in the ascending smoke the magical speech of the priest made visible the Imaginations uttered in the Word. Thus the path upward to the divine powers became externally visible in the sacrificial smoke. Two possibilities arose. "In this way it came about that the upward effort of human forces toward divine forces was experienced, was revealed, either in what was spoken into the sacrificial smoke or directly through the intonation of the magical, cultic Word."[17]

The human being became one with the airy element and through it with the cosmos. The priest and the participants experienced the Word in their astral body. With the passing of time those who practiced the cultus had only a very vague experience of it. However, no matter how worthy the celebrant there was and still always is something spiritually present, at least if the liturgy has been correctly preserved. In origin, the Semi-New Mysteries were performed by the Bodhisattvas, highly evolved human beings, who worked as emissaries of the Moon Teachers of Wisdom. They were the purely human initiates who started Mystery centers the world over. The transition from the Semi-Ancient to the Semi-New Mysteries is cardinal to an understanding of the Mexican Mysteries at the transition time of our era.

The Transition at the Time of Golgotha

The Mysteries celebrated long before Golgotha, particularly the so-called Southern Mysteries, were predominantly Summer Mysteries; they were Mysteries of ecstasy.[18] What we will talk about below refers primarily to the Southern Mysteries as they developed in Egypt and Meso-potamia, and continued to influence European culture and—in a modi-fied way—what was occurring in America. That this element applies to Mesoamerican culture can be ascertained from our exploration of Mayan and later manifestations of Mesoamerican spirituality, particularly in rela-tion to the ever-present central question of the Year God, surviving in both Toltec and Aztec spirituality. Additionally, Mayan civilization marked the transition, as we will see later, from the Semi-Ancient Mysteries to the Semi-New Mysteries as is visible in the central ceremonial ritual of the "vision-serpent."

In the times long before Golgotha humankind received their thoughts with vivid imaginations from the world of spirit. Thoughts and pictures came together in such a way that the recipients knew they were commun-ing with spiritual beings and that the thoughts weren't their personal possession. They were not received in full ego-consciousness and there-fore came with no effort. In those Mysteries knowledge and faith were one; knowledge acted with the primary strength of faith. Likewise science, art, and religion were not separated.

However, over time the leaders began to progressively separate some thoughts and offer a way for individual apprehension of the thoughts. In fact the initiates offered these thoughts back to the higher beings. This was done at Midsummer because at that time the earth is more connected to the whole spiritual environment that surrounds it, and people more easily connects with the cosmic environment. If this were not done the Mystery pupils would have been exposed to the Luciferic temptation, leading back to the past.

The initiates offered the thoughts back to the upper gods by entering the ceremonies wearing the symbols of wisdom and removing them one at a time. At the end of the ceremony they had returned to being a regular person who needed to acquire the wisdom anew in the course of the year. So a time of wisdom alternated with a time of ignorance at the other end of the year.

The candidates to initiation were taught to read the "Book of Nature." This meant the ability to read in every manifestation of nature a revela-tion of the secrets of the universe and their relevance for human life. The initiates communicated the inspirations they received from the so-called Year God. This Year God belonged to the rank of the Archai or Primal Powers. Through the Year God the initiate was able to read something from the buds sprouting in spring, something else from the flowers blossoming later, yet other revelations from the fruits ripening in summer and fall, and from the bare trees in winter. In the spring the initiates could understand how the forces of the universe shape the human physical body. In the summer they were able to read and understand the secrets concerning plant life and the human etheric body. In autumn they deciphered the forms that animals take as well as their seasonal behaviors, instincts and drives. This also brought knowledge of the secrets of the human astral body. During winter initiates experienced a deepening of their inner lives through spiritual activity and exertion. They came closer to the secrets of their egos. Their attention was drawn from the outer world to the depths of their inner beings. This culminated in the experience of the Midnight Sun, the beholding of the sun through the surface of the earth. This was possible because in winter the earth is inwardly spiritualized.

The above was true until the 8th and 9th centuries BC when the thoughts that came down to humankind grew darker. This was compensated by human beings' ability to acquire their own thoughts, which was an important transition of consciousness. For the initiates the Midwinter festival was filled with the sadness of knowing that humans could not find their egos in earthly life. It was a feeling of being forsaken by the cosmos. This feeling became stronger the closer in time to the incarnation of Christ, but was accompanied with the prophetic knowledge of the coming of the Christ to earth that would bring healing to humanity's estrangement from the cosmos. It was known that the festival of sorrow would be changed into one of inner joy.

Before the time of Golgotha thoughts were experienced like we do breathing at present. In the time leading to Golgotha and subsequently, thoughts were felt more like the blood that dwells and circulates in our veins; they were thus felt as more earthly and more personal. This shift in consciousness in the manner of experiencing human thinking was reflected in a shift of importance between summer and winter solstices. Human thoughts were now in danger of falling prey to Ahriman. Now the human being—wanting to experience the divine anew—needed to connect with the Mysteries of the incarnated deity, and that was best done at the opposite time of the year, at Midwinter. This was so because after Golgotha the Christ Being that once dwelt in the sun was now united with the earth. So now instead of moving outwards into the cosmos at Midsummer, the human soul had to deepen inwardly, to connect with and spiritualize the forces that worked from below. Whereas before the priests had enacted sacrifices for others, now the Christmas Mysteries were, in Steiner's terms, "more democratic." In these Mysteries what mattered was the ability to share in the experience with others.

Night and Day Consciousness

Another change of consciousness occurred in a particularly marked way among the ancient Hebrews, who after all were preparing the ground for the incarnation of the Christ. While the Hebrews were promoting the new emerging faculty of thinking, they still received their revelations in particularly vivid dreams. In these clairvoyant dreams Jahve, whose name they were forbidden to pronounce, spoke to them through the Archangel Michael, His countenance.[19] For this reason those seeking initiation called Jahve's revelation "the night revelation." So, they became aware that in ordinary consciousness they could not reach to the divine; the secrets of existence could only be reached in another state of consciousness. They also knew that during the day only Luciferic beings accompanied them in their consciousness. The creator beings communicated when human beings entered the consciousness of the night, or in the parts of them that were unconscious during day consciousness. This is why Jahve was called "the Ruler of the Night," and Michael "Jahve's countenance" or "Jahve's Servant."

A change occurred at the time of the Mystery of Golgotha: now the earth needed the human being to progress. In degrees Michael could awaken consciousness of the spiritual world not just in sleep but also in ordinary consciousness. For this to happen there had to be a time of transition. And in this time of transition there was what Steiner calls "a dark night of knowledge." Michael went from being the one who offered the revelation by night to inspire the human being in day consciousness. He went from being a night-spirit to a day-spirit at the time of Golgotha. This was also the time in which the Ahrimanic element acquired progressively more importance.

What occurred among the Hebrews and in other parts of the world acquired a particular coloration in Mesoamerica, given its more pronounced Atlantean consciousness. So, what is said above serves as a parallel. Nevertheless, we will see changes in the nature of the Mysteries (from Ancient to Semi-New Mysteries), in the nature and function of the Year God, and a shift from night to day consciousness. These are more pronounced in some cultures than in others.

Cultural Innovations: Language, Writing and Calendar

The cultural changes that most concern us here are language, writing and the calendar. In Atlantean time there existed a primal root language common to all. Consonants arose from the need of the soul to convey expression for outer impressions. Vowels mirrored the inner experiences of the soul, such as joy, pleasure, pain, or sadness. The Angels who had completed their development on Old Moon inspired this original language. However, diversity could not have developed if the Angels alone had played their influence. The "retarded angels," who had not completed their development, played their role by working through special teachers. We owe the development of different languages out of a primordial language to what Steiner calls "great, enlightening teachers."[20]

A little clarification is necessary here in order to characterize the differences between the normally developed Angels and those who had not achieved their full development on Old Moon. Those who did not go through a full development were Luciferic beings, which we can picture as beings standing between the Angels and humanity. They form the lowest rung of Luciferic beings. Although these beings are the source of evil, they are not evil per se. We owe the possibility of differentiation of cultures through language to the Luciferic angels. Since they did not complete their evolution on the Old Moon, these Luciferic beings were able to incorporate in human bodies during earth evolution. In Lemurian and especially Atlantean times, ordinary human beings lived side by side with a number of individuals who bore such Luciferic angelic beings in their innermost core. The incarnated Luciferic beings created cultures in various places.

In contrast to language that has a common origin in time for humanity, writing appeared at different points in time in various civilizations and took on very different forms. The need for writing corresponds to the desire to preserve the experience of and connection with the revelation of the spirit. As long as these experiences could be continuously renewed there was no need to preserve memory of them in a fixed form. The pictorial writing of hieroglyphs of Egypt represented the images that were first experienced inwardly. The much more abstract alphabet itself was introduced only much later, around 1500 BC.

Early calendars were tied to the sun and moon, and only later would planetary cycles begin to play a part. The ancient Egyptian Calendar, known as the *Annus Vagus* or "Wandering Year," had 365 days, divided into 12 months of 30 days each, plus 5 extra days at the end of the year. A month consisted of 3 ten-day "weeks." This system was in use by 2400 BC, and possibly before. The experience of time was originally accompanied by a lively feeling for the planetary rhythms reflecting the guidance of the gods. Later on, when this knowledge was lost, time was experienced as the repetition of the same, as a mechanical alternation and recurrence of immutably predetermined laws.

II: NATIVE AMERICAN CONSCIOUSNESS

The Native American lived—and to quite an extent still lives—in a type of consciousness that retained many aspects of Atlantean consciousness. Steiner talks about Atlantean consciousness in relation to the idea of the Tau. In English and German this word is similar to dew. Of Tau Steiner says: "The wisdom of Atlantis is embodied in water in a drop of dew. The German word Tau is nothing more than the old Atlantean sound. So we should look with reverence and devotion at every dewdrop glittering from a blade of grass as a holy legacy from that age in which the connection between humanity and the Gods was not yet severed."[21] What Steiner calls the Tau is what the Native American expresses as "Great Spirit." The T cross, symbol of the Tau, is in fact very widespread in Olmec, Mayan, Incan, and other American civilizations.

How the Native American envisions the earth itself is quite telling in this regard. In North America the earth is called Turtle Island by the Algonquians and many other groups. We have seen that this idea does not differ from the way in which the world was seen by early Atlanteans, for whom the gods dwelled in the waters all around the continent of Atlantis. For the Native American of old, and even of the present, ocean and heaven were co-substantial. Interestingly, green and blue are also often called by the same name. Among many Mayan tribes the same word indicates water, winter, rain, and vegetation. All the rivers emerge from Tlalocan, the earthly paradise. The floating earth is imagined as a monster and called Itzam-cab-ain, great crocodile.[22]

The Native Americans live fully in the Atlantean picture-consciousness. Their etheric body—much less connected with the physical body—communicates to them images imbued with life. Once again let us look at the Mayan worldview. The sun sets through a cave to the west and emerges through another on the east. The heavens are supported by the world tree, erected upon four pillars (also called bearers) symbolized by the four highest mountains of the region. The World Tree means literally "raised-up sky" (Wakah-Chan). The mountains are what the pyramids became later: a natural pedestal for the gods. The present-day Chortis (Ethnic Maya) believe that clouds come from the highest mountains. The cloud—called water-snake—forms a container that empties through the snout. Water gets transferred from one mountain to another. This concept is pictorially represented by birds resting on the top of a mountain and carrying cloud banners. The birds symbolize the spirit of the clouds.

The power of the ether body and its closer association with the astral body brought about two natural consequences. The life of feelings was more closely associated with the phenomena of growth. In the past the lower astral could influence the growth of the body, hence the manifestation of giants and dwarves and all other Atlantean human forms. This will be apparent in the earliest ages of American humanity and the frequent reference of Mesoamerican and other American legends to past races of giants.

Like the Atlanteans, the Native Americans have a prodigious memory. This is why retrieving understanding of present-day ritual and practices offers insight into the religions of ancient times. Memory worked differently from how it works at present. An example will illustrate this. Concerning the famous Mexican Codices discovered at the time of the Conquest or shortly after, Doris Heyden conveys what Don Fernando de Alva Ixtlilxochitl, descendant of the famous Nezahualcoyotl, offered to the understanding of the interpretation of the sacred or historical texts.[23] Don Fernando stated that the tlamantine or "learned priests" of the Aztecs availed themselves of the songs that accompanied the sacred texts. The words and rhythm of the songs elucidated much of the pictures of the texts. He emphasized that one could only be understood with the help of the other: "[the visual images] gave true meaning to the songs, since these were composed with metaphors, similes, and allegories." Further supporting this theory is this quote of a Nahuatl scholar:

I sing the pictures of the book
And see them spread out;
I am an elegant bird
For I make the codices speak
Within the house of pictures.[24]

A final consequence of this particular consciousness of the Native American is its ready access to the world of the departed souls and the ancestors. In the figure of speech "All Our Relations" are included not only the living but also the line of ancestors. In his famous speech, Chief Seattle contrasts Native American consciousness with Western consciousness, not only in relation to its living perception of the reality of the spiritual world behind nature, but very much so on the basis of his living connection with all of those who have gone before him.

Popol Vuh: History of a Document

We could not venture to write this book were it not for the existence of the Mayan document known as Popol Vuh. The images and events described in the sacred text will allow us to reconstruct first American mythology, then the history of the Maya and Toltecs. In this first part we will only be concerned with the story of the gods and the Ages of Mesoamerican humanity.

With good reason, the Popol Vuh has been called the Mesoamerican Bible. Its most likely meaning is "Book of Council." It is in fact a depiction of the central events of American history. No other indigenous document is as encompassing as the Popol Vuh. Four other Maya-Quiché documents include common parts of its history, but none of these, nor any other one, spans such a vast timeline as the Popol Vuh.

Adrian Recinos believes it was originally taken down a few years after the Spanish conquest. It is estimated that the document was written in 1544. The original document could have been written in Mayan hieroglyphs by one or various authors of the lineages that once ruled the Quiché: the Cauecs, the Great Houses, or the Lord Quiché. Father Ximenez, a Dominican monk, first translated it in 1688 after Mayan natives showed him the text. The monk affirms that the Maya grew up listening to and memorizing the contents of the Popol Vuh, although only the priests were qualified for interpreting it.

The French abbot, Etienne Brasseur de Beaubourg, probably possessed the book after its mysterious disappearance from the Library of Guatemala in 1858—the date coinciding with his visit to the country. He proceeded to write a French translation in 1861. The original version was then rediscovered in the Newbury Library in Chicago in 1941, by Adrian Recinos who wrote a second, more complete and exact Spanish translation. The first English translation of the Spanish text was the work of S. G. Morley and

D. Goetz in 1950. Only in 1985 was the original Mayan text translated to English by D. Tedlock.

The document is a continuous narrative with no subdivisions or stated structure. It was only through later translations that it received its present subdivision into chapters. One thing stands out nevertheless. A single event is the clear transition between myth and history, characterized by the resurrection of the central duo of heroes, the Twins Hunahpu and Ixbalamqué, whom we will discuss in greater detail later. That event is mirrored in the macro-cosmos with the so-called "Dawning," a new evolutionary step accompanied by the acquisition of a new consciousness. It is in fact the transition into a historical consciousness.

Throughout the narrative appear what seem to be dislocations and repetitions. The sequence of events seems to move back and forth in time. It does so according to a definite structure. First we are told about the days of Creation, an equivalent of the Bible's Genesis, then about the four ages of humanity—the four stages of consciousness undergone by the Native Americans. The Fourth Age is only alluded to, in Part I, Chapters 1 to 3 (Recinos and Morley/Goetz versions). To each age correspond definite types of social organization. A second part tells us of the divine interventions in human affairs, first by the so-called Ahpus, then by the Twins, followed by the beginning of the Fourth Age (Part I, Chapters 4 to 9, and Part II). The third and fourth sections narrate the historical development undergone by the Quiché nation shortly before and after the Fourth Age (Parts III and IV).

The whole of the odyssey of the Popol Vuh revolves around the vertical axis of heaven, earth, and underworld—the perennial motif of all Meso-American mythology. We will now enter into the images of the first part of the document, depicting the ages of humankind to which the Popol Vuh devotes only three chapters. In this the help of R. Girard will assist us.

A little discussion of Girard's life and methodology will underline the value of the Popol Vuh as a research tool. Before his groundbreaking research, indigenous documents were considered inaccessible to scientific study. Girard met considerable resistance from the Mayan elders, and only after more than twenty years of mutual acquaintance was he able to gain their trust, receive their insights, and be admitted to their ceremonies. Through Girard's work, it is the Chorti and Quiché-Maya tribes who express themselves about their own worldview and past. This is the truly unprecedented dimension of his work.

Four Ages: The Narrative of the Popol Vuh

Throughout this work I have availed myself of the 1947 translation of Adrian Recinos, *Popol Vuh: las antiguas historias del Quiché*; the more recent English version by D. Tedlock, *Popol Vuh: The Definitive Edition of the Mayan Book of the Dawn of Life and the Glories of Gods and Kings*; and Goetz and Morley's translation of Recinos's Spanish version, *Popol Vuh: The Sacred Book of the Ancient Quiché Maya*.[25]

The Popol Vuh portends to be the revelation of the gods, which it proceeds to enumerate. The preamble describes the division of the book between the deeds of the gods and the subsequent human history. Mention is made of an original Popol Vuh that no longer exists. According to the text, in the original was clearly visible "the coming from the other side of the sea [likely reference to Atlantis] and the narration of our obscurity, and our life" (Preamble).

The Popol Vuh begins in the same way as the Book of Genesis. The earth was not yet created and air and water were the only two elements present. It was still night. The world was set in motion by the Progenitors—the Great Mother and the Great Father—and the duo Tepeu and Gucumatz, who were in the waters. In the heaven was Heart of Heaven, also called Huracan. Heart of Heaven is one and threefold, formed of Caculha Huracan, the lightning, Chipi Caculha, the small flash, Raxa Caculha, the thunder.[26] Tepeu and Gucumatz deliberated together on how to bring light and life. From the heavens came forth the creative word of Heart of Heaven. From the mutual deliberation and wishes of the gods and through their creative word, the earth sprang forth. Later the mountains, valleys, and trees arose. Tepeu and Gucumatz addressed Heart of Heaven in rejoicing. The latter replied, "Our creation will be concluded."

What follows is the creation of human beings. There were three stages and three failures. The fourth successful attempt is elaborated in much more detail later in the text, throughout Parts I and II.

The first stage was the creation of the "brutes," beings that lived very close to the animalistic stage. Each of them was assigned his own territory. The gods begged the brutes to call on their creators, to hallow their names. But none of them could speak, although each uttered different sounds. After a second trial the gods realized their failure. They decreed that the brutes would be of benefit for their flesh, that they would have to sacrifice themselves for others, becoming in effect animals.

Still, the gods yearned for a being that could call on their name and bring them sustenance. The second human being was thus created from earth and mud, but it lacked cohesion and strength. It could speak but had no reason, nor could he multiply. The gods undid their creation and now called on the help of the pair of ancients, Ixpiyacoc and Ixmucane, described as diviners and soothsayers. They had to create mortal man. This was the stage of the creation of Wood Man, the mannequins made of wood. They resembled men, and could talk, procreate, and spread over the earth. Their feet and hands weren't fully formed, nor did they have blood or fat. They lacked a soul, reason, and any memory of their creators. Their forgetfulness was the source of their disgrace. That is why Heart of Heaven caused a flood that brought about the end of Wood Man.

At the stage of Third Man, for the first time the Popol Vuh mentions an explicit differentiation of the sexes. Man's flesh was made from *tzite*, a bean, the woman from *tule*, a reed. However, human beings still lacked thought, and did not remember to honor the gods. A dark, endless rain caused their ruin this time. Not only the elements rebelled against humanity—so did the utensils and the domesticated animals. Pots, pans, grinding stones, and dogs complained of having been mistreated by their owners. The animals and utensils wanted the humans to experience the pain they endured. Humanity was thus annihilated. Only the monkeys in the woods survived as descendents of that age. We will discuss the Fourth Age in greater detail throughout much of the rest of the book.

The Four Ages and Evolution of Consciousness

American interpretation of history has been mired in insurmountable difficulties. With the nearly absolute absence of dates in the time before our era it is almost impossible to give mythologies their due and place events in a context of time. The Popol Vuh allows us to lay the foundations of the stages of development of pre-historical and historical American civilizations. That stages of development and stages of consciousness of humanity do not coincide will become obvious through some basic observation. The present day Native Americans differ greatly among themselves through their social organization, religious practices, worldviews, etc. The inhabitants of the Tierra del Fuego live at a stage of development antedating the introduction of religious ritual. So did the Yahi and their last representative, Ishi. Nomadic cultures, such as the Apache or Sioux, differ from agricultural societies such as the Pueblos. Consciousness did not evolve homogeneously throughout the continent. Added to this, different waves of immigration succeeded each other throughout the centuries.

We will call attention to the difference between the stages of development of various civilizations and stages of consciousness by calling the first one Age (First Age, Second Age, etc.) and the second one Man (First Man, Second Man, etc.). First Man is a stage of consciousness originating from the First Age but subsisting through all the subsequent Ages. In the present Fourth Age, all the stages of consciousness co-exist; thus we have First Man, Second Man. Third Man, and Fourth Man. The reader needs to keep in mind that the process of evolution of consciousness is an ongoing one. At no stage does it fully replicate the past. The Fueguiños, inhabiting the southern tip of the Americas, do not possess the same pre-religious consciousness or practices that were widespread when all of America was still at their stage of development.

To be able to follow the stages of development of consciousness we need to refer to a homogeneous group. To be able furthermore to place these in a chronology, we need to refer to one such process of development that was brought to completion at the major turning points of American development. Such is the process described in the Popol Vuh because of the central role played in Mesoamerica by Mayan civilization. What the Popol Vuh shows, unlike many other mythologies of the continent, is the complete unfolding of four successive stages of consciousness and their full achievement. The Fourth Age marks the full achievement of historical consciousness. This stage was first attained by Mayan civilization, as we will see later. How the Aztecs could claim to have reached further to the stage of a Fifth Sun is a matter that will be elucidated in chapter nine.

A further difficulty in the present analysis lies in the continuous waves of migration. We have seen above that already before the end of the Atlantean times there were migrations from the sinking continent. Later migratory waves came from Asia; they are the ones that history mostly acknowledges. In more recent times as research begins to highlight more and more, there have also been migrations reaching the Americas from Europe. The races most often mentioned in this context are the Celts, Phoenicians, Babylonians, and Hebrews. We will consider some of these migrations in later chapters, particularly in the seventh. Otherwise we can consider that the agent of change won't be as important as the nature of the change of consciousness and the stage of development to which it corresponds.

Steiner has described the development of humanity from the times of Lemuria, through Atlantis, to the development of the present post-Atlantean epoch. These descriptions will serve here as a parallel frame of reference. We must keep in mind that the orderly development of the epochs of civilization (Polaris, Hyperborea, Lemuria, Atlantis, present earth) is differentiated all over the earth. While Atlantis was undergoing its own evolution, other areas of the earth were inhabited, and were undergoing a parallel evolution. There isn't one sequence of development that applies all over the globe, but rather particular sequences according to the different prehistorical developments that occurred in any geographical area.

There is general agreement between archaeologists and the native documents of Central and South America as far as the first three ages are concerned (see tableau on p. 52). The Ages have also been called the Suns or Worlds. In different places of the Popol Vuh we are told of the Dawning. This event refers as much as to an external occurrence as it does correspond to a change of consciousness. For some ethnic groups such as the Hopis, each successive change of consciousness is seen as another Dawning or, in their terms, an "Emergence."

In order to amplify the understanding of the four ages we will refer to the Popol Vuh, Part I, Chapters 1 to 3. To this will be added the record of archaeology. What follows is a short summary of the narrative of the Three Ages up to the beginning of the Fourth, with the help of Girard's added research.[27]

First Age: The Giants

During the First Age humans still lived within a paradisiacal world with no knowledge of evil. There was no real social structure and the division in moieties or clans did not exist yet. Life was organized in small blood-related, patrilineal groups. Girard calls this a purely individualistic stage. We actually prefer to call it pre-individualistic, since it precedes sexual differentiation and later evolution of individuality. Life was lived in simple communion with the spiritual world. People, we are told, had a sense of the presence of the creator. There was as yet no ritual because there was no need for religion. Nor was there any ceremony of burial of the dead. In fact, spiritual science indicates that people did not go through the cycle of incarnation and excarnation. We are also told that they had no faculty of speech: "Speak our names, praise us, your mother, your father.... But they could not make them speak like men; they only hissed, screamed, cackled; they were unable to make words and each screamed in a different way" (Popol Vuh, Part I, Chapter 2). First Man did not know pottery and did not build houses or temples but dwelt in caves.

This stage corresponds—at least in terms of consciousness—to the early stages of Lemurians, who spiritual science tells us had no faculty of speech but transmitted thought through a kind of telepathy. Memory had not yet developed. Lemurians had power over the forces of their body; they could for example increase their strength through their will. Theirs was a "religion of the will." Those who held power were venerated by the others. The episode of Vucub Caquix and his sons—which refers to First Man (rather than First Age)—will highlight this titanic strength. Of Lemuria, Steiner says that the majority of humanity could only be qualified as merely reaching an animal stage. We see therefore that what the Popol Vuh defines as human of the First Age is equivalent to humanity at the early Lemurian stage of development.

The end of the First Age comes with humans' transformation into animals—those that incarnated too soon. "Accept your destiny: your flesh shall be torn to pieces. So shall it be. This shall be your lot" (Part I, Chapter 2). Humanity of the First Age still existed in later times. It is native knowledge that not all the First Men disappeared or were transformed into animals. We will see an example of it in the next chapter of the Popol Vuh with the episode of Vucub Caquix.

Second Age: Religion

Humans of the Second Age knew how to speak but lacked understanding. They are called Mud Man in the sacred text. Girard defined the Second Age as patriarchal and collective. The social organization evolved to the level of moieties, practicing so-called exogamic marriage outside of one's moiety. The simplest unit is the macro-family of three generations. Property is held in common. The village has become the political unity and is now ruled by a council of chiefs. The gods that play a role in this period are what the Popol Vuh calls the Ahpus. The social organization is hinted at in the episode of Vucub Caquix, where humans of the Second Age (or Second Man in the specific episode) is represented by the "Four Hundred Boys," 400 (20 x 20) standing for a very large number in Mayan esotericism. This way of characterizing the group specifies at once the patriarchal and collective nature of the social organism. At this stage the sons inherit the moral and intellectual qualities of their progenitors.

Other innovations result from the Second Age. Most emblematic is the introduction of pottery, symbolic of the name Mud Man. Here we see a sign of the progressive movement from the prevailing Atlantean element of water toward the element of earth. Pottery is a further stage of dominion over the solid element. It will be followed in time with the use of wood and later stone in sculpture and architecture. The Ahpus introduce the arts, singing and painting in particular. Dancing probably dates from this period too. The first cultivated plants are roots: yucca, jicama, sweet potato, taro, etc. Maize hasn't been introduced yet!

This Second Age had many similarities with the second part of Lemuria. Memory had developed but there was as yet no capacity for logical thinking. Language had its beginnings and so had singing and dancing, and the cultivation of plants for foodstuffs. The Popol Vuh points to a first knowledge of good and evil. With time the Second Age brought the transition from nomadic to sedentary life and the movement toward matriarchal society.

Overall the transition from First to Second Age was a small one. Its main result was the formation of a social structure. The only heroes of this age were the Four Hundred Boys; no true individuals are mentioned. The second Age ended with a flood. The Third Age will introduce much more radical changes.

Third Age: Matriarchy

The Third Age is the age of "Wood Man." The Quiché text indicates that man is made of the "wood" of *tzite*, a bean, and woman is made of *tule*, a reed used for making mats. Both plants originate from Guatemala. For the first time man is clearly distinguished from woman. The name Wood Man is associated with the fact that humans enter the time of wooden implements, and of wooden sculpture.

The gods ask the help of Ixmucane and Ixpiyacoc, a couple of diviners. Ixpiyacoc, the male figure, plays a passive role in Mayan mythology. Ixmucane, the active one, indicates the transition from a patriarchal, or rather pre-individual, worldview into a matriarchal regime. Succession happens on the mother's side. The Grandmother (Ixmucane) is the head of the clan. Men have a politico-military role. We now see three generations: Ixmucane and Ixpiyacoc, Hun and Vucub Hunahpu (the so-called Ahpus), Hun Batz and Hun Chouen. The latter live with the Grandmother. At this stage the Ahpus initiate their descent into the Underworld. Before leaving, they ask Hun Batz and Hun Chouen to continue cultivating the arts and keep the fire in the hearth going, as well as "the warmth in the heart of your grandmother" (Part II, Chapter 2).

Hun Batz and Hun Chouen are the guides of this age. Their nature is still that of divine guides. They are musicians, singers, painters, sculptors, jewelers, dice players, and ball players (Part II, Chapter 1). The effects of their innovations are dramatic. The Third Age starts with the domestication of animals and the true beginnings of horticulture. Maize, beans, and probably also the squash are introduced, and they will constitute the staple foods of all the generations to come. Smoking follows the cultivation of tobacco. Other important cultivated plants are cocoa and copal (burned as incense). With cotton comes the art of weaving. The grindstone is also introduced in this period. Curiously it is called *camé*, as are the lords who rule in the later part of the Third Age.

Camé is an important name in the Third Age. Evil, now active in the world, is referred to through the presence of the adversary clan of Xibalba and its leaders, Hun Camé and Vucub Camé. We are told that the *tucurs* (magicians, literally owls) carry out human sacrifice inaugurated by the Camé. The task of the Third Age is to develop knowledge of the Underworld. The process will only be completed at the end of the Third Age with the episode of the descent of the Twins to the Underworld. We now find reference to the first use of torture by ants and thorns (as in the episode of the infancy of Hunahpu and Ixbalamqué). Human sacrifice appears in the form of decapitation (as in the death of the Hun Hunahpu) and quartering. Cannibalism also originates from this cultural horizon. Later, human sacrifice evolves toward the forms with organ removal.

In the religious field we witness the veneration of the dead and the appearance of the god of death. The dead are now buried in permanent cemeteries. There also develops the practice of secondary burial with exhumation of the bones, which are later hung on a tree. This goes together with the idea that the soul resides in the bones. Mummification is a practice that goes in the same direction and that mostly developed in South America. As we can see, humanity of this age wrestle with the question of immortality, which will only be resolved in the following age. Doubts about the immortality of the soul are accompanied by an intensifying dread of death and of the "end of times." The New Fire Ceremony—celebrated every 52 years—is a vestige of this dread of death and of the end of times, as will appear more clearly when we turn to the study of Mesoamerican astrology.

The end result of the above evolution is the differentiation of the three worlds common to much of American mythology: heavens, earth, and underworld. The fall from the original state of union with the gods is accompanied by knowledge of the soul as that which weaves between the world of the spirit and the world of body and matter. The upper world is the world of spirit, that which lives beyond good and evil. The underworld is where good and evil are both present—it is the world of the soul. It should not be understood as a negative world, an equivalent of doctrinal hell, but rather as the world through which the soul evolves in its way to the land of the spirit. This is reflected in the fact that the dead are both sought under the earth or above in mountains or clouds; these are steps of their journey in the afterlife.

The priesthood becomes hereditary. The priest is also a healer and can predict the future. He is the shaman who can abandon his body through the intermediary of an animal guide. The introduction of animal sacrifice occurs also during this time—turkeys being the animal of choice. The first calendars are lunar, reflecting the importance of matriarchy.

The Third Age corresponds in many ways to the end of Lemuria and the transition into Atlantis. At this stage appear the beginnings of language, the predominant role of women, the domestication of animals and the introduction of agriculture, as well as the use of sacrificial animals. The end of the Third Age comes through a black rain (Part II, Chapter 3) and the rebellion of animals and utensils against humanity. It isn't clear whether the end of the age comes through rain or volcanic eruptions. However, references to volcanic and tectonic phenomena are clearly expressed in the chapter of Vucub Caquix, during the Third Age. At the end of the age Hun Batz and Hun Chouen are transformed into monkeys. The two will later represent the vices of idleness and envy in the Fourth Age.

Fourth Age

The Fourth Age will occupy us specifically in chapter 6. For the moment we can specify that it marks the transition from mythical to historical consciousness. The story of the three previous ages indicates which qualities humans lacked and needed to develop. During the First Age the human being is a mere brute and has no faculty of speech. During the Second Age the human can be compared to a mere lump of mud and has no memory. During the Third Age the human is like a wooden statue; no faculty of understanding, and lack of blood indicates lack of will. The ingredients that humanity needs to develop are spiritual: the power to speak, to remember, and to think. Maize Man, who has all the above qualities, inaugurates the Fourth Age. Maize Man's fate is associated with a whole new development of agriculture, intimately connected with ritual life and astrology.

Moral development is one way of looking at the deeper meanings of the Popol Vuh. Good and evil don't have merely a set role. They are only relative terms. The good of one epoch becomes the evil of the following one. The shaman/priest of the third epoch becomes the sorcerer of the fourth period. Hun Batz and Hun Chouen are the guides of the Third Age. By resisting the rise of the Twins they came to embody the vices of the next period: laziness, cruelty, and envy. This does not mean that they do not have a lawful place even in the Fourth Age. There they are the patrons of the arts and of merriment. The four representatives of First Age become the cosmic bearers of the following ages. Nothing is static in the Popol Vuh. All truly corresponds to the reality of the spiritual development of races and peoples.

Girard highlights the fact that archaeology and indigenous sources are in agreement as far as the first three ages are concerned. To these three horizons Girard adds the horizon of the Fourth Age and Mayan patriarchy. Modern archaeology does not stress the differences of level of development reached by the Maya in relation to their contemporary cultures as Girard does in following the inner logic of the Popol Vuh. This is summarized in the following tableau:

According to Archaeologists	According to the Popol Vuh	Developments
1st Horizon: Pre-historic	*1st Age:* "Brutes"	Hunter-gatherers
2nd Horizon: Archaic	*2nd Age:* "Mud Man" "Four Hundred Boys"	Invention of pottery, early development of Agriculture
3rd Horizon: Formative	*3rd Age:* "Wood Man," Matriarchy	Sacred Calendar Calendar Round, maize cultivation
Classic Maya	*4th Age:* "Maize Man," Patriarchy	Long Count, second maize crop

It is now possible to try to find a time frame for the four successive epochs. There are no strict correspondences between the four Ages and the epochs defined by Steiner; there are only parallels. The Ancient Toltecs—who emigrated from Atlantis before the Flood—carried an Atlantean consciousness to a continent that had not yet received the civilizing impulse of Atlantis. We find therefore mostly pre-Atlantean traits in the early populations of Mesoamerica. The First Age would correspond to this original American population. Whether living at the time of Atlantis or earlier, it remained at a pre–Atlantean stage of consciousness. The Second Age sees the beginning of a social organization, most likely the one introduced by the Ancient Toltecs in their first emigration from Atlantis. The Third Age appears through the rise of Olmec civilization, as we will see in the images of the Popol Vuh. It is the main thesis of this book that the Fourth Age in Mesoamerica was ushered by the Maya at the time of Christ. The demonstration of the above theses is the subject of the following chapters.

The terminology referring to the periods of Mesoamerican history varies slightly according to authors or schools of thought. Thus, for example, what is Late Formative for some can be found as Proto-Classic for others. In order to keep homogeneity throughout the work we will refer to the following terminology:

Before 1500 BC:	Archaic
1500–800 BC:	Early Formative: onset of Olmec civilization
800–300 BC:	Middle Formative
300 BC–0:	Late Formative
AD 0–200:	Proto-Classic: rise of Mayan and Teotihuacan civilizations
AD 200–600:	Early Classic
AD 600–900:	Late Classic
AD 900–1200:	Terminal Classic/Early Post-Classic
AD 1200–Conquest (1519):	Late Post-Classic: rise of the Aztecs

For our purposes, First and Second Age are the periods that can be defined as Archaic, the Third Age closely corresponds with the rise of the Olmec and the Formative; the Fourth Age corresponds to the rise of Mayan civilization.

The different Ages bring with them different kinds of consciousness. To the original Lemurians and the Atlantean immigrants were added the waves of migration of the post-Atlantean times before and after the time of Christ. They form a complex chapter in the history of the Americas, one that lies beyond the scope of the present work. We will nevertheless explore the influences that reached Central America through Asia via the Bering Strait, and from Phoenicia and Palestine. To sum up then, the Four Ages give us a valid key of interpretation of the spiritual evolution of American humanity, a blueprint of development that receives confirmation from the anthropological record of North and South America. The Popol Vuh refers more to stages of consciousness than to historical migrations, because its focus is the central event of the Dawning and the spiritual forces that either opposed it or worked toward its realization.

The Four Ages and the Challenge of Post-Atlantean Time

Part II of the Popol Vuh explains in imaginative language the nature of the changes that occurred during the Fourth Age. It is the thesis of this book that the initiate of the Americas brought about the Fourth Age. Therefore we will deal in depth with the Fourth Age in chapters 6 and 7. At this moment it will be sufficient to indicate the progression of consciousness that can be followed from the First to the Fourth Age.

The Fourth Age is inaugurated by the Dawning and is the Age of Maize Man. Of the Ahpus that initiate the first descent to the Underworld, we are reminded that they are born in darkness. The Twins inaugurate the solar age. The change can be compared to a re-quickening of the earth. The Chilam Balam of Chumayel states: "The month [meaning the new astrology] was created when the earth awoke."[28] This leads us to believe that the Native American perceived at this stage important changes in the aura of the earth. Dawning and awakening on the earthly level further correspond to important changes of consciousness.

The Native American Atlantean-like consciousness had to undergo a dual process. On one hand it had to progressively penetrate the earth element, the element of space. Significantly the Second Man is Man of Mud, who did not quite reach a solid state. Next is Man of Wood, and we are told that only the last human had blood. As a Man of Maize he belongs to heaven, earth, and underworld just like the maize plant does at different stages of its development. The latter part of the Popol Vuh makes this notion very clear. The former sculptures of the continent make the words of the Popol Vuh understandable: "they had no extremities." The first sculptures show a very rudimentary knowledge of anatomy: the extremities are barely present. It is primarily at the stage of classical Mayan sculpture that the human body reaches the highest harmony of measure and proportion, fully representing human anatomy. It seems as though American Man gradually gains possession and consciousness of the full nature of the earthly element that permeates his body, as his consciousness progressively withdraws from the divine element of the environment.

The second process concerns the human being's relationship to time. The Fall from Paradise occurs at the end of the First Age. The pristine stage of union reached in the First Age leads us to the last stage of knowledge of immortality attained by Man of Maize. The "brute" doesn't need religion because he is in contact with the divinity. The Men of the Second and Third Age discover through memory the link between generations, initiate the rituals of burial, and inaugurate the era of religious practices. Man of the Third Age struggles with the notions of the underworld and of mortality. Here appears the problem of the finiteness of time. From this originates the dread of the extinction of the world so aptly depicted with the New Fire ceremony, as we will see in the chapters about the Toltecs and the Aztecs. The astronomy of these two civilizations cannot depict the certainty of the continuity of time. That the Maya inaugurate another stage of civilization is highlighted by the resurrection of their solar god, Hunahpu, and the lunar counterpart, Ixbalamqué. What would appear as a mere symbol in the myth becomes a reality in the fact that the Maya are the first to devise a calendar that is no longer cyclical. It moves forward into eternity, because it is now based on a galactic point of reference.

Accompanying this movement of fall and redemption is the movement of separation between heaven and earth. From a world of waters and air we move into the creation of earth and mountains. Later in the Second Age, but especially in the Third Age, the Native American discovers the underworld. This movement deepens with the growing strength of the Camé and the Lords of Xibalba. Good and evil stand in full antagonism. The integration of underworld, earth, and upper-world can only occur through the integration of human and divine elements in the figures of the Twins. It is their resurrection that brings a new world and a new consciousness, accompanied by the event of the Dawning.

The Four Ages in North and South America

Knowledge of the Four Worlds echoes with variations in the traditions of both North and South America. We will take the Hopi and the Inca as an example of each. We must keep in mind that the correspondence is only indicative since each civilization had its own development, comes from a different background, and met with different migrating populations and defining changes of civilization. Therefore, the changes of consciousness do not necessarily occur at the same points in time.

In Hopi mythology, during the First Age Spider Woman created four male beings, then four females.[29] These first people could neither speak nor reproduce. This age knew of no sickness and no evil; people were still pure and happy. The end of the First World came from the human beings using "their vibratory centers," i.e., supernatural faculties, for selfish purposes. The world was destroyed by fire.

During the Second World people could still talk to each other from the center of their heads. They started to quarrel, and war and greed broke out in their ranks. Humanity had to defend itself from wild animals. The Second World was destroyed by cold and ice.

The Third World saw the emergence of big cities and civilizations. People started to use their reproductive faculties in evil ways. This world was destroyed by the Flood and some of its people were saved by Spider Woman. They had to undergo repeated migrations. The protector of the Third Age was the important Hopi god Masaw, a Guardian figure. Having lost humility, Masaw was appointed god of death and of the underworld by the supreme god Taiowa.

Masaw was also the deity who asked the Hopi to undertake their migrations before he could become their leader in the Fourth Age. Each group had to follow its own star before reaching its destination. The Fourth World wasn't "beautiful and easy" like the previous ones but was the first world that has height and depth, heat and cold, beauty and ugliness.

The Hopi portray the transition from one world to the next as an "emergence." It is as if each stage from the First to the Fourth World were a progressive movement from darkness toward the light of day. This worldview is replicated in the structure of the ceremonial kiva that has a hole in the ground, called *sipapu*, to indicate the place of emergence from a previous world, and a ladder leading to an opening in the ceiling, in the direction of the next world.

Girard indicates that Andean cultures also subdivided their cultural development into four ages. Some of their early historians preserved the tradition, the most complete version being given by Guaman Poma.[30] The First Age, Pakanmok Runa, starts with a land inhabited with wild animals and monsters such as giants, dwarves, and ghosts. The "People of the Dawn" were the first to conquer the land. They were nomads dwelling in caves. They lived off berries and buried their dead without any ceremonies.

The Second Age is the Age of the Wan Runa (indigenous people). The god Alpamanta Rurac made the creatures of the Second Age out of mud. This period marked the beginning of sedentary life and agricultural activity. Human beings abandoned caves for the first dwellings called *pukullo*. The invention of pottery was attributed to the gods. The people adored the lightning god Illapa, their symbol of life and death; the *kuntur* (condor), bird of the sun; and *kuri poma*, the golden lion. The idea of the underworld was fully born. At this time arrived the god Tonapa or Tarapaca. The Second Age ended with a flood and the rebellion of the domestic animals and utensils.

The Third Age is called the Age of the Purun Runa. The land was used more intensively. There were more cultivated plants, and llama and alpaca were domesticated. Cooperative work reached a climax. Among the inventions of the age were weaving and metal work. There was the use of drums and flutes, but still no writing. Another typical introduction of this age was the ritual use of fermented drinks. The sovereigns, called Capac Apo, were carried in a litter, a characteristic of the Third Age that survives in many cultures.

The Fourth Age is the time of the Auka Runa, "people of the times of war." The internal struggles of the previous age reached a climax. This was the time of the fortified cities called *pukaras*. The farmers left the lowlands to take refuge in the high plateau. During this age the practices of cannibalism and human sacrifice, even with removal of the heart, reached a peak. The dead were buried with their food and goods, the men sometimes with their women. From our perspective we can see that even though this was called a Fourth Age, it was in reality only a stage of decadence of the Third Age. The three previous ages have similarities and correspondences with the ages of the Popol Vuh, although the Andean Second Age corresponds more closely to the Mesoamerican Third Age. This is to be expected, given the possible differences between the continents.

CHAPTER 3

POPOL VUH: THE DEEDS
OF THE GREAT SPIRIT

W E WILL let the Popol Vuh yield as much insight and knowledge
as possible before trying to add any interpretation that could be offered
through the insight of spiritual science. In order to reach that stage we will
explore first the stage of the Third Age, of which the descent of the Ahpus
to the Underworld captures the essence.

After the fourth chapter of Part I the Popol Vuh tells us of the deeds of
the gods, in particular the Ahpus and the Twins, Hunahpu and Ixbalamqué. The narrative goes back and forth between the Twins first, then the
Ahpus, and the Twins again afterward. At the end of the story of the Ahpus
we are told that the Twins are their descendants. This is one of the reasons
to believe that the first episode of the Twins occurs in time after the story
of the Ahpus. But there are more reasons than that.

In the first episode of the Twins they are confronted by the giants,
called Vucub Caquix and Chimalmat, and their two sons, Zipacna and
Capracan. These giants are representatives of a patriarchal age (the only
woman, Chimalmat, is barely mentioned) and more particularly the First
Age. Are they men of the First Age, or First Man of a later age? Having
seen what characterizes the different ages we can find clues in the text. The
text refers to the presence of Men of the Second Age—the Four Hundred
Boys—who have adopted a communal lifestyle. The text also mentions
the use of *chicha*, a fermented maize alcohol. Both maize and fermented
beverages appeared in the Third Age. To make things clearer, in referring
to the giants, the Popol Vuh also states: "Truly, they are clear examples
of those people who drowned, and their nature is that of supernatural
beings" (Part I, Chapter 4). This is a precise reference to the fact that the

giants are representatives of First Man at a later point in time. This places us in time at the Third Age, and the active presence of the elderly Ixmu-cané and Ixpiyacoc further confirms the whole tableau.

We see how important it has been to be able to recognize the different ages and their characteristics. The story of the gods' confrontation with the opposing forces is thus divided in two according to the kinds of beings that they confront. This is the inner logic of the Popol Vuh. In the first part (Part I, Chapters 4 to 9) the Twins confront the forces of the heights, the Giant Vucub Caquix and his sons. In Part II, first the Ahpus and then the Twins confront the opposing force of the depths, the lords of Xibalba. In fact the whole of Part II of the Popol Vuh is concerned with confronting the forces of Xibalba. However, all of the episodes of the Twins occur during the same age, the third one. So does the descent of the Ahpus into the underworld.

It is finally understandable why Vucub Caquix has been presented first and the whole of the story pertaining to the lords of Xibalba comes later. The progressive gods are challenged from two sides. The first is the less serious threat of the return to the past. The second is a much more diffi-cult confrontation, upon which depends the emergence of the Fourth Age. We will modify the order of the Popol Vuh in order to follow the events more sequentially.

Who are the main characters in this divine plot? Of the Ahpus we are told that they play all day long and that they are sages and diviners. The fact that they don't work makes it obvious that they are gods. They are distinguished as Hun Hunahpu (1 Hunahpu) and Vucub Hunahpu (7 Hunahpu). They appear as two beings; in reality they are the numerals of seven gods, a usual Mayan way to present the gods. We will see it on other occasions: Hun Chouen (One Artisan) and Hun Batz (One Monkey) are the divine guides of the age. The situation is different for the Twins Hunahpu and Ixbalamqué. They are the sons of the Ahpus and of Ixquic, resulting from the union of a god with a woman. They are the sons of a virgin. This is a familiar theme of Mesoamerican and American mythol-ogy, as we have seen in chapter 1. The Twins are both human and divine. We will see later that the duality of twins is a way to distinguish different realities. In other words, the Twins can be seen as an imaginative device, similar to what we saw in Hopi mythology where we find a Youth and an Echo, two seemingly unrelated entities. In effect the Twins will have to struggle with the lords of the underworld as humans. We are told of the

Twins' birth as well as of their infancy, needless details for all the other gods. The lords of the underworld are separated in the Camé and their subordinates, the Lords of Xibalba. The author is indebted for many insights into this part of the narrative by the work of both Rafael Girard and Nahum Megged.[1]

The Narrative

Part II of the Mayan text starts with a genealogy of the Ahpus Hun Hunahpu and Vucub Hunahpu. They descended from the ancient diviners Ixpiyacoc and Ixmucané. From the Ahpus descended Hun Batz and Hun Chouen. Their mother was called Ixbaquiyalo, who was the wife of Hun Hunahpu, but she is never mentioned again in the book. Hun Batz and Hun Chouen were diviners and wise men. The brothers were devoted to the arts: flute playing, singing, hunting with the blowgun, painting, sculpting, jewelry, and gold-work.

Hun Hunahpu and Vucub Hunahpu spent their time playing at dice and at the ball game. Having gone to play ball on the way to the realm of Xibalba they were heard by Hun Camé and Vucub Camé in the realm of the underworld. Their play disturbed the lords. The Camé wanted to call the two gods to the underworld because they desired the adornments and gear that the Ahpus used for the ball game. Therefore the Camé sent messengers with an invitation to play ball in their realm and a request that the Ahpus bring their gear. Before leaving the Ahpus communicated to the grandmother, Ixmucané, their decision to go to Xibalba. To the sons Hun Batz and Hun Chouen they entrusted the care of the grandmother and the cultivation of the arts.

The Ahpus went down a steep stairway leading toward the underworld. They arrived at an underground river in the canyons called Nuzivan Cul and Cuzivan, and crossed it. They later crossed another river that passed through thorny bushes, a river of blood without drinking of it, and a final river. They went on further to where four paths met: one was red, the second black, the third white, and the last yellow. The black path told them: "I am the path you need to take, that will lead you to the Lord."

Upon arriving at the council hall of Xibalba they met two wooden mannequins. Taking them for the lords they saluted them, causing the hilarity of the Lords of Xibalba. Having introduced themselves the lords offered the visitors stone seats. Unaware that the seats were hot the two awakened to the surprise, causing again the jollity of the hosts. The lords now submitted the Ahpus to the first of many tests: the Cave of Darkness. The Ahpus were each given a lit pine torch and a lit cigar. Their task was to keep the place lit and return all the objects whole the next day. The next day, when torches and cigars had been consumed, the Twins were condemned to being sacrificed. After doing this and before burial, the head of Hun Hunahpu was hung on a tree. Simultaneously with the placing of the head, this tree bore fruit for the first time. However, the original head could not be distinguished from the rest of the fruits.

The Descent of the Ahpus to the Underworld

The descent of the Ahpus inaugurates a new age, indicated when they tell Hun Batz and Hun Chouen, sons of Hun Hunahpu: "Keep on playing the flute and singing, painting and carving; warm our house and warm the heart of our Grandmother" (Part II, Chapter 2). This episode marks an important transition. This is the American equivalent of the Twilight of the Gods. The Elohim leave their original dwelling. In consolation they send to humanity their sons as guides to help them reconnect with the spiritual worlds through religion and the arts. The guides, Hun Batz and Hun Chouen, are most likely human beings acting completely out of divine inspiration. Their lives have no recorded biography, apart from their demise at the end of the Third Age.

The episode of the Ahpus contrasts with the two episodes of the Twins. The Ahpus lack wisdom, cunning, and knowledge of the laws of earth. Their adventure in the realm of Xibalba looks like a naïve rout. The Ahpus play the ball game on the surface of the earth. They do not know that they are playing above the realm of Xibalba.

Whether the Ahpus play the ball game is not said. Still the confrontation appears in other terms. They come to meet the world of death that they do not know, shown by the successive stages. At first they are shown the mannequins, which they do not differentiate from the living; they salute them, causing the derision of the Xibalbans. Finally, at the end of their trials the Ahpus are told, "This very day you shall disappear and your memory will be obliterated." This is the further trial by which the Ahpus are induced to believe that there is nothing after death, no resurrection.

The above is the first superficial message of the episode. That this is not all appears after a second reading of the text. The gods of the heavens visit their counterparts but leave their ball and gear at home. In effect they do not give their enemies any of their attributes, the powers that the Camé want to acquire. The Ahpus' demise is only a preliminary exploration of the realm of death. The gods need to know about Xibalba and human death.

The Ahpus are defeated in the Cave of Darkness. This is a test that requires them to maintain light in the darkness. They fail because they cannot maintain consciousness in the realm of death. Thus they are sacrificed. The text specifies that Hun Hunahpu is beheaded and his body is buried together with the body of Vucub Hunahpu. It is already clear that Hun Hunahpu's function is differentiated from Vucub Hunahpu's. This idea will reappear frequently.

The head of Hun Hunahpu is placed on the fork of a tree. The first seeds of resurrection are planted in the realm of Xibalba. The text says: "And having put the head in the tree, instantly the tree, which had never borne fruit before the head of Hun Hunahpu was placed among its branches, was covered with fruit. And this calabash tree, it is said, is the one which we now call the head of Hun-Hunahpu" (Part II, Chapter 2). The tree, which has never fruited, becomes a Tree of Life or World Tree. Head and gourd are linguistically equivalent: head is *ahpu*, and so is chief.

The end of the descent into the underworld reinforces the feeling that a twilight of the gods has occurred. The Ahpus have worked at reducing the gap between the heavens and the underworld that they do not comprehend. American humanity seems to fall prey to the Camé, although on the other hand Hun Batz and Hun Chouen continue to offer guidance and inspiration. The stage is set for a confrontation between the lords of the underworld and the guiding powers of the Third Age. The Ahpus, seemingly defeated, have preserved their power from the lords of the underworld and sown life in the underworld. This life represented by the gourds on the tree is the beginning of the next stage of conquest of the realm of death.

The Lords of Xibalba are presented to us as beings capable of inflicting diseases upon the human race (Part II, Chapter 1). Thus the Lords Xiquiripat and Cuchumaquic "caused the shedding of blood of men"; Ahalpuh and Ahalgana "made men swell and make pus gush forth from their legs and stain their faces yellow." They remind us of the image that Steiner paints of the supersensible being Quetzalcoatl, a spirit that he describes as similar to Goethe's Mephistopheles, essentially an Ahrimanic being.[2] He further characterizes him thus: "His symbol was similar to the Mercury staff to be found in the Eastern Hemisphere, the spirit who could disseminate malignant disease through certain magic forces. He could inflict them upon those whom he wished to injure in order to separate them from the relatively good god, Tezcatlipoca."[3]

On all accounts the seven Ahpus, also called Heart of Heaven, are the equivalent in Western tradition of the seven Elohim. Let us hear what Steiner has to say in this context:

> The Indians then took over with them to the West all that was great in the Atlantean culture. What was the greatest of all to the Indian? It was that he was still able dimly to sense something of the ancient greatness and majesty of a period which existed in the old Atlantean epoch, in which the division of the races had hardly begun, in which men could look up to the sun and perceive the Spirits of Form (Elohim) as if through a sea of mist. Through an ocean of mist the Atlantean gazed up at that which to him was not divided into six or seven, but which acted together. This co-operative action of the seven Spirits of Form was called by the Atlanteans the Great Spirit who revealed himself to man in ancient Atlantis.[4]

The transition to earth evolution was marked by the separation of the Elohim Yahve from the six remaining Elohim. Six of the normal Spirits of Form resided in the Sun while Yahve exerted his influence from the Moon, and assumed the leading role. The Popol Vuh is announcing the changing conditions of the times and the transition of consciousness undergone, by describing the Ahpus looking with interest to an earth that they do not fully comprehend. The descent of the Ahpus corresponds to a twilight of the gods and a dimming of the Atlantean-like perception of the world brought about by the growing reality of the underworld and its powers.

CHAPTER 4

THE THIRD AGE

T HE TRANSITION between Second and Third Age is marked first and foremost by an increasing separation between the human and the divine. The shaman is now the intermediary between his fellow human beings and the gods. Knowledge of good and evil also deepens and with it the apprehension of the underworld or soul realm as well as the heavens or higher spiritual worlds. Let us keep in mind that this division of underworld and higher spiritual world concerns the realms of soul and spirit much more specifically than it does the good and evil of traditional Western theology.

The clearest indication of the transition from the Second Age to the Third Age is the passage from an egalitarian age to a religious/hierarchical society. This is why the Popol Vuh refers to Man of the Second Age, surviving in later periods, as the Four Hundred Boys: four hundred, 20 x 20, is the number that stands for very large or infinite in Mayan esotericism. This social transition occurred in Mesoamerica, according to the historical record, around 1500 to 1200 BC. The civilization that ushered these changes was the Olmec, the one that has been defined the "mother culture" of Mesoamerica. Let us turn to the imaginative content of the Popol Vuh before we seek confirmation in the historical record.

To substantiate our claim about the initial spiritual thrust of the Third Age is harder than it is in relation to the Fourth Age. The reason for this lies in the nature of our present studies. The Popol Vuh presents a firm point of reference in imaginative terms. Image after image builds up a picture of the nature of the transition occurring first and foremost at the time of the Fourth Age. To characterize the Fourth Age the author needed first of all to find a point of reference in time that allowed us to place the transition between Third and Fourth Age. Once that had been secured it was possible then to use the imaginative content of Olmec art and everything that anthropology, linguistics, archaeology, and archaeoastrology have brought to light in respect to the Olmecs and all other societies that can be presently characterized as Third Man, i.e., the consciousness of the Third Age as it has survived to the present. Comparing Olmec with present-day Third Man often offers confirmation of the imaginations of the Popol Vuh.

Olmec is the name that researchers have given to that civilization whose most clear traces have survived in southern Veracruz and western Tabasco along the Atlantic coast of Mexico. Olmeca was the name with which the Aztecs referred to the region. The Olmecs have also been identified with the so-called "Middle Formative Ceremonial Complex." "Formative" is the archaeological term that corresponds to the Third Age in historical terms.

Recent research substantiates the fact that before the Olmecs there were essentially egalitarian societies with no social stratification.[1] The latter was thus one of the hallmark changes introduced by the Olmecs. Historians divide Olmec history from a Pre-Olmec to an Epi-Olmec periods with the following approximate ranges of time:

- – Pre-Olmec: 1500–1200 BC
- – Initial Olmec: 1200–900 BC
- – Intermediate Olmec: 900–600 BC
- – Terminal Olmec and Epi-Olmec: 600 BC–1 AD[2]

The earliest evidence of human occupation near the important Olmec site of La Venta, in the so-called "Olmec heartland" in Mexico's southern Gulf Coast area, has been dated to the Pre-Olmec period. The next phase, Initial Olmec, was accompanied by the growth of the important centers of La Venta, Los Cerros, and San Lorenzo, and perhaps already Tres Zapotes. The site of San Lorenzo was short lived and had practically collapsed even before the end of this period.

During the Intermediate Olmec new sites developed, such as Rio Pesquero and San Martin Pajapan. Olmec influence spread from the north of Mexico to as far south as El Salvador and Costa Rica. This influence manifested in complex settlement patterns going from towns to hamlets, craft workshops or local shrines, unified by a social/political economic system, at least at the regional level.

Interestingly, this culture that influenced so much of Mesoamerican social life waned quite abruptly around 400 BC, in the period that has been called Terminal Olmec. This was the time of the demise of La Venta, and of San Lorenzo that had apparently been reoccupied. The period that followed is called Epi-Olmec. Although Olmec iconography persisted, it was a time of decline. Of interest to our analysis is the fact that at the very end of this time appeared the earliest dated stelae in Tres Zapotes and other early inscriptions in the western part of the Olmec territory.

There is no doubt that Olmec influence reached its apogee in the so-called Olmec heartland on the Gulf Coast. There is reason to believe, however, that Olmec culture did not originate from the Gulf Coast but rather from the Pacific Coast. Let us follow the evidence that points in this direction.

FROM SECOND TO THIRD AGE: OLMEC ORIGIN

Our guiding thread through the transition from Second to Third Age comes from looking at the development of the calendar and the rise of agriculture. As we will have abundant occasions to elucidate, the so-called "Sacred Calendar" of 260 days is closely associated in time and function with the development of agriculture and particularly with the cultivation of maize. Where was it that the first agricultural society thrived in Mesoamerica? In the Sacred Calendar is a knowledge that encompasses the awareness of the movements of heavenly bodies, the use of mathematical skills, and the perfecting of the agricultural cycle of maize. The difficulty in planting maize lay in avoiding drying out or flooding of the seed. Maize demanded great awareness of the timing of the rains. Let us therefore look more closely at the development of agriculture in Mesoamerica.

It has been estimated that by 5000 BC about 10% of the diet came from domesticated plants. In 1500 BC that rose up to 35%.[3] In unusually favored agricultural areas the surplus of food made it possible to support a level of labor diversification not possible in other areas. This is what occurred in the Old World in the Valley of the Nile, of the Tigris and Euphrates, and the Indus Valley in Pakistan. Although the soils of the Mexican Gulf Coast plain are fertile, due to their calcareous nature water often lies in depth and is not immediately available. However, all the conditions for abundant agriculture were gathered in the Soconusco, the region of the Pacific Coast lying between southern Mexico and western Guatemala.

German naturalist Hans Gadow (1855–1928) thought that the Sacred Calendar had to originate from tropical lowlands, because of the names of alligator, monkey, iguana, tapir, etc. that are often mentioned. Vincent Malmström focuses on the Soconusco region of the Pacific coast because it has the right geography, the right astronomy, the biology and history that match the Sacred Calendar. He acknowledges others who had come to similar conclusions: Zelia Nuttall in 1928 and Ola Apenes in 1936, though both of them had fallen into the "Copan trap," placing the origin of the Sacred Calendar in Copan. That city is situated at the same latitude of the Soconusco, but further to the east. Girard also recognizes the central importance of the Soconusco in the elaboration of the calendar, although in doing so he mostly focuses on the elaboration of the "Long Count," the crowning refinement of the Sacred Calendar.

The Soconusco gathers all the ideal conditions not only for the cultivation of maize but also for the development of agricultural surpluses that could support the development of civilization. At its largest the Soconusco extends for 200 miles NW–SE from latitudes 13° to 17° along the Pacific coast of southern Mexico and western Guatemala, at a width of 30 miles.

These 6,000 square miles comprise an area of incredible ecological diversity due to ample geographical variations. In this region we move from sea level to an elevation of 13,000 feet: the highest mountain, Tajamulco, is 13,845' high and is situated 20 miles from the Mexican border. On the Mexican side the soil is granite; south of the border it is of volcanic origin. Even though the Mexican soils are poor, they are favored by a good climate.

The temperature fluctuates between 80° and 86°F. Rain comes in a monsoonal pattern with a monthly average of 5"–6". From December to April there is a growing moisture deficit of 22". This amount is more than made up by the end of June. The maximum occurs in September, then the rainfall tapers off in November. Because of this pattern the streams run all year long and the vegetation cover is a lush tropical forest. Maize can be cultivated up to 2,600'. There is a high degree of ecological diversity going from coastal mangroves to tropical forest and *paramo* (a treeless alpine plateau). The very rich fauna abounds with fish, shrimp, mussels, turtles, and aquatic birds and on land tapirs, deer, peccary, etc. With such a rich diversity of food supply the indigenous populations could easily free a great part of their time from work obligations.

From 7000 to 1800 BC people in the region lived in a nomadic lifestyle. The earliest permanent settlements, accompanied by stratified social structures and sophisticated pottery, arose in the Early Formative starting around 1800 BC, the earliest recorded date in Mesoamerica. The periods before the establishment of Olmec influence according to John E. Clark are: Barra period (1850–1650 BC) Lacona period (1650–1500 BC), Ocos period (1500–1350 BC) and Cherla period (1350–1200 BC).[4]

The first evidence of agriculture appears in the Lacona period. The first to be cultivated—due to their ease—were the roots and tubers. By the end of the period maize appeared as the dominant crop. This is why Clark suggested calling these people the Mokaya, signifying "people of the corn" in Mixe-Zoque language. Cacao was also probably exploited by this time. From retrieved ceramics there is some evidence that Lacona influence spread north to Oaxaca and west to the lowlands of Gulf Coast plains through the Tehuantepec isthmus.[5]

From about 1600 BC settlements arose along the Soconusco, which was in fact one of the most heavily populated regions of Mesoamerica. Let us look at three very closely located archaeological sites: Paso de la Amada, Cantón Corralito, and Ojo de Agua. In Paso de la Amada archaeologists have found one of the earliest palaces and the oldest ball court, dating at around 1600 BC.[6]

David Cheetham calls Cantón Corralito "America's first true colony."[7] The place, first explored in 1985, had been a chiefdom center of the Mokaya people. Their tradition came to an abrupt end in about 1200 BC, when Olmec artifacts first appear in the region. Cantón Corrallito covered at least 600 acres by 1000 BC. There are thousands of Olmec-style objects unlike those found anywhere else in Mesoamerica outside of the Olmec heartland along the Gulf Coast. Up to 20% of the pottery analyzed on site came from San Lorenzo, one of the earliest and most important Olmec ceremonial centers. It has been hypothesized that Cantón Corralito was an administrative center of the Olmecs in the region and may have been inhabited by Gulf Olmecs. The occupation of the colony ended by 1000 BC due to flooding by the nearby Coatan River.

Ojo de Agua, at least 250 acres in size, may be the first planned ceremonial center in Mesoamerica and the first with pyramids.[8] The sophisticated pottery of the area dates from 1800 BC. Surprisingly, though it was one of the earlier potteries it produced items of high quality. Early pottery existed elsewhere (e.g., Guerrero) but was much more crude. Ojo de Agua also has a series of earthen mounds. Mounds 5 and 7, suggesting the form of pyramids, may be the earliest pyramids in Mesoamerica. Others do not appear until the creation of La Venta (built around 1200 BC), a second important Olmec center.

There are other signs of the development of high culture in the region of the Soconusco: the first concerns the development of monumental sculpture not unlike the well known Olmec; the other, otherwise unknown in Mesoamerica, is evidence of knowledge of magnetism.

Possibly as far back as the Barra period (1850–1650 BC) the people of Soconusco started erecting monumental sculptures to their chiefs.[9] These sculptures are hard to date because it is argued that they have been moved. Some researchers indicate that they go back to as far as 2000 BC; others place them at around 1200–800 BC and even as late as 500 BC. The statues are situated on the Guatemalan side of the Soconusco, due to the presence there of basalt which is much easier to sculpt than Mexican granite. The rudiments of a body or a head were represented in large rounded boulders of 5' or more in diameter. The outlines were etched in bas-relief with minimal carving. They have been dubbed "fat boys" even though their gender is not recognizable. Most of the time these figures hold their hands wrapped around their bodies so that they nearly come together over the center of the abdomen.

Many of the fat boys are magnetized, as are a number of other sculptures found throughout the region.[10] Eleven statues have been found in La Democracia, Guatemala: four sculptures of human bodies and six of human heads have magnetic properties. In El Baul two statues possessing magnetic properties have also been discovered. One of them represents two men sitting in cross-legged position over a bench. Two north magnetic poles are located where their arms cross and two south poles under the bench. A nearby jaguar has two north magnetic poles in its paws with no detected south poles. A magnetic statue, which could either be that of a turtle head or a frog body, has also been found in Izapa. It has a strong north polarity in its snout and an equally strong south polarity in the extreme back of the head so that it can be compared to a giant bar magnet.

Some generalities emerge in the patterns of magnetization. If the sculpture is a head it is usually magnetized on the right temple; if a body the magnetic pole is usually near the navel.[11] However, nothing has been introduced in the rocks at these points; these are just the places where a higher concentration of magnetite or magnetic iron ore naturally occurs. Usually an opposite pole of attraction exists barely more than 4" away. In the example of the head if magnetic forces enter above the right ear, they leave below it. If they enter the body at the left of the navel, they will leave it to the right of it. Thus, most of the times there is a kind of U-shaped magnetic field. As puzzling and interesting as knowledge of magnetism may have been for the people of Soconusco, we are still in the dark concerning the practical application of or reason for this kind of knowledge.

On the basis of many of these discoveries, many wonder if Olmec culture had its origin in the Soconusco. To elucidate this matter further we will turn to other supporting evidence.

Prior to 1200 BC the so-called Mokaya culture existed in the Soconusco. Through the isthmus the Olmecs initiated cultural exchanges around 1200 BC. The Mokaya subsequently adopted all of the Olmec ceremonial motifs in the use of their pottery. The egalitarian Mokaya society evolved according to Olmec religious stratification, although it still maintained autonomous regional features. That a new consciousness spread appears in the fact that the new stratification persisted for more than twelve centuries.[12]

We have already pointed to the appearance of elaborate pottery as far back as 1800 BC in the Barra period. Between 1350 and 1200 BC archaeologists speak of the Cherla period in which the "Olmec influence" is inferred from the idea that the Olmecs had moved south from the Gulf Coast. This is not supported by archaeological evidence; rather, there is evidence that the opposite occurred. The Ocos style ceramic (of the Lacona period) appears to have spread northward at that time! Ocos is close to Izapa to the south.[13]

The oldest ceremonial center of the Olmecs is San Lorenzo, dating to 1350 BC during the time of the early Cherla phase of the Soconusco. San Lorenzo is also the center that is in most direct proximity to the Soconusco through the Tehuantepec isthmus. This may attest to the northward move of the Zoque-speaking people of Soconusco. The absence of any intermediate settlements is easy to explain given the aridity of the Tehuantepec isthmus. For people used to humid environments and agriculture, nothing like their original habitat appeared until they reached the other side of the divide, where San Lorenzo is placed on a river.

Finally we can look at linguistic evidence. M. Swadesh argues that pre-Mayan language was spoken throughout the Gulf Coast as far back as 1500 BC. He argues that the Huastec (far north of Veracruz) were separated from the Yucatec (spoken in Campeche and Yucatan regions) during the 13th century BC. This would most likely have occurred through the intrusion in the middle of the group of a non-Maya speaking group.[14] This intrusion could have its origin in the Zoque group coming from Soconusco and spreading to the north. It is almost certain on a linguistic basis that this migration took place.

Another major component of the claim that the Olmec civilization originated in the Soconusco comes from the elaboration of the "Short Count," which gives rise to the 52-year cycle so central to all Mesoamerican astronomies before the appearance of the Maya Long Count, and for many ethnic groups even after that. Various Olmec sites align to the sunset of August 13 over prominent mountains. August 13 is the date of the zenith sun in Izapa. This is also the date of the Mayan beginning of time. We will return to this aspect after looking at Olmec religion and iconography.[15]

Olmec Civilization

Whether the Soconusco hypothesis is true or not does not alter everything that follows in relation to the importance of the Olmecs. What was the most visible change introduced by Olmec culture? Many historians define it as a sudden cultural influx with no known formal precedents, nor gradual development.[16] Likewise, the whole pantheon of Olmec human/animal creatures, appearing in the statuary, was present from the very beginning. At the time shortly following the Olmec spread, various phenomena took place almost simultaneously. This was the time of proliferation of cities. San Lorenzo and La Venta had hundreds and even thousands of inhabitants. The increase of population was made possible by technological revolutions: new farming techniques such as the use of terracing and irrigation, hybridization of cultivars, introduction of the back-strap loom, and most likely the shaman's knowledge of astronomy and the astronomical/religious calendar known as the "Sacred Calendar." The hybridization of cultivated plants through cross-fertilization and grafting was most likely the task of the shaman and one of the central revolutions of the Third Age.[17]

Linda Schele speaks of an Olmec Complex embodying shared cosmology, symbolic arrays, artistic style, and ritual performances that were combined with local versions. Thus, groups from different regions, speaking different languages, comprised the Olmec Complex. One of the ways the cultural influence seems to have spread is through the Olmec use of small portable objects.

Olmec cosmo-vision was reflected in their ceremonial centers. The layout of their cities was never wholly visible to human eyes, because it seems to have been intended for the gods. Their sophisticated views were encompassed in a coherent art style. They invented monumental sculpture and inaugurated the ritual use of caves, mountaintops, and springs. In effect it is Olmec art and iconography that can allow us to come closer to grasping some aspects of the Olmec mystery. Let us turn to this aspect at present.

Olmec Art and Cosmology

The Olmecs introduced momentous technological and artistic changes in Mesoamerican culture. In the architectural realm Central America owes to them the introduction of the *talud* (the incline between two horizontal planes as used in many subsequent Toltec and Mayan pyramids), the use of the column, and the introduction of works of hydraulic engineering. The Olmec have left us elaborate drainage systems in their major ceremonial centers (e.g., La Venta, San Lorenzo, Laguna de los Cerros). The ceremonial center of San Lorenzo can give us an idea of the size of the Olmec revolution. Natural topography was modified with the construction of six artificial ridges on the north, south, and west sides. An estimated 67,000 cubic meters of soil were needed to create a platform 650 feet long, 160 feet wide and 20 feet high! This was only one of the many ceremonial centers! San Lorenzo also had a 650-foot drainage system carved out of basalt and ten colossal heads.

The famous colossal heads were among the first artistic objects to draw attention to the Olmec culture. Most of them belong to an era between 1200 and 600 BC. They are very harmonious—all except the later ones— and were constructed with the golden mean proportion. They have broad noses, thick lips, and elongated ears adorned with earrings. The most amazing element of their construction is not simply their size but the fact that the rocks they were built of came from a considerable distance.[18] Some authors, Neil Baldwin among them, believe that the colossal statues represented sacred rulers.[19]

The Olmec revolution cannot be measured merely by the grandeur of its most visible achievements. It can be appreciated down to the smallest artifacts. The treatment of jade is the most indicative in this regard. Although a very hard and difficult material to carve, the Olmecs could sculpt it with amazing accuracy and place minute perforations in it. The stone was polished beautifully. This led Michael Coe to express himself thus: "No matter how small the object, it always looks much larger than it really is." In effect, it can be said that the Olmecs imbued civilization with a whole new set of meanings.

Olmec civilization had a surprisingly novel artistic style, with dominant traits such as: human bodies with feline heads, jaguar-like masks, grooved or notched foreheads, prominent canines, pronounced upper lips, small feline noses, etc. Archaeologists sense that Olmec art played an almost exclusively sacred role (an exception to this is most likely found in the seemingly more mundane representations in clay). This would explain why jade and greenstone objects were buried under the ceremonial court of La Venta, and why many objects were buried in caches and burials. The layout of the ceremonial centers themselves speaks of an art that only the gods can fully apprehend in its totality. Incidentally, this is also a characteristic that is found in other parts of Mesoamerica and in Andean culture.

On the basis of the many cultures that have retained typical Third Age social organizations, archaeologists deduce that much of Olmec art was intended for being carried on journeys. Through the art objects shamans could introduce new meanings and symbols to other ethnic groups. Even today, among the Cuna of Panama and the Chocó of Colombia, art is for the most part ritually functional. The shaman carries with himself those objects that he will use for his rituals. Some of them will be discarded after the ceremony; the others will be kept in boxes or bundles for ulterior use. The objects have a role of "spirit helpers"; they help the shaman in the performance of divinations, cures, or any other ritual. Thus the art did and still does extend soul and natural powers.[20]

Olmec art is a curious mix of naturalism and abstraction. It is not however realistic, as it can be seen by the fact that the head to body ratios of the adult are 1 to 4 rather than the more natural 1 to 7. Rather, Olmec art almost always conveys a sense of the supernatural. Carolyn Tate sees in this art an emphasis on the study of inner transformation and how it is manifested outwardly.[21] Olmec faces often display a very strict symmetry and an idealized geometrical beauty rather than faithful realistic proportions. Overall they are more concerned with the archetype of divine ecstasy than with individual traits. This is sometimes reinforced by the carved signs in the sculptures that represent symbols of the underworld and its thresholds. Some interesting standing figures—particularly those of La Venta Offering 4—are portrayed in the pose of cultic ecstasy. They stand with legs slightly flexed, knees bent and the spine in relaxed position. The gaze, also relaxed, points to a far distant point or is most likely directed inwardly. The La Venta figures "meditate" next to cosmic axis effigies.

The Olmec artist must have been second to the priest alone in status. So lengthy must have been the production of artifacts that the artist most likely had to retire from society in order to produce an effigy of the supernatural. He must perforce have communicated with the other world. This necessity was still acknowledged in 16th century Yucatan: the Mayan artist who then received a commission went to the temple to meditate in order to receive inspiration.[22]

Olmec Iconography

Having approached the general aspects of Olmec art let us turn now to its themes, which can be divided into mythic images and representations of the human figure. According to B. de la Fuente there are 3 groups of Olmec images.[23] To the first belong the following mythic images:

- Very few, deteriorated monuments represent the union of a jaguar and a woman, a union that may have produced the so-called "were-jaguars," part animal and part human. Karl Taube contests this interpretation and sees the sculptures as an image of human sacrifice, the jaguar being the masked shaman.[24]
- Human figures emerging from the interior of a cave of those large monoliths that have been called "altars." One of those is the famous La Venta Altar 4, of which more will be said further (figure 1).
- Human figures with highly stylized, mask-like heads, holding babies. The inert posture of the children suggests human sacrifice.

Figure 1: Altar 4 of La Venta

To a second group belong figures mostly representing supernatural beings or shamans. In these the animal and imaginary characteristics are mostly concentrated in the head and face. Sometimes claws substitute hands and feet. Among them are the so-called "jaguar babies" recognizable by the thick upper lip curled back with large bifurcated canines protruding through the mouth, and a broad flattened nose (figure 2).

To a third group belong human figures that can be divided in three types:

- Men under supernatural protection: e.g., figures wearing elaborate "were-jaguar" headdresses over human heads.
- Mediators: seated human figures with individualized expressions, some feline traits, and a supernatural aura surrounding them. They may be figures of initiates.
- Colossal heads: their eyes, opened to slits, seem to express the condition of a dead individual. This could also indicate that the highest initiates may have carried their influence over the other shamans even after their death (figure 3).

Figure 2: jaguar baby   **Figure 3: colossal head**

Jaguar and Eagle

When they are present, jaguar features form a continuum between the most purely human forms with just a jaguar mouth, a middle stage of interpenetration, and an almost complete animal metamorphosis. The jaguar traits are thus integral parts of the individuals portrayed rather than masks added to them. Peter T. Furst concludes that the statues portray stages of transformation. Practically everywhere, he notes, they depict the convulsions of a tortured grimace, implying a gesture of effort. It is the depiction of the shamanic transformation that is in effect physically and emotionally demanding. Richard Burger has come to the same conclusions in regard to the Chavin culture of the Andes, which probably played a parallel role to the Olmec at the same point in time.[25]

What is recognizable in the artistic record is confirmed by present day anthropology. The Third Age, we will remember, is preserved to a degree, although in a transformed fashion, in modern day "Third Man." Thus, many tribes of the Amazon call themselves "Jaguar People" and claim descent from jaguar ancestors. They may also call their territory "Land of the Jaguar." For some of them the first jaguar people were both animal and human; others consider themselves actual jaguars. The shaman, as guardian of the tribe, is the jaguar per excellence. Throughout Mesoamerica and South America words for shaman and jaguar are either the same or similar—and this is also the case for many Mayan tribes. This is because the jaguar is the shaman's spirit companion (*nagual*). It is through the help of the jaguar that the shaman goes to the spiritual world. It is often a journey fraught with the perils of an encounter with all the unredeemed soul beings. The journey is also portrayed as the shaman's fight with the jaguar. From all of the above it may seem surprising however that few or no tribes consider the jaguar a deity. They may define him a "master of the species"—thus a powerful being but rarely a god. Why this is so is a matter to which we will return later.

Indications of the way in which the shamanic flight is achieved also come from the record of anthropology. The preparation for the shamanic transformation was and still is achieved through the use of psychotropic substances, among which tobacco plays a key role. It was either inhaled through the nose or made into wads of leaf and lime for chewing—a little like coca is still prepared in the Andes. The native tobacco is much stronger than the known cultivated varieties, and its ingestion leads to an aggressive altered state that is reminiscent of the poses depicted in Olmec figurines of the shaman in the various stages of transformation. Tobacco leads to hyper-alertness and wakefulness, similar to coca. The so-called "Olmec spoons" could have been instruments for inhaling tobacco and other hallucinogenic substances. They are often given the shape of birds, a theme that is evocative of the shaman's journey. The bird is in fact another complementary dimension of this spirit journey, as we will realize further.

A puzzling shamanic posture is the so-called "acrobat pose." It is portrayed in stelae by a personage with the feet above the head. One such figure from Tlalilco (close to Mexico City) was found together with a stone mirror and "divining bundle," most likely attributes of power (figure 4a). From other acrobat depictions it is apparent that the figure represents a shaman/ruler. Thus, he appears either associated with the eagle that indicates the shamanic flight, or with the sprout-topped headdress, a symbol of power. Examples of the acrobat pose are also known to anthropology. The Tacana of Eastern Bolivia use somersaulting as a technique for inducing shamanic trance. To some degree the same is practiced by the Huichols of Mexico.[26] Final confirmation of this acrobat pose appears in Olmec statuary, as in San Lorenzo monument 16, in an altar of Rio Pesquero or in the "Shook Panel" of San Antonio Suchitepequez (figure 4b).[27]

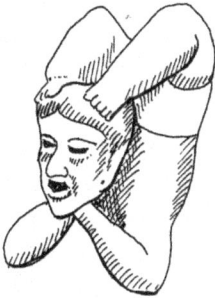

Figure 4a: acrobat pose   **Figure 4b: Shook Panel**

Who then is this jaguar that is defined as neither a god nor a human being? Let us approach in stages this figure that is familiar to spiritual science. The jaguar is an animal that lives in the forest, where he is the most feared of all animals. He is a good swimmer and he leaps with ease. He is active both day and night. He is then an animal that lives at the boundary of the elements—the mediator between opposites and between the elements. This image is reinforced by an addition that has appeared more clearly to recent research. The jaguar has an alter ego in the figure of the eagle. All that has been said about the jaguar applies—though to a lesser degree—to the eagle.

In fact, a combination of jaguar and eagle appears both in Olmec culture and in its Andean counterpart, Chavin. The harpy eagle—the one that most resembles Olmec representations—is the largest of all American eagles. A male can weigh 9 to 10 lbs, a female from 15 to 20. The head is garlanded by a collar of feathers. What has previously been said about the jaguar is mirrored in the harpy eagle. Given its size and raptorial habits he is in fact often called the "jaguar of the sky." The shamans also transform themselves into eagles in their sacred journeys. The Mojo tribe of Bolivia and the Bororo of Central Brazil link the jaguar and the harpy eagle as spirit companions of both shamans and rulers.[28] Both jaguar and harpy eagle are closely associated with thunder, whose messengers they are in the heavens. This merged identity would explain why the Olmec jaguar has the so-called "flame eye brows." These would really be the harpy eagle's feather crest. What further confirms the above hypothesis is the fact that jaguars are sometimes represented with feathers on their back.

We have now further elements which allow us to characterize the jaguar/eagle. Let us look at a final iconographic element that will further reveal the jaguar's nature and why he is neither a god nor a human being. This will appear from an exploration of the themes of La Venta Altar 4 (see figure 1). The altar is a large monolith that should actually be called a throne. It represents a ruler sitting on a throne. He appears under an arch, as if emerging from under the ground. The arch is surmounted by a jaguar mouth with fangs and the cross bands that, as Girard explains, refer to the place in the heavens that is the intersection of the ecliptic and the Milky Way, a very significant cosmic threshold in Mesoamerican world-view. Thus the ruler is placed between two thresholds: one pointing to the underworld, the other to the heavens. The shaman ruler himself wears a bird helmet that points to the eagle.

We have already seen eagle and jaguar—or more precisely lion—in another context. These are the Lion and Eagle spirits that worked as groups souls in Lemurian and Atlantean times. It is not surprising to find them among populations that have retained the Atlantean consciousness. Jaguar/Lion and Eagle spirits are actually a generality of American cosmology. They are diffused in the iconography even where they are not present in the fauna, indicating that they are something more than naturalistic references or imported symbols. For populations that have retained the earlier cosmic orientation of Atlantean times it is not too surprising not to encounter the manifestation of the Bull spirits, or their local equivalents, that complete the image of the sphinx. Thus, we could say that for the Native American, eagle and jaguar represented a sort of simplified sphinx of the Native American human archetype.

In another sense the jaguar/eagle plays the role of the one that Rudolf Steiner has called the "Guardian of the Threshold." It is the Guardian who guides the shaman to soul and spiritual worlds. It is the Guardian who tests the disciple's readiness to cross the threshold; hence the spirit journey has the quality of test for the shaman/ruler, and hence the dangers to the shaman attempting spirit flight.

We can now turn to the spiritual beings whom the shaman met while journeying to the other world.

Celestial Dragon

The first being we will look at is the one that appears most abundantly in Olmec iconography, the so-called Celestial Dragon. It is represented either full-figured or with the symbolic shortcut of the "paw-wing," a composite of human hand, animal paw, and bird's wing, indicating that this being moves between worlds (figure 5). K. A. Taube calls it the "avian serpent" because apart from feathers he often has beak and wings. Sky cross-bands (St. Andrew's Crosses) are often placed in the mouth of the dragon portrayed frontally. Another associated symbol is the diamond-shaped symbol, precursor of the Mayan Venus/Lamat hieroglyph. This is the symbol that evolved into the quincunx, the four-pointed star with a central point (figure 6). The crested brow is another of the attributes of the avian serpent. In addition, it often has a fang.

Figure 5: Olmec dragon   Figure 6: Venus / Lamat symbol

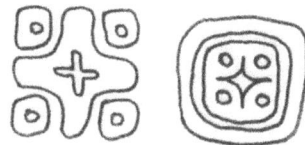

K. A. Taube studied the head symbols that give the best diagnostic of the being.[29] In many Early Formative artistic samples the paw-wing appears just behind the head as if it were an appendage of the cheek or neck. This was still the case during the Middle Formative. The paw-wing is more of a wing than a paw. That is why the majority of avian serpents of the Early

Formative have a paw-wing turned upward to represent feathered wings. In fact the paw-wing may be the symbol for wind, and by extension of clouds and rain. This is therefore the being who brings the rain, and K. A. Taube argues that he is the ancestor of Quetzalcoatl. Further indication of the correctness of this interpretation is its frequent association with waves and standing water. La Venta Monument 19 obviously represents a snake surmounted by a flame-browed head (figure 7). Immediately under and to the side are two *quetzal* birds facing a central sky band. Note in passing the appearance of quetzals in close association to the being of Quetzalcoatl.

The association of quetzal with the avian serpent can be easily understood due to the use of the green feathers of the bird—a symbol for water, rain, and growth. Quetzal "feather bundles" are a symbol evocative of sprouting growth, like grass or maize shoots. This is why quetzal feathers commonly appear in the costumes of Mesoamerican maize deities. This association is well documented throughout Mesoamerica. Olmec sculptures of rulers represent feather bundles commonly seen in sculptures. See in this regard the individual of San Miguel Amuco (Guerrero) dressed as an avian serpent with the bundle under his left arm. The bundle in the hands of figures of dignitaries, further metamorphosed in Mayan times, was thought of as a torch; however, it is a symbol for water and growth (figure 8).

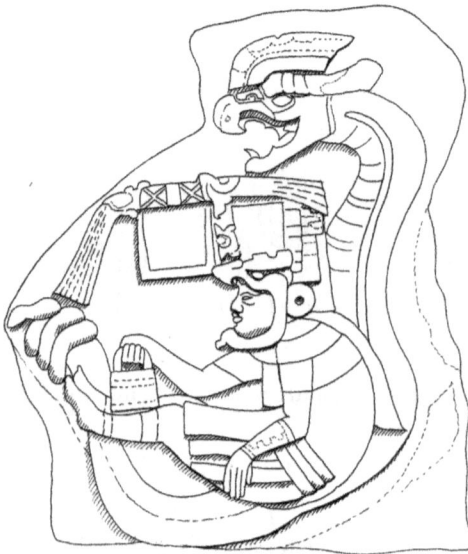

Figure 7: La Venta Monument 19   **Figure 8: feather bundles**

Terrestrial Dragon

Let us look at a second, less familiar creature: the so-called "terrestrial dragon." The caiman is a well-known symbol that followed the early symbol of the turtle, standing for the mass of land emerging from the waters. An image of this dragon is found in La Venta Monument 6 (figure 9). This monument is a sarcophagus of the ruler depicting the fact that he was buried in the earth. This and other figures have L-shaped eyes when seen frontally, both topped with "flame eyebrows" and gumlines with down-turning brackets. In the Middle Formative the earth was represented by a line of gum brackets or a single in-turning gum bracket (figure 10). The latter symbolism, further stylized, is the most universal identification of the Earth dragon and a gaping maw was used to represent access to the underworld. Occasionally, celestial and terrestrial dragons are shown together to form either two separate creatures or a monster with both celestial and earthly traits.

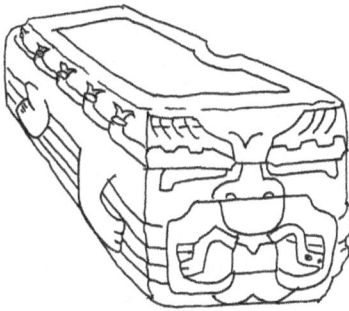

Figure 9: La Venta Monument 6   **Figure 10: earth/gum brackets**

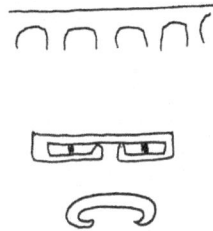

W. M. Stirling turns our attention to the upper portion of Tres Zapotes Stela D portraying two profile-facing jaguar heads. Sky bands contain both jaguar and serpent imagery. In La Venta Monument 80 a great cosmic jaguar holds a bicephalic serpent in its mouth (figure 11). In earlier Olmec art the serpents are represented as hanging from the corners of the jaguar's mouth. The serpents appear in rope-like form. This is also the case in other sculptures, as in La Venta Monument 80, Los Soldados Monument 1, and San Lorenzo Monument 37. Whether the serpents are seen as two creatures or one, one aspect remains consistent: their link to the jaguar, not only through some of the motifs of the serpents themselves (fangs, flame eyebrows, etc.) but also through the central role of the jaguar in uniting them. We can now

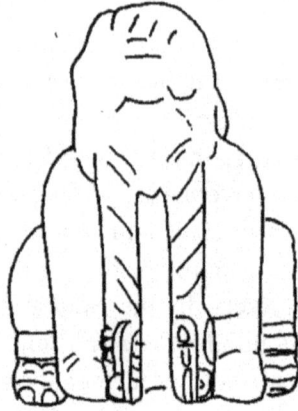

Figure 11: jaguar holding bicephalic serpent in his mouth

say that the two serpents, or the bicephalic serpent, represent the elements and the deities that rule over them. Not surprisingly, it is air and water in the figure of Quetzalcoatl. Earth is the predominant element of the earth dragon. There is no indication that fire has yet an existence of its own. The above should not surprise us in view of the prevailing Atlantean consciousness of the time. Only in later Ages would Mesoamerican consciousness reach further in the knowledge of the elements. The fire element was a very well known reality of the consciousness of the Aztecs, as in the figure of Xiucoatl, the "fire serpent," and the role it plays in the birth of their patron hero Huitzilopochtli, or in the New Fire Ceremony.

There is a further realm beyond the elements of air, water, and earth that we have just characterized: the realm of the Rain God Chac. According to K. A. Taube, the Rain God appears represented as often as the celestial dragon.[30] He too is heavily imbued with jaguar imagery. The culmination of representations of Chac occurs during the so-called Late Formative, the period that ushers in the Fourth Age. Let us look at some of his identifying characteristics: down-turning snout, a single pointed tooth, and a curling whisker at the back of the mouth.

Most telling are the details on top of the head. Often there are volutes of gently curving forms, or a couple of scrolls flowing in opposite directions identified as *muyal* or cloud in Mayan languages. In its most simple stylization the clouds take the shape of a lemniscate or "lazy S." In abbreviated form, the Rain God may just appear as a feather-crested eye or a lazy-S from which falls a trilobate raindrop. In such a way, rain was equated with the tears of the god. Once again we find here a representation of the Tau, the Great Spirit. The above iconography, coupled with other abundant anthropological observations, points to the role of the shaman/king as the preserver of the order of the natural world. Certainly, he played an important role in calling for the rains in agriculture. His knowledge of astrology also played a central role in agriculture.

The shaman/ruler was also identified with the World Tree, the cosmic foundation of the world. The World Tree has been represented as an upended supernatural saurian whose tail and upper body sprout vegetation (for example in Izapa), or simply as sprouting maize. Simplified to the extreme it appears as a trefoil—symbol of the maize sprout—worn in the headdress of the shaman. Oftentimes the ruler is the central figure surrounded by the four maize plants of the four directions. Seen together they form the famous quincunx figure that survived to the time of the Aztecs (see figure 6).

The rulers are identified as those who stand at the cosmic center and the interface of natural and supernatural worlds. This is why they are often represented resting on reptilian legs, i.e., resting on the physical world of the Earth Dragon (figure 12). Bound sprouts or cuttings appear in the form of "torches" that they hold in their arms. The bundles are often associated with the so-called "knuckle dusters," identified as instruments for bloodletting. Knuckle dusters may have been large conch shells. The two objects— bundles and knuckle dusters—are now recognized as symbols of

Figure 12: Celt of Rio Pesquero   Figure 13: Monument San Martin Pajapan

authority. The shaman was then the authority who could raise the World Tree, setting and preserving the balance between the physical world, soul (underworld), and spiritual worlds. In this regard see the life-size figures of San Martin Pajapan: the shaman wears an anthropomorphic headdress and in his hands he holds a post in the position a person would be in the act of trying to raise it (figure 13).

More than its iconography, the element that placed Olmec civilization in the context of its prophetic future was the Sacred Calendar in its link to the maize god, the god who underwent death and resurrection.

Olmec Astronomy

Olmec culture has defined the notion of Mesoamerica itself, which corresponds to the original area of spread of the culture of maize. Wherever Olmec civilization reached, maize cultivation and the Sacred Calendar followed. What we are about to illustrate comes from what was later preserved by the Maya.

Mayan astronomy presents a certain complexity. In order to understand the Native American worldview we need to get a deeper understanding of it. We will introduce some very basic elements now, before returning to an in-depth analysis of the most esoteric aspects of the Mayan calendar in the Fourth Age chapter. Before the appearance of the so-called Long Count in the Fourth Age—and for most cultures even after that—the two main calendars of the year were:

- The *Haab*, or solar year of 365 days divided into 18 months of 20 days each, with 5 extra days at the end of the year, the so-called five "days of affliction." It is also called a "Vague Year," since it is short of about 6 hours in relation to the true year.
- The *Tzolkin* or "Sacred Calendar" composed of 260 days, which are the permutations of 20 signs (the same of the 20 days of the Haab) and 13 numerals. It runs from February to the end of October and then is absent for 105 days until the beginning date is reached again. This is the static Tzolkin, but there is also a "dynamic Tzolkin."

In origin the Tzolkin was a fixed calendar that anchored the community work in the maize fields (called *milpa*) with religious celebrations. The Tzolkin tied together myth, rituals, astronomy, and the agricultural practices of maize cultivation. The dynamic Tzolkin was also used in conjunction with the Haab as the revolving wheels of a clock in what is known as the "Calendar Round." In this instance every dynamic Tzolkin followed each other without end. This meant that to every day of the year corresponded a date of the Haab and a date of the Tzolkin. Every 52 years (52 x 365 = 73 x 260 = 18.980 days) the two wheels of this calendar returned to the initial positions of both Haab and Tzolkin. The number 52 is important as we will see in the civilizations of Central Mexico, where it was known for the ritual of the New Fire, occurring every 52 years and associated with the dread of the end of time. The Toltec and Aztec worlds were tied to this conception of time. For the populations who only knew the Calendar Round, time still had a cyclical connotation, and eternity as a concept was unknown.

A possible reason for the number 260 lies in the relationship between Venus in relation to the earth and Venus in relation to the Sun. Venus' synodic cycle takes between 584 and 585 days. At the end of the cycle the planet finds itself back in the same position on the ecliptic. Venus' revolution around the sun takes between 224 and 225 days. The ratio of the two cycles (585/225) is exactly 2.6, which multiplied by 100 gives us the number of the Tzolkin. This is a plausible hypothesis for a calendar where Sun and Venus played the two most important roles.

To the Maya, who did not know fractions, the use of the Tzolkin allowed to anchor their calendar in a precise way with the movements of the planets in the universe. The Tzolkin has remarkable properties. Forty-six Tzolkins represent exactly 405 lunar revolutions, 65 cycles of Venus correspond to 146 Tzolkins, 50 revolutions of Mars correspond to 153 Tzolkins, and 104 of Mercury's revolution corresponded to 115 periods of the Tzolkin' s interval between the two zenith passages of the sun.[31] Many more properties were attached to the Tzolkin and the Mayan calendar. The interested reader can find some challenging thoughts in the book *Mayan Prophecies*.[32] Clearly this was not the result of a trial and error system but the initiatory knowledge of higher laws at work in the universe. However, there was one element that the conjunction of Haab and Tzolkin could not compensate for: the phenomenon of the precession of the equinoxes, according to which every 72 years the sun rises 1° behind in the constellations of the zodiac.

The Vague Year and the Sacred Calendar could not offer a rigorous accounting of time. Every four years in effect an extra leap day offsets the regular time interval between solstices and equinoxes, and this difference accrues further over larger periods of time. One way to calibrate the calendar in order to correct for the discrepancy between the Haab and astronomic year was done by observing within the temples the position of the sun at the time of the solstices. This could be done by placing pyramids in alignment in such a way that the solstice sun would rise or set on the peak of the highest mountain of the horizon on such date. Malmström detects in San Lorenzo an alignment to the mountain Zempoaltepec on the sunset of winter solstice. In La Venta, the Volcan San Martin probably served as the marker for the summer solstice sunset. The layout of Laguna de los Cerros (sited northwest of San Lorenzo) results from the compromise of a placement on a river and an alignment to the summer solstice sunrise over Cerro Santa Marta. Tres Zapotes is oriented to Volcan San Martin's summer solstice sunrise.[33]

In addition to the solstices, in tropical areas there are other phenomena clearly recognizable and measurable in the course of the year. These are the two yearly times in which the sun shines exactly overhead, from the zenith. At latitudes 23° 5', both north and south of the equator, the sun reaches the zenith during the summer solstice. In the latitudes between the two extremes the sun intersects the zenith twice, before and after the summer solstice. The zenith passages could be ascertained through the use of gnomons—simple, exactly vertical stone rods planted in the ground. Only on the days of the zenith sun did the gnomon shed no shadow at noon.

One of the most significant dates in Mesoamerica is that of August 13; this is the beginning date of Mayan Long Count, but it appears likely that the date itself did not originate with the Mayan civilization. August 13 is the date of the zenith sun at latitude 14° 15' in the Soconusco. At this latitude lies Izapa, of which much will be said in relation to the Fourth Age. Cerro de las Mesas' site aligns to the sunset of August 13 over the Orizaba peak. Later structures built at La Venta deviated some 23° 5' from the site's axis which aims to 8° west of north. The orthogonal axes of this orientation marked the sunset of August 13 on the western horizon.[34]

Polar Astronomy: An Initiation Center of the Olmecs

There are three major Olmec sites in Southern Mexico, in close proximity to the Gulf Coast. La Venta is the largest of the three and seemingly the most important. It is situated on a two-square-mile island of the Tonala River, in the plains of northern Tabasco. Given its geographic situation it could not have supported a large population. Its location and construction indicate that it must have been reserved for ceremonial uses.

La Venta has a strictly symmetrical arrangement around an axis 8° west of north. To achieve this exact orientation the builders had to undertake extensive additional earth fills, since the axis diverges from the island's central ridge. This is a first indication that there was a deliberate intention behind the orientation of the buildings.

The very large pyramid has a unique fluted cone shape. It is a perfect platform for observation of the night sky. In the climatic and topographic situation of La Venta, the pyramid was needed in order to reach above the tropical tree canopy. To the astronomer-priest fell the task of finding the relation between the time of the year and the celestial configurations of the night sky, in order to indicate times for planting, burning, harvesting, etc. This he could do by correlating the patterns of rain with the astrological observations. The pyramid allowed precise astronomical observations for these goals.

Since La Venta is situated at 18° north latitude, the stars within 18 degrees of the north celestial pole would never set. The star Polaris of Ursa Minor is the best approximation of the north celestial pole at the present time. However at the time of the Olmecs, the celestial pole was just a point in space. The easiest point of reference in the heavens was the Big Dipper, whose main four stars of the "bowl" were all located within 18 degrees of the celestial pole. They were therefore visible year-round. It is M. P. Hatch's hypothesis that the La Venta site was oriented toward the Big Dipper, and particularly toward the four stars of the "bowl" called Alpha, Beta, Gamma, and Delta Ursae Majoris.[35] These stars make a perfect time clock and can be used as "pointers" to determine the north celestial pole. The ideal time to start the time computation was on the night of the summer solstice. At midnight of June 21, 2000 BC, the center of the bowl lay exactly on the meridian (the imaginary north to south line in the sky). In that same night, directly south of Ursa Major and also on the meridian lay the star Gamma Cygni—the center star of Cygnus, a constellation with a rough X form. The two constellations crossed the meridian at midnight. Such an event was rather spectacular and served to mark a significant moment of the year.

The very same night of the summer solstice, the Pleiades were rising above the horizon, almost due east. Opposite to them Scorpio would be setting on the horizon. Leo would play the equivalent role of Cygnus at midnight of the winter solstice. Thus the four constellations of Cygnus, Pleiades, Leo, and Scorpio would have allowed the recognition of summer solstice, fall equinox, winter solstice, and spring equinox.

M. P. Hatch believes that the typical square upper lip of the Olmec jaguar represents the bowl of the dipper (see figure 3). She also believes to have recognized the symbols for Cygnus (St. Andrew's cross) for Leo (a crescent) and for the Pleiades (three circles in cluster).[36] Her explanation has the merit of depicting the various positions of the stars in a correct way at different times of the year. The puzzling knowledge and use of the magnetic properties incorporated in sculptures, mentioned earlier, lends some additional weight to the hypothesis of the so-called "Polar God." Finally, the hypothesis of the importance of Ursa Major gains further weight when gauged against the growing evidence of the importance of the Southern Cross in Andean Civilizations during the two millennia before our era. The constellation may in fact have served as the aspect of the measuring operative system upon whose proportions buildings and cities were built, for which C. Milla Villena cogently argues.[37]

The precession of the equinoxes is a very precise and predictable phenomenon for the stars on the ecliptic. It is much less so for the stars around the celestial pole. The declination of the four stars of the bowl decreased slowly between the period of 2000 to 1000 BC, and twice as fast between 1000 and 500 BC. In 600 BC Ursa Major was sinking much further below the horizon than previously. The meridian transit was delayed by 1 hour 20' for Alpha Ursae Majoris. For this and other astronomical reasons connected with the precession of the equinoxes, it seems that by 600 BC La Venta had ceased to fill the purpose for which it had been built.

We have seen how the notion of time was central for Mesoamerican humanity. Cosmology and inner life formed an indissoluble entity. Losing understanding of the connection with time meant questioning the soul's essence. In fact it was exactly this process that led in the Third Age to the agonizing twilight of the gods, with the wrenching question of mortality and the fate of the soul. Only the Fourth Age brought a solution to the riddle of immortality of the soul and eternity in time. The necessity to change astrological points of reference is probably what the Popol Vuh calls the fall of Vucub Caquix. Astronomically, this Luciferic figure corresponds to Ursa Major, reinforcing the possibility of M. P. Hatch's La Venta hypothesis. The fall is a good image for the drift of the constellation in space, due to the precession of the equinoxes. This phenomenon also coincides in time with the mythological descent of the Ahpus to the underworld. By the time of the Twins, Pole Star astronomy was a science looking back to the past, a longing for a condition that did not hold true any longer.

Olmec Culture: Between Past and Future

How did Olmec culture come to such a sudden demise? Roman Piña Chan has studied closely the colossal Olmec heads mostly found in the largest ceremonial centers.[38] Most of them were carved between 1200 and 600 BC. As we have mentioned earlier, they are very harmonious in their proportions, in fact built closely according to the Golden Mean. This guiding canon no longer appears in the later heads built after 600 BC. This observation seems to confirm in the artistic realm what we know from archaeology. The Olmec civilization was subject to a cultural decline from at least 400 BC. The hypothesis of the Fall of Ursa Major/Seven Macaw offers an explanation of the modality of this demise. Another indication of cultural decline is the portrayal in the Popol Vuh of the transformation of the priesthood of the Third Age into monkeys, in effect making explicit that before the advent of the Twins the priesthood had lost relevance.

As the Popol Vuh indicates, the Third Age presided over a "twilight of the gods." In its language this is the "descent of the Ahpus to the Underworld." The twilight of the gods in a wider sense begins with the onset of the "time of darkness" or Kali Yuga, beginning in 3100 BC with the loss of clairvoyant abilities, manifesting earliest in the civilizations of Egypt and Babylonia.[39] In earlier times the Egyptians knew that the gods had ruled and taught them. By saying that the gods had been their teachers they meant that in a clairvoyant state they reached to their teachers who did not incarnate in physical human bodies. At the time of the Ancient Egyptians the initiates could perceive the level of the Angels who could only appear in an etheric body and therefore could only be perceived by clairvoyant individuals. This meant that the individuals who received guidance were assured of the reliability of the wisdom thus communicated. There was a very direct link between this wisdom and the spiritual world.

This direct connection with the spiritual world started to wane in Egyptian culture and even more so in Chaldean-Babylonian culture. The first leader that the Egyptians acknowledged as more human than divine was called Menes. It was then that the possibility of error entered civilization because now human beings had to rely on the instrument of the brain. Egyptian culture played an emblematic role at the time of Kali Yuga in as much as it was guided at different times by the Angels, the retarded angels, or simple human beings. The role of the retarded beings played a part in the idea of mummification, which implied that the preservation of the body was important in the evolution of the soul after death.[40]

At the same point in time of the beginning of Kali Yuga, starting with Chaldean/Mesopotamian cultures the shrinking of the etheric body set the stage for a change of consciousness. Individuals and cultures could either accept the change or rebel against it and cling to outmoded clairvoyance in a decadent fashion.

Even though the Age of Darkness initiated in 3101 bc, what is known as the twilight of the gods starts around 1250 bc, a turning point for Hebrew and Greek civilizations marked by the Exodus and the Trojan wars. In mythological terms this was expressed in the death of Osiris, Adonis, or Tammuz (Egypt / Phoenicia / Babylonia). Later, myths appeared indicating the resurrection of the god. The new consciousness followed in greater part by Greek and Hebrew civilizations stood in stark contrast with the practices of Mesopotamian, Egyptian, and Phoenician neighbors. Abraham introduced offerings of bread and wine, representing a movement away from blood offerings to plant and soul offerings—a spiritualization of sacrifice. Likewise, circumcision implied a moving away from the sexual ecstasy that allowed humans to recapture in a decadent fashion the old forces of clairvoyance, thus encouraging the newborn faculty of thinking. The Dionysian intoxication of the Phoenicians—with human sacrifice in its most decadent manifestation—intensified the "giant" nature of atavistic clairvoyance in order to project it into the future.[41]

Hebrew culture promoted the forces of the moon and the earth of their god Yahweh, rather than the old forces of the sun. These were the forces for the acquisition of freedom and the forming of an independent human ego, reached at the cost of a further severance from the solar reality of the spirit. Contrary to this progression, when the Moon mysteries fell into decadence in Mesopotamia the priests retrieved old faculties of perception through the practice of the sacrifice of the firstborn.

Among the Israelites inheritance itself was changing in nature. The new goal was to serve the promotion of the forces of thinking that were to carry into the future, rather than preservation of old faculties of clairvoyance that were now tainted. This was why Jacob bypassed Esau's right as firstborn. He did this through cunning, the further proof of the rise of the intellect.

The Olmecs were a civilization poised between the past, from which it still drew its inspiration, and a coming time that was about to introduce a sizeable change of consciousness. We can find evidence of this attachment to the primordial past in various parts of Olmec culture. In art it appears in the famous "jaguar baby" motif. It is also discernable in the figures of inert babies, whose posture and demeanor is evocative of human sacrifice. Remains of disarticulated children bodies have been found at El Manatí springs.[42] A similar fascination was devoted to hunchbacks, dwarves, and to the figure of deformed fetuses. Figures of hunchbacks emerging from mouths of beasts seem to indicate that they traveled back and forth between worlds. The same is true of dwarves: a dwarf burial in La Venta's Offering 1943-M in Mound A-3 is positioned in between the ruler's tomb C and the underworld sea of the sunken courtyard.[43] This, together with the recovery of Olmec dwarf thrones, reinforces the idea that the dwarves had a function of messengers to the Underworld for the rulers. Finally, head deformation served the purpose of preserving earlier forms of consciousness. It is visible in the pear-shaped head of many sculptures.

The record of archaeology confirms the claims of the Popol Vuh. The great culture that preceded the Maya was the Olmecs. Before them all of Mesoamerica had societies working along egalitarian principles. It was the time of the Four Hundred Boys according to the sacred book. The Olmecs introduced a whole new culture that went from the egalitarian societies of the Four Hundred Boys to the societies of the Third Age. No culture exposed to this change reverted back to its original state. Moreover, there is no indication that this was done by force; rather it was as if different cultures borrowed the knowledge of the Olmecs. An indication of this lies in the fact that some of the most famous Olmec art—the famous Olmec axes found in Oaxaca—are not found in the Olmec heartland.[44] It seems therefore that diverse cultures superimposed the Olmec values and world-view to their original background, while maintaining political autonomy from the areas where the main ceremonial centers are found.

Olmec culture introduced a completely new cultural qualitative shift, one that was made most clearly visible in arts in which no formal precedent has been detected. They came as if out of divine inspiration. This new art, as well as the introduction of the Sacred Calendar, is the revolution introduced by Hun Batz and Hun Chouen, whom the Popol Vuh describes as artists and wise men.

Olmec civilization prepared Mesoamerica for the future with the ritual cultivation of maize. The ritual year of the Tzolkin outlines a prophetic path from death to resurrection. The maize god points the way to the questions that dominate the minds and hearts of the Third Age: Does the soul survive death? Will time and civilization continue? Will there be eternity? The Olmec Sacred Calendar built the foundation upon which the Maya further elaborated the astronomy of resurrection and eternity.

Olmec civilization prepared the ground for the coming of the initiate of the Americas and the inauguration of the Fourth Age. However, this mission came to at least a partial standstill in the period of decadence starting from around 400 BC How decadence and preservation played themselves out in practice is difficult to establish. The end of Olmec culture introduced the practices of infant sacrifice in order to recapture the ability of atavistic clairvoyance that was progressively being lost. Serving the same purpose was the practice of human sacrifice with organ removal, of which more will be said in the following chapters.

The advent of a new consciousness that the Olmecs only prophesied: this is the theme of the succeeding chapter in the Popol Vuh. In their deeds the Twins, inaugurators of a new age, prevent the continuation of the impulses of the past and guard against an acceleration toward the future brought in by the practice of human sacrifice with organ removal. Let us turn to this double challenge.

CHAPTER 5

Popol Vuh: The Deeds of the Twins

W E WILL NOW LOOK at the deeds of the Twins that form the heart of the mythological part of the Popol Vuh, the part that deals with the deeds of the gods (Parts I and II).

The Miraculous Conception of the Twins (Part II, Chapter 3)

After the death of the Ahpus, the Xibalbans placed a ban on the fruit of the tree of life and forbade anyone to approach it. However, Ixquic, daughter of Cuchumaquic, lord of Xibalba decided to go see the tree at the place of Pucbal-Chah. Seeing the maiden at the foot of the tree, Hun Hunahpu asked her whether she desired of the fruit of the tree. Since this was her wish, he asked her to extend her arm toward the head. Hun Hunahpu spit on her hand, and where the saliva fell it was immediately absorbed. The head declared that through the spit the god has impregnated the maiden and he foretold that he would have spiritual heirs through her. This is how the Twins Hunahpu and Ixbalamqué were conceived.

After six months of pregnancy Ixquic's father perceived her state and believed that she had been dishonored. Upon being interrogated Ixquic denied having met any men. The answer reinforced the initial suspicion and Ixquic was condemned to being sacrificed by having her heart removed. Four messengers were sent to do the deed. To them Ixquic revealed the truth about her pregnancy. The messengers agreed to save her, and in order to deceive the lords the maiden conceived the idea of substituting the heart, required as a proof of sacrifice, with the coagulated red sap of the blood tree. Ixquic admonished the magicians to cease the practice of human sacrifice. She prophesied that in the future sacrifice would only require the blood of animals. Upon returning to their lords the messengers set the false heart over a fire and succeeded in deceiving the Camé. After that they left the service of the lords and joined Ixquic.

Birth and Infancy of the Twins (Part II, Chapters 4 and 5)

When she was about to give birth, Ixquic joined Ixmucané and her grandsons, Hun Batz and Hun Chouen. To the Grandmother she revealed that she carried the seed of her son, Hun Hunahpu. Ixmucané did not believe her message. Instead she sent her on an impossible errand of filling a large net with grains of maize. Arriving on the field the young woman discovered one lone single plant of maize. Filled with sorrow she addressed the deities of maize and of nature, admitting her sins and invoking their help. She then took the silks of the maize and laid them down on the net as if they were maize cobs. Suddenly the net filled up with grain. The animals of the field helped Ixquic carry back the harvest. The Grandmother, disbelieving the maiden's claim, went to the field and found out that Ixquic had spoken the truth. She then realized that only her son could have made such a miracle possible and finally accepted her daughter in law.

Soon after Ixquic gave birth to the Twins Hunahpu and Ixbalamqué. The two could not sleep and kept the Grandmother awake. Hun Batz and Hun Chouen placed them on an anthill and later over thorny bushes. Their envy and jealousy caused them to desire the Twins' death. They knew in their heart the importance of the Twins, but could not reconcile themselves to the idea of someone who would carry their message further. The Twins grew up accustomed to the Grandmother's neglect and the brothers' spitefulness. They faithfully brought back the fruit of their hunting but received little food in exchange. Even though the Twins were aware of all of this they suffered it with tolerance.

One day the Twins returned home without game and told the Grandmother that the birds that they had hunted had remained hanging on a tree. Hun Batz and Hun Chouen agreed to help their younger brothers, unaware that the Twins wanted to teach them a lesson for all the suffering imposed on them. They went together to the foot of the tree called Canté, where innumerable birds were singing. Hun Batz and Hun Chouen climbed the tree to take down the birds that the Twins hunted. All of a sudden the tree started growing up and the two found themselves unable to come down. Startled and afraid they asked the Twins what to do and were told to take off their pants, tie them around their waist and let the ends dangle off their back. Having done this they were instantly transformed into monkeys and started acting likewise. The Twins returned home and told the Grandmother that something had happened to her grandsons and that this would be a test of her strength. Hunahpu and Ixbalamqué started playing on their flute and drums and calling on the two monkeys. Hun Batz and Hun Chouen arrived and danced to the music causing the hilarity of the old woman. The Twins reproached the Grandmother for having chased the grandsons away. They told her that they would call again on the two monkeys and asked her to refrain from laughing. Twice more the Twins played their instruments and the monkeys responded to their call. Their antics were more than the grandmother could endure without laughter and again they ran away. When the Twins played their instruments for a fourth time their elder brothers no longer responded. Hun Batz and Hun Chouen were thus punished for their pride and envy. They did not want to make way for the new times and had placed obstacles on the way of their younger brothers.

The Twins now inaugurated the work in the maize fields. They did it as divine beings without the need to toil and with the help of the animals. They took up their tools and asked the Grandmother to bring them lunch when it was time. When the Twins went to the field, the hoe started working on its own to remove trees and shrubs. The mourning dove on the top of a tree was ready to alert them to Ixmucané's arrival. Meanwhile they hunted with their blowguns. When the dove sang to alert them the Twins rubbed themselves in soil and sawdust to pretend that they had been working. When they returned home after work they pretended likewise that they were very tired. The next day they returned to the field only to find all their work undone and the trees and plants grown back. They repeated the operations of the previous day and decided to hold watch over the field overnight. At midnight they surprised the animals that were invoking the spirits of the plants and calling them to rise again. They could not get hold of the lion and the panther, and of the deer and rabbit they caught only the tails. Neither could they lay their hands on any other animal except the rat. They first wrapped him in a cloth, and then they squeezed his head, burned his tail in the fire, and tried to drown him. Trying to save his life, the rat told them that he should not die at their hand nor should the Twins work in the fields. The rat revealed to them the secret of the ball game gear that the Ahpus left in the rafters of the hut and that the Grandmother kept secret from the Twins. Together with the rat the Twins devised a plan to come in possession of the ball gear. They returned to the hut at noon hiding the rat with them. They asked the Grandmother for their food and later told her that they were very thirsty. The Grandmother went to the river to fill a jar. The Twins instructed the mosquito to delay the Grandmother by perforating the water jar. Meanwhile the rat climbed onto the rafters and by chewing at the ropes that held the gear together, he released all of it. The youths took the gear and immediately went to hide it on the path that led to the ball court. Going to the river they also helped the Grandmother fix the hole in the jar.

The Confrontation with the Giants (Part I, Chapters 3 to 9)

Before the Dawning, there existed a very proud being by the name of Vucub Caquix, whose name means Seven Macaw. The sun and moon were still veiled, as it were, and Vucub Caquix called himself the sun and the moon. Obviously he was not the sun, nor could he see very far. Only his teeth and eyes shone like the sun. He could pretend to that status because the true sun hadn't dawned yet. Vucub Caquix had a wife, Chimalmat, and two sons, Zipacná and Capracan. Zipacná could create and destroy mountains and boasted: "I am he who made the earth." Capracan caused earthquakes, claiming: "I shake the heavens and move the earth."

The Twins lamented the state of affairs. They planned to destroy Vucub Caquix and his progeny. Vucub Caquix had a tree of nance from which he derived nourishment daily. The Twins hid close to the tree when Vucub Caquix climbed it to fetch fruits. With their blowguns they wounded him in the jaw, causing his fall. When Hunahpu approached him, Seven Macaw tore off his arm. Seven Macaw felt pain in his teeth, but knew that the Twins would have to return to recover the arm.

The Twins went to seek the help of the two diviners, Ixmucané and Ixpiyacoc. With them they devised a plan. The old couple would pretend to be tooth healers and the grandparents of two orphaned children. Together they all went to the house of Vucub Caquix, still afflicted by his tooth pain. When they met the lord, the grandparents begged for alms in exchange for their services and skills as surgeons. The ancients offered to replace the teeth with others made of ground bone. In reality they replaced them with grains of white maize, causing the teeth to lose their original brilliance. Finally they also removed the eyes, the last insignia of splendor of the lord. This is how Seven Macaw and his wife Chimalmat died and the Twins recovered the severed arm. The ancient ones helped to set Hunahpu's arm back in place. The Twins proceeded further, happy to have fulfilled the wishes of Heart of Heaven. The Twins now confronted Seven Macaw's sons, but before that the sacred text interjects an episode concerning one of them, Zipacná.

Zipacná was bathing along the shore of a river, when he saw the Four Hundred Boys passing by, attempting to carry a trunk that they wanted to use as the center beam of their house. They had difficulty moving the trunk because it was very heavy. After inquiring about their activity the giant offered to help them. The boys asked Zipacná about his parents and he told them he had none; therefore they gave him shelter in exchange for more help the next day. In reality the Four Hundred Boys felt intimidated and worried because of his strength. They devised a plan to get rid of the giant. With the pretext of having to set the beam in the ground they dug a hole and asked Zipacná to place himself in it in order to help them. They actually intended to bury him. The giant, having heard of their plan, pretended to go along with it. Once in the hole he dug a shelter to the side of it. When all was done the giant called the boys to tell them that the work was finished. The boys hurled the post with strength intending to crush Zipacná. The latter cried pretending to have been hurt. Zipacná pushed the pretense further by giving part of his hair and his nails to the ants, who carried them to the surface. This was proof enough of Zipacná's death for the boys. The Four Hundred Boys rejoiced at the news and relaxed their guard by drinking chicha. On the third day, when the boys had fallen into a drunken stupor, Zipacná brought down the beam and the whole house over them. None of them survived and tradition says that they were later incorporated into the constellation of the Pleiades.

The Twins were angered by the deaths of the Four Hundred Boys. They decided to approach Zipacná, who used to bathe by the shore of the river in search of fish and crabs that he fed on. The Twins built an imitation of a large crab, and they placed it at the feet of the mountain called Meavan. Later they placed themselves in the path of the giant and asked him questions about his activities. When he told them that he was hunting for food, they indicated that they could show him the way to an enormous crab of which they said they were afraid. They pretended not to want to see it again, only to yield to Zipacná's repeated entreaties. When the giant dove in to take hold of the crab the Twins brought the mountain down on him. Zipacná was converted into stone. It was now the turn of the second son, Capracan.

The giant Capracan was busy kicking down mountains with his feet. The Twins approached him, inquiring about his activities. They feigned being orphans who ignored their origin and told him of the existence of a large mountain toward the east. They asked him in disbelief whether he was able to bring it down. Filled with curiosity the giant asked to be led to the mountain. On the way there the Twins hunted for birds. They didn't need their blowguns because they could hunt them down just with their breath, causing the giant's admiration. After stopping to rest, the Twins roasted the birds over the fire and covered with chalk the one they wanted to give to Capracan. In an act of imitative magic, by covering the bird with earth, they wanted to bring about the giant's burial. Capracan was enticed by the cooked food that he was not used to, since he only ate raw foods. After eating the bird, the giant felt greatly debilitated. He had lost his strength and the Twins tied him up and buried him.

The Call to the Underworld (Part II, Chapters 6 and 7)

Delighted about their discovery, the Twins went to the ball court, the very same where their fathers used to play. Once more the lords of Xibalba heard them play, and disturbed by the noise sent messengers to the hut of the Grandmother. They told her that the lords wished to see the Twins a week hence and asked that they bring their ball gear. Although filled with anxiety, the Grandmother pondered on how to send the message to her grandsons. At that moment a louse fell on her skirt. Picking him up, she asked him to go see the Twins and entrusted to him the message of the lords. On the way to accomplish his errand the louse met the frog and told him of his task. They agreed that the frog could swallow the louse and carry the message faster. Further along the way the frog met with the snake and told him of his mission. Again they agreed that the message would arrive faster if the snake swallowed the frog, and he proceeded to do so. Finally, the snake met the falcon who swallowed him in order to carry the message faster. The latter arrived at the ball court and the Twins, hearing his call, hunted him down, hurting him in the eye. The wounded bird announced that he was carrying a message, but he needed healing first of all. The Twins applied some rubber from the ball and a medicinal herb onto his wounded eye. Instantly the bird was healed. The falcon vomited the snake and the snake the frog. The frog tried to eject the louse but couldn't. The Twins kicked him in the back, then looked into his mouth and found the louse behind his teeth. They realized that the frog hadn't swallowed him but had just pretended to. The frog was punished by becoming food for snakes ever since. The louse finally gave the message to the Twins and told them of the sorrow of the Grandmother. The Twins returned to their hut to take leave of her. To console Ixmucané they planted two maize plants inside the house. They foretold that the old woman would be able to know by the fate of the plants whether her grandsons were alive or dead. The two maize plants were set in the dry earth.

The Descent to the Underworld and the Trials (Part II, Chapters 8-11)

The Twins retraced the path taken by the Ahpus before them. They went down the steep stairway and across the same rivers. The text specifies that they did not touch the waters because they laid down their blowguns as bridges. Finally they also arrived at the crossroads with the four paths. The Twins sent before them their ally the mosquito with orders to sting each of the lords in turn. The mosquito first stung the two mannequins, extracting no answer, and then the other lords. Each time one was stung the lords addressed him with his name asking what had happened. Through this ruse the Twins heard the names of each of the lords of Xibalba.

When they arrived in Xibalba the lords asked the Twins to greet the mannequins. The Twins avoided the trap and started greeting each lord with his name. The lords were taken aback by this, since they wanted their names to be kept secret and they did not know the identity of the Twins. They then offered the Twins the hot seats, but the Twins saw through the lords' deceit and refused.

Like their fathers before them, the Twins had to submit to the test of the Cave of Darkness. Like the Ahpus, they were given a lit torch of pinewood and a lit cigar with the request to return them whole the next morning. The Twins did not light up the torch but put macaw feathers on its tip, and they placed glowworms on top of their cigars. In this way they fulfilled the lords' request the next morning. The Xibalbans, angered by their success, inquired about the identity of the Twins but did not receive any answers from them. The Twins were now challenged to a ball game. Although the lords used their own ball, the Twins defeated them. For the second game the Twins used their ball, and defeated the lords again. The task that the lords set for the Twins the next night seemed impossible to perform. They had to gather four gourds with flowers: one of red, one of white, one of yellow, and a fourth of another kind of bloom. Twins had to perform this while locked in the Cave of Knives, the second torment of Xibalba. The

Twins promised the knives the flesh of animals instead of human sacrifices. As for the flowers, they called upon the ants to cut them and bring them back to them. The lords had entrusted the care of Xibalba's garden to two guardians. But neither one of them noticed that the ants were robbing them of their flowers. The ants climbed the trees and cut the flowers down and later collected them. The lords felt defeated and challenged the Twins to another ball game, but nobody won this time.

The next test of the Twins was the Cave of Cold. The Twins overcame it by burning old stumps and survived to the next morning. The fourth trial came with the Cave of the Jaguars. Hunahpu and Ixbalamqué survived it by throwing bones to the animals. The fifth was the Cave of Fire where the Twins endured the scorching heat. The final test was given in the Cave of the Bats. Since the bats' wings cut like knives, the Twins hid by sleeping inside their blowguns. Seeing that they could not reach them, the bats were waiting close to the blowgun's orifice. The Twins were curious to know whether the sun had dawned. Hunahpu's curiosity got the best of him and he put his head out of the blowgun to inquire about the sun. A bat decapitated him with a fell swoop. Not hearing the voice of Hunahpu, Ixbalamqué realized that they had been defeated. The Camé rejoiced and ordered that the head be hung over the ball court.

Ixbalamqué called on the help of all the animals, asking them to go fetch their own favorite food. The only one remaining behind was the turtle; when he reached the extremity of the body of Hunahpu, he assumed the form of the head. The gods of heaven came to the rescue and helped carve the face out of the turtle so that finally the head could talk again. The sun was about to dawn and the gods wanted to delay it. For this they entrusted the turkey vulture, who performed the task successfully. Ixbalamqué now advised Hunahpu about the coming ball game. "Do not do anything," he said, "I will do everything." Meanwhile Ixbalamqué also entrusted the rabbit with the task of waiting for the ball when it would go off the court.

When the sun arose the Twins survived unscathed. The lords now called a game in which Hunahpu's head served as the ball. Ixbalamqué was the first to seize it. It looked like the ball was going to go through the ring but then it stopped and it directed itself toward the oak grove where the rabbit was waiting, pretending to run with the ball. When the Camé set after him, Ixbalamqué replaced the turtle head with the true head and set the false head on the ball court. After the lords found the substitute ball they resumed playing. Ixbalamqué threw a rock at the turtle ball, which came down crashing and breaking into thousand pieces. The Camé were humiliated and defeated.

Death and Resurrection of the Twins (Part II, Chapters 12-14)

Having survived all the trials the Twins now devised another plan to defeat the Xibalbans. They called on the diviners, Xulu and Pacam. They told them that the lords intended to throw them into an oven. The sages were to mislead the lords as to the manner of disposing of the bodies of the Twins. They had to pretend that the only way to get rid of them was to grind their bodies to ashes and throw them in the river. The Twins then took leave of the sages knowing that they were going to their death. They directed themselves toward the fire that the lords were tending and willingly threw themselves into it. The lords of the underworld rejoiced and called on the help of Xulu and Pacam. The two carried out Twins' plan and made sure that the ashes of the Twins were dispersed in the waters of the river.

On the fifth day the Twins were seen in the water with the appearance of fish-men. The next day they presented themselves as paupers to the Lords of Xibalba. They told the lords that they could entertain them with their dances and with many other prodigious feats. They could burn houses and restore them to their original condition, or kill and then resuscitate each other. The Xibalbans accepted the show and marveled at their performance. Word of this came to Hun and Vucub Camé who also wanted to witness such skills. The Twins feigned not daring to perform for the chiefs of the Xibalbans. The lords wanted to know where the two came from, and again the Twins feigned ignorance about their origin. They initiated their performance, and started doing feats at the lords' request. They first cut to pieces their dog and resuscitated it, and then burned their house and brought it back to normal. Finally, they sacrificed a man and removed his heart and later resuscitated him. Astounded, the lords asked them to repeat the last performance on each other. Ixbalamqué sacrificed Hunahpu and then revived him. "Do the same with us!" they finally requested. The Twins did as asked, obviously without resuscitating the lords. The text specifies that the supreme chief of the lords had died. On hearing this, the other lords fled, all except one who begged for forgiveness. After hiding in a canyon, the lords were discovered and they surrendered to the Twins.

Upon having defeated the Camé, the Twins revealed their identity and declared they had come to avenge the death of the Ahpus. The lords of Xibalba asked for clemency. The Twins decreed that the lords would have to abstain from the ball game. They would have to confine themselves to the manual arts and the crafts and would be unable to sway the minds of righteous men. Only the wicked, those who gave themselves to vice, would listen to them.

Meanwhile the Grandmother, mourning the death of the Twins, saw the two plants of maize revive in her hut, after they had died at the time of the Twins' death. Hunahpu and Ixbalamqué reinstated the memory of the Ahpus and promised them that they would be the first ones to be adored by the faithful people. Then when the sun was at its highest the Twins ascended to the heavens, one becoming the sun, the other the moon. At this moment the dome of the heavens and the face of the earth lit up. The Four Hundred Boys were resuscitated and turned into stars.

The Being of the Twins

The chapters concerning the life and deeds of the Twins Hunahpu and Ixbalamqué are the most well known of the Popol Vuh. In them arises the focal point of the myth that marks the transition from the Third Age into the Fourth Age. The Twins usher in the time of the Dawning, accompanied by a new stage of consciousness for American humanity. The continuation of the stage of descent is indicated by the names of the beings. Hunahpu, the more important of the Twins, inherits the name and qualities of his predecessor Hun Hunahpu. He is the solar being and his weapon of choice—the blowgun—represents the solar ray, hence all the miracles that ensue from its use. After completing their deeds the Twins inaugurate the era of the Man of Maize.

The Twins are the sons of earthly Ixquic, daughter of Cuchumaquic, a lord of Xibalba. In Ixquic's name appears etymologically the word *quic*, which means blood. *Ix* means earth. *Cuchumaquic* means "Blood Gatherer." The Popol Vuh qualifies him in these terms: "There are the lords named House Corner and Blood Gatherer. And this is their commission: to draw blood from people" (Part II, Chapter 1). The Twins are conceived when the head of Hunahpu lets some drops of saliva fall unto the palm of Ixquic's hand. This is the origin of the virgin birth. The drop of saliva, like the drop of water that fertilizes the ground, is another expression of the dewdrop: the totality of the being of Tau—the Great Spirit—that the

Ahpus embody. Hunahpu and maize will share a common fate from this moment onwards. Hunahpu, like the crop, is born in the underworld. The drop of water is the same one that fertilizes the crop in the field.

The mother already points to the mission of her sons. To the messengers sent to ensure that she will be sacrificed and have her heart removed, Ixquic shows the use of copal as a substitute for heart sacrifice. The burning of the substance will replace the heart sacrifice; soul sacrifice supersedes human sacrifice. Ixquic conceives the Twins who inherit the characteristics of their father. From the beginning it is clear that they are sent to continue the mission of the Ahpus. This time they are to take with them the earth knowledge that they received from their mother.

Even before the miraculous birth of the Twins there are clear indications that we are entering an age of transition. The Grandmother cannot accept Ixquic since she is the daughter of a Xibalban. She thinks her sons have died in Xibalba and cannot accept Ixquic's claim that she bears Hun Hunahpu's children. Ixquic claims, "Nevertheless it is true that I am your daughter-in-law; I have been for a long-time. I belong to Hun Hunahpu. They live in what I carry, Hun Hunahpu and Vucub Hunahpu are not dead; they will return to show themselves clearly. And you shall see their image in what I bring to you." Notice here how the author uses interchangeably one entity alone or the two together. The Grandmother replies, "Furthermore you are an impostor; my sons of whom you speak are already dead" (Part II, Chapter 4).

The recognition of Ixquic by the Grandmother only comes after she gives Ixquic an impossible task: filling a net with maize from one single plant. Ixquic takes the hair of the maize and fills the net with maize cobs. The image possibly points to a new stage of the cultivation of maize that the Maya introduced. Before completing this deed Ixquic enacts the Ritual of Confession, through which the maiden calls on Chabal, guardian of the maize, and a trinity of goddesses whose names all start with Ix, the prefix indicating the earth. To them Ixquic says: "I am under obligation because of many faults." Thus she recognizes her human nature and her sin, but through the beings that she carries in her womb she can bring about the miracle of the maize. From this sign Ixmucané can recognize that Ixquic bears her grandsons and is finally able to accept the newcomer.

The end of Ixquic's trials is also the end of her active role. The Twins' trials begin where hers end. Their birth occurs in the woods, far from the hut of the Grandmother, in keeping with the habits of the Third Age. The birth of Hunahpu—and by extension of the Twins—is said to occur at the winter solstice. This is born out by the fact that the civil calendar that corresponds to his regency rules during the wintertime of the year (the tropical dry season).

The Twins now face the opposition of the older brothers. Hun Batz and Hun Chouen are the leaders of a whole epoch. Humanity of that age saw the work of the guides of humankind in the figure of the leaders that represented them. Thus Hun Batz and Hun Chouen are most likely the leaders that represent the gods on earth. The fact that one of them is called One Artisan and the other One Monkey points to the beginning and to the end of an age just like the Popol Vuh represents it. At the end of the Third Age Hun Batz and Hun Chouen embody the vices of that period: cruelty, envy, and indolence. They will be later transformed into monkeys. What follows is in effect a summary of the decadent practices that they can inflict upon the Twins. This is summarized in one sentence of the Popol Vuh: "Now, what Hun Batz and Hun Chouen wished was that they [Hunahpu and Ixbalamqué] would die there on the anthill, or on the thistles. They wished this because of the hatred and envy Hun Batz and Hun Chouen felt for them" (Part II, Chapter 5). The two torments inflicted upon the Twins were tortures by means of which enemies were tested during the Third Age: the torture by ants and by thorns.[1]

The Twins bear the torments imposed on them by their brothers. In the words of the sacred text we hear: "But they did not become angry, nor did they become vexed, but suffered silently, because they knew their rank, and they understood everything clearly" (Part II, Chapter 5). From the words of the myth we can understand that a new age is beginning. The forces of heredity alone won't be enough to sustain the individual. The Twins and their brothers all share the same heredity. Hun Batz and Hun Chouen show themselves unworthy of it and are transformed into animals. The Twins show that it is not their heredity alone that qualifies them to lead humanity to a new age, but also their merits. In effect Hunahpu and Ixbalamqué are hunters and farmers. That their farming is not common farming is obvious from the text. They can count on the help of the elementals. The Twins' power over the animal realm will appear throughout the sacred text, especially in the trials of Xibalba and in the final ball game.

Hunahpu and Ixbalamqué inaugurate the beginning of a patriarchal age. They assure that they will take care of the Grandmother (Part II, Chapter 5). From now on men will work in the fields and maize cultivation will be further perfected, becoming central to the whole ensuing civilization.

The Danger of the Past

The confrontation with the giants occurs at a time when there was not yet light. The Popol Vuh tells us: "It was cloudy and twilight then on the face of the earth. There was no sun yet...The sky and the earth existed, but the faces of the sun and moon were covered" (Part 1, Chapter 4). The name Vucub Caquix, literally translated, means Seven Macaw. In astrological terms, Mayan tradition equates him to the Big Dipper. His wife corresponds to the constellation of Ursa Minor, the Small Dipper. His son's name, Zipacná, refers to a mythological animal with the features of a crocodile.2 The name fits the description of a being who is said to fish for crabs. Zipacná's brother is Capracan, or Earthquake.

We have therefore a heterogeneous assembly of beings. What they all have in common is their primitive consciousness. They hunt or gather and have titanic strength that allows them to bring down mountains. Their uniting trait is their ambition to be more than they are. Vucub Caquix is represented by the macaw, a parrot that mimics and imitates. Similarly to the giants, he pretends to be more than he is. Seven Macaw asserts: "So, then, I am the sun, I am the moon, for all humankind. So shall it be, because I can see very far" (Part I, Chapter 4). Zipacná says: "I am he who made the earth" (Part I, Chapter 5). Capracan: "I demolish the mountains" (Part I, Chapter 9). Thus it is pride that colors the three beings. This pride is accompanied by strength but lacks cunning. The Twins can easily lure them into traps and overcome them through magic. Incorporating an earthly element into their beings neutralizes them all. A bird smeared with chalk causes the death of Capracan, whereas Zipacná is crushed under a mountain and Vucub Caquix's teeth and eyes are replaced with maize, which is the symbol of human involvement with the tasks of earth.

As Father Ximenez intuited, the giants are representatives of a previous age through whom act Luciferic beings.3 They are endowed with titanic strength and use it in their fight against the Twins, as in the episode of the tearing of the arm of Hunahpu. They lose to the Twins because their existence is foreign to the reality of earth. When the Twins, with the help of Ixmucané and Ixpiyacoc, remove Vucub Caquix's teeth and eyes, the giant says: "It is not well that you pull my teeth because it is only with them that I am a lord and all my ornaments are my teeth and my eyes." Soon after these are removed the text says: "Instantly his features sagged and he no longer looked like a lord" (Part I, Chapter 6). The only true strength of Lucifer was semblance that resided in those parts of the body that can reflect the light of the sun: the teeth and eyes.

An interesting episode interjected in the narrative is Zipacná's fight against the Four Hundred Boys. Here we see a confrontation between Man of the First Age and Man of the Second Age. The Four Hundred Boys make communal decisions in order to eliminate Zipacná whom they fear because of his strength. The latter can preempt their intentions through his atavistic faculties of perception, his ability to "see very far."

Representatives of all three ages are present in the portion of the Popol Vuh that we are studying. After looking back to the challenges of the past, the Popol Vuh directs our attention to the more pressing tests of the present and future, those posed by the lords of Xibalba. From the heights of the mountains the Popol Vuh leads us to the depths of the underworld.

The Second Descent to the Underworld

Before descending into the underworld the Twins have faced all the evils of the preceding First and Second Ages. They have defeated the giants and the Luciferic forces that stood behind them. The action now moves away from mountains and volcanoes toward the belly of the earth, the realm of the lords of Xibalba.

Before attending to their mission in the underworld, the Twins perform a very indicative symbolic action for the Grandmother. They plant two stalks of maize in the middle of the house. The text specifies that they were planted in the dry earth! With this gesture the Twins unite their fate with the fate of the maize. The latter's growth will not only depend on natural elements but also on the life of the Twins, and therefore later from religious ceremonies. In the calendar this is reflected by two similar signs called *kin* (day/sun) and *kan* (maize). They are both represented by a circle and, according to Girard, they both correspond to the head of Hunahpu.[4]

The Twins go to the underworld in the same way their fathers went before them. However, they cross the rivers over their solar blowgun and they also sleep in their blowgun. This insulates them from contact with the underworld. The Twins have benefited from the experience of the Ahpus. They also possess the element of earth in their make-up. Contrary to their forefathers they have taken with them their gear, but they avoid giving out their names, i.e., their essences. In turn they manage to figure out the names of their adversaries, thanks to the help of the mosquito. Of the mosquito the Popol Vuh later says that it is a "hair that Hunahpu plucked out of his shinbone" (Part II, Chapter 8). Unlike the Ahpus they are now able to perceive the mannequins for what they are. They also know that they have to refuse the lords' ball and use their own in the ball game.

After winning the game the Twins relinquish their right to claim the sacrifice of the lords' life. This indicates that human sacrifice is in use at this point of time and that the lords of Xibalba or their tukurs performed them on vanquished enemies. The Twins have come to Xibalba not only with the desire to defeat the Camé, but also with the intent to inaugurate a new era, one without human sacrifice. The rest of the odyssey will further confirm this point.

In the underworld the Twins have to undergo various tests, six caves and a final ball game. Additionally there are ball games in between the tests of the caves, but none as important as the final one. In the Cave of Darkness the Twins manage to maintain the light without burning out the cigar. To accomplish this they avail themselves of the power of the tail feathers of the macaw. Lucifer (Seven Macaw), whom they have met and overcome, is the one that can help their consciousness stay awake in the darkness. Lucifer thus finds his rightful place in evolution.

The second test is the Cave of Knives. Apparently two tests are going on at the same time. One is posed by the danger of the knives. The other is the seemingly impossible task of retrieving flowers from the guarded garden of the lords. The flint knives are pacified by the Twins' promise that from now on they will be able to survive on animal meat. The lords of Xibalba receive the flowers they required through the intermediary of the ants who collected them for the Twins. Animals and flowers will now replace human sacrifice; the two parts of the test bear an inner relationship. In essence the Twins recognize the necessity of suffering in the order of creation, but they redirect it to the sacrifice of the animals and plants, as well as inner sacrifice.

The next test is the Cave of Cold that the Twins overcome by burning tree trunks. The fourth cave is that of the jaguars. Ixbalamqué is co-substantial with the jaguars and the forces of the night; therefore they cannot defeat him. The jaguar god, an instrument of the forces turned decadent that we see often depicted, particularly in Olmec statuary, is now made to work with the progressive deities. Finally, not even the Cave of Fire can destroy Hunahpu, a solar being.

The turning point of the tests of the caves comes with the final one, the Cave of Bats. The celestial bat cuts off Hunahpu's head in one swoop.

The decapitation of Hunahpu recapitulates Hun Hunahpu's earlier one. Hunahpu's fault has been his impatience in waiting for the dawn or Dawning. The Cave of Bats is the polar trial to the first one, the Cave of Darkness. In the Cave of Bats the Dawning is about to occur now that Hunahpu has been decapitated. This is a "False Dawning" that the Camé want to inaugurate but that the Twins have to delay. The god Tohil wants to instate the False Dawning in place of the "True Dawning." The Popol Vuh talks about it at length in Part III. At this point all of creation and Heart of Heaven (the Ahpus) come to the rescue of the Twins. It is only when the Twins have relinquished all their powers that Heart of Heaven can intervene. The vulture is sent to prevent the Dawning that the lords of Xibalba want to bring about.

The last cave is followed by a ball game that the lords of Xibalba want to play with Hunahpu's head. It takes the collaboration of the animal realm to make a false head in order to replace the hero's head. This is only a first stage. The Twins cannot forestall their death, but this time it will come through a voluntary choice.

Hunahpu and Ixbalamqué return to Xibalba after their initial trials, because their goal is not simply to survive the ordeals of the caves but to change the whole of evolution and counter the impulse of the Camé. The Twins trick the lords into killing them through fire and throw themselves in it willingly. We are told later that their ashes are spread into the river. The Twins reappear as fish-men after five days. Much esoteric symbolism is hidden in these few lines. The young maize god is also called God[5] because it takes five days for the maize to germinate in the Soconusco region. Fish is the *nagual* or animal representative of the young maize god. Here again the Twins share the destiny of maize. The whole of the myth is permeated with images from the natural world in which the Maya are immersed.

The apotheosis of the Twins, their resurrection, is their elevation to and identification with the sun and moon. In other words we are told that the Dawning has finally occurred. Not only the sun but also the stars appear. The Chorti Maya still identify Hunahpu as the Dawn God, a name that we have seen appear in other legends. Dawn God really stands for God of the Dawning. The Atlantean-like consciousness of the Native American has completed its descent from the watery element of Tlalocan, their original paradise, into the fullness of earth. This is what some traditions, for example the Collao mythology of Bolivia, call the Second Creation. We have already quoted in chapter two the Chilam Balam's book about the "creation of the *uinal*" (month, or astrology by extension). There we are told that the creation of the month occurred "when the earth, as well as the rocks and the trees awoke." A second translation says: "The uinal was created, the earth was created; sky, earth, trees, and rocks were set in order...."[5] The two translations are not saying different things. The indigenous compare the Dawning, a new awakening, to a new creation. In Hopi terminology the dawning is called the "emergence from the underworld." These are simply different imaginative ways to convey a similar change that occurred in the aura of the earth.

Something else has become clearer from the text of the Popol Vuh: the different functions of Hunahpu and Ixbalamqué. In all the episodes it is Hunahpu who plays the active role. It is Hunahpu who loses his arm to Vucub Caquix; it is he who loses his head in the Cave of Bats. Ixbalamqué simply accompanies him. Hunahpu turns into the sun, Ixbalamqué, according to his more human nature (co-substantiality with the jaguar) turns into the moon, whom the indigenous see intimately connected to the realm of earth, via the substance of water. Hunahpu, the solar entity, avails himself of the human companion or human body of Ixbalamqué. Does the story portray two different entities: a god in the figure of Hunahpu, a man in the figure of Ixbalamqué? Or does it portray two interpenetrating essences? It may not be possible to bring an ultimate answer to this question. Nevertheless, certain vases of the classical Maya period portray Ixbalamqué with a beard, accentuating his human dimension. Such is the case for a famous rendering of the maize god resurrecting from a turtle carapace, aided by Hunahpu and Ixbalamqué. The Twins stand on either side of the carapace and Ixbalamqué is recognizable by his beard (see figure 1, p. 157).

The portrayal of the duality of Christ and initiate in the image of the Twins may correspond in more than one way to the working of the initiate with the Christ. Steiner's research about the interaction of the disciples with the Christ can shed some light in this matter. Most of this appears in his *Fifth Gospel* cycle, where Steiner offers insights that make some Bible passages more intelligible. The first revelation concerns the fact that during the last three years of his ministry, the body of Jesus was not always present when the Christ manifested himself to the disciples. However, the spirit would appear clothed in an etheric body in such a way that it was not always possible for the disciples to know whether he was physically present or not.[6] With the passing of time and toward the coming of his death, the

Christ acquired the ability to speak through his disciples. The disciple in question would be transfigured. His face would change in such a way that the outsiders believed it was the Christ who spoke. At that time, the Christ himself would look quite ordinary to the onlookers.[7] In the lectures on the Saint Mark Gospel Steiner tells us that this is what he discovered in relation to Christ's conversation with the Sadducees.[8] This explains the difficulty of the Pharisees in recognizing Jesus among the others and their need to have Judas kiss him in order to arrest the right man. If the above was true of the disciples, all the more would we expect the same of the highest of initiates that was to conduct Christ's ministry in the Americas.

Two immediate consequences stem from the Twins' resurrection. The natives' fear of death caused by the twilight of the gods (descent of the Ahpus) is now overcome by the resurrection of the Twins—proof of the immortality of the soul. In the cycle of maize, their staple food and center of their economy, humanity of the Fourth Age perceived the annual rebirth of their sun deity. The Popol Vuh emphasizes this link. The resurrection of the Twins is mirrored by the fate of the maize in the Grandmother's house. The maize dies first and then sprouts a second time when the Twins resurrect. Furthermore, as we will later see in more detail, this is mirrored by the fact that precise astronomical knowledge allowed the Maya to cultivate two maize crops a year. From an economic perspective this implies a qualitative change in a civilization now able to sustain a higher population.

The conclusion of the Twins' odyssey comes with the defeat of the Camé. Here a few things are elucidated about the powers of evil. Only one of the sevenfold beings is specifically killed. We hear in effect: "And so it happened that they first sacrificed the one, who was the chief and lord, the one called Hun Camé, king of Xibalba," and further, "And when Hun Camé was dead, they overpowered Vucub Camé, and they did not bring either back to life" (Part II, Chapter 13).[9] Here again we see a being of a twofold (or more precisely sevenfold) nature, a device that we have seen used before. He is designated by the first and last numerals, but it is also made clear that one being has supremacy. The text differentiates the Xibalbans from the Camé. The Xibalbans are spared. After their defeat the sacred text specifies of the lords of Xibalba: "Their power in the olden days was not much. They only liked to do evil to men in those times. In truth, in those days, they did not have the category of gods" (Part II, Chapter 14). The Xibalbans and Camé are human beings, inspired by regressive spiritual beings—but human beings nevertheless. From now onwards their role will be to attend to secular functions. They will have the choice to become artisans and produce pottery or grindstones. They will have no access to the ball game or any religious ceremonial function. They will only be able to attract those who give themselves up to vices. Evil therefore has been confined to its natural function in the furtherance of world evolution. The Xibalbans will be able to test human virtue, not to set the standards of civilization. Evil will not reign sovereign as it did at the height of the practice of human sacrifice.

The Twins can finally disclose their identity. They can claim the heritage of the Ahpus and redirect the people to praise the Ahpus, instead of the gods of the underworld. Heaven, earth, and underworld have found a new relationship with each other. The turning point of American history—the transition into historical times—has occurred.

CHAPTER 6

THE FOURTH AGE

T HE BEGINNING of the Fourth Age has unique dimensions in the history of Mesoamerica. No mythology other than the Mayan, and no record other than that of the Popol Vuh, clearly elaborates this event in such detail. Few other American cultures have shown such a dramatic inner and outer transformation as the one witnessed by the Maya at this point in time. In order to render this phenomenon visible we will have to penetrate Mayan cosmovision deeper and deeper. Later we will see how geographical and archaeological indications of modem history fit with Mayan esoteric knowledge. These findings will be examined later in light of Steiner's assertions of 1916 concerning the Mexican Mysteries.

Two beings, or groups of beings, made possible the transition from the Third to the Fourth Age: the Ahpus and the Twins. The religion and life of the Fourth Age revolve around them. The events that the Popol Vuh narrates are reflected by the important changes that Mayan civilization brought about in all fields of knowledge. We will look at many aspects of this culture's development, in order to corroborate the imaginative language of the sacred text and find its deeper meaning between the lines of recorded history.

The Dawning: Turning Point of Time

The Dawning was a momentous event both for the earth and for those who witnessed it. The earth was quickened and the eyes of the people were opened to a new reality. It effectively amounted to a new creation. Perceptions of reality and consciousness are here intimately linked. Atlantean consciousness did not perceive colors and outlines as a modem person does. Rather, objects appeared like pictures, interweaving into each other, and no clear outlines were perceived.

We have seen how Native American consciousness can be defined as Atlantean. Steiner offers us another example of how consciousness in ancient times differed from modern consciousness even in the post-Atlantean age, in the case of the ancient Chaldeans at the important transition time of the onset of Kali Yuga. The Chaldeans, descendents of the original Sumerians, had a different perception of their surroundings. They were unaware of the difference between the sunlight of the day and its absence at night. They perceived the sun as black, surrounded by a beautiful aura. Similarly to the Native Americans, they imagined that it descended at night into a funnel.[1] At this point in time some of the Chaldeans were beginning to perceive more fully physical reality, while still retaining perception of some of the spiritual realities behind it. This signified a transition from night- to day-consciousness. Revelation received in the dream or sleep state, in union with the gods, had to give way to communication received in full consciousness.

Chaldean and Mayan consciousnesses vastly differed and therefore the above example can only serve to illustrate parallels. What is important to realize is that different stages of consciousness are accompanied with different kinds and degrees of perception of the world. Steiner's observations give us further encouragement to realize that the Popol Vuh is trying to express a deeper dimension of reality. It does not have any use for symbolic thinking. Thus the Dawning truly corresponds to the emergence into a new stage of consciousness and perception. This explains why it was perceived as a new creation.

We will observe a different state of consciousness when we examine the history of the Quiché Maya. Without going further, their history takes on a set direction when they hesitate to wait for the Dawning. The text says: "Our first mothers and fathers did not yet have wood nor stones to keep; but their hearts were tired of waiting for the sun" (Part III, Chapter 4). The forerunners of the Quiché separated from the rest of the Maya before the critical event of the Dawning and, as the Popol Vuh underlines, developed a different relationship with this momentous event than the bulk of the Maya.

In the prelude to the Dawning the Popol Vuh deals with the matter of evil and its dual manifestation. The Giants can destroy and provoke events similar to natural catastrophes. On the other hand the Xibalbans can bring illness and death. Both sets of beings resort to strength or cunning. Seven Macaw severs Hunahpu's arm, the Camé decapitate both Hun Hunahpu and Hunahpu. The Ahpus and the Twins accept the necessity of sacrifice. This is made clear at the climax of the odyssey of the Twins. Their death in the fire of the oven is undertaken willingly. The Xibalbans and Vucub Caquix act solely for themselves to the point of pretending to be gods. The Twins reinstate the cult of the Ahpus, as will later appear upon a closer look at Mayan religion, calendar, and astronomy.

History bears out the changes in consciousness accompanying the Maya revolution. Human sacrifice is present in the pre-classical period, but absent from the Fourth Age for a few centuries at least. It is not practiced by the Maya until the 4th century AD, and is only re-introduced gradually, with alternate success, until it reaches a peak with the arrival of the Toltecs in the Yucatan and the foundation of the Mayapan League during the 11th century. Moreover, the sacrifices here mentioned did not entail organ removal, at least not until the time of the League.

In America, the fate of the individual was intimately linked with the tribe or ethnic group. The Quiché bear a collective fate as a nation. They differ from the other Mayan tribes of Cakchiquels, Rabinal, Tzotzil, etc. in relation to the gods they follow. Nevertheless the Popol Vuh points to the beginning of individual choice. Ixquic, a Xibalban, has chosen to transgress her father's wishes and has rebelled against the necessity of human sacrifice. She has borne the Twins who will later bring the end of the rule of her people.

The matter of individual choice echoes the imperative to abandon idolatry that Manu enjoined his followers in the fifth post-Atlantean epoch: "You shall follow the God of whom you cannot make engraved images." This is the imperative that accompanies the time of the Dawning. Expecting the Dawning requires the development of the forces of faith, placed against the waning strength of the old divine revelation in which the knowledge stemming from revelation was synonymous with faith. Expecting the Dawning without having the outer support of the gods is similar to the trials of the tribes Israel for whom outer success was not automatically linked to the favor of God. Trials and failures set the stage for the development of new forces of the soul. The expectation of the Dawning is a time of great inner trial, especially for the priests who were to lead their people.

Agrarian God and Solar God

The resurrection of the Twins was preceded by the reinstatement of the cult of the Ahpus, which had been perverted by the Camé. The Camé had in fact overcome the cult of the Ahpus. This is how the Popol Vuh describes the deed of the Twins: "And here is how they [Twins] extolled the memory of their fathers, whom they had left there in the place of sacrifice at the ball court: 'You shall be invoked,' their sons said to them, when they fortified their heart. 'You shall be the first to arise, and you shall be the first to be worshipped by the sons of the noblemen, by the civilized vassals. Your names shall not be lost. So it shall be!' they told their fathers and thus consoled themselves. 'We are the avengers of your death, of the pains and sorrows which they caused you'" (Part II, Chapter 14).

The text also emphasizes that the earlier demise of the Ahpus and elevation of the Camé corresponded with the apogee of human sacrifice. The cult of the Ahpus, or Great Spirit, had been debased by the Camé. The sevenfold being of the Ahpus became the sevenfold Camé. The Xibalbans' Great Spirit is in reality an Ahrimanic being.

The place of the Ahpus and the Twins in the Fourth Age is reflected in the division of the year. The rainy season is the one corresponding to the Sacred Calendar and it is the time of the so-called Agrarian God— the resuscitated Ahpus. The dry season is the season of the civil calendar and of the Solar God. The transition between the two occurs at Yaxkin (October 25th), sometimes erroneously thought to be the New Year. In reality it is the festival of the New Sun. Yaxkin commemorates the Dawning and the point in time of the Twins' resurrection. The year is therefore divided in two parts. The Agrarian God of the origins is commemorated and celebrated during the time of the growth of maize. The Solar God, ruling during the dry season, is also called the Tribal God, reflecting the fact that it is he, more than the Agrarian God, who differentiates the tribes. The Solar God inaugurates the history of each tribe.

In fact, a much deeper knowledge is imbedded in the division of the year than appears at first sight. We find clues of it in the Popol Vuh in the apotheosis of the Twins. The sun that rises in the heavens at the time of the Dawning is a spiritual being. The Popol Vuh makes it clear by indicating that it is more than the physical sun: "Like a man was the sun when it showed itself" (Part III, Chapter 9). This is not an incidental figure of speech. In fact the same appears quite clearly in the narratives of the

Dawning in South America. The Spanish chronicler Molina says in this regard: "At the time that it was about to arise, the sun, in the image of a very resplendent man, called out to the Incas...."[2]

In the myths of North and South America deeper truths are hidden that are only known to spiritual science, particularly in relation to the Mystery of Golgotha. Steiner has indicated in many instances that at the crucifixion Jesus' blood pouring into the earth had an enduring effect for the future of the planet. The earth would have dried up had it not been for the sacrificial deed of Christ and the pouring of his blood into the earth. Seen spiritually, after Christ's death the earth became a shining being radiating light into its surroundings, and it became possible for each human being to experience this light in himself. "When Jesus died on the cross at Golgotha something was born to the Earth that before had existed only in the cosmos. The death of Jesus of Nazareth was the birth of the all-prevailing cosmic love within the Earth's sphere."[3] In clairvoyant experience the initiates of Ireland detected this change in the earth's aura, thereby understanding the magnitude of an event which they could not have witnessed historically.[4] Much the same occurred in America, at least among the Maya.

The Dawning was a cosmic event. It was reflected through changes in human consciousness that the priesthood of the Mexican Mysteries carefully prepared and that the deeds of the Twins ushered in. There was nothing automatic in the nature of this change. Part III of the Popol Vuh will bear further evidence to this aspect of Mesoamerican history. The deed of Christ, and of the American initiate, offered in freedom the possibility of a new evolutionary course.

The Dawning divides the year in two, because two beings rule over their respective part of the year. The dry season is the time of Hunahpu, and to it corresponds the knowledge of the historical deed of the initiate on behalf of the Christ—the solar spirit. This is also what introduces historical consciousness among the Maya. On the other hand the rainy season is the one that reflects primarily of the initiate counterpart.

The Solar God—the Christ—now fulfills the task earlier performed by the Year God. In Steiner's words, "Christ has taken upon Himself tasks which had formerly in earthly evolution been fulfilled by the 'Year God.' In this transition from the 'Year God' to Christ, that is, in the transition from a more natural to a purely spiritual experience of the cycle of the year...."[5]

The initiate plays the role of the Guardian of the Threshold, aptly represented in many ways. He represents the Thunder and Lightning God of the agricultural cycle. In Mesoamerican culture, to be struck by lightning (and survive) is a proof of the favor of the gods and of being able to bear initiation. It is the initiate who educates his people in the rigidly codified communal tasks of the fields. He forms the link between the Atlantean past of the Great Spirit and the historical times of the solar spirit. The Sacred Calendar can be compared to a path of education that leads the individual to the yearly recognition of the event of the Dawning among the Maya. The initiate, as a Guardian of the Threshold, leads the individual from Atlantean into post-Atlantean consciousness in the course of the year.

The role of the two beings is indicated in the image of Hunahpu and Ixbalamqué's apotheosis as the new sun and moon. This enigmatic role of sun and moon is known to spiritual science in the realm of life after death. Once the soul is freed from the body it expands into the cosmos. Until it reaches the sphere of the moon it is involved in what is called the kamaloca stage. It is a phase of burning out of all the attachments that the soul still has toward its previous life on earth. It experiences the consequences of all its deeds in the previous life. The sphere of the moon forms the boundary between the experiences of kamaloca and the entrance into the realm of the inner planets, Mercury and Venus, later followed by entrance into the sphere of the Sun. The Sun forms the gateway toward the realm of the purely spiritual sphere. Before that, our life in the spiritual world only allows us to meet those we were previously associated with on earth, or those with whom we shared common religious and spiritual beliefs. In the Sun sphere we can connect on a purely human basis—in as much as we have made this our concern on earth—which means in as much as we have penetrated our life with the impulse of the Christ, the Higher Guardian of the Threshold. It is through the Lower Guardian of the Threshold that we can penetrate into the first rungs of the spiritual realms, the soul world. Through meeting consciously with the Higher Guardian we can enter the spiritual world proper and can devote our life to the betterment of all other human beings on earth.

Moon and sun stand in this relationship with each other and with the Lower and Higher Guardian of the Thresholds. This makes it more understandable why the realm of earth extends as far as the moon for the Maya and other indigenous people. Under this light Ixbalamqué and Hunahpu play successive roles in the education of their people. It is the initiate who guides his people through the stages of the collective spiritual-practical education of the Sacred Calendar. Christ/Hunahpu is the archetype of individual development that follows Yaxkin, time of the Dawning.

The so-called Tzolkin—creation of the Third Age—is a Sacred Calendar, which in the Fourth Age links the deeds of the Twins and their descent to Xibalba with the cultivation of maize. It is a calendar of religious-agricultural practices accompanying the cultivation of maize tied to astronomical observations. Its cycle of 260 days goes from February to the end of October. The civil year comprises the remaining 105 days of the year. Even climatologically, the time of the Sacred Calendar, corresponding to the rainy season, echoes the conditions of Atlantean humanity. Yaxkin is the divider between the pre-historic cycle of nature and the historic time of culture. Thus, for example, the festivals of Kukulkan or other historical figures are celebrated during the dry season. Between the two seasons, at the time of Yaxkin, stands the resurrection of the Twins and the commemoration of the Dawning, which effectively inaugurates history. During the dry season there is no cult of the Agrarian God.

Agrarian God and Solar God have other very distinct complementary characteristics. The cult of the Agrarian God is performed at night, therefore in similar conditions of consciousness to those preceding the Dawning. The Solar God's rituals are conducted at midday. The agrarian priest literally receives his knowledge from the stars. Before the conquest it was the solar priest who kept the sacred books. To him belonged the realms of history and science. The ballgame was played during the dry season, particularly around the time of the winter solstice, in honor of the Solar God.

The two priests reflect the reality of two types of consciousness. The work on the fields is done collectively. The agrarian priests work in a group, at whose head stands the *"horchan"* (snake-head). The solar priest, called *kin*, (sun, day) acts alone. Individualism inaugurated by Hunahpu survives side by side with group consciousness of the earlier epochs. Interestingly, this same structure of the priesthood was still kept, fifteen centuries later, by the Aztecs. Before Christ the gift of atavistic clairvoyance depended upon heredity. In the time of preparation for the incarnation of Christ the Hebrew people were no longer strictly respecting heredity laws, in an effort to encourage the development of the new faculty of thinking over and against the simple preservation of atavistic faculties.[6]

The pre-Hispanic Maya called their Solar God Kinich Ahau. The Agrarian God was called Itzamat-ul, meaning "the one who receives the grace," or "dew from heaven," another confirmation of the Tau essence of the Ahpus.[7] The duo of Agrarian and Solar (or other, non-solar, Tribal Gods) accompanies all of Mesoamerican religions and civilizations that we will study later on. Among the Toltecs we have Tlaloc (Agrarian God) and Quetzalcoatl (Tribal God); the Aztecs honored Tlaloc (Agrarian God) and Huitchilopochtli (Tribal God).

What differentiates the tribes is mainly the Tribal God, whether the Christ or another being. We can ask ourselves if the relation to the Agrarian God remained the same in the course of time. Or were the different tribes worshipping gods of different epochs? We will see this matter when we come to the history of the tribes in chapter 1 of Part II.

A New Look at the Sacred and Civil Calendars

We will now explore the deeper meanings of the sacred and civil calendars in relation to the previous ages and more in depth in relation to the Fourth Age. The Tzolkin tied together myth, rituals, astronomy, and the agricultural practices of maize cultivation. The number twenty is central to its architecture. The month, called *uinal*, has twenty days and this unity is called the *Ahau* or lord (solar deity). Twenty is the sum of fingers and toes; it is the measure of those who have fully incarnated into their extremities.

Both sacred and civil calendars start with the five "days of affliction" or "days without name" that complete the year of 365 days. Girard illustrates the correspondence of the four Ages with the phases of the calendar:

- "Pralaya," the five "days of affliction," February 8 to 12: the state preceding the formation of time and the universe.
- First Age, starting on February 12: creation of the universe and time.
- Second Age, starting with the opening of the rainy season on May 1: the creation of the plants.
- Third Age, with a turning point on August 12: on this date the "bending of the maize," for the drying of the cob, has a symbolic correspondence with the "binding of years," typical ceremony of the Third Age.
- Fourth Age, historical celebrations and inauguration of the dry season starting at Yaxkin (October 25): the Dawning.[8]

The sacred year of the Tzolkin gathers interesting properties. There are two successive periods of 40 days between February 8 to May 1, then twice 52 days from the first zenith passage of the sun to summer solstice and from the summer solstice to the second zenith passage (August 12). We can summarize the above as follows:

From Feb 8 to March 21: 40 days
From March 21 to May 1 (1st zenith passage): 40 days
From May 1 to Summer Solstice: 52 days
From Summer Solstice to August 12 (2nd zenith passage): 52 days.[9]

On a larger scale 52 years is the time that completes a Calendar Round that was commemorated with the New Fire Ceremony in Toltec and Aztec civilizations.

The agricultural tasks are performed on days that the priests have found favorable. There are propitious days for sowing, clearing the milpa, harvesting, storing, etc. Maize occupies a central place in the indigenous understanding of the spiritual world. Its birth, death, and resurrection imbue every part of the Sacred Calendar with meaning. The yearly ceremonial cycle and the pantheon of the gods cannot be understood without it. The maize needs for its growth both the physical operations performed in the fields, and the subtle energies brought in through the yearly ceremonial life. In order to further find our way into a mythology that will reverberate throughout another fifteen centuries of Mesoamerican history, we need to understand who are the numeral gods and their various equivalent names. They are an integral part of the Sacred Calendar.

All Mayan and Mesoamerican gods are referred to as numeral gods for which Girard has elucidated much of the terminology. Among these we have already seen God 5, the Young Maize God, and God 7, corresponding to the seven Ahpus. Another two numbers are important in order to have a basic understanding of Mayan numerology: the numbers 13 and 9. God 13 is the god of the heavens, while God 9 indicates the underworld. God 7 operates on the surface of the earth as the Agrarian God.

God 13 appears in the Chilam Balam represented with his body standing over the Tree of Life (figure 1).[10] God 13 is planted on the earth, the head stretching to the heavens. In some representations the head of the Agrarian God appears in the middle, with 6 stars on each side. We see here the grouping of 6 + 1 + 6. The Agrarian God or God 7 stands at the middle

Figure 1: from the Chilam Balam

of a progression forming his number from either side. The Maya actually count 13 constellations of the zodiac. This was the thesis of H. J. Spinden in 1916, which has since been confirmed by others.[11]

God 7 refers to the 7 Ahpus or the undivided 7 Elohim. Another way to envision God 7 has to do with the sun's yearly movement on the horizon. The intersolstitial cross marks the four observable extremes of the sun at the solstices: the highest and lowest sunrise and sunset elongations. These are the pillars over which is built the house of the heavens. The four corners with the three daily positions of the sun form again the number 7. The three daily positions are toward the east (ascent), center (corresponding with zenith twice a year in tropical areas) and toward the west (descent). Schematically this is represented as follows:

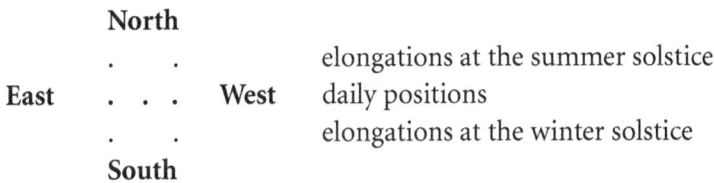

	North		
	. .		elongations at the summer solstice
East	. . .	**West**	daily positions
	. .		elongations at the winter solstice
	South		

The God 7, in following the destiny of maize, meets with God 9, deity of the underworld. God 9 is represented by the nine Lords of the Night: in their series are included the God of Cold and the God of Death. The origin of the number nine is more obscure than the others. Girard sees it in the equivalence that the Maya attribute to the numbers three and nine. For the Maya, in the underworld is expressed the reality of the number three: the union of male and female principles and the young maize that results from it. The nine gods could otherwise correspond with the nine layers of the underworld that Steiner describes in his work.[12] There were nine layers of the underworld in correspondence to the thirteen layers of the heavens.

We can now look at the development of maize and how it is associated with the deeds of the gods. God 7, the Agrarian God, presides over the cycle of maize as we have seen previously. Upon being laid in the ground the maize kernel undergoes a process of dissolution, of death. At this stage he is equated with the God of Cold. With him the god of maize has to fight a strenuous battle, the same that man faces in going to the underworld. The Agrarian God sends the rains acting in concert with the primordial Saturn/Fire God (of the underworld) who gives the warmth for the young seed to germinate. The grain of maize dying in the earth is equated with Tezcatlipoca, the god who transforms himself in order to feed humanity. He is represented with a flint, the prototype of the sacrificial knife used for animal sacrifice, and represented in axes and knives with human faces.[13]

As the maize develops its first two leaves it is equated with God 5, the Solar God having resurrected. The number 5 indicates the 5 days that it takes maize to germinate in the Soconusco. As the plant of maize develops, its spirit progressively withdraws. Manifestation and spirit potential are polar opposites forming two ends of a spectrum. The end of the agricultural cycle is the beginning of the regency of the Solar God. At this stage the maize is "de-sanctified" since it has reached its maximum physical manifestation.

The Maya and all Mesoamerican cultures after them, perfected in the calendar the symbolism of their cosmology. This can be seen in relation to the cardinal dates of the Tzolkin. The first numeral day associated with the beginning of the Tzolkin is not 1 but 7 (e.g., 7 Ahau, meaning 7 Lord, or 7 Chouen meaning 7 Monkey), reflecting the fact that the Sacred Calendar is ruled by the Agrarian God or God 7. The passage of the sun at the zenith corresponds to a day 9 of the Tzolkin. This inaugurates the descent of the sun to the underworld in agreement with the symbolism of the number 9. Finally, the closure of the Tzolkin occurs on a day 13, commemorating the resurrection of the Twins.[14]

In the following tableau the Tzolkin is associated with the numeral gods and with the episodes of the Popol Vuh that equate maize with the deeds of the Twins, or God 5.

— February 8: inauguration of the Sacred Calendar. First movement of the sun. God 7 (Agrarian God) leads the calendar wheel.

– March 21: equinox. Solar God descends to earth. Institution of the Hearth Fire, the hearth set at the center of the universe, symbolizing the original creation. Burning of the weeds in the milpas.

– April 30 - May 1: sun passage at the zenith. This corresponds with the descent of the sun to the underworld. The underworld is symbolized by God 9. Beginning of the rainy season and the Pleiades reach their zenith. Rituals of attraction of the rains. Mythologically this corresponds with the sacrifice of the Ahpus, the origin of the Tree of Life, the fecundation of Ixquic. Before sowing there is observation of strict sexual abstinence, showing once more how maize is not just the product of natural forces but a co-creation of the human beings with the gods. The first crop of maize is called fire maize (*"milpa de fuego"*).

– June 21: summer solstice. Maximum precipitation.

– July 25: dry period. Preparation of the fields for the second milpa. Ritual request for temporary suspension of the rains.

– August 12: second sun passage to the zenith. Bending of the first milpa and sowing of the second maize. The folding of the corn indicates the closing of a cycle. It also serves as the archetype for a larger cycle and the so-called "binding of the years" that was evoked in the New Fire Ceremony performed every 52 years. The position of the Milky Way indicates the time of the second sowing. Before the zenith sun there is the well-known phenomenon of the Perseid meteor shower, starting on August 11 and reaching a climax on August 12.

– September (first 3 weeks): seeds of the second maize crop sown among the stalks of the first crop. This crop yields 2/3 of the first crop but requires much less work.

– October 24 at midnight: end of agricultural calendar and cycle. Desanctification of maize. Dark period ends. The gods come out of the underworld. The return of the gods to the heavens is what is meant by the numeral God 13. Yaxkin occurs on day 13 of the Tzolkin.

– October 25: commemoration of the Dawning, start of the hundred days of rest and hunting. Festival of the dead and solar festivals. Elevation of Hunahpu to the status of Solar God.

– December, before the solstice: *doblada* (bending) of the second crop.

- December 21: winter solstice, festival of harvest. This was the
  time of the celebration of the ballgame.[15]

We can now introduce two other tools of the calendar: the Count of the
Nine Lords of the Night, and the Lunar Year.

- COUNT OF THE NINE LORDS OF THE NIGHT. Each of the Nine
  Lords rules over each following night in an endless succession.
  Each lord rules exactly 20 times over the 180 days between the
  first zenith passage of the sun on May 1 and the closure of the
  Tzolkin. They accompany the cycle of maize from sowing to the
  completion of the Sacred Calendar.
- LUNAR YEAR. This is a calendar of 177 days, approximately one
  half of the solar year. The beginning of the dry season and the
  beginning of the rainy season are the start of each lunar year.

Solar God and Ball Game

According to colonial sources the ball game was only played in the
dry season, around the winter solstice, in honor of the Solar God.[16] J. M.
Jenkins indicates that the ball court was called *Pom Hexel Hom* which he
translates: "offerings and resurrection in the ball court graveyard." M. T.
Uriarte confirms that *Hom* means both tomb and ball court.[17] Linguistic
indications confirm what simple observation can detect. The ball courts
are usually sunk in the ground. Their topography reinforces what the
Popol Vuh tells us about them: that they were entrances to the underworld. They are often depicted in codices with a cross dividing them into
four equal parts, e.g., in Codex Columbino and Codex Borbonicus. The
division of the heavens and the earth into four quadrants corresponds to
the elevation of the house of the heavens above the earth, whose foundations lie at the four furthest east and west elongations of the sun at the
solstices.

The field's form greatly evolved through the centuries. It went from
being an open-ended field to the classical I shape. During the game the
players hit the ball, symbol of the sun, toward the opposing team on the
other half of the field. The game, played with a rubber ball, was fast and
dangerous. The players, who had to throw themselves on the ground, were
protected with gloves and kneepads. They could not touch the ball with
head, feet or arms. It seems that they wore yokes around their waist with

which they could also hit the ball.[18] The purpose of the game was to place the ball in a goal ring.

As is indicated in the images of the Popol Vuh, historians for the most part think that the ball game represented a battle between the forces of light and of darkness. From the context of the Popol Vuh, which mentions the repeated ball games the Lords of Xibalba play against the Twins, it is likely that the game is a celebration of solar rebirth at the annual level. We will see in chapter 6 that it may have had a larger cosmic significance in relation to larger cycles of time.

Ball courts are found as far south as Western Salvador. They spread north of Central Mexico without reaching the northern border. An island outside their geographical distribution is found in Arizona and New Mexico. Possibly the oldest ball court is the one found in 1995 at Paso de la Amada in Chiapas, dated between 1400 and 1250 BC. M. Coe indicates that in San Lorenzo appears the first purposefully built Olmec ball court.[19]

Curiously in the famous city of Teotihuacan—whose history will occupy us in chapter 1 of Part II—no ball courts have been found. Later, the game also disappeared from the Mayan lowlands. In the late Classic Maya period ball courts were rebuilt in the very same areas, and even the exact locations, of the old ones. This denotes a desire to maintain a connection with the past.[20] Schele and Freidel point to the obvious differences in the markers of the ball court: some portray mythical scenes between the Lords of Xibalba and the Twins, while others depict prisoners, skulls, and human sacrifice.[21] In its most elevated form the game celebrated the deeds of the Twins. In its later manifestations the ball game acquired a new militaristic symbolism, for example in Tula and Chichen Itza, an aspect of the late Toltec civilization. There were no less than 6 ball courts in Tula; there, as in Chichen Itza, they were associated with skull-racks. The courts were associated with war symbolism and the game was accompanied by human sacrifice during Aztec time as well.

The Revolution of the Long Count

We have mentioned that the Haab of 365 days and the Sacred Calendar of 260 days gave rise to the "short count," more well-known as the Calendar Round. The dynamic Tzolkin was used in conjunction with the Haab as the revolving wheels of a clock in the cycle of 52 years. Every 52 years the two wheels of this calendar returned to the initial positions of both Haab and Tzolkin. This was a time of truth; the priests wondered if and how they could recalibrate the calendar. This act was sanctioned in the ritual of the New Fire, associated with the dread of the end of time. The Toltec and Aztec worlds were still tied to this conception of time. For the populations who only knew the Calendar Round time still had a cyclical connotation, and eternity as a concept was unknown. The death of the Ahpus in the underworld was much more than a figure of speech; it was the condition of soul of the Mesoamerican Third Age seeking a new relationship with the spirit. The anxiety preceding the New Fire ceremony was the outer reflection of a condition of soul. The resurrection of the Twins was the reality that superseded the death of the Ahpus. The Maya inaugurated the new consciousness of the Fourth Age, in which their calendar played a central role. Resurrection of the Ahpus and the concept of eternity in the calendar are complementary aspects of new dimension of hope inaugurated by the deed of the Twins.

The Mayan Long Count is based once again on the sacred number 20. The order units upon which the calendar was based are:

 – *kin* (sun): one day
 – *uinal* (moon: roughly month): bundle of 20 *kins*
 – *tun*: 18 (rather than 20) bundles of *uinals* or 360 days
 – *katun*: bundle of 20 *tuns* or 7,200 days
 – *baktun*: bundle of 20 *katuns* or 144,000 days (roughly more than 394 years)
 – Great Cycle of 13 *baktuns* or 5,125 years.

In this system a Calendar Round corresponds exactly to 2 *katuns*, 12 *tuns* and 13 *uinals*. Dates found on stelae are written in descending order of magnitude, starting from the larger cycles of time.

The Maya were now relying on another cycle, the Long Count of 5,125 years, rather than 52 years. In the present system every day of that cycle was unique; after 5,125 years the cycle started again, just as it had done after 52 years in the Calendar Round. To all practical purposes this is the equivalent of eternity, since it goes much further than the human life span. A Great Cycle was considered one World Age. There is a very similar, notable precedent to the Mayan great cycle: ancient Indians preserved knowledge of the 5000 year epochs called Krita Yuga, Treta Yuga, Dvapara Yuga, and Kali Yuga. The latter—the Dark Age—started in 3101 BC and went to AD 1899. The present Mayan Great Cycle started on August 13, 3114 BC, and it will end on December 21, 2012. Indian and Mayan cycles are thus closely aligned. This explains the meaning of the 2012 date as the expected beginning of a New Age, the end of a Kali Yuga, or Age of Darkness. The present age that began in 1899 marks the beginning of the Indian Satya Yuga or Age of Light. The Indian Age of Light and the coming Maya Great Cycle are designations of a very unique time in human history. Steiner, referring to the prophecies of all traditions, comments: "This is indeed the time of great decisions—the great crisis to which the sacred books of all time have referred—for in reality the present time is meant."[22]

August 13, as we remember, is the date of the second zenith passage of the sun. The date 3114 BC commemorates the birth of Venus, according to Mayan tradition. The paramount role that Venus plays in all of Mesoamerican worldviews confirms the enduring inheritance of the Atlantean Venus Mysteries.

The famous Maya scholar M. D. Coe asserts that the Mayan calendar with the Long Count had reached its definite form in the 1st century BC. Whether this was a Mayan or an Olmec achievement is something that he leaves open to debate.[23] With the invention of the Long Count appear the dated stelae of Mayan culture, recording historical events. The stela is thus the functional counterpart of the New Fire Ceremony. The people of the Fourth Age do not need the New Fire Ceremony because they have the Long Count, which they use for recording events on their stelae. The New Fire Ceremony is in fact unknown to most Maya and their descendents.

It is of great interest for our study to look at the dates and distribution of the earliest Long Count dates. These are the following:

- Stela 2 of Chiapa de Corzo: Dec. 10, 36 BC
- Stela C of Tres Zapotes: Sept. 5, 32 BC
- Stela 1 of El Baul: either March 6, AD 37 or July 21, AD 11 (not unequivocal yet!)
- Stela 5 of Abaj Takalik: 2 dates of May 22, AD 103 and June 6, AD 126

Of the six stelae with the earliest recorded dates, two came from Guatemalan Soconusco, three from the Olmec area, and one from halfway in between, so that it is hard to ascertain from this evidence where in this axis the Long Count originated.[24]

Long Count and Competing Astronomies of Mesoamerica

The matter with which astronomy struggled is the difference between the solar year of 365 days and the sidereal year that adds six hours to it every year. Accountable for this addition is the movement of the sun through the signs of the zodiac during the time that has been called the Platonic year of 25,920 years. In other words, the sun does not return after a year to the exact same place it occupied in the heavens the previous year. Every 72 years it moves a degree further on the ecliptic. This phenomenon is known as the precession of the equinoxes. It seems that three ways to deal with the problem or to compensate for it were devised in successive steps. The first one was offered by the Olmec civilization; the second one was in use during the succeeding Teotihuacan, Toltec, and Aztec civilizations; finally, the Maya achieved the invention of the Long Count.

There is evidence to indicate that the early Olmecs anchored the solar year to the sidereal year through reference to Ursa Major, identified in the Popol Vuh as Vucub Caquix, as we have seen in reference to the Third Age. The Toltecs and Aztecs made use of so-called zenith astrology. The Maya could move on to a galactic astrology, where earthly rhythms were solidly anchored within the rhythms of the cosmos. We have turned our attention previously to polar astronomy; we will look now at zenith astronomy.

In the tropical areas, the yearly path of the sun makes an arc across the heavens that intersects the zenith on two occasions. In the summer, between these two passages at the zenith, the sun shines from the northern sky. It was a very remarkable phenomenon—one that allowed the agricultural cycle to be anchored within the course of the year. It also allowed early astronomers periodically to correct the discrepancy due to the precession of the equinoxes. The recognition of the shift between the expected zenith passage and the actual one allowed the priests to periodically re-align the solar year with the sidereal year.

The easiest way to recognize the zenith passage was through the use of the "gnomon." The simplest version of it is a pole placed in exact vertical position: when the sun is at the zenith, the gnomon casts no shadow. Another more precise and elaborate way to detect the zenith passage uses an astronomical chamber called "zenith chamber." This is a subterranean space connected to the surface by a long vertical shaft. The sunrays will penetrate through the whole length of the shaft only when the sun shines exactly at the zenith. Such chambers have been found in some of the more important places of Mexico, e.g., Teotihuacan, Monte Alban, and Xochicalco.[25] We will return to zenith astronomy when we look in more detail at Toltec and Aztec civilizations. There, the basic idea described above is woven with additional cosmological motifs.

We have seen how central was the notion of time for the Mesoamerican. Cosmology and inner life formed an indissoluble entity. Losing understanding of the connection with time meant questioning the soul's essence. In fact it was exactly this process that led in the Third Age to the agonizing twilight of the gods with the wrenching question of mortality and the fate of the soul. Only the Fourth Age brought a solution to the riddle of immortality of the soul and eternity in time. The necessity to change astrological points of reference is probably what the Popol Vuh calls the fall of Vucub Caquix, mirrored in the heavens by the drifting in space of Ursa Major due to the phenomenon of the precession of the equinoxes. This coincides in time with the mythological descent of the Ahpus to the underworld. By the time of the Twins, Pole Star astronomy was a science looking back to the past, a longing for a condition that no longer held true.

In essence two kinds of astronomy show us complementary tendencies. The first looks back to the past. It is a knowledge that held validity during a certain period of time, then progressively lost its connection with reality. Was it still applied at the end of the Third Age and was that also an aspect of the struggle of the Twins to bring in the new world view? It would be difficult to answer that question. On the historical level we know that the Olmec center of Tres Zapotes, near the Gulf Coast of Mexico, was still in function in the second century BC. This is an indication that although Olmec civilization was waning, polar god astronomy may still have had a following.

Zenith astronomy is intimately tied with a cyclical notion of time: the 52 years of the Calendar Round. Another aspect is also apparent. Zenith astronomy holds true only within the tropics, that is to say within a latitude of 23° 5' north or south of the equator. More specifically, zenith passage is intimately bound with *exact* latitude: only two places on the same latitude will have identical zenith passages. The use of the zenith as a reference point therefore intimately binds astronomical observations to the latitude.

The earliest astronomy was bound to time; the later one was limited in space. Only Mayan astrology emancipated itself to quite a degree from time and space constraints and could thus be called a "galactic astronomy." The fear of a universe drifting in space or the need to renew the "contract with time" through the New Fire Ceremony was overcome by the notion of eternity, firmly established by the Long Count.

To understand Mayan astronomy more fully let us look at some concepts that the Maya contributed to Mesoamerican worldview. The

Milky Way was compared by the Native Americans (and still is) to a gigantic snake. After the arrival of the conquistadors, it was called Santiago—a term derived from the path of Compostela which was said to follow the Milky Way. The ecliptic intersects the Milky Way between the constellations of Taurus and Gemini and, at the opposite end of the heavens, in Sagittarius. In July at midnight, the Milky Way is at its zenith and it forms a cross with the ecliptic in the constellations of Taurus and Gemini. This cross was seen as the intersection of a pair of two-headed snakes, and was represented by a swastika, the equivalent of a moving cross. It is a cross that rotates during the night, contrary to the fixed astronomic cross formed by the axis of solstice sunrise and sunset points in space.

At the opposite time of the year, during the Winter Solstice, the Milky Way crosses the ecliptic in Sagittarius at a 61° angle. This is the time of the celebration of the rebirth of the solar being Hunahpu. In Sagittarius the Milky Way forms an expansion, a bulge. At the opposite end of Taurus/Gemini the Milky Way is at its thinnest. Seen from the perspective of the universe, our Galaxy is at its widest expanse exactly in Sagittarius. In Sagittarius the Milky Way forms a dark rift, almost completely surrounded by the white light of the stars. The Maya saw this place as a womb of creation. The ecliptic zodiac passes through the Milky Way in Sagittarius, very close to where the Galactic Center is located. The Galactic Center is about 26,000 light years away from Earth. The above is a central theme of the new galactic astronomy—one that we will see abundantly used in Izapa. The new galactic astronomy, based upon the observation of the Milky Way and the ecliptic, superseded the two approaches of polar and zenith astronomy.

The changes of cosmovision reflected in the Long Count had their counterpart in the new social organization. One and the other are intimately intertwined and tied in time to the life and deeds of the Twins. This is also the conclusion of Schele and Friedel. In reviewing the Mayan revolution they conclude, "it is no coincidence that Maya kingship and Maya writing emerged simultaneously in the century before our Common Era, for the technology of writing served the hierarchical institutions of Maya life." This feat was accomplished in the short space of one century![26]

Maya Kingship and Civilization

Ancient Maya civilization most likely took form between the Late Formative (300 BC–0) and the Proto-Classic (0–AD 200), but more particularly the second part. This was a time of intensified agriculture and other technological advances, accompanied by an exponential growth of population. Central to this growth, Girard argues, was the introduction of the second crop of maize. It seems that this was also the time that saw the rise of swamp and river agriculture with the development of the system of raised beds that survived to the time of the Aztecs. Schele and Friedel indicate that some of these formed royal farms in which labor was given as tribute. This would explain why the nobility was also called *Ah Nab* (Water Lily People).[27]

It was believed thus far that writing came to the fore around AD 250-300 during the Maya Classic period. Newer findings refer to a succession of scripts; from an early Olmec writing going back to 900 BC, to a later "Isthmian" or "Epi-Olmec" writing, to the final, more well known Mayan writing that appears profusely in Classic stelae.[28] In these facts we find confirmation that writing closely follows the use of a calendar, and that either serve for the preservation of atavistic knowledge at a time when memory cannot transmit it any longer down the line of generations. It is not surprising therefore to find confirmation of the fact that writing already existed—even if at a limited level of use—at the time in which the Sacred Calendar was introduced by the Olmecs. Thus, the Maya did not invent writing: they simply brought it to a whole new level of development, and generalized its use.

In architecture and art the Maya also introduced new significant elements. Massive pyramids appeared in the lowlands. It is estimated that around the first century AD the architectural innovation of corbel vaulting also appeared. These advances are further confirmation of the role of the initiate in arts and knowledge, as we know it from legends.

The ceremonial center of Izapa may have been the place of introduction of the stelae. Its stelae, which do not bear a date, may point to a sort of first historical or primordial event, the one that is depicted in the images of the Popol Vuh relative to the life of the Twins. They may not need dating because they do not refer to rulers but to a first initiate and to a beginning of time, more precisely to the beginning of the Fourth Age. They may be the very link in time between mythical and historical consciousness. We will review these stelae in detail when we look more closely at the important site of Izapa.

In San Bartolo, a very remote and forested region of El Peten northeast of Guatemala, a mural of very high quality has been found resembling those of Classic Mayan style. It has been dated to AD 100-200, which makes it one of the earliest of the Mayan murals. The complex mythological imagery represents the Maize God. No earlier examples have been found in Mayan areas; others are known from the Late Classic period. Experts at the Yale Peabody Museum define this as potentially one of the most significant discoveries in Maya archaeology in the last several decades.[29]

Let us look now at the social revolution introduced through the establishment of kingship and the city-state. In the Proto-classic emerged the title Ahau, referring to the Solar God. Before this time there was mounting social tension. Generalized trade was generating a flow of wealth that was unequally distributed, and social differences exacerbated tensions. Leadership was becoming more and more hierarchical. The institution of Ahau preserved and gave another meaning to social hierarchy.

The king was the *ahau* of the *ahauob*, the nobility. The *ahauob* ruled subordinate units, and under them were the *cahal*, or lesser nobles. Early kings viewed themselves as brothers descending from the same mythical ancestors. Inheritance was predominantly given to the elder son, but the fact that it was also given to other sons in many cases shows that the support of the nobility was important. Departure from strict inheritance is an important factor to which we have alluded previously. The kingship gave rise to the appearance of large towns in the southern zone, such as Uaxactun, Cerros, and El Mirador. The number of kingdoms evolved from around a dozen in first century BC to as many as 60 in the eighth century AD.[30]

The Mayan political system was in many ways an analogue of the Greek city-states. It presented itself as a unified whole to the outsiders. Most kingdoms were organized hierarchically around a main center or capital, with subsidiary sites ranging from cities or palace compounds to hamlets and farms. Interestingly, early Mayan kingdoms did not maintain a standing army. This state of co-existence may have stemmed from the power of the idea of brotherhood among the kings.

The king was ultimately the re-embodiment of the Twins and he reenacted their triumph over death. This is why all kings descended from an original ancestor. The overriding metaphor of kingship was kinship with the original founders and the gods behind them. This may be the reason why early rulers left little records as far as their identities![31] The Fourth Age introduced the division between the Sacred Year and the Civil Year. There was a division between tasks and functions of the priesthood that we can surmise from surviving tradition. However, kingship has not survived with it. According to the surviving division of the year, the original king most likely was its ultimate civil authority, corresponding to the time of the civil year. Thus the Fourth Age introduces the separation of the roles of king and priests that had been one and the same during the Third Age.

The Maya inaugurated the transition from matriarchy to what is generally called a patriarchy. It could be argued that it is a mixed matriarchy-patriarchy, since blood membership was reckoned through males, marriage membership through females. Lineages derived from a common ancestor and were grouped into clans. Clan organization crossed over differences in social prestige and wealth. Following primogeniture, lineage was ranked according to its distance from the central axis of the firstborn of a clan. Lineages were ranked in function of the central lineage of the king's bloodline. The descendants of the closest relatives of the king thus formed the lineages of the nobles. A very similar arrangement was in vigor at the time of the Incas.[32]

Let us look at the town of Cerros, which experienced the institution of kingship at the time of its inception. Interestingly, it is located in Southern Yucatan just north of Belize, on the ocean, far from the original cultural centers. When Cerros adopted kingship, irreversible changes occurred in less than two generations. It was a paradigm shift. Urban renewal was undertaken around 50 BC and Cerros went from being a village of fishermen to a kingdom. This implies, according to Schele and Friedel, that emissaries and artists had previously come to Cerros to usher this cultural revolution.[33]

The axis of the town ran north to south with a ball court at the southern end. After building on the north-south axis, Cerros extended its buildings on the east-west axis. The main temple—called First Temple—shows the place where four large tree trunks were set. With these the king commemorated the event of the raising of the sky, an event that occurred at the beginning of creation. Four great masks were placed on either side of the stairs, on two platforms before the top of the temple. There was a correspondence between the placement of the four masks and their meanings: rising sun and morning star were placed to the east; setting sun and evening star to the west. In this representation, the sun was seen rising and setting above the waters of the ocean. The king first spiraled in clockwise to enter the inner sanctum and spiraled out anticlockwise. It was in the inner sanctum that he fasted and received visions from his communications with underworld and heavens. Here he would also enter in communication with his ancestors. Coming out of the sanctum of the pyramid he traced a circular path from east to west and north to south, imitating the movement of sun and Venus.

Larger, later structures allowed the king to perform his ceremonies openly, while still privately enough, surrounded by other priests and dignitaries. A lower plaza at the base of the temple allowed in a larger group. There was a final lower plaza that could accommodate a much larger crowd. The king, after his ceremonies, would come down the stairs and be seen first by the nobility and then by all. These three levels of initiation and participation are likewise present and clearly marked in Inca ceremonial centers, as for example in the Island of the Sun's access to the sacred rock where the sun was said to have emerged.

That Mayan civilization represented a watershed is also signified by the name *chan* that they gave themselves. Both Girard, through ethnological research, and Schele and Freidel,[34] from an archaeological perspective, confirm that the word *chan* (Cholan) or *can* (Yucatec) stood for both sky and snake. The rulers of the Maya freely exchanged the titles for sky and snake in their titles and names. Both glyphs were read in the same way. Girard argues that the term *chan* better represents Mayan culture than the term Maya, derived from the League of Mayapan ten centuries later.

Chan points to the serpent of heaven. The serpent of heaven is also the path of access between human and sacred worlds. In the Palenque sarcophagus of Lord Pacal the serpent wrapped around the horizontal branch of the tree-cross represents the ecliptic, and quite accurately so, since it has two intersecting points with the horizontal beam. It seems to point to the path that leads from the human world to the world of the gods through the portals of Gemini and Sagittarius.

The vision serpent was the conduit of communication between the Mayan ruler and the world of spirit. A lintel of Yaxchilan shows Lady Xoc, during and following bloodletting from the tongue. The blood was collected in a bowl, where it impregnated strips of paper. These were set afire and Lady Xoc had a vision of an ancestor in the rising smoke.[35] This indicates that through the blood the rulers could acquire powers of vision into the past or the future. However, we know that the Popol Vuh contrasts natural offerings through the fact that the Twins repudiate the heart sacrifice and bloodletting that is the ruse of the gods in order to wait for the hidden reintroduction of human sacrifice. The records seem to indicate the return of the practice of bloodletting later in time. However, the vision obtained in the rising of the smoke is the hallmark of the new kind of Mysteries introduced by the Maya; the Mysteries of the Sacred Word. These are the ones that Steiner characterized as the Semi-new Mysteries. This is then the deeper aspect of the Mayan revolution and the reason why they called themselves snakes. This transition is also marked by the emphasis placed on the winter solstice that is now the time of the celebration of the festival of Hunahpu, the Solar God. This is another important step of transition into the Semi-new Mysteries—no longer celebrating mysteries of ecstasy at the summer solstice, associated with the Year God, but celebrating the new consciousness of the Christ who has descended from the sun to the earth.

The transition within the Mysteries is visible in the elaboration of the new calendar. Sacred Calendar and Haab are preceded by the so-called "days of affliction" or "days without name" that complete the year of 365 days. This is a calendar form typical of the Ancient and Semi-Ancient Mysteries that had not yet reached the ability to fathom astronomical science. The difference between the astronomical year and the calendar brought about the appearance of the remaining five sacred days, which had a special significance for cultic purposes especially in the attainment of transubstantiated substances or leavens to be used during the rest of the year. The Long Count that is anchored to a new perception of the heavenly revolutions enshrines the achievement of new human faculties that can be attained through the Semi-new Mysteries. However, the Sacred Calendar and the accompanying celebration of the five days of affliction endured and played a subsidiary role in Mayan cosmology alongside the Long Count.

Geography of the Life of the Twins in the Popol Vuh

That the Popol Vuh is not just a "story" is borne out by something even more tangible than the change of consciousness it depicts in relation to the advent of the Fourth Age. The contents of the myth point to a very specific geographic area of Mesoamerica. They also point to a very narrow window of time. The Mayan document is quite precise about the events concerning the deeds of the Twins, in relation to Vucub Caquix and the Lords of Xibalba. Caquizahay, the "house of the Macaws," according to Brasseur de Beaubourg, is the village of Alotenango in the region of Alta Verapaz, on the western part of Guatemala's Pacific coast.[36] Dennis Tedlock believes the bend of Rio Negro (or Chixoy) north of Rabinal to be the site of the mountain Meavan, where the Twins buried the giant Zipacna.[37] The mountains quoted in the Popol Vuh in relation to the

Giants are: Chicac, Hunahpu, Pecul, Yuxcanul, Macamob, and Huliznab. They correspond to Volcano of Fire, Volcano of Water, Volcano of Santa Maria, Cerro Quemado, and Zunil. Except for the last one, which remains unknown, the others are all located in Alta Verapaz.[38]

And what about Xibalba? The ball game court is located in Nim Xor Carchah. This place, mentioned in the *Anales de los Xahil*, is located once more in Alta Verapaz. In the region there is a widespread phenomenon of rivers disappearing underground for part of their course. Finally the people referred to as the "Ah Tza" and "Ah Tukur" are believed by Brasseur de Beaubourg to refer to the Itzae tribes and the tukurs of Tecolotlan, who inhabit Verapaz.[39]

More evidence pointing to the Pacific coast at the border between Guatemala and Mexico appears from the information provided in the Book of Council. All the fauna mentioned in the text is present in the area, such as lizard, jaguar, rattlesnake, and conches of the family of the Spondilus. The tapir is exclusively present there. In the botanical realm the evidence is even more abundant. We find there the cacao, zapote, pataxte, anona, iocotas, matasanos, gourd, copal, the trees of nantze and ceiba, copal, cotton, caoutchouc, tobacco, and beans that the book mentions. Finally, maize was developed from some of the original wild cultivars in the west of Guatemala. This is most likely the original Tamoanchan, the mythic land of the origin, although this word may also stand for the earlier origin of Atlantis.

We will now try to identify a ceremonial center that played a key role for the establishment of the Fourth Age. We will do this by looking at the limitations already imposed upon us by the Tzolkin, and by the conditions we have found to be true about the Fourth Age. Something needs to be reiterated here in order to avoid later confusion. The Tzolkin and Long Count very likely originate from the same geographical area. However, they are not simultaneous: about ten centuries elapsed between one and the other. At present we are looking for the place of origin of the images of the Popol Vuh, whose conditions also match the cultivation requirements of maize as they are described in the Tzolkin.

Given the time constraints associated with certain astronomical phenomena (e.g., 105 days between two sun zenith passages) the Tzolkin could only have originated within a certain given latitude, between 14° 15' and 15° 15' North. This is the latitude that corresponds to the region of the Soconusco. At that latitude further to the east we also find Copan, the greatest ceremonial center of the Classic Maya period. Art reached the apex of its expression in the monuments and statuary present there. The further from Copan and its parallel, the more difficult it became for the priests to harmonize astrological calculations with the constraints of the Tzolkin. In fact, Copan was used as a point of reference in order to correct the calculations.[40] Was Copan then the original Mystery Center at the turning point of American history? Although astronomical calculations were correct in Copan, its climatic conditions did not correspond to the ones that the Popol Vuh describes as favorable to the two consecutive crops of maize. Additionally Copan was not founded until the fourth century AD.

To find all the conditions we are seeking we have to move along the Copan parallel toward the coast. There we can find total correspondence between the ceremonial cycle of the year and the agricultural practices of maize. This is the area that corresponds to the city of Tapachula, Chiapas, in Mexico, a few miles from the Guatemalan border. It is close to here that we find the puzzling center of Izapa, known by the archaeologists as the turning point and link between different civilizations at the beginning of our era. This small site with little known ruins, but with incredible relevance for the history of Mesoamerica, was founded in the second and third centuries before our era.

Modern day access to the ruins of Izapa is not easy. No tourist buses assault the ruins. In fact, for the whole time I visited them, I was the only visitor there with my guide. The guards at each separate block of ruins returned from their occupations with animals or farm work to open a gate and give us access. I must have been one of the very rare visitors on a warm but breezy February day. On some levels the visit did not meet my expectations. The important stelae sheltered under aluminum roofing are very faint and barely visible in the light of day. I could hardly detect the drawings I had seen reproduced so many times. At times I could not recognize the stela at all.

This is Izapa, a very important archaeological site in the history of Mesoamerica. In contrast to the famous Teotihuacan or Tenochtitlan, which we will see later, nothing outwardly indicates the importance of the place. In its minimalism, Izapa is very sober and elegant. We can see that everything had a purpose and nothing was added in order to display pomp and magnificence.

The ruins reveal that Izapa was most likely exclusively a ceremonial site where very few people lived, a true Mystery Center. It was first built in the Late Formative (300 BC–0). Most of the actual constructions (Groups A,

B, E) date from the so-called "Guillen Phase" (300–50 BC). At that time the major Olmec centers on the Atlantic coast were in decline. The important Group F, which includes a pyramid and a ball court, dates from the following phases called Hato (50 BC–AD 100) and Itstapa (AD 100–250).[41]

The Mystery Center's artistic expression marks a turning point. It has been said to be a critical culture in the transition from Olmecs to Maya. In Izapa are found motifs later present in Teotihuacan and in the Zapotec civilization of Monte Alban. The center's influence is also felt in Kaminaljuyu, a major pre-Classic site of Guatemala.

Figure 2: Stela 25, Izapa   Figure 3: Stela 10, Izapa

What is it that gives this presently neglected site such importance? Part of it may have been its geographic location, close to the isthmus of Tehuantepec, which granted easy passage between north and south. However, there is much more than this. Izapa, to all appearances, is the place where the images of the Popol Vuh first appear recorded in ceremonial stelae. These are stelae with no recorded dates, unlike the most common kinds of stelae. Barba de Piña Chan has identified fifteen stelae portraying episodes of the Popol Vuh. Among the most recognizable are:

Stela 5: primordial creation scene
Stela 25: Hunahpu's arm torn off by Seven Macaw (figure 2)
Stela 89: Capracan tied by the Twins
Stela 10: Ixquic's impregnation by Hun Hunahpu (figure 3)

Stela 12: the two maize canes growing in the Grandmother's hut

Stela 21: Xibalban Lord cutting the head of Hun Hunahpu in the Cave of Bats

Stela 60: final defeat and sacrifice of the Xibalban Lords

Stelae 22 and 67: scenes of the Twins' death and resurrection (figure 4)

Stela 9: Twins' resurrection and ascent[42] (see figure 3, chapter 7, p. 170)

Figure 4: Stela 67, Izapa

It has become more and more evident that the Popol Vuh is a truly central esoteric document for Mesoamerica, if not for the whole of the Americas. The Sacred Calendar, as it was further evolved in the Fourth Age, is the yearly re-creation of the deeds of the Twins, and these deeds follow closely the cultivation of maize. The presence of the stelae point to Izapa as the Mystery Center of origin of the Popol Vuh and Long Count. The time span during which Izapa was built lends further weight to the hypothesis. We will substantiate this claim in what follows and in the next chapter.

Izapa and the Olmec Mystery

Izapa is puzzling. How can such a small place have long-lasting effects over the whole of the region and beyond? Here we touch upon a clear "symptom" in the sense of which Steiner spoke in historical terms. The ruins, in themselves rather deceptive, are a symptom of something deeper than the historical record can unearth. Through Izapa a fountain-spring of spiritual renewal was at work in America. It is then no wonder that so many historical developments point toward this small, unspectacular site. Science can confirm its importance without shedding full understanding of the facts. As to the nature of the spiritual renewal that took place in Izapa, we cannot go any further for the moment than to unearth more evidence.

The famous Maya archaeologist M. D. Coe recognizes the role of Izapa in relation to the Olmec and Maya in the following terms: "Crucial to the problem of how higher culture came about among the Maya is the Izapan civilization, for it occupies a middle ground in time and in space between the early stages of the Olmec civilization and the Early Classic Maya. Its hallmark is an elaborate art-style found on monuments scattered over a wide zone, from Tres Zapotes (Olmec) on the Veracruz coast, to the Pacific plain of Chiapas and Guatemala, and up into the Guatemala City area."[43]

Girard's research allows us to come closer to understanding the enigma of the evolution between the Olmec and the Maya. The Miraflores art of the Pacific, which blossomed from 250 BC to AD 250, displays both an Olmec character and traits that will later appear in the Mayan Classic period (AD 250–600). Artistic links can be seen between Miraflores, Santa Lucia Cotzumalguapa (Soconusco), and the Olmec La Venta on the Atlantic coast. The region of Soconusco, of which Izapa is part, represents a more advanced culture than the regions around it, but is very similar to the culture of La Venta. As seen previously, a stela with the date 31 BC has been found in Tres Zapotes (Atlantic coast), dated four years after the one found in El Baul and five years after the one found at Chiapa de Corzo, both on the opposite coast.

Other similarities in artistic style exist between Maya and Olmec. Many artistic elements are common to both civilizations: the cross, the Tau, the ceiba tree (tree of life), the swastika, the hair-dress with feathers, the Olmec mouth and ears, the *kan* glyph for maize, etc. On the basis of all of the evidence Girard concludes that it is difficult to tell where Olmec stops and Maya begins. E. J. Palacios concurs that there is only one original Olmec culture from which arose the Maya and the Zapotecs, who then developed independently.[44]

Why is it then that the reality of such a continuity has baffled the archaeologists? To get closer to an answer we can look at the problem from an aesthetic perspective. Glen Williamson has looked at the differences between Olmec and Izapan art. In some of the Olmec art he detects a very strong element of fear; it is clearly present in the Olmec babies, very likely sacrificial victims. Izapa marks, according to Williamson, a transition to a "sun-oriented art." He concludes that Mayan art represents an explosion of life after a period that was dominated by fear and death.[45] This would be a confirmation of the message of the Popol Vuh. Some observations by Girard go in the same direction. The young Maize God has panther traits in the Olmec La Venta. In the Miraflores art, its zoomorphic representation was the fish that symbolizes the foetus in the womb—once again a qualitatively different image.[46]

A different art and a different world outlook in two cultures that form a continuity: this is a very plausible explanation to the Olmec-Maya riddle. In between the two cultures stand an event and a place that completely changed the spiritual/cultural values. We could dismiss all the above judgments as mere feelings, far from objective reality. Still, it is undeniable that the onlooker receives a very different impression from the contrasting kinds of art and is touched by the beauty expressed in Izapa. In the words of another researcher who has been touched by the beauty of Izapan art: "The profound cosmology hidden within Izapa's pictographic code represents a great flowering of knowledge, an era of great visionary openness and achievement that may have eroded into bland secular dogmas by the time the Classic Maya appeared on the scene."[47]

Between Maya and Olmecs stood a turning point of time. In the space of a century sweeping cultural changes moved through Mesoamerica. The new form of initiation undergone by the Mayan king marks the transition to a new form of consciousness. This corresponds to the stage that arose in what Steiner calls the Semi-new Mysteries. The ritual was intoned in the Sacred Word and made visible in the vision serpent. Such was the importance of this new revelation that the Maya called themselves *chan*, serpents. Natural offerings replaced the practice of human sacrifice of the decadent stage of Olmec culture. This change corresponds to the central imagination of the descent of the Twins to Xibalba, their death and resurrection.

The old dread of death and the end of time was now accompanied by the new knowledge of the immortality that follows resurrection, the central image of the Dawning in the Popol Vuh. Writing and the calendar were the two inventions that underscored the change of consciousness that Mayan civilization introduced. On the whole this corresponded to the rise of a historical consciousness, sanctioned in the central role of the stelae.

The new calendar was based on cycles far longer than the 52-year Calendar Round, but that was simply a consequence of the new form. Its foundation was the knowledge of the precession of the equinoxes, which allowed a calendar of far more precision than the Calendar Round. The Long Count probably made possible a revolution in the agricultural field, at least in the Soconusco, through the introduction of the second maize crop. This change allowed an expansion of population at the outset of the Fourth Age.

Ixbalamqué became the archetype for all the new kings who considered themselves brothers to him. The establishment of the city-state and kingship were closely associated with the new form of initiation. Mayan culture rested on the movement of social differentiation that accompanied the rise of Olmec civilization and to which it gave new, deeper meaning. This was the revolutionary essence of the Mayan city-state.

We can now move this exploration further by turning to Steiner's research into the nature of the Mexican Mysteries. Through his revelations and with the help of Mayan esotericism we can come closer to the enigma of the figure of the American initiate.

CHAPTER 7

IXBALAMQUÉ: INITIATE
OF THE AMERICAS

I N ORDER TO LOOK at the Mexican Mysteries, we will widen our gaze to encompass the general evolution of the Mysteries after the destruction of Atlantis. After the Flood, humanity prepared for a new step in the dissemination of knowledge through the Mysteries. What had been one single source of knowledge—albeit divided according to the planetary Mysteries—formed two streams, a northern one and a southern one.[1]

The northern stream moved through England, the north of France, Scandinavia, Russia, and from there into Asia and India. These were people more adapted to the use of the outer senses. They were turned toward external perception of the macrocosm, following what could be called a Sun path. Their gods belonged to the upper gods, gods of the macrocosm. The northern people built in their bodily form an image of the spirit, and lived in the world of the Christ, the world of space and of the zodiac. In the world of space is represented that which is above good and evil. The Christ did not descend to earth by the path of time, but from the path of space. He was surrounded by the twelve apostles, as the earth is surrounded by the twelve signs of the zodiac.

The southern stream went through Spain to Africa, Egypt, and Arabia. Their gods belonged to the underworld; they were rulers of the soul life. Osiris, the divinity that human beings find on passing through the gate of death, does not live in the external sense world. The meeting with the gods of the underworld leads to the rising of consciousness. Southern people created the invisible soul-image of the godhead in their inner life. This was therefore a path of purification of humanity's moral life. The gods of the inner life aroused either fear and terror or trust and benevolence, depending on humanity's stage of development. The spiritual world of the southern peoples is called the world of Lucifer, the "light-bearer." In contrast to the Sun Path this was a Luciferic Path. It is the number seven that leads us from space into time, toward the gods of the Luciferic realm. Seven is the number linked with human development, as in the seven-year phases. It is also linked with the aeons of planetary development or the stages of development in Atlantis or in our present post-Atlantean epoch. The Christ being can be understood in His totality through the union of the two streams.[2]

America did not follow this general evolution, nor did part of Asia, particularly what corresponds to present-day China. Both America and China preserved the old Atlantean consciousness. The Popol Vuh has allowed us to see how this happened through the four successive Ages. In the West, the unity of Atlantean consciousness was preserved also in Ireland, or more exactly in old Hibernia, as we will see further on in the chapter.

In order to deepen our understanding of the Mexican Mysteries we will gather many different strands. We will weave in Mayan and Anthroposophical knowledge of the Mexican Mysteries. Since these Mysteries preserved the last of Atlantean knowledge, we will explore other similar, earlier Mysteries, such as earlier American Mysteries or the Mysteries of Hibernia. We will also turn to a historical analysis of the interactions between the old and new worlds, particularly the place occupied by Hebrew and Phoenician/Babylonian impulses in the New World. This approach has a double purpose. It will allow us to discern similarities and differences between the Mysteries, before highlighting the uniqueness of the Mexican Mysteries, and lead us on the way to identifying Vitzliputzli, the initiate of the Americas.

Spiritual Scientific Background to the Mexican Mysteries[2]

We know from Steiner that in the West arose one who was an opponent of the Great Spirit, but nevertheless was connected to it. His name sounded something like Taotl. Steiner defines him as a distortion of the Great Spirit, a being who did not descend into physical incarnation. The Popol Vuh indicates an episode that sets the stage for the Taotl forces in the event of the first descent of the Ahpus to the underworld. In it we see the Elohim—the Seven Ahpus—descending to earth. The nature of the Ahpus undergoes a transformation later concluded by the resurrection of the Twins. Their descent awakens a deep fear of death. Those who cling to the previous memory of the Ahpus are now in reality referring to retarded beings who have taken their place—the Camé.

The Lords of Xibalba revere the seven Camé. In the hierarchy of Xibalba the Popol Vuh calls them the "supreme judges" (Part II, Chapter 1). It is here most likely that we find the equivalent of the Taotl being of whom Steiner speaks. The Twins suppress this cult to reinstate the seven Ahpus, the Great Spirit in a new form. They are subordinated to Hunahpu, the Solar Spirit of the Christ.

As we have seen previously, Steiner mentions another regressive spirit, known under the name of Quetzalcoatl. He qualifies him as Mephistophelean, which is to say essentially Ahrimanic. In effect he says, "His symbol was similar to the Mercury staff found in the Eastern Hemisphere, the spirit who could disseminate malignant diseases through certain magic forces. He could inflict them upon those he wished to injure in order to separate them from the relatively good god, Tezcatlipoca." The cult of Quetzalcoatl was not public, but esoteric. It contributed to the furtherance of Ahrimanic impulses in America. The Popol Vuh confirms the presence of this being with the portrayal of the Lords of Xibalba, each of them described according to the diseases that he can inflict upon humanity. Ten of them are mentioned in Part II, Chapter 1 of the Popol Vuh.[4] Quetzalcoatl's cult continued after the time of Christ. His name is well known and connected to many myths that presently survive in the collective imagination. Quetzalcoatl too did not incarnate: he only reached down into an etheric body. We will return to this being in the following chapters.

Opposed to the esoteric Taotl and Quetzalcoatl mysteries was the cult of Tezcatlipoca. This being belonged to a much lower hierarchy than Taotl, but he was partly connected through his qualities to the Yahweh God, one of the Elohim. Tezcatlipoca's cult—originally esoteric—aimed at the establishment of a Yahweh religion, parallel to the one that was then developing in Palestine. It soon became purely exoteric. We have seen that the descent of the Ahpus left Hun Batz and Hun Chouen to lead humanity through the arts and all outer cultural manifestations. The brothers cared for the Grandmother and, by extension, for the whole of the matriarchy in the absence of the Great Spirit. They were both artists and wise men. In them we find the cult of Tezcatlipoca, with its mixed qualities and the ultimate movement toward corruption that the Popol Vuh symbolizes with the transformation of the two guides into monkeys. Their impulse loses its original strength without turning into any clearly decadent Mystery.

Rather, it is supplanted by the Taotl and Quetzalcoatl Mysteries. Mayan esotericism confirms what Steiner found through spiritual research in the names of the guides of the Third Age. As the first name—Hun Batz—implies, the guide is initially the man of wisdom. At the other end stands One Monkey, the image of the Mystery emptied out and stripped of its meaning.

The cult of two beings within the precincts of the Mysteries accompanies Mesoamerican spirituality through the succeeding stages. The decadent Mysteries of the Third Age venerated Taotl/Camé and Quetzalcoatl. The Popol Vuh inaugurates the cult of the Agrarian God—the resurrected Ahpus—and of the Twins. Other following cultures of very different natures also cultivated the dual worship. The Toltecs and the Aztecs revered in Tlaloc the being that took on the function of the Ahpus. Additionally the Toltecs revered Quetzalcoatl and the Aztecs Huitchilopochtli. We will return to these matters in more detail in chapters 1 and 2 of Part II.

The central ritual of the decadent Mexican Mysteries was the performance of human sacrifice through excision of the stomach from a live individual. Following such practices the victims would relinquish the desire to incarnate and bear a human ego. The victim's soul at the moment of dying drew the initiate with itself into the realm that was to be established beyond earth. Steiner concludes: "The earth would gradually have become desolate, having upon it only the force of death, whereas any living souls would have departed to found another planet under the leadership of Lucifer and Ahriman." The decadent priesthood, and above all its highest black magician, possessed a knowledge of and mastery over the working of the forces of death in everything living. The withdrawal of the souls from the reality of earth was then the ultimate goal of the Mexican Mysteries.

We may pause for a moment over the mention of sacrifice with excision of the stomach. This may come as a surprise to many, since it is beyond doubt that it was the heart that the Aztecs removed. About this second type of sacrifice we have redundant information. We must remember that Steiner's insights are the result of spiritual research into one of the deepest secrets of the decadent Mysteries, moreover of Mysteries whose knowledge had to be wiped out by Vitzliputzli for the sake of earth evolution. On this point a scientific interpretation of history can say very little. We will return to it only at the end of our exploration when we will be able to compare the decadent Mysteries of two different epochs: the time of Christ and the Aztec civilization in the fifteenth century.

To understand the nature of this transition we can look at how Steiner defines it. After the vanquishing of the Mysteries of Taotl, the decadent Mexican Mysteries of the times of Christ, he tells us that:

Nothing survived from these regions of what might have lived on if the Mysteries of Taotl had borne fruit. The forces left over from the impulses that lived in these Mysteries survived only in the etheric world. They still exist subsensibly, belonging to what would be seen if, in the sphere of the spirit, one could light a paper over a solfatara.

Later on in the same lecture cycle the thought is thus completed:

Nevertheless, so much force remained that a further attack could have been made upon the fifth epoch, having as its aim so to mechanize the earth that the resulting culture would not only have culminated in a mass of purely mechanical contrivances but would have made human beings themselves into such pure homunculi that their egos would have departed.

We therefore have to do with two separate phenomena and epochs. In between the two the Popol Vuh confirms what Steiner tells us. Human sacrifice with its ritualistic and esoteric aspects was banned. This does not mean that other kinds of human sacrifice were not performed in between times. Other human beings were effectively sacrificed, but the priests most likely could not avail themselves of the knowledge of the forces of the organs as they had done before the time of the Christ and would later do at the times of Chichen Itza and of the Aztecs.

We will now confine our gaze to the time of Christ, and to the initiate Vitzliputzli, whom we are told was born in the year 1 AD. Steiner does not confirm Vitzliputzli's virgin birth; he just confirms a tradition. This is an important distinction to be made. According to tradition, it is a "feathered being," an etheric entity, who has impregnated the mother. Steiner defines Vitzliputzli both as an initiate and as a "supersensible being in a human form." Once again the parallels with the Mayan text are surprising. The Popol Vuh equates its major turning point with the abolition of human sacrifice brought about by a being or duality of beings—the Twins—born of the virgin Ixquic and of the Great Spirit. Vitzliputzli lived between the years AD 1 and 33, replicating Jesus Christ's life span. The year AD 30—

inaugurating Christ's ministry—saw the beginning of the initiate's three-year confrontation with the individual whom Steiner calls the "super-magician." The battle ended with the crucifixion of the magician. With this death it is not only the dark priest who was obliterated, but also the knowledge he possessed. It is remarkable once again to follow this parallel in the Popol Vuh, where it is portrayed in the overcoming of the powers of the underworld. The resurrected Twins enact performances of death and resurrection in front of the Camé. The Camé know everything about death and its powers, but they do not comprehend the forces of life through resurrection that they all the more covet. By making use of this power the Twins can overcome the Camé. It is one of them specifically—Hun Camé, their lord—who is killed. The other being, Vucub Camé, completing the sevenfold entity, is overpowered. On the other hand the Xibalbans, corresponding to the priesthood of Quetzalcoatl, are allowed to continue taking part in evolution, but now in a more limited fashion than before. Evil cannot reign unrestrained any longer. It has recovered its rightful place in world evolution. The death of the magician imposes a ban on his soul throughout the whole epoch until the following age of the Consciousness Soul.

The Dawning is the reflection of the deeds of Christ and of the initiate Vitzliputzli in the aura of the earth and the consciousness of the Native American. This could explain the different stages of development of Mayan esotericism. The Mysteries of the Third Age prepared the knowledge of the incarnation of Christ through the sacred cultivation of maize enshrined in the Tzolkin. They announced His coming. The time of waiting for the Dawning was a time of testing and also the final, most intense stage of the twilight of the old gods. Seen under that light the experiences of anguish depicted in Part III of the Popol Vuh acquire more meaning. Finally, the Maya inaugurated the Fourth Age and the cult of the Solar God.

Steiner has not told us much about the process of initiation within the precinct of the progressive Mexican Mysteries inaugurated by Vitzliputzli. The two lectures of 1916 are all that we have in this regard, and they are mostly concerned with the decadent mysteries. However he was aware of the nature of the progressive mysteries, and mentioned it on at least one occasion. This is what he says of them in a lecture of the cycle *Karmic Relationships*: "These [Mexican] Mysteries had at one time been a factor of great significance in America but had then become decadent, with the result that conceptions of the rites, and their ritual enactment, had become thoroughly childish in comparison with the *grandeur of earlier times*" (italics added).[5]

It is in a sense unfortunate that Steiner could only draw from Aztec sources at the time when he talked about the Mexican Mysteries, as argues Stephen Clarke.[6] The Popol Vuh had not been found again in his lifetime, and the previous translations of the text were probably only accessible to specialists. The being Vitzliputzli does in effect correspond to the initiate Ixbalamqué, but from an Aztec perspective. However, the name Vitzliputzli corresponds to a wholly new decadent interpretation of the initiate, as it will clearly appear from the chapter on the Aztecs. Ixbalamqué, also called Yax Balam, is a much better name choice for the initiate since it is the name given him by the Maya, at the time of Christ. We will adopt it in the rest of this exploration.

We will now explore the process of initiation in what will be a hypothesis, resting on the knowledge of Mesoamerican astronomy and cosmology. In order to tentatively identify the nature of the being Vitzliputzli/Ixbalamqué, as far as it is possible through anthroposophical knowledge, we will turn to little known aspects of the American past. They will reveal that there have been more contacts between the Old and New Worlds than we usually believe.

Old World and New World Interactions

That there have been at least three early sources of immigration from Europe to America before Columbus seems more and more certain. We will confine our scope to the evidence of Phoenician and Semitic migrations. The Celtic immigration will not concern us in this context. To introduce such a historical perspective we will only point to the most significant and symptomatic discoveries. More evidence is amply presented in the notes to the text. What seems like a detour will deepen our understanding of the spiritual battle that was raging in America at the time of Vitzliputzli, and its connections with the Old World.

Babylonian Impulses via Phoenicia

All the evidence of a Phoenician presence in the American continent has often been downplayed, only to grow with time to a point that is now difficult to ignore. We will present part of that material as well as the even more surprising possibility of a small Semitic presence in some parts of America.

That America, as a vast island in the Atlantic, was known to the ancients is a fact reported by many writers and historians. Aristotle in 360 BC mentions a fertile, wooded country beyond the Pillars of Hercules. This island was in fact so hospitable that many Carthaginians (originally Phoenicians) had gone there and some had remained.[7] In 21 BC Diodorus says quite the same, adding that the Phoenicians had kept the existence of such a land a secret. Aelianus (~AD 200) confirms this last point, saying that the huge island was common knowledge among the Phoenicians of Cadiz. Plutarch, in AD 70, mentions that at the latitude of Britain lay islands beyond which was found a great continent. Many other writers report of a land beyond the Atlantic.[8] In fact, according to Diodorus, the Phoenicians may have known of America as early as the 11th century BC. Other indirect evidence is the knowledge of the Sargasso Sea and the patterns of the trade winds blowing toward America.[9]

The Phoenicians were the merchants of the Mediterranean and far beyond. They were a mercurial people, trading in culture as they did in goods. They had contacts with and offered their services to Egyptian, Libyan, Babylonian (Hittite, and later Assyrian), and Persian merchant fleets. These versatile people borrowed from the fields of astronomy, mathematics, and religion. The alliances and common commercial undertakings brokered by the Phoenicians are the most plausible explanation for numerous inscriptions in Egyptian, Libyan, and Punic-Phoenician in the Americas. Some of these appear simultaneously in the same location.[10] The Phoenicians were probably one of the few societies with the knowledge and ability to sail to the New World, but others could have reached it with their help.

To give an idea of Phoenician investment in maritime affairs it may suffice to say that a quinquireme (a boat with five rowers per oar) needed a crew of 250 rowers. Together with the rest of the sailors this meant a total crew of 400.[11] In their commercial pursuits the Phoenicians traveled as far as Britain, Africa, the Azores, and the Canary Islands. Carthaginian coins have been found on Corvo, the westernmost island of the Azores.[12] Between the years 609 to 593 BC, during the reign of Necho, ruler of Egypt, the Phoenicians circumnavigated Africa. The periplus of Hanno is widely acknowledged as authentic today. Comparing this with the protracted forty-year effort by the Portuguese to reach Sierra Leone at the time of Henry the Navigator, gives us an idea of the level of naval expertise that the Phoenicians had reached. Phoenician inscriptions have been found on the Canary Islands; from there a storm could easily have swept their boats toward the Big Island of the Atlantic Sea.

Indirect Phoenician evidence is scattered throughout the Americas. It appears first of all in artistic representations. On a huge stela of La

Venta appears what the archaeologists call an "Uncle Sam figure" with high-bridged nose and beard. He wears shoes with painted toes in a style that the Phoenicians had borrowed from the Assyrians. Clay head figurines found on the Rio Balsas (between the states of Guerrero and Michoacan) have long beards and a way of presenting the hair very much like the Assyrian-Babylonian style, reminiscent of the god Melkarth. The most puzzling indications of Old World influence are artifacts showing knowledge of the wheel. Small, wheeled toys have been discovered in tombs at the Olmec Tres Zapotes, Monte del Fraile (near the Popocatepetl summit in central Mexico) and at Remojadas. They bear great similarities to a Phoenician miniature chariot held at the Louvre.[13] Knowledge of the wheel points by necessity to the Old World. Other evidence concerns the recovery of roll-seals used for commercial deals, equivalent to the ones used by the Phoenicians, and ceramic jugs and amphorae of the same composition and consistency as those excavated from Portugal and Spain, where Phoenicians were also present.[14]

Carthage was in origin a Phoenician colony, which later emancipated itself from the mother country and started its own commercial empire. Carthaginian coins have been found along the coasts and the shores of navigable rivers of the Americas. The coins date from the fourth to the third century BC. A limestone horse's head, carved like Carthage's coat of arms, has been found in North Salem, New York; it matches the design that appears in Carthaginian coins. Finally, what appears as Phoenician mass reproductions of Babylonian artifacts have been found at Cuenca, Ecuador.[15]

To understand Phoenician and primarily Carthaginian expeditions and immigration to the New World we need to know a little of Phoenician history. Carthage was founded in 825 BC on the coast of present day Tunisia. It soon became independent. Phoenicia struggled long to free itself from Assyrian domination during the 7th century BC. These years may have been propitious for the settling of a colony in the New World.[16]

Professor Barry Fell helps to shed some light on the possible aims and motivations of the later Carthaginian presence on the continent through recovery of their currency and mass-produced artifacts. By the beginning of the 3rd century BC, Carthage had adjusted the weights of its own coinage to match those used in Cyprus and Egypt. Carthage also exerted total control over the supply of tin, a metal that was essential for producing the bronze used for weapons and for Roman coinage.

Carthage lacked the timber necessary for its fleet. Around 300 BC we witness the minting of large amounts of coins in electrum—an alloy of gold to which a small amount of silver has been added. At this time, the Syracusan emblem of Arethusa disappeared and was replaced by the goddess Tanith, the Phoenician equivalent of Astarte. This coinage ceased to be struck after 241 BC, the year that marked the end of the First Punic War. The years between 300 and 241 BC marked a sudden expansion of Carthaginian gold holdings. The Carthaginians had developed a market of Egyptian, Assyrian, and Semitic art produced in the Phoenician factories of Cyprus. Fell believes that these items were exclusively intended for trade by the Carthaginians based in Carthage or Spain, with the Amerindians. The dates of contact between this supposed contact between the Americas and Carthage match the sudden influx of gold to the city. The Amerindians would probably part from their gold in exchange for the bronze artifacts. The gold coinage would serve to pay the mercenaries hired among Greeks or Libyans. There may have been another trade in the American northeast with the Algonquians: iron cutting tools or bronze art replicas for lumber to build ships.[17]

Semitic Evidence in the New World

The traces left by the Hebrew presence in the Americas are not as abundant but just as surprising as the Phoenician ones. The Jewish nation hardly mustered the naval might of Tyre, Sidon, or Carthage. However, we know from history that at the time of King Solomon, the Hebrews had entered into an alliance with Hiram, the Phoenician king. There is abundant mention of naval operations throughout the Old Testament, especially in Book 2 of Chronicles and Book 1 of Kings. There we are informed of the facts that the allies disposed of vessels of considerable tonnage (2 Chr 8:18). Hiram sent experienced sailors, together with the servants of Solomon, as we are told in 1 Kings 9:28. The fleets sailed to Ophir (India) in one direction and to Tarshish or Tartessos—a Phoenician colony in Spain—in the other (2 Chr 9:10). 1 Kings 10:22 confirms that the two nations had their navies side by side at Tarshish. The collaboration between the two cultures had far-reaching consequences.[18]

D. A. Deal has studied the ruins of a city at Hidden Mountain in Las Lunas, New Mexico. He found what appears to be a camp laid out in military fashion, very similar to Lachish, a fortified city of Judea. Las Lunas also contains a ceremonial center. A tablet of the Ten Commandments written in Paleo-Hebrew was recovered at the site. A zodiac map, carved in stone, shows a solar eclipse in Virgo at 3 p.m. in the month of September; Mars, Jupiter, and Mercury were in close proximity to the sun. This configuration occurred on 9/18/106 BC, a date that corresponds with the kind of writing found on the inscriptions.[19]

Las Lunas is not the only site in America bearing Hebrew inscriptions. Another tablet found in Newark, Ohio, contains the Ten Commandments in Hebrew. It is known as the Ohio Decalogue. In a burial mound at Bat Creek, Tennessee was found a tablet with an inscription in a Hebraic script in use in the Middle East around AD 100. It is a grave memorial reading: "I pray you Yah (have) pity." Finally, two tablets containing invocations to Baal have been found in West Virginia: the Grave Creek Stone of Moundsville, and the so-called Braxton Tablet.[20] The mention of both Yahweh and Baal reflect the very real ongoing spiritual struggle between the two deities for the soul of the Hebrew people.

Alexander von Wuthenau has researched all traces of non-American presence in Mesoamerica. What led him on this path was the repeated discovery of pottery and statuary with exact anthropological representations of non-native races. He found evidence of Semitic, Phoenician, Celtic, and African presences. The African presence could simply have followed the Phoenicians, who had African slaves and were at one point allied with the Libyans. Of interest to us in the present context is the so-called Phylactery Stela of Tepatlaxco, Veracruz, Mexico. In this stela a bearded figure is represented with a cord wound seven times around the arm and three times around the middle finger. This is a correct display of the Jewish phylactery or tefillin, which are worn while reciting the weekday morning prayers.[21]

The idea of racial mixes is not the exclusive claim of little known or unconventional researchers like von Wuthenau. Some mainstream historians, like Nigel Davies, recognize the presence of both Negroid and "Uncle Sam" traits—pointing to the Semitic element—in Olmec statuary.[22] Olmec representations show us both the Olmec type dominating the "Uncle Sam" or vice-versa, indicating that there were evolving kinds of relationships.

All the archaeological research confirms Wuthenau's conclusion that, for the most part, the Semitic presence in the continent was much more limited in time than the Phoenician. It was highest in the period between 500 BC to AD 200. Of added interest is the presence of the glyph of the number 1 in connection with Semitic-looking people. Thus, for example, the Bat Creek inscription in Tennessee reads: "Year One of the Golden Age of the Jews."[23]

Progressive and Decadent Mysteries in the Middle East
and in the New World

In the religious field, the most fascinating discoveries concern the shared presence of gods on the two sides of the Atlantic. Humbaba or Baal, associated with the deities of the underworld of the Middle East, is very similar to the American Fire God, as can be seen from the extensive ceramic samples that von Wuthenau has collected and compared.[24] The Fire God will play a considerable role later in time in Mesoamerica.

Old World and New World both preserve relics of the Carthaginian goddess Tanit (equivalent to the Phoenician Astarte). Her sign, consisting of a triangle with a disc and a crescent, has been found in Deerpark, and at Hawk's Nest Mountain, New York. Tanit's elaborate symbols from Carthaginian tombstones match corresponding petroglyphs in Colorado. Finally, a metal urn in Phoenician-Egyptian style, depicting Astarte and datable from around 600 BC, has been discovered in New York State at the junction of Chenango and Susquehanna rivers.[25]

The presence of the gods of the Old World and their American counterparts seems to show that a spiritual battle was waged on both sides of the ocean. Phoenicians and Hebrews had undergone various kinds of relationships in the Middle East. We mentioned a first era of collaboration between them at the time of King Solomon. This close alliance between the two nations—which had ample repercussions on economic and military levels—could not have occurred without a rapprochement at the spiritual level. The reigns of Solomon and David probably restored a unity of cult of the original Jehovah deity. Such is the opinion of T. C. Johnson[26] and also the implicit record of the Bible.

Things changed in Phoenicia when the High Priest Ethbaal (899–867 BC) seized power. As a fanatic priest of Astarte he spread the practice of infanticide. Upon marrying his daughter Jezebel to Ahab, king of Israel, he sent with her four hundred priests of Baal and four hundred priests of Astarte. Jezebel induced Ahab to build a temple to Baal-Melkarth, in front of which stood a stone sculpture of Baal. The nation of Israel relinquished the worship of Yehovah as we also hear in the second Book of Kings: "And they caused their sons and daughters to pass through the fire, and used divination, and enchantment" (2 Kings, 17:16-17). The deity was now adored in carved images, like an idol. Ritual infanticide was carried out regularly and consumed in fire. The sacrifices occurred either annually, for special occasions, or as an offering to appease the gods after major calamities.

This point in time saw the testing of the Hebrew nation in their belief of Yahweh. In the old times the favors of the gods were known by the fate incurred by the tribes or the whole nation. Through famines, plagues, and wars the gods expressed their anger. The new cult of Yahweh required that the individual see his fate separately from the deeds of the gods. The Hebrew nation was called upon to follow its god Yahweh and be faithful to him regardless of the tests that would come. External events were not to be taken as proof of the god's pleasure or displeasure. It was in this time of trial that the Hebrews embraced the cult of Baal.

The spirit of Elijah operated against this state of affairs through the individualities of Naboth, and later Elisha. This confrontation culminated in Elijah-Naboth's standing against the four hundred and fifty priests and prophets of Baal. This is how Steiner describes the height of the performances of the priests of Baal: "The ecstatic exercises are carried to such lengths that the hands and other parts of the body are cut with knives until the blood flows, so as to increase still further the awesome character of the spectacle evoked by these followers of Baal, under the frenzied stimulus of the dancing and the music."[27] The power emanating from the being of Elijah-Naboth overcame the priesthood of Baal, putting an end to its hold over the Hebrew nation. The dimension of the challenge to the nation of Israel is made clear in 1 Kings 16:31-33: "And as if it had been a light thing for him to walk in the sins of Jeroboam, the son of Nebat, he took for wife Jezebel the daughter of Ethbaal, king of the Sidonians, and went and served Baal, and worshipped him. And Ahab made an Asherah. Ahab did more to provoke the Lord, the god of Israel, to anger than all the kings of Israel who were before him." Ahab was leading his people down the road of black magic. Elijah enabled the Hebrews to overcome this threat.

A similar kind of black magic to that accompanying the cults of Baal and Astarte seems to have emerged in the New World five or more centuries later. Spiritual practices take hold of different civilizations without the need of a physical instrument to carry them from one place to the other. After all, what is needed for a similarity of cults is the influence of same or similar spiritual influences. However, when the evidence of the presence of Middle Eastern populations is accompanied with their ritual objects and practices, it is legitimate to think of some level of direct influence. A practice that accompanied the decadent Babylonian-Phoenician mysteries was the practice of cranial deformation, also abundantly found in Mesoamerica, beginning with the Olmecs.[28] Self-mutilation, infanticide, cranial deformation, and divination are practices that the people of Israel were exhorted to avoid, in the spiritual struggle pitting Yahweh worship against the Baal-Astarte cults. Numerous references to this subject appear especially in the Book of Leviticus, the Second Book of Kings and Judges. There the people of Israel are exhorted not to practice head deformation, blood-letting, child sacrifice, etc.[29] All these practices were also present in the New World.

What reached a culmination in the Old World found more extreme conditions in the Americas and was developed to a paroxysm not yet possible in the Middle East. In America, the stronger magnetic forces of the earth act with greater strength upon the so-called Ahrimanic or geographic double. This helps to explain the added strength of the Mexican Mysteries when compared with their Babylonian counterpart. On our continent the decadent mysteries evolved further toward human sacrifice with specific organ removal and the demonic knowledge it conferred to the High Priest. Here also arose the forces opposing these decadent mysteries, and the center of Izapa from which they spread.

Individuality of the Initiate: a Hypothesis

What follows moves into the realm of hypothesis: all we have is supporting evidence. Present research shows us that the presence of Phoenicians and Hebrews on this continent will have to be recognized in time. The weight of proof is abundant and substantial. What is also striking is how, although widespread, the presence of Hebrews and Phoenicians focused primarily in two different areas: the Atlantic and the Pacific coasts. The Hebrew presence was highest on the Pacific coast and finally points toward the center of Izapa. Was it then possible as the many legends say that the prophet was really bearded? Could we look for his arrival from the west? We should give credit to the legends of many natives that testify, as Alexander Von Humboldt recorded in three instances, that the transformation of their civilization was due to "persons differing from themselves in appearance and descent."[30] Andean traditions attest that Viracocha was white and had a flowing beard, and so he was depicted in the statues found at the time of the conquest. This was probably the reason for the natives to address the conquistadors as Viracocha, the name they gave both to their god and their cultural hero.[31]

According to the archaeological record, the mysteries of Izapa were prepared over a few centuries. As the discoveries regarding the Sacred Calendar denote, there were different stages of evolution of the Mysteries. The Sacred Calendar was developed first in relation to the cultivation of maize. The Long Count was added afterward. Some cultures already knew of the Sacred Calendar, when they separated from the original Mayan civilization, as Parts III and IV of the Popol Vuh underline. Only the Mayan civilization reaped the full benefits of the preparation of the Mysteries of Izapa leading to the elaboration of the Long Count.

The analysis of the Popol Vuh has brought us closer to the Mystery of the being of the Twins. They are said to be the sons of a virgin. We should not forget that the Popol Vuh conveys imaginative pictures, not necessarily literal realities. Steiner in fact stops short of confirming the virgin birth. The Popol Vuh speaks about two beings that work as one: Hunahpu and Ixbalamqué. We have already identified Hunahpu as the solar being. Ixbalamqué, as the suffix Ix denotes, is his earthly-lunar counterpart. That he is the human counterpart, and most likely the initiate, is indirectly confirmed by the fact that in Mayan artistic objects Ixbalamqué is often represented as a bearded personage. Such is the case in various Late Classic objects, as for example, the well-known "resurrection vase" that shows the resurrection of the Maize God from the carapace of a turtle and the Twins on both sides of it (figure 1). The iconography therefore places side by side the initiate and the solar being. And we can ask ourselves about the identity of this initiate.

Figure 1: resurrection vase

What follows can only be a hypothesis. The initiate of the Americas is most likely that being who stood closest to the Christ Sun during Atlantean times, since Native American consciousness lived strongly in the afterglow of what had been the reality of Atlantis. The great initiate Manu is an obvious choice, since he is that being who led the Sun oracles of Atlantis. He prepared the way for the survival of those who did not partake of the decadent oracles cultivating practices of black magic. It was this black magic which led to the demise of the Atlantean continent through the famous Flood, portrayed in the Old Testament and traditions that survive in the Americas and elsewhere. The divine Manu is also the highest of initiates, the only one whom we could imagine standing at the side of Christ at the time of Golgotha. Is this the one to whom Steiner refers as a "supersensible being in a human form"? If he were the one, Manu would be seen carrying further the role he had fulfilled in Atlantis. At that time he had preserved the purity of the Sun Oracle, whose teachings stood against the decadent practices of other Mysteries. At the time of Golgotha the decadent Mysteries had intensified and the returning Manu would have continued to lead those who preserved his memory from Atlantean times past a new cultural impasse, pitting the powers of the Sun God against the decadent Mysteries of the Fire God.

There is another striking similarity between the deeds of Manu at the end of Atlantis and those that appeared in the Mysteries of Izapa. After leading his people through the Flood in the episode of Noah and the building of the ark, those who survived Atlantean civilization witnessed the conditions of the new world with the Sun in the heavens and the rainbow. The rainbow was not known in Atlantis in the conditions of the more liquid/misty atmosphere there prevailing. The post-Atlantean times are accompanied with new conditions of existence and novel sensory perceptions on behalf of those who survived Atlantis, therefore the experience of the rainbow. Not surprisingly the Maya, without mentioning the rainbow, explicitly mention the phenomenon of the Dawning, associated with the appearance of Sun and Moon in the firmament of the heavens, a new way to perceive the physical environment. This phenomenon is closely associated with the first traces of a historical consciousness.

Finally, all of the above may explain an element that remains puzzling no matter how one may look at it: the fact that the initiate is bearded, or that he is called Viracocha in the Andes, a name that also denotes racial characteristics. This will remain a mystery, but another fact acquires a different light under the lens of our explorations. The ancient Hebrews hardly had colonial ambitions, and their settlements hardly point to anything of that nature. Their presence in America may be attributed to spiritual reasons. It may point to preparations for the momentous event that reverberated from the Middle East to the Americas forever changing the fate of Earth evolution. The documented physical connection between old and new worlds could be related to the preparation and coordination of events known to the initiates for centuries before the incarnation of Christ.

At the time of the crucifixion on Golgotha there was what Steiner describes as a darkening of the Earth, possibly an eclipse of the Sun. At that time the vitality of all living beings decreased. Steiner could not tell if it was an eclipse or darkness caused by mighty cloud formations.[32] He comments: "While this change happened on the Earth, also in the physical sense, the Christ spirit entered into the living Earth aura. Through the death of Christ Jesus, the Earth received the Christ impulse."[33] At the time when the body was laid on the earth there was an earthquake in the region. The body of Christ was taken into the earth and the next morning the tomb was empty. Steiner indicates that this was the moment in which the Christ being and his "all prevailing cosmic love" penetrated the earth through and through; they were reborn within the Earth.

While the Christ descended into the underworld after his death, the American initiate was fighting through the power of Christ against this realm of the underworld, which held sway in the New World. The Christ came to conquer death and offer new life through his resurrection. Through his deed of the descent into the underworld, he announced the future direction of humanity's struggle to redeem evil. It is this second aspect that Ixbalamqué prefigures, as an initiate, for the future of humankind. At the first level of the confrontation evil cannot be redeemed but banned until a later age. In this context Ixbalamqué's life becomes a mystery of the human initiation in the theater of the world. His deed announces the birth of a new consciousness, which is reflected outwardly by the Dawning.

As we are told in the legend of the Popocatepetl and similar ones mentioned in the first chapter in relation to Mesoamerica, the Prophet has to first perform a deed in order to perceive the future evolution of the earth. At the summit of Popocatepetl, the Prophet had first seen the future resurgence of human sacrifice, before entrusting himself to the Great Spirit and being able to foresee a further evolution in store for the earth. We will return to this matter later when we will offer evidence of the further evolution of the Mexican or, we could say, American Mysteries at the time of the Consciousness Soul.

We have tried to unveil an American event equivalent in its significance and coincident in time with the life, death, and resurrection of Jesus Christ. This is a symptom in the sense spoken by Steiner, i.e., an event whose roots lie deep under the surface of history, an event where the spiritual world manifests itself into the physical. In proportion to their importance, the two simultaneous events are not only symptoms, but can be qualified as a "central event." Central events require long historical preparation and bring long-term consequences over the following centuries and millennia.

Clearly the deeds of Ixbalamqué were only possible because on the other side of the earth the Christ had incarnated as a human being. To history the two events are equally puzzling. An endless flow of ink has been poured, volumes and volumes written, about the reality and authenticity of all the events connected with the life of Christ. A deed like the death and resurrection of Christ is a deed that the spiritual worlds bestowed upon humanity for its own progress. In keeping with the gift of human freedom, the Christ did not perform a miracle to force humanity to believe and take on a new path. Therefore, the recognition of the event is a step that human beings have to accomplish in their own souls. History can show the changes that have followed the life of Christ, but it cannot prove Christ's life, even less His resurrection. It can barely point to the historical dimension, not to the spiritual dimensions of His life. Once we recreate an understanding of the latter inwardly, we can illuminate history with a new understanding.

As with Christ, the same is true with the deed of Ixbalamqué. The Popol Vuh turns our gaze to an important event that occurred in a very precise part of Mexico-Guatemala. It also points to the very narrow time window of the 1st century BC and the 1st century AD. The ceremonial site of Izapa gathers all the conditions for having been the initiatory center of the progressive Mexican Mysteries. There we find woven together all the elements of Mesoamerican esotericism: the deeds of the Twins as described in the Popol Vuh and depicted in the ceremonial stelae, the coincidence of the Tzolkin with the local climate, and finally the origin of the Long Count and of the new astronomy. Additionally Izapa is situated in a key location that connects the Atlantic Coast with the Pacific Coast through the isthmus of Tehuantepec.

Izapa, or more broadly speaking the whole of Guatemala and South-ern Mexico, play an important role for the whole of the Americas, as P. Dixon points out.[34] Here the Eastern Pacific overreaches itself to almost touch the Western Atlantic. This forms a sort of planetary cross of earth and water elements, closely associated to a strong presence of volcanic phenomena. Dixon calls it a "continental heart located above the equator." Izapa is thus placed in a central place of the America's etheric geography. At a closer look it also stands in the unique environment of the Soconusco. Both these elements contributed to its role in the Mysteries that modified America's evolution and history.

No matter how much all the elements of the life of the Twins point to a precise place and time, their deeds and identity are shielded from direct enquiry. The last three years of the confrontation of the super-magician with Ixbalamqué remain, as a supersensible deed, solely accessible to spiritual research. The Popol Vuh mentions the death of Hun Camé. The crucifixion is not mentioned explicitly; nevertheless Hun Camé dies after he requests that the Twins perform the mystery of death and resurrection on him. So, even here, we find a strong confirmation in the direction of Steiner's research. Izapa's outstanding Stela 67, portraying a bearded figure holding a cross in each hand, could be an allusion to this mystery (see figure 4, chapter 6, p. 139).

The earthly life of Christ influenced western civilization for the following centuries. Whether animated with progressive and construc-tive or decadent and destructive goals, all the churches, heresies, and cultural movements constantly referred to the point in time of Christ's incarnation. They did so even when animated by intentions contrary to the essence and being of the Christ. No other worldview could have substituted for this one and been accepted. We will see the same to be true for the following centuries in America. Fifteen centuries later, the Aztecs could only spread a religion of human sacrifice under the guise of following and renewing the message of the Prophet. The Iroquois, with-out following this knowledge in full consciousness, were still acting under its reverberations.

We can now turn to a second strand of our study: the characterization of the Mexican Mysteries themselves. Before doing this we will turn to other, earlier Mysteries that preserved the unity of Atlantean knowledge, in which the path outward toward the macrocosmos was present at the same time as the descent into the microcosmos of the soul.

The Last Atlantean Mysteries

Before launching into the new territory of the progressive Mexican Mysteries, we want to add some ground under our feet, as it were. We will first look at the nature of an earlier Native American initiation through the eyes of Grace Cooke—the conscious memories of a previous initiation on the American continent, which took place in the Southern hemisphere a few millennia before our times. We will then examine the nature of the Hibernian Mysteries.

An Initiation Process in Early America

It is now known that South American civilization preceded Mesoamerica. The first organized ceremonial centers were present along the Peruvian coast already in the third millennium BC. These are most likely the ones to which Grace Cooke refers. The leader of these Mysteries was called Menes, a term reminiscent of Manes and Manu, the high initiate who led humankind out of Atlantis. The process of initiation was divided into three stages. First, the pupil had to undergo seven years of training of the physical body. He would have to face severe tests of strength and endurance. It was a preparation, testing the courage of the neophyte.

In the second stage came instruction based on the observation of natural phenomena, studying and meditating on nature. The neophyte would learn to observe weather formations for entire days and nights. He was also taught the arts of agriculture and animal husbandry. At this time of human development humanity had more direct power over nature through its etheric body and could influence nature from within. Thus the second period was in all degrees a type of course in natural science as applied to the ordering of human existence.

At the final stage, the pupil was taken to a cave high on a mountain and left for a long time of silence and meditation. Grace Cooke, referring to her own previous incarnation, evokes:

> This was the sharpest ordeal ... I had to face legions of elementals and wrestle with them, to overcome or be overcome. Again and again these creatures of the underworld tempted me with all manner of bribes to put myself in their hands, to surrender my faith and trust in God or eternal good: in return for which they would bestow on me power to work the strange magic of the Lucifers, great powers over earth itself and its people, over the people of the inner world even.[35]

The third part of the initiation lasted two years and ended with tests experienced in two different temples. Here the disciple would be alternatively exposed to great heat and intense cold. The training protected the flesh from these extremes and taught the disciple how to use the power of thought in order to heal injuries and illnesses. In women, this initiation brought about the attainment of prophetic vision.

From the above, the Atlantean nature of this initiation process is apparent. In addition lingering Lemurian elements continue, particularly the differentiation of the role of women. The inner and outer aspects of initiation weave into each other at different times. As in the Hibernian Mysteries analyzed below (but here more literally), tests of heat and cold play an important part, and the development of prophetic vision also marks the last step of the process.

Preservation of Atlantean Knowledge in Hibernia

From Steiner we know that the Hibernian Mysteries played an important role for a long time before our era. The Mysteries of Hibernia existed in a place roughly equivalent to modern Ireland. These Mysteries were preserved by the succeeding culture of Druids and Bards in a different form. Through them they were still present in a pale reflection at the time of the foundation of Christianity.

The Hibernian Mysteries preserved most faithfully the ancient wisdom-teaching of the Atlantean peoples.[36] These Mysteries were some of the deeper mysteries of antiquity. Steiner expresses the difficulty of perceiving them even clairvoyantly. He also stresses that they could neither be approached through ordinary historical research, nor with historical clairvoyance. He qualifies these Mysteries as Great Mysteries, the last Great Mysteries which expressed human and cosmic secrets.[37]

In the context of this study, regarding these Mysteries we can say that the preparation of the pupil led him to a state of complete despair in his search for the truth. At the same time he could find no reality behind the phenomena of sense perception. The subsequent phases of initiation brought him in front of two statues of gigantic size: one male, the other female. In front of the male statue the aspiring initiate felt as if consumed by heat. He felt what it would be if the Sun alone worked in the cosmos. In front of the female statue he was filled with imaginations of the Earth in winter and acquired the feeling of what it would be if the Moon alone worked in the cosmos. This first phase of the ritual led the pupil to perceive that the male statue was conveying to him the idea of science, whereas the female statue was indicating the role of art. This meeting with science and art led to the pupil perceiving the form of Christ. The priest who directed him to the Christ-picture said to him: "Receive the Word and the Power of this Being into thy heart." Another priest said: "And receive from Him what the two images wished to give thee—Science and Art." Later in his initiation, the pupil could draw the two experiences together. What the pupil had achieved was a twofold process. On one hand he could reach outwardly into the farthest cosmic spaces. On the other he could plunge deeply into his soul. When he could master these processes and recognize them, a twofold set of experiences opened up to the candidate to initiation. When he learned to control his movement out into cosmic spaces, he was led into the past evolutionary stages of the Earth. When he learned to control his inner dreaming, outer physical heat was felt to be the same as soul heat. In his consciousness he was transported into the future evolutionary stages of earth existence. This glimpse into the future was accompanied with the distressing experience of knowing that he had to overcome his lower ego, which could otherwise be the source of evil.

What became of the preservation of old Atlantean knowledge after the time of Christ? We know that on one side the Hibernian Mysteries partly continued in the Arthurian Stream founded by the initiate known as Merlin in 1100 BC, which continued roughly until the ninth century AD. However, the old atavistic clairvoyance was now dimmed.

Of the Mysteries of Hibernia and their offshoots Steiner further says that while the Mystery of Golgotha occurred on earth, on the island of Hibernia this event was experienced spiritually in the aura of the earth. The events of Golgotha were experienced in pictures at the same time in which they occurred historically. The same seems to have been the case in America, although with a qualitatively different experience. It is less surprising therefore that both Popol Vuh and Inca esotericism (through the chronicler Molina) associated the presence of the human-sun being with the event of the Dawning.

With the benefit of having explored other Mysteries that preserved the Atlantean knowledge we can now return to the Mysteries of Izapa.

Izapa and a Possible Initiation Path

We will now follow a possible initiation path into the mysteries of Izapa. Much of this exploration is made possible through the research work of J. M. Jenkins.[38]

As we have seen previously, during the winter solstice the Milky Way crosses the sun's path on the ecliptic in Sagittarius. This is the time of the celebration of the rebirth of the solar being and hero, Hunahpu. It is in Sagittarius that the Milky Way forms a dark rift, almost completely surrounded by the white light of the stars. This place, pointing to the center of the galaxy, was seen by the Maya as a womb of creation. This is a central theme of the new galactic astronomy that we will see abundantly used in Izapa. This new astronomy, based upon the observation of the Milky Way and the ecliptic, supersedes the two approaches of polar and zenith astronomy in Izapa. Let us see how.

Izapa has a particular geography. To its north are situated the two volcanoes Tacana and Tajumulco, to its south the ocean. In the polarity of heavens and underworld, the ocean represents the underworld. The ceremonial site is the symbolic middle ground between heights and depths. The north-south axis offers a first layer of meaning to the design of the city.

Izapa is located at 14°15' latitude. The celestial pole is situated 14° above the horizon. In the northern direction, slightly to the east of it, is situated the volcano Tacana. A cleft closely situated to the east of the summit served as a marker for the rising of the Big Dipper, from around 300 BC to the beginning of our era. At the December solstice, the Big Dipper was visible for the whole night, when the sun was at its lowest. At the opposite time of year, during the summer solstice, the Big Dipper was not visible at night and the sun was at its highest. The winter solstice was the moment of the rebirth of the sun and of its representative, Hunahpu. The volcano Tacana, situated to the north, symbolizes the polar region. Consequently, the polar astronomy belongs to the region and direction of the north.

Let us now look closer at zenith astronomy. At first sight zenith astrology would have no directional quality, since it points away from earth to the heavens above. However, in the Mesoamerican worldview there was a correspondence between the north-south axis and the zenith-nadir axis. The south is equivalent to the underworld, the north to the heavens. The north is equivalent to up, the south to down. Therefore, zenith astrology also referred to the north.

Finally, galactic astronomy looked symbolically to the sunrise of the December solstice, toward the southeast, perpendicularly to the northern direction: the Tacana volcano is situated at 23° east of north, the December sunrise horizon at 23° south of east. Most of the monuments in the site of Izapa are oriented in these directions. In December 100 BC, the Milky Way rose parallel over the horizon, two hours before the December solstice sun. What J. M. Jenkins has discovered through computer simulation is the fact that at Izapa, looking to the southeast, the sun will rise within the rift of the Milky Way in the year 2012, a very unique occurrence. On the December solstice, the sun will appear as if reborn from the center of the galaxy. The year 2012 is particularly significant in the Mayan calendar as the end-date of the present Great Cycle. Here is yet a further confirmation that Izapa has a central place in the origin of the Long Count. The dark rift of the Milky Way has still other symbolic associations. It is the place where the head of Hun Hunahpu stood on top of the cosmic tree, and it is also the place of the re-birth of the Twins. The Great Cycle that started in 3114 BC ends in 2012 BC. As already mentioned, this cycle is in close correspondence to the cycle of Kali Yuga, from the Indian esoteric tradition, which extends from 3101 BC to AD 1899. Here is a further possible indication that the Maya looked at the end of the cycle as an end of a time of darkness.

Modern day Quiché Maya still call the dark rift *Xibalba be,* or the "road to the underworld." So the Mayan end-date of the present Great Cycle has many added meanings. The meeting of the sun in the dark rift of the Milky Way in 2012 indicates a future rebirth of the solar deity. It is also what the Maya define as the cosmic reunion of First Father and First Mother—the union of heaven and earth—that points to a movement of redemption of the underworld.

Two concepts face each other in the iconography of Izapa: the rebirth of the maize/sun deity during the agricultural cycle, and the rebirth of the sun god during the yearly and cosmic cycles. One refers to the earthly aspect of the sun deity, the other to the cosmic aspect. These twin concepts are represented in ways that may cause confusion at times. In Izapa, the Milky Way is represented in a variety of ways. A recurrent one is the caiman, with the mouth pointing toward Sagittarius and the tail toward the thinner part of the Milky Way in Taurus/Gemini. Stela 25 of Izapa portrays the heavens on the day of the December solstice (see figure 2 chapter 6, p. 138). At that time, the head of the caiman (the largest part of the Milky Way, the dark rift) looks to the nadir, and is situated under the horizon. The tail of the caiman (the thinnest part of the Milky Way in Taurus/Gemini) is overhead.[39]

The dialogue between north and south summarizes the deeds of the Twins, their double confrontation with Vucub Caquix and the Lords of Xibalba. This theme of the Popol Vuh is woven within the iconographic content of the stelae. The Popol Vuh provided simultaneous contact with mythical realities and their astronomical counterparts. Let us now "walk" the Izapa ruins in chronological order, in what could have been the astronomical/cosmological initiation into the Mexican Mysteries.

The message of the transition from one form of astronomy to another one is sculpted in stone from group to group:

- Group A, built from 300 to 50 BC and thus the oldest, is the one that reveals the fall of Seven Macaw, the Polar God. By the year 300 BC, in effect Ursa Major had already considerably drifted away from its proximity to the heavenly north pole.
- Group B, used simultaneously and shortly after Group A, clearly treats the theme of zenith astronomy.
- Group E is an intermediate group of the same age as A and B, whose main theme is the Father/Mother polarity.
- Group F, dated 50 BC to AD 100, is the most recent and celebrates galactic astronomy. It is the only one with a ball court! Note here too the coincidence in time between the dating of the building and the timing of the Dawning as the transition into our era.

The imaginations of the Popol Vuh and the orientation of the stelae and monuments will allow us to decode the essential meaning of the groups. Although most of the monuments in one group point in one direction, a significant one may point to another, and complete the message of each particular group. The placement of a stela within a group offers other valuable indications: central stelae are often the most important ones. The final layer of interpretation resides in the Mayan hieroglyphs and symbolic representations. We have seen some of them with the moving cross or swastika, the two-headed serpent, the cosmic caiman, etc.

We will now envision an initiation path that moves from Group A, to group B, Group E and finally to group F. Keep in mind that there is only circumstantial evidence for this progression. Nevertheless the path through the iconography of these groups will reveal the importance of Izapa, and the central place of the message of the Popol Vuh in the role of the sacred place.

Group A: The Fall of Seven Macaw

Group A is a group comprised of four platforms, three of which are oriented north-south, the northernmost toward the December Solstice sunrise. All of the carved monuments are north or south of the platforms, except for Stela 27, oriented toward the December Solstice horizon. Stela 5 is the most fully carved document of all Izapa stelae. V. Garth Norman calls it a "supernarrative." It is understood to depict events from different world Ages that we have seen in part I of the Popol Vuh. It portrays a sky panel at the top, the sacred tree in the middle and water scrolls at the bottom. At the base of the tree there are seven human figures, and further up deities or spiritual beings. The iconography at the bottom is the same used in other places to indicate the flood. This is another reason for acknowledging the stela as a portrayal of Mayan creation. It is a fitting introduction to the esoteric content of the Popol Vuh that concerns the three previous ages. Stela 7 depicts Seven Macaw in upward flight and Stela 2 an early stage of the fall of Seven Macaw. Here he is depicted as standing above the sacred tree, but in a reversed position with head down. The Hero Twins appear on each side in a movement indicating with their arms a downward motion of the god. The same theme reappears in Stela 4, this time with a single being in the act of striking an inverted, falling Seven Macaw with a club (figure 2). Stelae 2 and 4 stand in the central positions of their respective north and south platforms.

Figure 2: Stela 4, Izapa

To the east of Stela 4, Stela 25, already mentioned, shows the Milky Way as the cosmic caiman and Hunahpu without the arm that has been torn by Seven Macaw. He holds a staff, with the polar god as a macaw sitting on top of it. The important Stela 27 is a representation of the galactic cosmic center of the dark rift of the Milky Way. Pointing as it does to the December solstice, it works as a final reminder that Seven Macaw is fallen, but there is a new astronomy and a new god. Stela 27 stands as an answer to all the other stelae. It points toward the Group B.

Of added interest to our analysis is the correspondence in time of Group A with the reality of Olmec decline. At the time in which Group A was built—around AD 300—the Olmec worldview was waning and most likely so was polar astronomy due to the "fall" of the Big Dipper, caused by the precession of the equinoxes.

Group B: the Transition to Zenith Astronomy

Group B includes Mound 30A, which is facing north. Carved stelae are present on the northern and western platforms. What draws the visitor's attention is the central location of three pillars and three stelae. The three pillars are surmounted by a ball. We have in them a simple representation of the sphere of the sun on the cosmic zenith axis—in other words a ceremonial gnomon, referring to zenith astronomy. Throne I stands in alignment with the central gnomon. The throne symbolizes the cosmic center in which the priest enters in connection with the spiritual world. The glyphs carved on it are placed at the four cosmic directions (summer and winter solstice sunrises and sunsets). Additionally, the positions of rising and setting zenith sun (due east and due west) are clearly marked in the middle of each side, as well as the zenith sun itself, at the intersection of the cross-bands carved on the middle of the throne.

Stelae 8, 9 and 10 stand facing the three gnomons. Stela 9, the central one, represents a solar deity carrying a human being to the zenith. This is reminiscent of the episode of the resurrection of Hunahpu (figure 3). Stelae 8 and 10 both denote a vertical polarity. In Stela 8 we see a figure of a ruler or priest sitting on a throne, located in the underworld. Stela 10 depicts the cosmic tree (see figure 3, chapter 6, p. 138). At its base is Ixquic giving birth to the Twins. Above the tree are cloud scrolls and among them is Hun Hunahpu, father of the Twins. This is the best possible representation of the dual nature of Hunahpu and Ixbalamqué.

Stela 11, situated on the western platform and facing the December Solstice, completes the message of the three previous stelae (figure 4). There, we see the solar deity reborn from a frog's mouth, another possible symbol of the underworld and the dark rift. The outstretched hands of the god, indicating the completion of a cycle, reinforce the message. Stela 11 indicates then a transition toward the galactic astronomy of Group F.

Figure 3: Stela 9, Izapa

Figure 4: Stela 11, Izapa

Group E: Cosmic Father / Cosmic Mother Union

Group E could form a prelude to Group F. The group's prominent features are Stelae 19 and 20, oriented toward the December Solstice sunrise. Stela 19 is a figurative representation of the female principle (figure 5). A v-shaped cleft bears in its center a circle with a rectangular indentation on the bottom, a representation of a womb. Stela 20 is what J. M. Jenkins calls a "phallic breechcloth" that possibly represents the male principle (figure 6). Stela 88, only partly preserved, may depict the fertilization of the female by the male principle on a cosmic level (figure 7). It is symbolized by the solar circle standing above the v-cleft, an image that could be pointing to the event of the December solstice of 2012. For the above reasons Group E could have been a prelude to the cosmic re-enactment performed during the ball game that we will see in the next group.

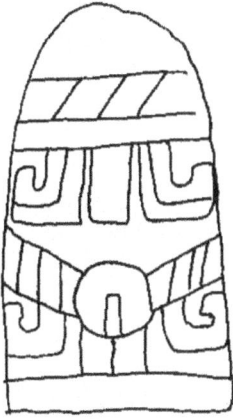

Figure 5: Stela 19, Izapa

Figure 6: Stela 20, Izapa

Figure 7: Stela 88, Izapa

Group F: The New Galactic Astronomy

Group F is oriented toward the December solstice sunrise, and its most prominent feature is the ball court. Group F was the one built latest in time and closest to the turning point of our era. It is significant that it was continuously used into the Classic Maya age and even into the Post-Classic, for a thousand years after its building. The ball court introduces us to the solar deity's cosmic dimension.

Stela 60, prominently placed to the east of the ball court, facing the west, depicts a victorious ball player dominating a fallen Vucub Caquix. It reconnects us to polar astronomy, but this time it states clearly that the era of Vucub Caquix has come to an end. Monument 4 is a zenith gnomon, the only monument reminding us of zenith astronomy. All the other carved monuments simply portray the new astronomy and the resurrection of the Sun God. In the ball court the candidates for initiation probably witnessed the re-enactment of the cosmic drama of the sun's resurrection. The end of the game, when the ball, representing the head of Hunahpu, went into the goal ring, indicated the death and rebirth of the sun god.

There are many other elements that complete the meaning of the ball court's cosmology. It is Stela 67, in the center of the northern wall of the court, which catches our interest and adds further food for thought (see figure 4, chapter 6, p. 139). It is quite unique among all the other carvings and deserves a closer look. What we see is a solar hero standing in a canoe. That he is human is further emphasized by the unequivocal presence of a beard. The canoe echoes the shape of the ball court, and points toward the rift of the Milky Way on the December 21, 2012 sunrise. This could correspond to the view that the Milky Way's Dark Rift moves in the heavens in relation to the precession of the equinoxes—a situation that is reflected on the horizon above, where the Milky Way progressively drifts toward the sunrise sun of the year 2012 (according to computer simulation enacted by J. M. Jenkins). V. G. Norman calls our attention to the two crosses that the figure holds in both hands, which are rarely portrayed anywhere else in Mesoamerican iconography. He equates them to the Egyptian ankh scepter, a symbol of life.[40] They actually more closely resemble the so-called Latin cross with a longer lower arm. This stela may give a hint of the solar hero, Ixbalamqué, and the reality of the two crucifixions: the one in Golgotha and the one in Mesoamerica. This is confirmed in Mesoamerican legends, where the prophet sometimes appears with the sign of the cross in either hand. The outstretched hands indicate the end of a cycle in Mayan symbolism.

We can now compare what we have gleaned from Izapan statuary and history with the insights that Rudolf Steiner has offered us from spiritual research.

The Nature of Izapan Initiation

We have brought forth two previous examples of survival of Atlantean mysteries in the post-Atlantean era. The first ones were the Hibernian mysteries. In America, more or less at the same time, there were the Mysteries of Menes, the ones described from previous life memories by G. Cooke. Many elements are common to the three streams of mysteries that we have described. In all of them, the inner path into the microcosm is accompanied by the outer path into the macrocosm. Knowledge of the past is accompanied with prophetic knowledge of the future. In its furthest implications Mystery knowledge affected the organization of social forms, agriculture, astronomy, and religious practices.

The initiation path of Izapa and the text of the Popol Vuh offer us various insights into the nature of the Mysteries. The Popol Vuh gives indications about the trials that preceded the final deeds of the Twins—trials that the highest initiate underwent. These are the trials of the six Caves, in some degree similar to what Grace Cooke describes of her initiation. These may have been part of the path of the disciples of the Izapa Mysteries, constituting the path into the microcosm. The other part is what remains engraved in the stelae: a grandiose survey of the path into the macrocosm, a cosmic history in stone that provided the disciple with an instruction into the remote past and distant future of American cosmology, looking forward until AD 2012.

What is it then that makes the emerging Mayan Mysteries unique? A clue has been offered in the Izapan ball court. The deeds of Vitzliputzli have been performed in the world. The Popol Vuh offers to the adept, within the precinct of the Mysteries, a view of his task in the world. Ixbalamqué and the solar being represented by the Twins have to overcome the dangers of Vucub Caquix and of the Lords of Xibalba. The Popol Vuh speaks before that of all the previous ages of humankind and the temptations undergone by humanity of the First, Second, and Third Age. To all of these correspond a trial and a test. Humanity fails each time, only to start again with new forces. The human being has to learn to work in co-creation with the gods. Maize, with which the Twins are identified in the agricultural cycle of the year, depends on human efforts for its growth. Unique among other cereal seeds is its incapacity to reproduce on its own. Through this imagery and many of its aspects the Mexican Mysteries seem to point to humanity's present and future co-creative role in concert with the gods.

The end date defining the present Great Cycle of 13 baktuns is the year 2012. The Mayan Mysteries are mysteries of the future. An element of this vision of the future appeared in the Legend of the Popocatepetl. There we saw the Prophet beholding in a vision the destruction of Tula, the Golden City. This was his trial. His faith, sustaining him, allowed him to regain the gift of prophecy and to perceive further into the future the coming of the new era and the rebirth of the golden city of Tula.

With these elements in mind, it becomes easier to identify the meaning of the end date and the rebirth of the Solar God. This we can only do with the help of spiritual science. The present time to which the Popol Vuh points is the time that Steiner defines as the time of the reappearance of the Christ in the etheric, the event that has also been called the Second Coming. Defined by Steiner, it is a progressively unfolding event that human beings will start experiencing from the year 1933. This point in time represents a growing aspect of modern spiritual co-creation. Precisely as humanity is able to bring the darkest horrors of unprecedented evil, so it is able to sustain the work of Christ in active co-creation. We will return to this aspect as we reach the conclusions of these studies.

Accompanying the ability to co-create with the gods is the risk of being led astray by alluring calls. The appeal of Vucub Caquix and the Lords of Xibalba is subtle and real. The Popol Vuh mentions almost as a surprise that the Lords of Xibalba are not real gods. Before that, it had led us to believe that they were. Whether they were or not does not cause great difference in the Native American soul. In effect, they were the tools of spiritual beings that their souls could perceive as clearly as physical reality. These retarding beings, acting through humans, posed a real threat to the progressive forces represented by the initiate and the Mysteries of Izapa.

The answers to the threats of Vucub Caquix and Xibalba survive to this day in the Mayan ritual year and its division between rainy season and dry season, Sacred Calendar and civil year. The iconographic message shows that the Twins have overcome the night god that Vucub Caquix's consciousness represents. The Twins' life accompanies the death and resurrection of maize, its life cycle. It is a new night consciousness that the priest of the agrarian god represents; we could call it a Christ-imbued night consciousness. The agrarian priest works with the night exclusively in the realm of the natural cycle and does so in commemorating the deeds of the Twins. The threat of Vucub Caquix, the night god, has been overcome. The agrarian god, hearkening to the days of Atlantis, rules exclusively over nature in close cooperation with the Twins who accompany the cycle of maize with their life. Nature, penetrated by the Christ-imbued deeds of the initiate, offers new resources to the human being and to civilization. On the other hand the solar god ushers in the new age of historical consciousness and culture, sowing the seeds of individuality most clearly visible in the conduct of the solar priest.

After Izapa, the subsequent history of Mesoamerica is followed by the inner struggles and doubts of discerning between the different calls that have all the appearance of legitimacy. Teotihuacan and Aztec worldviews are based on an apparent continuation of the tradition of the Popol Vuh. What is it that makes Teotihuacan different from the Toltecs of Tula, from the League of Mayapan, or from the Aztecs? We will look now at history, following the threads of The Popol Vuh, cosmology, and astronomy that have already allowed us to find our way into the Mysteries of Izapa. Knowledge of these central Mysteries will give us an orientation into later American history.

PART II

FROM THE TIME OF CHRIST TO THE CONQUEST

CHAPTER 1

Teotihuacan and
Toltec Influence

I: Teotihuacan Civilization

THE POPOL VUH has allowed us to have an overview of the ages of
development of America from a privileged standpoint. Its central myth
includes the life and times of Ixbalamqué at the turning point of American history. Part III of the Popol Vuh recapitulates the transition from the
Third Age into the Fourth Age from the human perspective. We are not
concerned anymore with the deeds of the gods but with the point of view
of the Maya Quiché and their ancestors. By a detour of fate, the Popol Vuh
allows us to see the links between the Mayan and Teotihuacan civilizations, the Toltecs of Tula, and the Mayapan League (Maya New Empire)
before the rise of the Aztecs. This is due to the particular ethnic group
whose history we are following—the Maya Quiché—whose history forms
a bridge with all the above-mentioned groups except the Aztecs.

Once more it will appear that the Popol Vuh sheds light on phenomena and spiritual modes of perception little accessible to modern Western
man, but absolutely real to the Native American consciousness. We cannot
dismiss its contents without losing the opportunity of seeing what is truly
unique about Native American history.

The period of time leading to the confrontation between Vitzliputzli
and the "super-magician" is preceded by the introduction of the Tzolkin
and the Mysteries of Izapa. It is a time of tremendous expectation, but also
a time of spiritual darkness and testing. Practically all of Part III of the
sacred book is dedicated to this turning point as it is perceived and experienced from the perspective of a particular tribe. Part IV reviews all of

the modern era. Thus we see Part III dealing in depth with a few centuries at most and Part IV giving us an overview of ten or more centuries. This is certainly a different way of looking at history than the western scientific one. The reason for this is simple to explain once we penetrate the depth of the Native American way of thinking. Part III deals with the most "spiritually charged" events of Quiché history. Part IV shows less drastic developments, although it covers parts of history that archaeologists and historians have investigated at great length, and which fill up most of Mesoamerican history books. The Popol Vuh is less concerned about the wars, building of cities, or the outer development of culture than with the spiritual trials of the people in their following of the god Tohil. The god's deeds and requests affect the life of the Quiché. This becomes clear in Part IV, where the book puts particular stress on the resurgence of human sacrifice and the response of the tribes to this phenomenon.

We will now follow the events of Mesoamerican history through the eyes of the sacred book and complete the picture with all the evidence gathered from the historical record. We are trying to make visible the process that Girard inaugurated. Only through a complement of Native American imaginative language and western scientific methodology can we fill in the picture of American history. We will turn to the spiritual events in the first place through the Popol Vuh. We will then find how they manifested in history.

The Quiché Maya and the Rise of the God Tohil

The Popol Vuh spends some time relating the origin of the Quiché. The way they partake of the birth of the Fourth Age—at least chronologically—comprises practically all of Part III. And here it is difficult at first to make way into the elements of the drama. In effect Part III returns to the central event of the Dawning, but now no longer from the perspective of the spiritual world—rather from the particular historic perspective of one indigenous group, the Maya Quiché. Having moved from the mythological into the historical part of the Popol Vuh, we will both follow the narrative and offer commentary as we move along.

We are told that the progenitors of the Quiché were formed of maize. This happened in Paxil and Cayala. Mention is given of cocoa, honey, *zapotes, anonas, nances,* and other tropical fruits (Part III, Chapter 1). All of this points to the "original paradise" of the Soconusco. The ancestors of the race are still special men; they are engendered by the gods: "It is said that they were made and formed, they had no mother, they had no father. They were only called men" (Part III, Chapter 2). The same is said later of the first four women in Chapter 3. This is exactly the process that describes the formation of man and woman of the Third Age. The four ancestors still have atavistic clairvoyance, but they lose it immediately. The gods deprive them of this gift: "Let their sight reach only to that which is near; let them see only a little of the face of the earth" (Part III, Chapter 2).

The indications become more precise when we are told that the Dawning has not yet occurred. "The speech of all was the same. They did not invoke wood nor stone, and they remembered the word of the Creator and the Maker, the Heart of Heaven, the Heart of Earth" (Part III, Chapter 3). Interestingly, two things are linked here: the tribes all still speak the same language, and do not worship idols.

The anticipation of the Dawning is a time of trial, and Chapter 3 describes the impatience of the tribes. A puzzling comment is also added. Although the text has referred to the tribes as speaking the same language, it also mentions that there are black and white men, people who speak different languages. What seems a contradiction to the preceding part is what archaeology bears out. Semitic or Middle Eastern people (the famous "Uncle Sam") as well as African types are portrayed in many different artistic ways. In this regard we have seen the work of von Wuthenau in chapter 7.

Chapter 4 forms a turning point. Many ideas are expressed in few pages. Here again it is specified initially that the Quiché did not yet adore idols. Only a page later we are told that Tohil approaches the Quiché: "And the first that appeared was Tohil, as this god was called, and Balam Quitze put him on his hack, in his chest" (Part III, Chapter 4). This seems to refer to an idol (put him on his back and in his chest). We are told that three of the Quiché lords adopt new gods. These are called by three different names at first, Tohil, Avilix, Hacavitz, and then equated to just one: Tohil. A symptomatic sentence then appears that clarifies everything that follows. "One only [Tohil] was the name of the god, and therefore the three Quiché [families] did not separate" (Part III, Chapter 4). At this point two phenomena appear simultaneously: migration and language differentiation. The Quiché migrate while other tribes remain in the Orient—the place of origin—and differentiation of the languages ensues. The tribes follow the mandates of the gods. The common language is changed according to the different spiritual beings followed, a reminder of the Bible's episode of the

Tower of Babel. The same is reiterated in Chapter 9: "Well, the speech of the C'akchiquel is different because the name of their god was different when they came from there, from Tulan-Zuyva." The tribes continue the migration, following Venus ("the luminary of the dawn").

Upon arriving at their destination, a new level of the drama is reached. The Quiché experience something new. They are exposed to cold and hail. The god Tohil comes to their aid with the gift of fire. That it is a gift is underscored in the text: "It is not known how it was made, because it was already burning when Balam Quitze and Balam Acah saw it" (Part III, Chapter 5). A cycle of dependence of the tribes toward their new god is set. Big thunderstorms blot out the fire and the god renews the gift. The text gives us the image of the Fire Drill—the god who turns on his single foot to light the fire, a popular representation of this divine being (Part III, Chapter 5). At the point when doubt enters the minds of the three leaders, a messenger comes to speak for Tohil. It is a messenger from Xibalba—the text specifies it clearly—although he speaks in the name of the Creator and Progenitor. The neighboring tribes, which have migrated to the same place, ask the Quiché for fire. Tohil responds: "Are they willing to give their waist and their armpits? Do they want me to embrace them?" (Part III, Chapter 5). This is a direct reference to human sacrifice and heart removal.[1] It is followed even more clearly by the following remark: "The Cakchiquel did not ask for the fire, because they did not want to give themselves up to be overcome, the way the other tribes had been overcome when they offered their breasts and their armpits that they should be opened. And this was the opening (of the breasts) about which Tohil had spoken; that they should sacrifice all the tribes before him, that they should tear out their hearts from their breasts" (Part III, Chapter 6). The Cakchiquel continued to follow their own god. Note here a reinforcement of the previous notions. The Cakchiquel remained faithful to their previous spiritual orientation, and developed a different language or maintained their previous one. By not following the god Tohil, they could also resist the gift of fire accompanied by the injunction to practice human sacrifice.

The Dawning has not occurred yet. The priests fast while they wait. In Tulan the tribes reach great power but they still have to migrate further. They continue to follow Venus. The climax of the Dawning draws near with the priests doubting and regretting the times before their migration, when all the tribes spoke the same language and were united.

The three gods ask to be concealed. They are hidden, two of them on top of the mountains, a third in a canyon. However, the doubt and affliction of the priests is great and actually reaches a climax at this point. "They did not sleep; they remained standing and great was the anxiety of their hearts and their stomachs for the coming of dawn and the day. There, too, they felt shame; they were overcome with great sorrow, great suffering, and they were oppressed with pain" (Part III, Chapter 8). The Dawning finally arrives but brings mixed results. "Instantly the surface was dried by the sun. Like a man was the sun when it showed itself and its face glowed when it dried the surface of the earth" (Part III, Chapter 9). The image of the Dawning is unmistakable. It is "like a man," an image of the resurrected Hunahpu. However, we are actually witnessing an anti-climax. The sun brings unbearable heat, as underlined by the words "Certainly it was not the same sun which we see, it is said in their old tales" (Part III, Chapter 9). The Dawning has come but it has brought excessive heat. No rejoicing follows the event, contrary to what we have seen in Part II of the Popol Vuh. The tribes are still in doubt and pain. Here the text adds a revelation. The god Tohil is the same as the one adored by the less civilized tribes, the one they call Yolcuat Quitzalcuat— the name that is also equivalent to Quetzalcoatl (Part III, Chapter 9). This was first indicated in the text with mention of the tribes following Venus, the luminary of Quetzalcoatl.

The Dawning has been followed by the doubt of the tribes and the transformation of the gods. The gods now ask the priests not to show them to the tribes with whom they are displeased. They request sacrifices of plants and the blood of the animals. They also request the blood of the priests, clear reference to the practice of bloodletting. Then begins what the Popol Vuh calls the persecution of the birds and the deer. The gods can speak through the power of the blood. "As soon as the blood had been drunk by the gods, the stones spoke, when the priests and sacrificers came, when they came to bring their offering" (Part III, Chapter 10). Part III closes with the mention that the priests hide and the people do not know where they are. Meanwhile, Tohil has promised them future glory and dominion over the tribes.

Part IV of the Popol Vuh continues after the Dawning and progresses toward the rise and victory of the Tohil priesthood. Soon, as before the Dawning, the priests reinstate human sacrifice. This time they are performed unbeknownst to the population. The priests act in such a way to lead the people to believe that the missing individuals have been attacked by wild mountain beasts. Nevertheless their deeds are discovered.

Soon after, the tribes decide upon a way to defeat the priesthood. They send two beautiful maidens to tempt the god's representative, who bathes in the river every day. Tohil does not fall into the trap and sends back the maidens with three capes for the lords. One has a painting of a jaguar, another of an eagle, and the third a painting of wasps. The first two lords wear the first two capes and nothing happens. The third is stung by a swarm of wasps while wearing the third cape.

Finally, the tribes decide to attack the Quiché and their lords. Here mention is given of tribes attacking with bows and arrows, an important detail. The Quiché overcome the attackers through works of magic. They build fortified walls and put mannequins on top of them, decorated with silver from the tribute paid by the subjected tribes. They also fill four large gourds with wasps and drones, and place them on the perimeter of the city. When the tribes attack the Quiché they are overcome through ruse and magic. The mannequins give them the false impression that there are only a few defenders. The bees and wasps are an obvious reference to magic, as in the previous episode. It is they who overcome the attackers. The tribes are thus brought to subjection.

The lords of the Quiché, having accomplished their mission, disappear. They return to the East, from whence they came. Thus ends the long history of the first generation of the Quiché Lords. They leave behind them the *Pizom-Gagal*, "Bundle of Greatness," that wraps the idol of their god. The tribes never unwrap it.

Separately from the lords, three of the sons also return to their ancestral land. They are led by Lord Naxcit, whom history also knows as Topiltzin Quetzalcoatl, the famous Toltec king. Here they first found the city of Chi-Quix, and later Chi-Izmachi (Chichen Itza), forming an alliance of three Houses: Cavec, Nihaib, and Ahau-Quiché. This is therefore an alliance of the Quiché with other tribes. In Chi-Izmachi occurs a general revolt and many are taken slaves. Human sacrifice is in vigor again and reaches new heights. So do orgies associated with the marriage of the daughters of the lords (Part IV, Chapter 7). The Quiché, living at Chi-Izmachi, have to abandon it and later found Gumarcaah. In this new place the might of the Quiché reaches its culmination with the arrival to power of Lord Gucumatz. This famous figure instills terror unto the other tribes. He is said to be able to go to heaven for seven days and descend to the underworld for seven days. He can take the form of the snake, jaguar, or eagle for seven days at a time (Part IV, Chapter 9). The story ends with the success of Tohil and his representatives Gucumatz and the Quiché Maya. The last chapter gives us a list of the generation of rulers of the Quiché.

Spiritual Aspects of Quiché History

Part III of the sacred text is full of indications of spiritual events. The Quiché partake of the new, intensive use of maize, as the innovation that precedes the beginning of the Fourth Age. They know of the Sacred Calendar. The four progenitors of the race, initially clairvoyant, lose their atavistic gifts. Hence comes their testing; they cannot perceive the spiritual reality behind the physical anymore, and now have to rely on their faith rather than on the manifestation of the favor of the gods. Everything points to a process that has started with the adoption of the Tzolkin, but has not reached completion. In effect the Dawning has not yet occurred.

That the drama is originally set in the "original paradise" of Soconusco is made clear through reference to the local vegetation. An important spiritual battle is occurring at this stage. The tribes are enjoined to resist idolatry. This is a point in time corresponding to the beginning of the post-Atlantean times that occurred earlier in other parts of the world. At that time it was Manu who said: "Until now you have seen those who have led you; but there are higher leaders whom you do not see. It is these leaders to whom you are subject. You shall carry the orders of the god whom you do not see; and you shall obey one of whom you can make no image to yourselves."[2] The advent of the Fourth Age accompanies the transition to a new consciousness. The Atlantean-like consciousness present in America reaches a further step into the full reality of the new, post-Atlantean earth. It is not easy to measure the extent of the challenge posed by the injunction to follow the "god whom you do not see" and forsake the idols.

Other events accompany the necessity of this change of consciousness. The tribes differentiate from each other. Their language reflects the spiritual reality of the being or beings they follow. The text is quite clear about the fact that different tribes speak different languages according to their gods. Interestingly, there is no mention of any generation of leaders during their stay in Tulan-Zuyva.

The impending coming of the Dawning brings about a spiritual confrontation highlighted by the dramatic cold and hail preceding the introduction of fire, and the different experience of the Dawning that brings unbearable heat. This is the frightening reality that accompanies the trial of having to wait for an invisible god. Fire is more than the physical fire. It is the gift of the gods that replaces the progressive loss of the capacity to make use of etheric energy that had been available in Atlantis. The Native American had retained that faculty, together with his Atlantean consciousness, long after the destruction of Atlantis. We have seen that the Quiché lords have been turned into more ordinary human beings, only able to "see close." Premature and exclusive reliance on the Fire God, replacing the loss of clairvoyance, ushers in this kind of "anti-Dawning"— a different experience of the same event that has been witnessed by the other Maya tribes in the Orient.

Let us look at the phenomena accompanying the gift of fire. The text mentions that nobody knew where it came from. The tribes cannot maintain it, and it is extinguished during the thunderstorms. It is divine intervention that renews it. In this image of the Popol Vuh the mythological origin of the link between fire and the renewal of time first appears, as it was later enshrined in the ritual of the New Fire ceremony. The tribes depend now on their god Tohil and have to accept his requests. The Fire God was represented as the one-footed deity, thought to occupy the zenith. The Aztecs identified him as Tezcatlipoca, the dark twin of Quetzalcoatl.[3] The god is represented pivoting on his single foot, an eloquent image of a fire-drill. His symbol was the serpent-footed scepter of rulership. Its rattle (*tzab*) contains the combined symbols of the sun and the Pleiades, and points up to the zenith. Interestingly, the word *tzab* in Maya indicates both rattle and Pleiades. Here the text mentions Tezcatlipoca: the god that guides the Third Age, the one that had ushered the Yahweh-like cult of the Olmecs. However, here he has been merged with and replaced by the Fire God.

In the image of the renewal of the fire we see the archetype of American humanity's dependence upon the regressive gods. The motion is set forth for the cyclical renewal of time, the same that still existed at the time of the Aztecs who practiced the New Fire Ceremony every fifty-two years. Once again, the Popol Vuh allows us to see the root causes of pervasive historical phenomena. The cultural-spiritual element of finite time is a reminder of the Third Age, and another indication that the Quiché ancestors had begun but not completed the process of transition into the Fourth Age. The fear of mortality, universal to the Third Age, now intensifies and becomes dread. This is reflected by a Dawning unlike the one known in the region of lzapa.

The gift of fire is accompanied by the requests for human sacrifice. As in the mythical part of the Popol Vuh (Part II), human sacrifice and its overcoming are centered on the event of the Dawning. Why then, are we told of the same event twice? The reason is quite simple. Part II of the Popol Vuh relates the event in the East—the place of origin of the new mysteries—in relation to the deeds of Ixbalamqué. There a full Dawning has taken place, accompanied by both the new consciousness of the Fourth Age and the adoption of the Long Count, overcoming the fear of mortality and the end of time. Part III narrates the same event from the perspective of tribes who have emigrated before the completion of the deeds of the initiate. Not only have they emigrated, but they have also adopted all the practices that the Popol Vuh condemns, particularly idolatry and human sacrifice. The Dawning takes place nevertheless, because it is a spiritual event affecting all of the Americas. Here we see its results upon a population that has resisted the consciousness of the Fourth Age. This is manifested in the first place with unusual physical symptoms such as excessive heat. However, just like in the Orient, the Dawning brings about the overcoming of human sacrifice. Doubt, deep anxiety, and regret pervade the mood of the priests themselves. They cannot perform their rituals openly. The adversarial powers are immobilized, but they are preparing their resurgence over the long term. For the moment, that means accepting the blood of animals and the blood voluntarily given by the priests, who have to hide the idols.

The Popol Vuh's assertion of the presence of the Fire God and his equivalence with Quetzalcoatl is a question that will be further explored in the next chapter. We will explore the matter in relation to the old Atlantean Mysteries. The Fire God or Old God is recognized by archaeologists as one of, if not the oldest, venerated gods in Mesoamerica. He is usually represented as an ancient man in a squatting position, carrying a great cylindrical vessel over his head. In Teotihuacan the god's statuary is abundant and acquires the classical form.[4]

Parts II and III form two completely juxtaposed imaginations. In Part II the sacred text has gone to great lengths to build the image of humanity co-creating with the gods. The Twins partake of human and divine in their essence. The Dawning brings about resurrection and with it the ideas of immortality of the soul and eternity of time in the new calendar and astronomy. Part III shows the rise of a new god, Tohil. The text offers us many clues as to his being. On the astronomical level it is the star of

Venus that the tribes follow. On a cultural level it is the god of those tribes that still live fully in the consciousness of the Third Age. The Popol Vuh finally specifies that it is the being whom we have met with the name of Quetzalcoatl, whom Steiner defined as Mephistophelean, mostly endowed with Ahrimanic attributes. He thwarts the development of the Fourth Age for the Maya Quiché ancestors. Quetzalcoatl, or Tohil, feeds off the blood, which is to say the etheric vitality of the tribes. At a time when new earth conditions limit the power of access to the etheric energy of the natural world, the regressive god himself feeds off human vital forces. In short, the whole image of progressively deeper dependence is fully developed in Part III. Instead of the new gift of co-creation, American humanity has the choice of falling into greater and greater dependence upon the gods. This precludes the possibility of experiencing immortality of the soul, and on the outer level is accompanied with the cyclical dread of the extinction of civilization or time itself. These phenomena reach full completion at the time of the Consciousness Soul, roughly equivalent to the time of the discovery of America by Columbus.

As do many other esoteric documents, the Popol Vuh constructs all the elements of this central contrast with genius. Nothing is gratuitous or redundant. The Fourth Age is announced in Part I. Part II brings a deepening of the central event of the Fourth Age with the event of the Dawning. Part III seems to move back in time, but this is what allows us to deepen the nature of the central event in a way that archetypally encompasses any in-between events that may have occurred in America. By illustrating the fully realized Dawning and what we can call an "anti-Dawning," the Popol Vuh gives us an idea of the gamut of phenomena that affected the whole continent at the time of transition into the Fourth Age. It would be impossible to know specifically all these events from the limited record that archaeology has preserved. The Dawning is a watershed. It is either the point of access to a new era, filled with the ideas of eternity and human co-creation with the gods, or a step back into the past, accompanied with accrued doubt, anguish, and dread of the end of time.

Part IV of the Popol Vuh is simply the logical conclusion of Part III. The tribes react to the practice of human sacrifice. Since they have not found complete access to the impulses of the Fourth Age, the progressive spread of the practice of human sacrifice will occur over time, albeit a long span of time. Everything that the Popol Vuh has quickly offered out in a synopsis is borne out by historical evidence. This is what we will follow next.

The Historical Record of the Quiché

Taking the Popol Vuh seriously has allowed Girard to highlight aspects of Mesoamerican history that are usually the subject of many hypotheses but few concrete certainties. To the record of the Popol Vuh Girard added the data provided by other historical indigenous documents, and finally the record of iconography, ritual, and astronomy.

Girard traces the migration of the Quiché from the area at the border between Guatemala and Mexico to the place that saw the rise of the civilization of Teotihuacan, and later of the historical Toltecs of Tula and Chichen Itza. In fact this is what also allows him to define as Toltec both the civilization of Teotihuacan (after the times of Christ) and the later Tula, as historians of old used to do and as the rest of this work will prove.[5] The movement of return to the ancestral homeland is the one that history knows as the Toltec migration to Yucatan and the formation of the League of Mayapan (also called New [Maya] Empire) with the three cities of Chichen Itza, Uxmal, and Mayapan. Let us find our way through such astonishing revelations and see their historical ground.

The Quiché separated from the forming pre-Maya and Mayan civilization at a time when the latter had developed the Tzolkin but not the Long Count. We have seen how the Popol Vuh indicated these events. Historically this situates us at the time of the Third Age, the time of the American twilight of the gods. The Teotihuacan civilization originated one to two centuries before our era in the high plateau of Central Mexico, near the present capital.

Teotihuacan has left us some of the most impressive pyramids and monumental work on the continent. The famous murals of the site describe a tropical environment, and depict the use of rubber (in the ball game), cacao, and the shell of strobylus, all of which are not found on the high plateau. The Rabinal Achi—a Quiché document—points to the Quiché being of the "Toltec race." Other indigenous documents and chronicles attest to the Toltec origin of the Quiché Maya, and Nahua traditions further confirm that the Toltecs were not originally from Mexico.[6]

The Toltecs of Teotihuacan subjected the nomadic tribes that entered the high plateau from the north—known as Chichimecas or old Nahua— in contrast to the later Nahua that formed the Mexica population, later called the Aztecs. Among these we recognize the streams of post-Atlantean immigration that proceeded from Asia, across the Bering Strait. In AD 583, Chalcatzin and Tlacamihtzin of the Chichimecs led a rebellion against the rulers of Teotihuacan. The war lasted eight years and led to the defeat of the Chichimecs. The rout caused the historical transition from theocracy to military rule. The episode takes a few chapters of the Popol Vuh, Part III. At this date the Chichimecs of the time emigrated to the south, where they are known as Pipil (Chiapas, Guatemala, and further south). Pipil traditions, recorded in the sixteenth century, remember their subjugation by the Toltecs in their original land for more than five centuries. After rebelling against them and being defeated, they mention having to emigrate toward the south.[7]

Teotihuacan was already a metropolis in the two centuries before our era. The Quiché had already found it inhabited. The first phase of the city goes from 200 BC to the turn of our era. According to current archaeology, it is the most impressive phase of construction. During this time were built the Pyramid of the Sun and the Pyramid of the Moon. Whether the two temples were originally dedicated to the sun and moon is a question that has not been positively answered. They may in fact have being dedicated to other deities.[8] What is of interest to us is the fact that different temples lay buried under newer ones, possibly indicating the disgrace of one god and the rise of another—an element that has puzzled archaeologists and historians. The Temple of Quetzalcoatl, inside the famous "Ciudadela," is attributed to the date AD 200. It was buried under later structures. Around the Temple of Quetzalcoatl were found the remains of 96 sacrificial victims of a probable estimated amount of more than two hundred.

Teotihuacan developed a large metropolis, and in social and technological organization surpassed the Maya. Its extension covered up to seven square miles. Trade and commerce developed to a degree unknown to the Maya. However, on the cultural level little was added to the horizon and culture of the Third Age. The city reached its last stage from AD 650 to 750. At this time, pottery and murals depict evidence of a rising militarism. They also point to the existence of military orders whose symbols were the jaguar and the eagle, a motif later adopted by the Aztecs.[9] The city was sacked in the eighth century and then abandoned. The topographic exposure and openness made Teotihuacan difficult to defend.

The Toltecs moved into Tula, not far from Teotihuacan to the northwest. The city had been founded shortly before in the seventh century. Tula literally means "Place of Rushes"; symbolically it also stands for metropolis. The word tula stood in fact for both cities. In the annals they are called Tullan-Teotihuacan and Tullan-Xicoctitlan.[10] The nomadic post-

Atlantean immigration continued flowing from the north and acquired more and more importance in the new city.

Tula embraced a decidedly militaristic regime. The cult of Quetzal-coatl/Tohil, which had occupied one or more phases of Teotihuacan, was reintroduced. The *Anales de Cuauhtitlan* tell us: "All the Arts of the Toltecs, their knowledge, everything came from Quetzalcoatl," confirming the record of the Popol Vuh.[11] The god became the patron deity of the city. The roles of king and priest seem at this stage to have been very closely linked, pointing to a return to the ideology of the Third Age. Topiltzin Quetzalcoatl is described in both functions. In fact, the king/priest was often identified with the name of the patron deity.

Tula was abandoned after the tenth or eleventh century. The Popol Vuh indicates that the rebellion against the practice of human sacrifice played an important role in the decision to abandon the city and return to the Orient. The *Anales de Cuauhtitlan* describe the inner struggle of the last ruler, Topiltzin Quetzalcoatl, against the demons and/or black magicians alluring him toward the practice of human sacrifice, against which he fought.[12] Among three black magicians who approach the ruler, we hear the first mention of Huitchilopochtli, the Aztec cultural hero that Steiner called Vitzliputzli.

Tula's art reached a far inferior quality than it had in Teotihuacan. Here we see the reintroduction of the ball courts. That the game had assumed a whole new meaning is testified by the associated presence of "skull-racks." Captives were sacrificed during the performances. The adoption of human sacrifice has been pointed out by the Popol Vuh, with the mention of ordinary sacrifice and flaying. Colonial sources add a third type of sacrifice, being shot by arrows. The re-introduction of human sacrifice occurred on a scale yet hardly comparable with the later excesses of the Aztecs. Neither was heart sacrifice yet practiced. Netzahualcoyotl, a Chichimec king, even temporarily suppressed human sacrifice.

The Toltecs returned to the mythical Orient, their place of origin, the area occupied by the Maya. Local traditions, recorded by Bartolomé de Las Casas, indicate that their leader Quetzalcoatl landed on the coast of Xicalango in present-day Campeche. The same ruler is called Naxcit by the Quiché and Cuculkan by the other Maya. The book of Telchac indicates the date AD 980 for his arrival.[13] Quetzalcoatl founded the League of Mayapan comprising Uxmal, Chichen Itza, and Mayapan, from which the term Maya was derived. The three cities witnessed different cultural influences. Uxmal was closest in style to earlier Mayan cities. Chichen Itza has been qualified as a sister-city to Tula; it was there that Toltec imprint was the strongest. Human sacrifice was soon reintroduced on a large scale, especially in Chichen Itza. That Maya and Toltec cultures could blend so easily and willingly can be more easily understood with recognition of an earlier common heritage.

Apart from the re-introduction of human sacrifice, the Toltecs brought in other cultural elements foreign to the Maya. The use of bow and arrow, as well as the new social classes of producers and merchants, were unknown to the Maya. In the religious field they introduced the cult of the dog and the deer, adopted from the Nahua. Finally they brought the ritual of Palo Volador, still practiced by the Quiché, but unknown to other Maya. The Palo Volador is a spectacular ceremony portraying the transformation of Hun Batz and Hun Chouen into monkeys. It is a functional replica of the New Fire Ceremony, since it portrays the episode situated at the end of the Third Age.

Teotihuacan's Cosmology

Teotihuacan's rigorous layout was endlessly repeated throughout the city and its neighborhoods. It persisted throughout the city's existence. The north-south axis was emphasized over the east-west. However, the famous Ciudadela did not lie within this major alignment. From north to south ran the so-called "Avenue of the Dead." Farthest to the north lay the Pyramid of the Moon (140' high), followed to the south by the Pyramid of the Sun (210' high). A cave situated under the Pyramid of the Sun emerges at the base of the western end, leading into a 338-foot-long tunnel whose center is situated under the summit of the pyramid.

The north-south direction was a reflection of the axis of heavens (north) to underworld (south), as we have seen in Izapa. The Rio San Juan and San Lorenzo were channeled east to west to accentuate the division between the upper part of the city to the north from the lower part with its Ciudadela. The mountains of Cerro Gordo to the north and Patlachique to the south formed, together with the rivers, the major topographic features of the city.

The Ciudadela, lying lower than the rest of the city, most likely represented the underworld, surrounded by the waters of the rivers. It was comprised of 12 platforms surrounding the central temple pyramid of Quetzalcoatl. The main plaza could host 100,000 people without much crowding. The temple of the Feathered Serpent was a unique building both for its time and for Mesoamerica in general. It showcased a unique alternation of rectilinear forms in six stages with three-dimensional sculptures of the square-headed Tlaloc heads and the famous protruding effigy sculptures of the feathered serpent. This may be the very first manifestation of the dual temple, representing both agrarian and tribal gods. An estimated two hundred sacrificed captives lay buried under its surface in what appears to have been a dedicatory offering. We will speak more of this later.

Teotihuacan's main north-south axis—best exemplified by the Avenue of the Dead—is oriented 15° 30' east of north. The other perpendicular but less prominent axis is the one of 16° 30' south of east. The Pyramid of the Sun is exactly perpendicular to the east-west axis of the Avenue of the Dead. From the western façade of the pyramid a sightline to the western horizon lies exactly on the 285° 30' (270 + 15° 30') azimuth. The western façade is aligned to the winter solstice sunrise over the Orizaba peak, the highest mountain of the region. However, the mountain is not visible from Teotihuacan. V. H. Malmström hypothesizes the use of a relay station, and found in this site evidence that suggests that the place was used as a shrine.[14] The orientation of the Avenue of the Dead and of the pyramid do not correspond to solstitial or zenith alignments at Teotihuacan, but rather to the 15° 30' alignment and to the August 13 date that we have already found in Olmec times. Observers at the pyramid could see the sun set on the western horizon on April 29 (or 30) and August 12 (or 13). These dates, 105 days apart, divide the year in 105/260 portions. August 13 is the famous beginning date—corresponding to the mythological birth of Venus—of the Maya. This is the zenith date for Izapa at latitude 15° 30'.[15] The zenith passages in Teotihuacan occurred on May 18 and July 26. It is obvious to think that this orientation had been imported to Teotihuacan. Once again, there was a deliberate effort in building a sacred city, not so much in a strategic place but rather in a topographical location that would align with all the most important calendrical dates of Mesoamerican cosmology. This is why Teotihuacan later proved to be indefensible as a city.

The heliacal rising of the Pleiades occurred in AD 150 on the 15° 30' alignment on May 18 (true zenith sun) after 40 days of invisibility. However, this changed over time and it occurred 20 days later under the Aztecs. The Pyramid of the Sun is perfectly aligned to the Pyramid of the

Moon on the north-south axis. This alignment with the meridian may have facilitated the observation of the zenith passage of stars overhead, such as the Pleiades, which played such a central part in Toltec and Aztec civilizations.

Human Sacrifice

The Temple of Quetzalcoatl conceals the clearest evidence of human sacrifice. It has long been a subject of speculation whether the practice was common in the metropolis of the Anahuac. It is only recently that Saburo Sugiyama has gathered conclusive evidence. Human sacrifice appears quite clearly in Aztec ideology, iconography, and archaeological artifacts, whereas it appears much more veiled in Teotihuacan's art and archaeology. All the evidence points to it but no single item clearly and unequivocally does.

At least three types of sacrifice have been placed in evidence:

- *Dismemberment*: four dismembered persons in association with an altar were found to the north of the Oaxaca Barrio. Another eight, placed in a well, were found in a complex adjacent to it.
- *Decapitation:* evidence strongly pointing to decapitation is visible in four skulls found north of the Ciudadela.
- *Infanticide:* fetuses and infants were found under altars in the Tlajinga 33 compound and also at the Tlamilolpa compound. A large number of infant burials were found at La Ventilla within a residential compound.[16]

Data indicate that human sacrifice was not exclusive of the highest strata of the population but practiced by various social strata. Iconographic representations of bloody rituals are found in paintings distributed in the living areas. These indicate a strong concern of the residents with sacrifice and/or self-sacrifice through bloodletting.

Besides the pyramid of Quetzalcoatl, the strongest candidates for retrieval of evidence of human sacrifice are the Pyramids of Sun and Moon. At the Pyramid of the Sun, a young child was buried at each of the four corners of the three lower pyramidal platforms that extended from the main body of the building. It is in fact suspected that there are more undetected burials under the pyramid. Inside the Pyramid of the Moon there were seven overlapping platforms and three dedicatory burials have been found. The burials inside the Pyramid of the Moon resemble those at the pyramid of Quetzalcoatl, evidence pointing to human sacrifice, but far smaller in scale.

No other sacrifices in Teotihuacan after the burials of the Temple of Quetzalcoatl reached the same scale. It seems there were more than 200 individuals buried under the structure. In Sugiyama's understanding the burials at the pyramid are the proof of mass-sacrificial rituals serving the purpose of the inauguration of the temple. The ceremony must have been quite imposing.

Among the individuals buried we find four categories:
- Males most likely of a high social status
- Males who probably had close relationships with the first group
- Individuals wearing collars with maxilla pendants, the most clearly military group
- Females wearing shell earplugs.[17]

However, all of the above groups seem to have been treated in an anonymous fashion, with little status differentiation. Individuality was minimally expressed. Only the people of the first category differentiate from the others by the form of the graves, position of the bodies, and the variety, quality, and quantity of offerings. In the central, apparently most important grave, twenty individuals were arranged in a highly symbolic mode, but once again with no clear differentiation of status. All of them are adorned with ornaments and buried with offerings. Many of the individuals have their arms tied behind their backs, a position that has been amply used in Mesoamerica to represent subjugated persons.

The disposition of the burials at the base of the Temple of Quetzalcoatl indicates most likely that they were part of a dedicatory burial program overlaid with cosmological and calendrical symbolism. The offerings were carefully distributed among the graves according to an overall master plan. The same planning appears from the production of offerings, to their placement within particular burials. The quality of the offerings, many of which came from foreign locations, indicates that the burials required some of the most expensive state investments. Among them are large obsidian knives, most likely used for sacrifice. Many obsidian figures represented Quetzalcoatl. There are also piercing tools that indicate their use for bloodletting. This latter retrieval sheds light on the use of the practice. In effect only one artistic representation shows high-ranking priests practicing bloodletting. The unusual concentration of projectile points, primarily among the women, at the burial complex manifests their martial role in the offerings. Ninety-five percent of the men in five graves carried slate disks, a diagnostic element for soldiers.

The same applies to the above-mentioned maxilla pendants, most likely used as trophies by the soldiers. They themselves may have been extracted through sacrifice.[18]

Sugiyama concludes that the burials at the temple of Quetzalcoatl may have been the earliest instance of association of the feathered serpent with warfare celebrated in grand scale. The Ciudadela reflected a new, albeit short-lived, political order. Different indications seem to confirm this. The first is the fact that the Ciudadela did not conform to the general layout of the city, leaving room for the hypothesis that it represented a new cosmology. Added to that was the fact that the temple was short-lived and that it laid buried under a later structure; likewise, the dedication burials were not repeated in the same way elsewhere. A first attempt at reintroducing human sacrifice was thus short-lived.

The above historical findings confirm the claims of the Popol Vuh. What history shows reflects the images of the Popol Vuh, where we are told that after the Dawning the priests had to limit themselves to bloodletting and the blood of animals for a time. Later, they returned to practicing human sacrifice surreptitiously. This would explain why the artistic record has so few explicit references to human sacrifice.

Let us now turn to the evidence associated with the cult of Quetzalcoatl, in order to ascertain his being.

Quetzalcoatl, Venus, and Zenith Astronomy

There is no doubt that Teotihuacan is the most impressive city and ceremonial center in all of North America. I had originally looked upon it as the possible center of the Mexican Mysteries given its monumental dimension. The Pyramid of the Moon and the Temple of Quetzalcoatl are four miles apart. From both summits of Sun and Moon Pyramids an unlimited vista is offered over the plateau and the ring of mountains that surround it. It is easy to feel like a creature out of place and out of time in such a context. It was clear that the people who had lived in Teotihuacan saw the world from another perspective. The words of the Popol Vuh, "In truth they were admirable men," (Part III, Chapter 2) acquire special weight.

The city follows the north-south direction of the Avenue of the Dead that links both pyramids to the Ciudadela at the southern extremity. The Ciudadela marks a step of return to a more human scale. At the Feathered Serpent Temple the sculptures of the two gods stand out in a truly unique way among all of Teotihuacan art. Izapa pales in front of the sheer dimension of the constructions of Teotihuacan. As in Izapa, there are no representations of rulers. The city was a sacred city, even though it hosted a large population, in fact a metropolis, quite unlike the Olmec La Venta or the Mayan Izapa.

The city of Teotihuacan forms the next link in time between the time of Christ that we have seen in Izapa, and the time of the conquest, when the Aztecs were still in power. It is the second of the three most significant initiation centers of Mesoamerica. The third, that will occupy us later, is Tenochtitlan, capital of the Aztec Empire.

Following Izapan tradition, we see clearly portrayed the duo of the agrarian god and the tribal god. Tlaloc is the new name of the deity that appeared in Izapa as God 7, or the Ahpus of the Third Age. As evolution progresses, so does the agrarian god. We will explore that progression, but first our attention will be turned to the new god. Quetzalcoatl is now a tribal god but not a solar god, as were the Twins or more specifically Hunahpu. Without anticipating further what we will see in the next chapter, the Aztecs too will keep the link with the tradition of the dual deity and will even inaugurate double platform temples. We will see the evolution from Izapa to the Toltecs coming to a culmination with the Aztecs.

It is of some interest that the Temple of Quetzalcoatl was superseded after the phase Teotihuacan II (finishing in AD 350). It seems that the ascent of Quetzalcoatl to the status of tribal god was fraught with ups and downs. We will now look at Quetzalcoatl in the successive developments of his cult. Steiner, referring to the time of Christ, explains that Quetzalcoatl did not incarnate. He only reached the level of the etheric. This is confirmed by the archaeological record. Up to Teotihuacan's classical phase the feathered serpent is solely a god.

What is almost unanimously agreed is the association between Quetzalcoatl's symbolism and the symbolism of the planet Venus. This is also the claim of the Popol Vuh. Venus was used for astronomical purposes associated with the course of the year and with agricultural practices. Teotihuacan tradition continued thus the tradition that linked the sacred calendar with Venus. This is primarily enshrined in the key relationship between the cycles of sun and Venus from which emerges the 2.6 proportion and the 260-day calendar. The Maya themselves acknowledged this cosmological link by indicating that the initial date of their Great Cycle— the year 3114—corresponded to the birth of Venus.

How could Venus, a planet, and therefore by definition erratic, be used as a point of reference? The answer has been given by various researchers. Venus presents itself as both morning star and evening star. Since it is one of the so-called inner planets, it gravitates in that portion of the sky closest to the sun, and is either visible early before sunrise or shortly after sunset. The cycle of Venus around the sun—the so-called synodic cycle—takes 584 days. Five of these cycles correspond almost exactly to eight years. Therefore, there is a cycle of eight years after which the phenomena of Venus' cycle repeat themselves at almost the same dates. (e.g., inferior or superior conjunctions, first visibility as morning or evening stars, etc.) There is yet another useful phenomenon rarely considered in present-day astronomy: the elongation. As Venus moves in the eastern or western sky it reaches maximum distances from the sun toward the north or the south. The maximum elongation is called an extreme. Venus as the morning star has a northern extreme and a southern extreme and so does Venus as an evening star. The cycle of the extremes has a regular correspondence with the seasonal phenomena of the year, particularly in the case of the evening star. Its northern extremes mark the beginning of the rainy season, the southern extremes the end of it.

There is yet a wider astronomical characterization of the feathered serpent in relation to the stars and Venus. The importance of the Pleiades in Mesoamerican or even North and South American cosmology has been widely acknowledged. To the Maya they are known as *tzab*, meaning the rattlesnake's rattle. The sun enters the Pleiades just at the beginning of the rainy season. The Pleiades are usually thought of in relation to Taurus. However, disregarding the ecliptic and the zodiac, they are closer to the constellation of Perseus. This is not a precedent, since the Babylonians had also viewed the Pleiades in this way. The water serpent, associated with the onset of the rainy season, has the corresponding shape of the constellation Perseus.[19] This observation is also confirmed by the murals of Tepantitla (Teotihuacan) where the feathered serpent is portrayed pouring water out of its mouth.[20] Therefore, the connection between the water serpent and Venus marks the beginning of the rainy season.

Sun and Venus actually vied for attention in yet other ways. Venus also competed symbolically to fulfill the conditions of the cycle of the Tzolkin, the Sacred Calendar. Venus's morning and evening visibility last on average 263 days, the approximate length of a Tzolkin (260 days). Its period of inferior invisibility—Venus between earth and sun—lasted on average eight days, though there are wide variations. Eight days was the span of time before the emergence of the first sprouts of corn at Teotihuacan's latitude and altitude. Thus a link was formed between Venus and maize, in the same way as it had been done in relation to the sun and the Twins through the contents of the Popol Vuh and the imagery of the Fourth Age in Izapa. Venus was now the being who plunged into the underworld for the time it took the maize to mature below the earth. It died and resurrected just like the Twins had done in Izapa. The morning star and the evening star became the equivalent of the Twins. The record of Teotihuacan shows silently what the Aztecs will later evolve to a further degree. Their testimonial has been recorded through many sources and will allow us to complete the process that had its beginning in Teotihuacan.

Venus alone could not have provided a correction factor between the yearly cycle of the sun and the sidereal year, a way to take into account the precession of the equinoxes. Teotihuacan's astronomical zenith chambers provide the rest of the answer. Three caves that were subterranean observatories have been discovered in the sacred city. Cave 1 of Teotihuacan, found 300 yards southeast of the Pyramid of the Sun, allowed for observation of zenith passages, solstices and equinoxes and the dates of February 9 and November 1. When the first rays of the sun enter the cave they illuminate the edge of a rough stela. Cave 2 marked everything as in Cave 1, with a stela inside serving the same purpose as in Cave 1, and also marked periods of 20 days around Feb. 12 and Oct. 30.[21]

Another prominent calendrical device proper to Teotihuacan and its influence is the use of so-called pecked crosses. They have been studied by archaeoastronomer Anthony Aveni. These crosses form a double-circular pattern centered on a pair of perpendicular axes. They are carved either on the rock, or on the floor of ceremonial buildings. They range from simple concentric circles to concentric Maltese crosses. An example of the latter is shown in figure 1. Pecked crosses tend to incorporate along their axes and quadrants sacred numbers such as 20, 13, and 9. Most often the extremities of the cross point to the cardinal directions.[22]

The pecked crosses could have been used for any of the following 3 functions:
- To count time
- As orientation devices
- As board games

Aveni only studies the first one. His insight came from comparing the pecked crosses to the quadripartite calendar wheels, also called quincunx, of the Codex Fejervari-Mayer (figure 2). This has the form of a juxtaposed large Maltese cross intersected by a smaller St. Andrew's cross. The outer rim of the design is marked with a total of 260 circles. Each segment of either cross counts 13 circles for a total of 20 segments. The sum of 260 represents thus the 20 months of 13 days of the Sacred Calendar (*Tonalpohualli* of the Aztecs) that follow each other in anti-clockwise sequence. The cosmogram unifies the two units of the calendar: the vague year of 360 days and the Sacred Calendar of 260 days giving birth to the Calendar Round. This form was also used for calculations involving the 52-year cycle, central to Aztec cosmology. Thus, Aztec cosmology seems to find a precedent in Teotihucan. The cross TEO 2 distinctly looks like the quincunx of the Codex Fejervari-Mayer. It is a set of three concentric Maltese crosses intersected by perpendicular axes. There are 260 elements in the outer perimeter. The cross most often repeats the numbers 5, 13, 18, and 20.

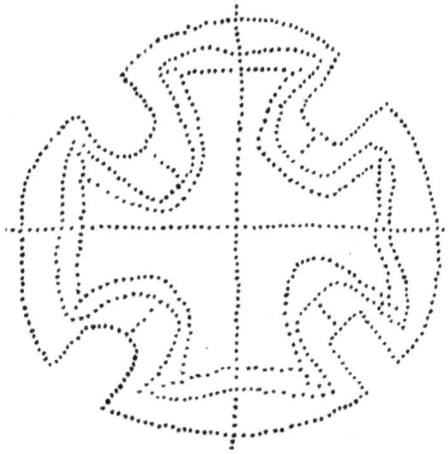

Figure 1: pecked cross

More than one cross recently found on the southeast side of the Pyramid of the Moon appears to have the Maltese cross design. Aveni concludes that it is quite clear that Teotihuacan is the place of origin of the motif. It is not surprising that they are present in the Guatemalan site of Kaminaljuyu, one of the places that shows the earliest Teotihuacan influence. On the basis of additional studies J. Broda concludes that the crosses known as TEO 1 and TEO 2 point to the four annual dates of February 5, April 29, August 13, and November 1.[23]

Quetzalcoatl as the War God

Where were the cults of Teotihuacan celebrated? The pyramids and the Temple of Quetzalcoatl were the obvious centers of reference. There may have been other centers concealed from view. Certainly a central one was the cave and tunnel situated under the Pyramid of the Sun. The tunnel, roofed and plastered, was divided into thirty sections ending in a ceremonial chamber in the shape of a four-leafed clover, containing a spring. Midway through the tunnel were two chambers opposite each other. The whole of 4 + 2 + 1 (tunnel) reproduces the symbolism of Chicomotzoc, whose meaning is "seven caves," the famed place of origin of the tribes in the Mexican high plateau.[24] The importance of the cave is underscored by the glyph symbol of Teotihuacan showing the two pyramids over a cave. In the last chamber of the tunnel have been found pottery pieces with anthropomorphic figures, one with the ornaments of a jaguar and the other of a bird.[25] These, together with other pottery and murals, suggest that the later Aztec military orders of Jaguar and Eagle may have had their origin in Teotihuacan. Note that the importance given to the cave marks a return to the practices of the Ancient Mysteries where the priest felt at one with the whole earth through his physical body.

Let us now look at the evolution of Quetzalcoatl imagery. Although prototypical forms of the feathered serpent appear as early as the pre-Classic, it is probably in the city's second phase (0 to AD 600) that the representations fill out and he appears as the rattlesnake covered with feathers—most dramatically in the center of the Ciudadela. Overall, representations of Quetzalcoatl are extremely rare in Teotihuacan until the Late Post-classic (after AD 600) when they start to proliferate. The later images often portray on their undersides representations of the earth monster, Tlaltecuhtli, the Earth Lord.[26]

A pivotal change occurs in between the 7th and 8th centuries, after the destruction of the city. For this we can turn to the city of Xochicalco, to the south of Mexico City, where we find the first human representations of Quetzalcoatl.[27] Here, contrary to Teotihuacan, the god is represented as a man. In the palace of Cacaxtla (Puebla Valley) appears very clearly the new war imagery associated with Quetzalcoatl. Two sculptural bas-reliefs—a man and a woman—portray sacrificial victims wearing five-lobed Venus aprons (figure 3). The male holds the five-lobed shell—a Venus symbol— in his hand and has a scorpion tail, imagery associated with the evening star and also a likely symbol of sacrifice. The figures are thus associated

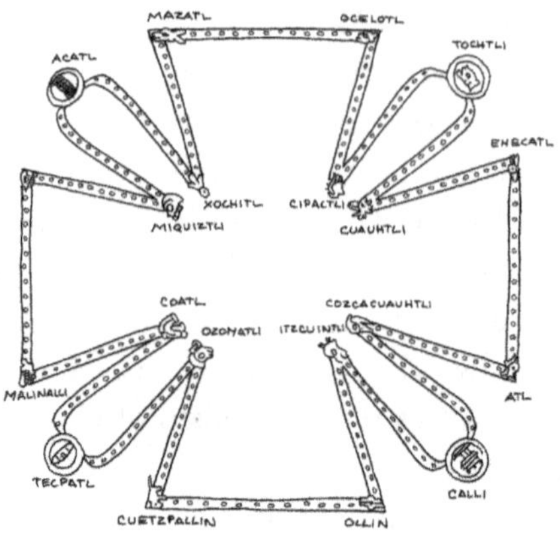

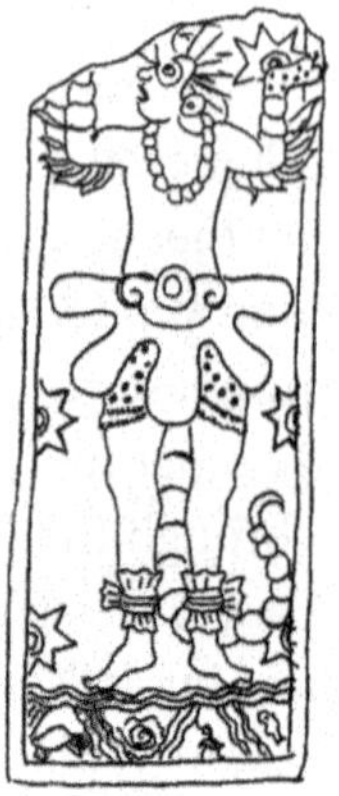

Figure 2 (left): Codex Feyervary-Mayer cosmogram
Figure 3 (right): sacrificial victim, Cacaxtla

with water and fertility symbolism on one hand, war and sacrifice on the other. Furthermore, Venus symbolism also replaces the so-called Mayan solar Kan crosses with corresponding Venus crosses.[28] The legends suggest that the man who led his people to the founding of Tula also bore the name Quetzalcoatl. Likewise, we have seen yet another ruler with the name of Topiltzin Quetzalcoatl, who led the Toltecs on the Mayan March to Yucatan. In Chichen Itza war-related symbolism reached its summit. Here it is that also appears the famous Caracol, a Venus observatory, built around the 9th-10th centuries AD.[29]

Ivan Sprajc concludes that the cult of Quetzalcoatl underwent a gradual but drastic transformation from an earlier stage, where the god was associated solely with agricultural and fertility themes, to a second phase where he was also associated with warfare and human sacrifice.[30] It appears clearly that the second theme, grafted upon the first, reflects purely ideological concerns: Quetzalcoatl imagery served as a justification for war and sacrifice. This phase of transformation of Quetzalcoatl was also accompanied in many places with a revival of the ball game. The city of El Tajin, for example, shows a complete worship of the god of death, abundantly portrayed. It has numerous ball courts and all the symbolism shows that it was an exclusively sacrificial game involving decapitation. The same is true of Tula, which had six ball courts. In Chichen Itza the ball courts are very similar to the ones of Tula, showing once again a similar cultural origin. Here they are associated with a profusion of emblems of death and skull-racks.

It is of further interest to look at the images of the deity Tlaloc as they evolve in time. E. Pasztory has examined at length the iconography of the agrarian god in Teotihuacan.[31] The god underwent an evolution from strictly natural symbolism to war symbolism. Let us look at the first stage. Tlaloc's typical representations have a number of constant elements: concentric rings representing the eyes, upper lip upturned at the corners, two long fangs in the corners of the mouth and three short ones in the middle. What Pasztory defines as Tlaloc A is the deity of the early Teotihuacan phases. Its symbolic representation is reptilian, a symbol of the earth. Tlaloc B reintroduces the jaguar traits, therefore becoming a deity of the underworld.

We come to the conclusion that under Toltec ideology Hunahpu was replaced by Quetzalcoatl and the solar connotation of Maya ideology was completely eclipsed. Likewise the Agrarian God suffered a complete transformation. However, this work has only been focusing on the larger protagonists of the Mesoamerican Mysteries. Many other players contributed to temper the polarity of Maya and Toltecs. When one turns the gaze closer to the ground, it may appear more clearly that other forces opposed Toltec ideology even in the Mexican high plateau. One such example is the city of Cholula.

Forces of Opposition: Cholula

Cholula is situated in the Puebla/Tlaxcala valley, east of Mexico City and just south of Cacaxtla in a very fertile plain, one considered among the most productive of Mexico. It is 62 miles southeast of Teotihuacan. Like Teotihuacan, the city was situated on the crossroads of many routes of commerce.

Although an important center of the Mexican high plateau—and very close to the Toltec capital—in Cholula militarism hardly ever played a part in the story, iconography, and symbolism of the city, even at the time of the Post-Classic. Cholula has been considered either a secondary center within the Teotihuacan empire or a separate polity. Some authors have assigned it the role of a port of trade between warring kingdoms.[32] There is reason to believe that Cholula acted independently of and in contrast to Teotihuacan.

Unlike the Toltec capital, Cholula was built entirely on a 24–26° east of north grid. The main pyramid faced the setting Sun on the summer solstice, thus making it a true pyramid of the Sun! It is very significant that a whole city gravitated around a different cosmology than Teotihuacan and that it survived the collapse of the metropolis and other affiliated centers.

Legends (Motolinia, Duran) indicate that the pyramid was built as a Tower of Babel. God stopped them by sending down a storm that cast down a great stone in the shape of a frog. This version is still held in San Andres Cholula. This was the oldest shrine, and most continuously in use the pre-Columbian world. There were many such centers throughout the Puebla/Tlaxcala valley, but Cholula was the only one to survive while the other ones were abandoned. By 200 BC, Cholula was the predominant center in the valley and at that time the building of the pyramid began.

The pyramid is called *Tlachihualtepetl* or "man-made mountain" and is the largest construction from pre-Columbian Mesoamerica. It measures more than 1300' on a side and covers about 40 acres at its base; the original mound measured at least 210' high, but the top is presently truncated.

The earliest structure under the great pyramid is of the Late Formative (just before the turn of our era) and was placed on the shore of a lake fed by springs. It was built on top of a spring, and a deep well leads to it. For the above reasons it was represented in the *Historia Tolteca-Chichimeca* with a froglike rain-deity on top of it. A colossal head in the so-called Patio of the Altars may in fact correspond to a stone frog altar. The drawings of the pyramid in the codices portray a large toad—symbol of fertility and regeneration—on top of the pyramid. In *Historia Tolteca-Chichimeca*, in addition to the toad, seven flowers are present, symbol of the Mixtec Sun deity and the Nahua deity Xochiquetzal, particularly linked to the Sun.[33] This is confirmed by the friar Duran, according to whom the Sun deity Tonacatecuhtli was worshipped on the pyramid, and this was still the case even in post-Classic times!

It is interesting to follow the stages of construction of the pyramid and its alternating fates. Although Cholula chronology is still partly problematic, here is what archaeologists believe at present.[34] The stages of building and changes that the pyramid underwent can be placed in roughly four periods:

STAGE 1: At this stage there seems to have been political/ideological affiliation to Teotihuacan. The initial temple measured 390' on a side and 55' high.

STAGE 2: At this stage the builders opted to ignore Teotihuacan building patterns. The pyramid measured 590' on a side and rose to 110' on nine levels. Each side was made up of steps so that one could walk to the top from every direction. There was a larger stairway counting 52 steps on the northern side, which had been structurally modified indicating that it may have been used as the main axis of ceremonial activity.

STAGE 3: This was probably the time when Teotihuacan was declining. The building expanded to 1150' on the side to reach a total height of 210'. Mc Cafferty hypothesizes that Cholula may have thus emphasized its rise to status of Teotihuacan's successor and signified it by building a pyramid unprecedented for its size. A rough monolith with a rectangular hole in its lower half, standing in front of the staircase, may have been used as a tool of observation of the solstice setting Sun.

STAGE 4: Post-Classic Time: With the arrival of the *Tolteca Chichimeca* (later leading to the Aztec rise), the pyramid lost its primacy. It was now associated with mountain worship and also as a shrine to a rain deity. There is evidence that the rededication of the pyramid did not occur peacefully. The sculptures of the final phase of the Patio of the Altars were thrown down and shattered. In fact, it has not been possible to find a finished façade from the final stage of the great pyramid. The fate of the pyramid corresponds to what may be called a ritual desecration. A new ceremonial center was built with a pyramid built to Quetzalcoatl. Late Post-Classic Cholula became thus the center of worship of the new deity. However, this may have been just a short passing phase.

Cholula kept on playing a role of opposition to Toltec and later Aztec ideology. Cortes, moving inland from the sea, repeatedly met in battle with the forces of Tlaxcala, at that time a confederation of four small kingdoms that had maintained a precarious independence from the Aztecs. Tlaxcala was being bled by the fight against the invaders, but the Spaniards were also considerably weakened. This is the reason for the alliance that Tlaxcala formed with the Spaniards against their bitter rivals, the Aztecs. This alliance was sealed by the marriage of the Tlaxcala commander's daughter to Pedro de Alvarado, Cortes' second in command.

In relation to its history it is interesting to note that the Sun pyramid became the second most important place for Christian pilgrimages after the Conquest. Pilgrims would come to the top of the pyramid to worship the *Virgen de los Remedios*, whom they petitioned for healing, for rains, and for agricultural fertility. Colonial period figures show the Virgin emerging from a *maguey*, plant of the *pulque*. The legend from which the cult originated is in some way similar to the more famous Guadalupe. [35]

II: TEOTIHUACAN INFLUENCE AMONG THE MAYA

The Maya and Teotihuacanos had been in contact since at least the first century BC, but according to Friedel and Schele, something quite different had occurred in the fourth century, during the Classic Period, on the occasion of the Tikal-Uaxactun war. This time the Maya adopted Teotihuacan ideology.[36]

David Stuart discusses the merits of two competing hypotheses about Teotihuacan influence upon the Mayan area in the Classic period:

- Externalist: overt and disruptive influence with direct military campaigns, if not political domination, to which Stuart mostly adheres.
- Internalist: local appropriation of Toltec ideology, as believed by Schele and Freidel, among others.

Stuart concedes that the reality is that political alliances and interactions could change quite rapidly, and so it is possible that both theories may be right in relation to different times.[37] It seems that at this stage empire was mostly based on winning over the enemy to the same god and ideology, rather than on physical domination from a central location.

David Stuart has proved the externalist scenario on the interpretation of hieroglyphs at both Copan and Tikal and neighboring cities. He believes, however, that the internalist scenario may have played a role after the fall of Teotihuacan. Let us look at Tikal, a very important city, where the first evidence of Teotihuacan ideology among the Maya surfaces.

The earliest recorded date of the site—AD 292—has been taken by many as the starting point of the Classic period. After Tikal, Mayan civilizations spread practically everywhere in the Peten, the region to the north of Guatemala. Frans Blom qualified the Old Empire as the "Peten Period." He called the New Empire the "Yucatan Period," since thisis where Mayan presence continued in the tenth to eleventh centuries.

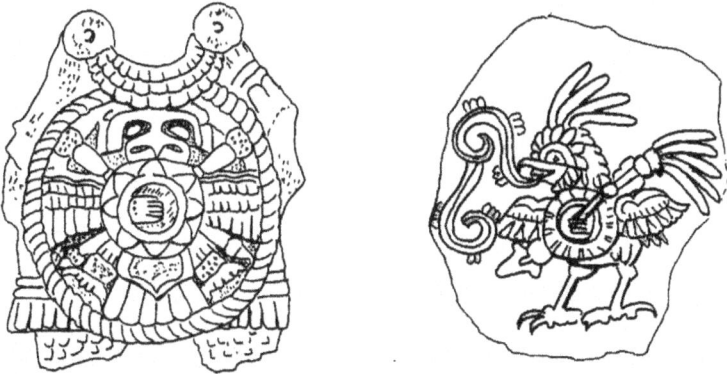

Figure 4: *"Lechuza y armas"* emblems, Teotihuacan

City-states of Mayan polity competed with each other, similar to Greek cities in their time. However, there was no tradition of standing armies. Battle was more of a matter of civic pride. The rivalry between Uaxactun and Tikal was resolved in AD 378 by means of a new kind of conflict, the one called the Tlaloc-Venus war, or sometimes just "Star Wars." The imagery and method was borrowed from the Teotihuacan civilization; with it came the new idea of conquest and submission of another city-state. The commemoration of the victory of Tikal appears on Uaxactun stela 5. There we find represented the first Tlaloc-Venus costume. It has a balloon shaped headdress and a spear thrower, quite a different costume from any other early Maya. The costume became the norm for the conqueror king. This new symbolism was borrowed from Teotihuacan, whose emissaries reached these areas at this time. Furthermore, other artistic elements appear directly influenced from Teotihuacan. Such is the case for the famous *lechuza y armas* (owl and weapons) symbol that is very common in Teotihuacan iconography (figure 4). It appears for example in the circular medallions worn on the collars of warrior figurines. It may have been the symbol of a warrior order similar to the later Eagle and Jaguar knights of the Aztecs.[38] Evidence of a Teotihuacan presence has surfaced in a cache in Tikal that includes what seems to be the remains of Teotihuacan residents of very high rank.[39] Other changes in sculpture and architecture followed the introduction of Venus-Tlaloc warfare. The markers that appear in the ball courts at this stage are not the typical early Classic markers. Rather they resemble motifs pictured in the murals of the Tlalocan in Teotihuacan. Until the fourth century AD, the Maya were constructing specialized observatories—such as the so-called Group E structures—for the observation of the sun. In Tikal, there is evidence that twin-pyramid groups replaced the Group E structures.[40]

Additional evidence in the written historical record of stelae, elicited through the work of David Stuart, supports the externalist thesis. The written record shows the appearance of a dynastic disruption. The new ruler coming to power in AD 378 appears as a Teotihuacano, and his father appears to be other than the previous king—to all appearances a foreigner.[41] A stone monument—reminiscent of feather-adorned ball court markers of Central Mexico (which did not exist in Teotihuacan!)—commemorates the arrival of Fire is Born in the year 378. This individual is mentioned as the envoy of a mysterious ruler, Spear-thrower Owl. The medallion at the top of the marker depicts an owl with the *atlatl* (spear-thrower). The motif corresponds once again to the *lechuza y armas* motif of Teotihuacan origin. Monuments predating the king in question were destroyed. In summary, Stuart concludes, the disruption to the monarchic succession was caused in a violent manner by the arrival of warriors from Teotihuacan in AD 378.

In Waka (El Peru) the local ruler Sun-faced Jaguar cemented an alliance with Fire is Born that resulted in the erection of a fire shrine sheltering the flame coming from Teotihuacan. This amounted to the recognition of the Fire God, the ultimate goal of Teotihuacan occupation.

After adopting this new cosmology, the Maya started timing their battles with the cycle of Venus and stationary points of Saturn and Jupiter. The new kind of war stripped the people not only of their king but also of their "portal," their contact with their ancestors. Mayan society was completely transformed. Up to that time there had been a coexistence of independent city-states. Beginning in the fifth century, Tikal gradually transformed into a Mayan superpower by forming alliances with cities down the Pasion River Valley up to Copan (present day Honduras). In the Campeche lowlands, the city of Calakmul rose to prominence in the sixth century and gradually became Tikal's bitter rival by enlisting allies throughout the Peten region, the Yucatan, and east to what is now Belize.

In 562 the new power defeated Tikal, although without subjugating it. Tikal recovered, and, less than twenty years later, eventually avenged itself over its archrival, which subsequently faltered. However, no clear winner emerged and Tikal suffered from the continuous state of war. The rivalry between the two split the Mayan world and has been equated to the Cold War of twentieth century.

Over time the warfare between the two cities brought all fortunes down. The population plummeted drastically. Artistic work decreased and so did hieroglyphic writing and the public recording of dates in Long Count. In Tikal the last recorded monument bears the date of AD 869.

That this was not a strictly Mayan/Toltec war of influence—rather a Solar/Venusian cultural war—is highlighted by other factors. Mayan Venus iconography traveled back to the Anahuac. In Cacaxtla and Xochicalco, in the Mexican high plateau, one can see the Mayan version of the Venus-Tlaloc complex.[42] In some places the Maya strove to regain their previous cultural hegemony. Let us see how this came to expression in Palenque, in a late attempt to offer a cultural revival to a dying culture.

Palenque Dynasty[43]

In Palenque efforts to revive traditional Mayan values are visible, particularly in the monarchy; however, these are also inextricably linked with Venus-Tlaloc symbolism. In the city Lord Chan-Bahlum (Snake-Jaguar) was crowned on January 10, AD 962. His Father Pacal (Shield) preceded him. These two kings of the late Classic brought an impulse of late renewal to the dynasty. They added monuments with daring innovative elements to the Mayan architecture, for example the famous Temple of the Inscriptions, Temple of the Cross, Temple of the Foliated Cross, and Temple of the Sun. These are the most expressive testimonies of Mayan cosmovision. However, they are part of a late effort to justify the charisma and power of kings at a time of decline. In Palenque we see the attempt to justify the king's rule through matrilineal rather than patrilineal descent. It was a successful short-term effort toward "creative mythology," at a time in which Mayan ideology was irretrievably tainted with the Toltec.

Pacal began this effort with the construction of the Temple of the Inscriptions. He had inherited the throne from his mother's side in violation of the patrilineal norm. Lady Kanal-Ikal (grandmother) and Lady Zac-Kuk were the only known women to have ruled as "kings," creating a serious ideological controversy for their descendents that Pacal set out to justify. Pacal was trying to establish an indisputable base for the acceptance of his and his successors' rule. He did this by linking astrological terms and dates, the lives of his ancestors, and the lives of the gods—in particular First Mother and First Father. In this new mythology the mother, Zac-Kuk, was equated with First Mother. Pacal was then the gods' offspring. Chan Bahlum, his successor, worked on the Temple of the Cross, the Temple of the Foliated Cross, and the Temple of the Sun, which all rise from the summit of pyramids. The Maya thought of their pyramids and temples as living mountains. Moving into the inner space of the temple, the king entered from the sacred mountain into the underworld where he would commune with the realm of Xibalba and with his ancestors. There he would hazard the perils of hell as his ancestors the Hero Twins had done. This journey of transformation is shown in the Temples. Chan Bahlum represents himself in the Temple of the Foliated Cross and in the Temple of the Sun as a large figure meeting with a smaller personage in the underworld. In Mayan convention, the larger figure was the ruling king communing in Xibalba with his father, a guarantee of the fact that power had been passed on from father to son.

The war-related imagery—warriors, captives, spears, bleeding jaguar heads, and dragons—continues in the Temple of the Sun, where the sun is represented as a Sun Jaguar shield with crossed spears and a throne with bleeding jaguar heads and bleeding dragons. The king holds the square shield of the Tlaloc/Venus warrior: thus he is the one who offers the gods both his own blood and the blood of captives.

The Temple of the Cross records the birth of First Mother and First Father, linking the dynasty with the primordial beginnings. This was done by linking the same date days of a cosmic cycle. The qualities of one were resumed in the other. By linking the birth, accession to power, and other significant biographical dates of the life of a king with the dates of cosmic events, the power of these events was re-actualized and made alive by the king himself. The king was not simply enlivened by this power; he actually embodied and retained these qualities beyond that point in time. He was therefore reborn as a god. Thus the linking with Zac-Kuk and First Mother served to justify a departure from the patrilineal line of descent by hearkening back to the time of Creation. It was a reenactment of it, a new Creation. Chan-Bahlum went further by linking himself with a supposed distant ancestor, the founder of the dynasty: Bahlum-Kuk, born in 993 BC and crowned on March 28, 967 BC.

Thus, he linked himself not with the time of the Dawning but with the Olmecs. Through the two kings a Mayan revival appeared in a curious blend of Mayan individualism and Venus military overtones. It was Mayan to the extent that it glorified a personal king but Venus/Teotihuacan-oriented in its symbolism. Palenque stands as a fitting archetype of Mayan promotion of over-individualism, when we compare it with the anonymity of the later Chichen Itza impulse. Nevertheless, such a strategy could hardly stall the fate of Maya civilization.

The Mayan Decline

The fall of the Maya of the Peten has long been considered an unsettled question. At presents we are able to fill in parts of the puzzle. Few dynasties lasted into the ninth century. Yet some states endured and grew in the northern end of the Yucatan.

Modern research has found patterns of changes during the Terminal Classic or Post-Classic sweeping from the southwest to the northeast, from the late 8th to the 10th centuries.[44] Patterns of political fragmentation, loss of political authority, and decrease of population (or influx of immigrants) moved from west to east and south to north. Rapid changes in cultural patterns were most pronounced in the western Peten. What suddenly collapsed was the kind of kingship that had been the hallmark of Mayan civilization. New forms of power emerged in its wake.

In the western Peten, changes cannot be attributed to population pressure or ecological disruption. Instead more was due to the strain of city antagonism that intensified after AD 600 and reached a culmination in AD 760, leading to a time of continual warfare, population migrating out, and the cessation of monumental art. Between AD 760 and 830 we see the abandonment of major centers and the building of fortified villages on hilltops. Centers like Palenque and Piedras Negras lost their prestige and imploded after their lords were defeated or captured by rival lords. Loss of authority of the lords undermined the belief that the ruler was in contact with the ancestors and the gods. Cities were rapidly abandoned and the political system never returned.

In the central and far northern Peten, the end of the Classic Period was more gradual. Here loss of political authority went hand in hand with a decline in monumental activity and decrease in population by AD 830–850. Southern Campeche and Calaxmul had been declining since the early 8th century. Calaxmul suffered great loss of population, and plummeted down to 10% of its original levels (late 7th century) by AD 850. This area seems to also have been affected by climate change and drought.

Contrary to the above areas, the period between AD 750 and 1100 is a period of great growth in northern Yucatan. The Puuc centers emerged in the mid 8th century. They likely incorporated Quetzalcoatl cults in their art and rituals and introduced new political structures—such as councils of lineage heads (*multepal*)—which became characteristic of Post-Classic states. This became even more prominent under the following kingdom of Chichen Itza. Puuc centers declined mostly in relation to the rise of Chichen Itza, which became the center of new cults and pilgrimage, thus outliving its rivals. These battles for supremacy were won with "rituals of termination," through which the city was ceremonially desecrated.

This pattern of ritual desecration had been inaugurated earlier among the Maya and may have been one of the final blows received by the city-state. In the summer of 2005, A. Demarest found evidence of a burial of Mayan nobles in the ancient city of Cancuen.[45] Fifty men, women, and children of the nobility were decapitated by pulling the head back and pushing a large spear through the chest into the spine. Many of these bodies were remarkably well preserved in the waters of a pool fed by a spring, and were recognizable by their jewelry. Others, such as the king and queen, were buried in shallow graves next to the pool. The royal couple was buried with their robes and adornments, their jade jewelry, necklaces of jaguar fangs, and rare shells. The king, Kan Maax, was recognizable through the necklace bearing his name and title, making it possible to identify the events to a date of around AD 800. By murdering the elite, placing their broken bodies in the ceremonial waters and methodically destroying palaces and monuments, Dr. Demarest speculated that the conquerors were "killing the city ritually." This is further confirmed by the invaders' defacing of all carved figures on Cancuen's monuments. The statues were toppled, face down.

This massacre could have been perpetrated by a neighboring tribe of the highlands, Demarest hypothesizes. The extermination of a vanquished royal family and nobility was a unique precedent in Mayan warfare in the Classic period. The death of the king and nobility spelled the end of the life of the trading city and had economic repercussions throughout the region. Within ten years of Cancuén's fall and abandonment, the same fate followed for the other cities on the Pasion River, with the exception of Seibal.

This is yet another example of how the Mayan decline was triggered in a particular instance. However, the particular modality does not alter the fundamental premise of the decline of the institution of the kingship and the demise of the cultural fruits of the Mayan Fourth Age, which led to the particular form of events in an unavoidable fashion. Cultural decline preceded physical decline.

Figure 5: Old God

Old themes, like the bound captive at the feet of the king, returned. Eventually the themes evolved toward further gruesomeness. The so-called Decapitator God appears in close association with the Tlaloc/Venus war symbolism. He has a trifurcated blade over his eye and he sits over a stool of human leg bones. In his hands he holds a severed human head. He is also called the Old God (figure 5).[46]

The end of the Classical period was often abrupt. It came through a humiliating defeat of the king or when the people turned their backs to the king. The complex swamp agricultural systems were neglected and nothing could be done to them in time of war. For that, the stability of a central government was necessary. It was in a larger sense a crisis of faith. By this time the Maya stopped building pyramids and stelae. Literacy and art continuously degraded. Writing in effect could not survive without the monarchy.

The movement of cultural decline, generalized throughout Mayan kingdoms, is most likely the cause of the demise of the whole civilization. Its survival in the Yucatan required a complete new cultural dimension, as we will see.

Chichen Itza

Yucatan saw the rise of the first large-scale empire, a new development among the Maya. By the end of the 8th century, a group of seafaring people held a series of strategic strongholds along the coast of Yucatan. These were the people called the Itzá, to whom the Chilam Balam refers. Eventually these merchant warriors established a permanent harbor in Isla Cerritos, north of the mouth of Rio Lagartos. After fighting the kingdoms of Cobá and Puuc, they eventually founded their capital in Chichen Itza, directly south but at some distance from Isla Cerritos. For a few centuries they ruled the north without rivals.

Chichen Itza ushered in a cultural revolution. From the beginning they used both Mayan and Mexican forms of expression. In fact at the beginning they also used Mayan hieroglyphic texts. However, after that they hardly used the written word and the stelae. Written history of the city covers a very short period. The earliest date is AD 867.[47] Chichen Itzá's texts also have a limited scope. They do not refer to the life of the ruler. Some of the texts refer to generations of siblings from matrilineal descent with no clear reference of rank among them. Their focus is upon rituals of dedication carried by groups of lords. One of the prominent images is of the bird that carves the chest of the victim to extract its heart, and the serpent that rises above the sacrifice.

Native chronicles of the Itzá indicate that they were ruled by groups of brothers, a brotherhood of princes. Likewise, bas-relief art in Chichen Itza mostly portrays large groups of people with no clearly individual leaders. Remarkable examples of these works are the Northwest Colonnade and the Temple of the Warriors, which for the most part portray warriors using the weapons of the Tlaloc warfare. In addition to the warriors, sorcerers or priests are depicted. There is also an intimidating Old Matriarch, probably a representative of the Moon Goddess. The prisoners are not stripped and humiliated as in the Southern Kingdoms. They are dressed in ways that differ little from their captors. The winners are as clearly Mayan as the losers.

The Maya of Chichen Itza did not attempt to portray individually the ruler sitting on the throne. The nobles all sit upon jaguar thrones. In the

Great Ball Court we see many figures of the characters known as Captain Sun Disk and Captain Serpent (figure 6). It appears that the insignia of these captains pertained to groups of people, not to any given individual. There are even captive captains, indicating that this was not exclusive to Chichen Itza. Enigmatically, the Itza constructed an empire without kings. In this however, they continued the earlier tradition of Teotihuacan. The kingship was displaced into objects and symbols, like the dead king sitting on a sun disk. Friedel and Schele conclude that Captain Sun Disk served as the image of the ancestral king presiding as a spirit.[48] There are clear references to heart sacrifices performed by warriors dressed as birds, possible members of the Eagle Order that we will find again in Aztec times. Others portray sacrifice by decapitation and by arrows. The ball court was used for sacrifice by decapitation and heads were collected on skull racks.

Figure 6: Captain Sun Disk (above), Captain Serpent (below)

At this point Quetzalcoatl, more than an instrument of communication with the other world, seems to become a symbol of the divinity of the state. It remained the object of the cult of Mayan-Toltec nobility until the Conquest. Chichen Itza was thus the capital of a kingdom without history. It had turned its back on the whole Mayan tradition of centuries and reverted to the matriarchy of the Third Age, with the added element of anonymity.

Another confirmation of the return to Teotihuacan tradition is the High Priest's Grave, a massive four-sided pyramid with feathered serpent balustrades. Interestingly, it was built over a cave like the Pyramid of the Sun in Teotihuacan, reinstating the Toltec theme of the cave as the place of origin.

What we have seen primarily through the evolution of Quetzalcoatl is the fact that a deity can evolve over time. Spiritual science teaches us that when evolution takes a further step forward, earlier spiritual beings acquire a regressive quality or are displaced by other opposing beings. This is also the nature of the changes undergone by Tlaloc, from agrarian to war deity. It is even clearer in the replacement of the solar deity Hunahpu with the Venus deity Quetzalcoatl.

Chichen Itza became heavily dependent on tribute or predation of its neighbors. With the decline of their neighbors, their own economy was heavily restricted and entered its terminal phase between AD 1050 and 1100.[49]

Conclusions

The archaeological record confirms at least the tendencies that the Popol Vuh has underlined. Human sacrifice was not practiced in the early days of Teotihuacan civilization. It reappeared in stages and in secretive fashion. Even though the dedication of the Temple of the Feathered Serpent sacrificed close to two hundred victims, this was a unique episode. The precedent was suppressed and the temple buried under a successive structure. The Popol Vuh's assertion that the priests had to hide their practices and abduct victims for their practices finds confirmation as well. In stages, the ideology of sacrifice was accepted more and more, and Teotihuacan became a militaristic regime. However, only occasionally do clear references to human sacrifice appear in Teotihuacan art. Official ideology did not glorify its practices as the later Chichen Itza and Aztecs did. Even at the time of Tula, human sacrifice was still resisted; witness the historical opposition of Topiltzin Quetzalcoatl.

Events take a decisive turn with the founding of the League of Mayapan and the rise of Chichen Itza. Here it seems that human sacrifice returns in strength, this time with the addition of heart sacrifice. This rising ideology will culminate in Aztec time.

While Toltec ideology rose, the Maya followed a descending curve. Teotihuacan influence played out into Mayan kingdoms with alternate fortunes. The Maya absorbed Toltec Venus ideology and often blended it into their own heritage, giving rise to hybrid forms of ideology. The contrast between Palenque and Chichen Itza best illustrates two extreme tendencies. Palenque's dynasty partly espoused Venus war symbolism, but it did so with an elaborate mythology legitimizing and exalting the monarch as the embodiment of the gods and linking the dynasty with all of Mayan history. It did so through resorting to all the wealth of Mayan astronomical knowledge. This was obviously a short-lived attempt, because the Mayan monarchy could only survive as a whole civilization uniting city-states. No single city could survive on its own. Nor could the fruits of the civilization—such as writing—survive in isolation. By the ninth and tenth centuries decline had reached most of Mayan civilization.

Chichen Itza's survival strategy was far more long-lived. In it we see the polar opposite of Palenque. The monarchs return to be the brothers of the same matrilineal families. There is no individual ruler, just as there was not one in Teotihuacan's long history. In fact, to some degree this is a return to the collective and anonymous social organization of the Second Age.

The gods seem to have a much more direct influence on Chichen Itza's ideology than do any single individuals. In the city the role played by the Fire God reaches new heights. It seems that here were introduced many new elements, like human sacrifice with heart removal. If we look at Chichen Itza from an evolutionary standpoint we see a movement of return to the consciousness of the early Atlantean times before its fourth epoch. This was the time preceding the intimations of ego-consciousness in which the individual felt its real being was held in the reality of the spiritual world and that the latter was more real than the world of the senses. Now, in a regressive way the individual lost himself in the dictates of a Fire God that deprived him of freedom, denied him access to the idea of immortality, and extolled the heavy price of heart sacrifice. It is not surprising that Chichen Itza's attempt at preserving Mayan writing was so short-lived. In Chichen Itza historical consciousness was not present.

Just as we saw that Mayan civilization ushered in the inauguration of the Semi-New Mysteries, Chichen Itza marked the return to the Semi-Old Mysteries. However, atavistic consciousness could no longer be achieved other than through regressive methods, such as blood-letting and human sacrifice. It was only in the blood that the Toltecs could achieve union with the sphere of revelation, and only in a regressive way. The stage was thus set for the intensification and new stage reached by the Aztecs. We will look at Aztec cosmology in contrast to the Iroquois worldview that arose to the north.

The Aztec Tribal God is Huitzilopochtli; the Iroquois initiate bringing complete renewal of his society is Deganawidah. Each of them is the fruit of a miraculous birth from a virgin. Both of them are civilizing heroes. The parallels between Aztecs and Iroquois go a step further. Both man-gods set the stage for consolidation of political power and formation of large political entities in the fifteenth century.

The Aztecs called their initial federation the Triple Alliance; the Iroquois formed the famous League of Five Nations (later, Six Nations). However, here the similarities stop and a gulf opens between the Aztec and Iroquois worldviews. Let us become acquainted with Aztec and Iroquois history and immerse ourselves in their respective worldviews. The Aztecs and Iroquois are representatives of completely new spiritual impulses that affected the whole of North and Central America. At the time of the Iroquois and Aztecs—the time leading to the development of the Consciousness Soul in Europe—South America witnessed the significant rise of the new civilization and empire of the Incas.[49]

CHAPTER 2

THE AZTECS

T HE POPOL VUH'S NARRATIVE reaches to the time of the Conquest, but it diverges from the part of history that we want to follow now. The Popol Vuh laid the basis for our understanding of Mayan and Toltec civilizations. We will further analyze in this chapter how the impulse that the Toltecs had set in motion evolved and underwent qualitative changes under the Aztecs. While doing so, the Aztecs took care to keep intact the links with Soconusco/Izapan traditions. These appear in the mythology, in the celebrations of the course of the year, in the dual worship of agrarian god and tribal god, and in the recognition of the initiate issued from a virgin birth. And yet the meaning of Popol Vuh Parts I and II completely changed in the process of adoption by Aztec culture. In North America, the Iroquois carried further the impulses of the time of Christ in a manner that does not seem apparently linked to the odyssey of the Twins. It takes a further analysis to discern those elements.

The analysis of Mesoamerican history has often been determined by comparisons between the contents of mythologies of successive civilizations. The meaning of a symbol or the relevance of a god is established by putting side-by-side Olmec material with Mayan, Toltec, and Aztec equivalents. Implied or assumed is the reasoning that the same god meant the same thing to different peoples at the distance of fifteen or more centuries. In terms of European history it would correspond to trying to understand who the Christ was from the historical documents of the first Christians, the ideas of the Reformation, the derivations of all the sects and heresies, and the records of the Inquisition. It is easy to come to the conclusion in this second instance that this would be an absurdity, especially since at times different groups fought each other to the death in the name of the Christ: suffice to think of the Third Crusade that the Catholic Church undertook against the Cathars. The situation is analogous in the Americas. Only the same civilization or two civilizations close in time and culture can furnish us with unequivocal conclusions about spiritual interpretations of the same deity. We have seen that even this must be done with caution; witness the radical spiritual transformation that occurred between Olmecs and Maya in the space of a century.

It was Girard's innovation to add to historical analysis the moral element of comparison. Few other researchers have taken this path, and none could see clearly through such a controversial matter without clear guidelines. In the absence of such guidelines it may be easier and more objective to cling to scientific "moral neutrality." Girard could lead us into an analysis of the moral question because he saw that even though different societies made different moral choices, they took care to provide a justification in doctrinal and cultural precedents. The Aztecs were no exception.

Notwithstanding Girard's Mayan pride that led him to minimize Mayan shortcomings, his approach is still valid. We will follow a similar path to his and point to the changes that have been introduced through time in the practices deriving from the same spiritual background. We will describe how this phenomenon occurred historically, how it was accompanied with the new imaginative material of myths and legends, and what cultural conditions made the changes possible.

War, Conquest, and Human Sacrifice

The Aztecs were first known as Mexica. Like many other nomad Nahua populations they came to the high plateau of the Anahuac of present day Mexico City from the north. They were the fruit of the continuing immigration that flowed to North America through the Bering Strait, and that we have qualified as post-Atlantean. They arrived at Tula in the year 1165 and later moved to Culhuacan where the ruler, Achitometl, allowed them to settle in the lands of Tizapan, provided they paid him tribute of canoes, labor, and mercenaries. Achitometl also gave them in marriage his daughter who could claim Toltec descent. For reasons that history ignores the Aztecs sacrificed the daughter and the Culhuacanos forced them to take refuge on the island of the lake Texcoco. There, Tenochtitlan was founded in 1325.

In Tenochtitlan the Aztecs were dominated by the Tepanecs, who similarly requested a tribute. A later ruler, Tezozomoc, doubled the amount of tribute. Already strained relations reached a breaking point when the Aztecs asked Maxtla, the son of Tezozomoc, permission to build a stone aqueduct. His refusal brought about an insurrection and the Aztecs, led by Izcoatl, defeated the Tepanecs in 1428. In order to do this they had allied with Texcoco and Tlacopan. In retaliation the Tepanecs now needed to pay a tribute of labor, land, and products to the Aztecs and their allies and they were not allowed to choose their own leader. The year 1428 is the turning point of Aztec rule.

The year 1428 is a pivotal date for Mesoamerican and indeed for American history. It marks the beginning of the Aztec Empire. We can now look closer at this single event of the formation of the Triple Alliance and its consequences. The momentous step of 1428 had probably been prepared for many years before. The ruler of the Alliance—the Tlaotani—was chosen by a council of warriors and priests, the so-called "Council of Four." What counted most were his military abilities and other religious criteria, not just heredity. Behind the figure of Izcoatl, the first ruler, stands tall the figure of Tlaclael, the highest priest.

Aztec society achieved a particular form of state in which religious, military, political, and economic functions were intimately connected with each other. The education of the priesthood and of the commoner was firmly held by the state. However, the keystone of the imperial social architecture laid a step above the simple concentration of all the functions of society under the hands of the state. Many city-states had already attempted such preliminary steps but none had set in place the possibility of empire, apart from Chichen Itza.

What made the Aztec state unique were the sweeping reforms introduced in 1428. In that year, Izcoatl—under what many see as the instigation of Tlaclael—burned all the earlier codices, the religious and historical documents. The justification for this act is offered in the Aztec migration myth originally published in *General History of the Things of New Spain,* Book 10, with the following words: "The history of it [the book] was saved, but it was burned when Izcoatl ruled in Mexico. A council of rulers of Mexico took place. They said: 'It is not necessary for all the common people to know of the writings; government will be defamed, and this will only spread sorcery in the land; for it containeth many falsehoods.'"[1] According to the native Tezozomoc and the Spanish Duran, Tlaclael was the man on whom power rested, rather than on the emperor.[2] He outlived three successive rulers who were either brothers or cousins.

An earlier custom had already been adopted of rewriting history through what some authors call "creative mythography." We saw it at work in the dynasty of Palenque. The legitimization of political authority through Toltec blood was the simplest example of such mythography. It allowed the justification of an uninterrupted spiritual legacy through physical descent. The rewriting of history is also achieved in myths and legends. The Aztecs did this by emphasizing their continuity with Teotihuacan, which the Aztecs imagined built by the gods (City of the Gods is the meaning of the Aztec word Teotihuacan) or by a race of giants. The city legitimized their continuity with primeval times through the legend of the Fifth Sun, as we will see later.

Aztec society was very stratified. The top of the pyramid was occupied by the nobility, in large part composed of the best warriors, the priesthood, and the *pochteca*, the equivalent of state merchants conducting foreign trade. Of particular interest to the present context is the training of warriors. Beginning in their adolescent years they were instructed to take captives and not to kill their enemies. One of the earliest requirements put on the young fighter was not to assist a companion in difficulty. Having proven his valor, the warrior accumulated civil responsibilities and functions of a more cultural nature, like the administration of schools. He was also given privileges, such as tax exoneration and the right to keep concubines. The commoner who offered many captives for human sacrifice could climb the social ladder.

Aztec economy was heavily dependent upon the tribute levied on the subjugated populations. The tribute supported a growing section of administrative professions, bureaucrats, soldiers, nobles, and priests. In time Aztec society grew top-heavy, leading to an endless cycle of war and conquest. Here is how the war was characterized from Aztec sources in the dialogue between Tlaclael and Moctezuma I: "Our god will feed himself with them [prisoners] as though he were eating warm tortillas, soft and tasty, straight out of the oven....And this war should be of such a nature that we do not endeavor to destroy the others totally. War must always continue, so that each time and whenever we wish and our god wishes to eat and feast, we may go there as one who goes to the market to buy something to eat...organized to obtain victims to offer our god Huitzilopochtli..."[3] The need for sacrificial captives and tribute for the nobility created the urge for more and more war campaigns. This obliged the armies to move farther and farther from the capital. The expansion met with logistical limits, both in depressed areas that could not provide a sizeable tribute, and in regions too far removed from the capital. The overly centralized state had become an obstacle to the desired imperialistic expansion.

Human Sacrifice

War's main purpose was the capture of sacrificial victims. Human sacrifice had returned and intensified in Aztec culture. This does not contradict Steiner's assertion that the power of the decadent Mexican Mysteries had been broken as far as the fourth post-Atlantean age was concerned. We must remember that Steiner referred to a particular form of human sacrifice, the one involving organ removal from a live victim with the consequent knowledge wrought by the priest. The appropriation of this knowledge was achieved most likely by Chichen Itza's priesthood. The Aztecs came to power in 1428, a few years after the symbolic beginning date of the fifth post-Atlantean age, the age of the Consciousness Soul, that Steiner places in 1413. As in the political sphere, Tlaclael had introduced sweeping changes in the religious/spiritual sphere.

The Toltecs had reintroduced the practice of human sacrifice, even the new sacrifice by removal of the heart. The year 1428 is once again a watershed date. What had been a practice limited to the order of the hundreds reached the historic heights of an estimated fifteen thousand sacrificial victims per year under the Aztecs. The dedication of the Temple of Tenochtitlan alone apparently required the death of more than ten thousand victims in four days.[4] Most important of all was the generalization of human sacrifice through removal of the heart from a live victim. This innovation also finds justification in the new mythology introduced by Tlaclael. A specific political structure existed on the basis of a particular worldview that supported it. We will now have a look at the imaginative contents of Aztec myth and legend and characterize them in relation to the Popol Vuh, with which Aztec tradition emphatically claims continuity.

Aztec Myth and the Rise of Huitzilopochtli

Huitzilopochtli is the man-become-god who accompanies the Aztecs in the mythical migration from Aztlan to Tenochtitlan. Let us now examine the myth of his virgin birth. The entire version is included in appendix 2.

The god is born on the hill of Coatepec, "Hill of Serpents." A woman by the name of Coatlicue is the mother of the Four Hundred Boys of the

South, known as Centzon Huitznahuac, and of their sister Coyolxauhqui. While she is doing penance in Coatepec, a ball of fine feathers falls on Coatlicue, which she picks up and places on her bosom. Consequently she is impregnated by a divine being. The Boys of the South believe that she has been dishonored and decide to put her to death. One of the gods, whose name is Cuauhuitlicac, reveals the plot to Huitzilopochtli, who is already communicating with his mother in the womb. Soon after birth, Huitzilopochtli puts on armor and gear and fights his opponents. His first victim is Coyolxauhqui whose head he severs with a "serpent of fire." Her body falls down the hill and is dismembered. Soon after, Huitzilopochtli pursues the Centzon Huiznahuac and annihilates them. Only a few, who escape the massacre, find their way to the south. The initial ferocity of the Four Hundred Boys is no match for the man-god. This is what the text says about the killing of the Four Hundred Boys: "The great warrior did more than defeat them…he obliterated their destiny…he introduced them into his destiny, he made them his own insignia." Huitzilopochtli wants to blot out their whole being, not just their bodies.

We can recognize some of the elements of the Popol Vuh in Huitzilopochtli's myth, as well as some major differences. The maiden is no longer impregnated by the Tau-drop of water but by the feather, a shift toward the air element. The Aztec hero is born full-grown: he requires no development. It is interesting to compare Hunahpu's deed with that of Huitzilopochtli. The Mayan solar god does away with human sacrifice. Human sacrifice, aptly described by Coyolxauhqui's dismemberment, is Huitzilopochtli's first act of life. In fact, Huitzilopochtli is a functional replica of the giant Zipacna of the Popol Vuh in the corresponding episode with the Four Hundred Boys. The myth has two different elements from the Popol Vuh, re-arranged and meshed together. The birth is the same as the Twins' birth; the deed is the same as is accomplished by Zipacna, the hero of the First Age, when he buries the Four Hundred Boys under their house.

The Aztec migration myth completes the justification for heart sacrifice. Ceremonial flaying and heart sacrifice appear in it as historical precedents. Heart sacrifice is first performed on Copil, a great sorcerer and son of the patron deity's sister, Malinalxoch. The text specifies: "They pursued each other with cunning and they captured Copil in Tepetzinco. When he was dead Huitzilopochtli cut off his head and slashed open his chest, he tore out his heart." Further in the text comes the flaying of the daughter of Achitometl, whom the Chichimec king of Culhuacan had previously given in marriage to the Mexica. The text sets the precedent for later ceremonies. It says, "Then Huitzilopochtli spoke...he said to them, 'O my fathers, I order you to slay the daughter of Achitometl and to flay her. When you have flayed her, you are to dress a priest in her skin.'"[5]

We will complete this review of mythological references with the myth of the creation of the sun and the moon. This is what the Aztecs call the "Birth of the Fifth Sun." Continuity with the tradition of the Popol Vuh is made manifest from the onset: "It is told that when yet all was in darkness, when yet no sun had shone and no dawn [Dawning] had broken—it is said—the gods gathered themselves together and took counsel among themselves there at Teotihuacan." The gods are awaiting the Dawning that will only come about if some of them will sacrifice themselves. Two of them—Tecuciztecatl and Nanauatzin—offer themselves by casting themselves into the fire. The eagle and the ocelot follow them. They do not die but are blackened by the flames. The two gods rise again in the heavens, Nanauatzin as the sun, Tecuciztecatl as the moon. This too is a familiar theme from the Popol Vuh, a parallel to the apotheosis of the Twins. Soon after, sun and moon stop on their path—at the time of the winter solstice— and all the gods decide to sacrifice themselves. It is the wind-god, Ecatl, who slays them and blows with strength in order to set the sun in motion.

The Fifth Sun is born in Teotihuacan. The Aztec myth therefore claims continuity with Toltec tradition. It is now clear that the Aztecs continued Toltec worldviews and pushed them to farther consequences. The Aztec Fifth Sun occurs immediately after the Fourth Sun of the Dawning. Nanauatzin is the Nahua version of the name Nanauac, given to Hunahpu by the Maya.[6] In this myth too, as in the myth of Huitzilopochtli and in the migration myth, there is an escalation of sacrifice until "all the gods died when the sun came into being."

Finally the mention of the ocelot and the eagle indicates the future importance of the Jaguar and Eagle knights. The text shows it thus: "From this event, [plunging into the fire] it is said, they took—from here was taken—the custom whereby was called and named one who was valiant, a warrior. The word quauhtli came first, it is told, because, as was said, the eagle first entered the fire. And the ocelot followed thereafter: thus it is said in one word—quauhtlocelotl because the latter fell into the fire after the eagle."

Aztec mythology shows a link with the traditions of the Popol Vuh. The written record also helps to shed some light on the element of continuity and escalation between Toltec and Aztec practices. We will now look at the place of ritual in Aztec life with an eye to similarities and differences with the traditions of the Popol Vuh.

Aztec Gods and Ritual

Early Mayan ritual, as it derived from the Popol Vuh, instituted the two parts of the year: the time of the sacred calendar, and the time of the civil year, with the corresponding cults of the agrarian god and of the solar god. According to the Spanish monk, Sahagun, the Aztecs maintained this division of the year and of the priesthood. The agrarian cult was called *Telpoch-calli*, the tribal cult *Calmenac*. In the Telpochcalli the priests worked, ate, and slept together. The pupils of the Calmenac went on the paths alone and slept alone.[7] This is confirmed by other sources. Tlaloc's rites were performed at night and the sacrifices occurred at midnight or before dawn. Huitzilopochtli ruled over the dry season, Tlaloc over the rainy season.[8] All of this faithfully reflects early Mayan tradition.

Aztec ritual modified old practices of the sacred calendar according to the new worldview. The odyssey of the maize received a new interpretation. What follows are examples of sacrifices and their relation to the cycle of maize and the deeds of the gods. The gestation of the young maize within the mother earth is performed in Aztec ritual with the flaying of a female victim whose skin envelops a young man. This represents the skin of the earth goddess Teteoinan or Toci enveloping Xipe, the young maize god. Girard sees a parallel of it in Mayan stelae where the young god is enveloped by a jaguar skin or emerges from the jaws of a jaguar. In another feast of Toci, called "Heart of Earth," earthly sexual intercourse was represented by impaled victims. The "Fiesta de los Elotes" (Festival of the New Maize) was celebrated by sacrificing a woman who represented Xilonen (maize at the stage of the young cob). The victim was decapitated on top of a pyramid and her heart removed.[9] Other sacrificial victims were thrown into the fire, thrown into the whirlpool of the lagoon of Pantitlan and drowned, locked up in caves, hurled from heights, strangled, entombed and starved, or given up to unequal gladiatorial combat. Finally many sacrifices were followed by ritual cannibalism. The sacrifices were just one part of Aztec blood offerings. All the population had to participate in some form of self-sacrifice or bloodletting envisioned as a penitential act. The thorns of the succulent plant, maguey, were used to draw blood from the earlobes. In other ways, blood was drawn from the tongue, ears, genitals, and other parts of the body.

A whole mystique surrounded human sacrifice that we will analyze here, since it allows us to penetrate the deeper essence of the practice. David Carrasco indicates: "Blood was called chalchiuh-atl (precious water). Human hearts were likened to fine burnished turquoise, and war was teoatl tlachinolli (divine liquid and burned things). War was the place 'where the jaguars roar, where feathered war bonnets heave about like foam in the waves.' Death on the battlefield was called xochimiquitzli (the flowery death)."[10] "Do not fear my heart! In the midst of the plain my heart craves death by the obsidian edge. Only this my heart craves: death in war..." wrote a Nahua poet.[11] A whole worldview emerges even just from these definitions. The relationships between gods and human beings stand at the opposite end of the idea of co-creation that we have brought forth among the Maya, most particularly the one that emerges from the pages of the Popol Vuh. Thus it is no surprise that blood offerings were called *nextlasoalioia* (payment of debt) or *nextlanlli* (debt paid).

In many sacrifices the victim itself was given the role of *ixiptla* or deity impersonator. Let us look at the example of the ritual performed at the end of the month of Toxcatl (May 4 to 23). The ceremonies were performed in expectation of the rainy season. The required impersonator of the deity Tezcatlipoca, chosen long ahead of time, was a young man as physically perfect as possible. His training required flute playing, speech, and flower carrying. During the last month, the *ixiptla* was given four young wives who symbolized fertility goddesses. The marriage represented the coming period of the earth's fertility, following the long period of drought.[12] Impersonators led a special life previous to their death. A whole mystique also surrounded the rapport between victim and executioner. Although referring to earlier forms of sacrifice, D. Gillette points out that the sacrificed enemy kings or nobles were considered like brothers of the victorious lords. The victims were said to be divine protectors of those who sent them to their death.[13] Human sacrifice could be made appealing to the victims themselves by inducing in them the illusion of the exalted role they performed or coaxing them with privileges that engendered tendencies toward escapism. In effect, what was instilled in them was the premature desire to leave the earth.

The examples of human sacrifice given earlier demonstrate that the rituals reconnected with the past. Although the forms were totally new, ceremonial life hearkened back to a common source, that of the Tzolkin and the Popol Vuh. The sacred calendar of 260 days was now called the

Tonalpohualli. It was used only as the dynamic calendar in conjunction with the year of 365 days. However some aspects of the static Tzolkin seem to have survived in time. A confirmation of this also comes from Aztec astronomy. Not far from Mexico City to the southwest lie the ruins of Malinalco. The site seems to have had primarily astronomical purposes. There, carved inside the rock, is a unique, monolithic temple. In the upper semi-circular shrine are two statues of an eagle symmetrically disposed around the statue of an ocelot. The three are placed on a semi-circular bench. Equidistant from the three, in the center of the circle, is another eagle carved on the floor. Through the door of the temple, the sun shines at right angles over the head of the central eagle on the day of the winter solstice, feast of the patron deity Huitzilopochtli. Here too there is accord with Mayan tradition that celebrated Hunahpu in the dry season. Another monolithic temple found nearby is the Structure IV, consisting of a large rectangular platform. It faces east where a stairway is located. The solar temple's orientation is such that the sun is in alignment with the axis of symmetry when it rises on the dates of February 13 and October 29. J. Galindo Trejo believes that other horizon markers indicated the dates of April 29 and August 13.[14] A consistent pattern emerges from all of these observations. Both sets of dates divide the year into a 260/105 relation, the interval of the sacred calendar. We are familiar with the dates of April 29 and August 13, dates of the sun's zenith passage—not in Malinalco but at Izapa's latitude! Finally December 21 is the date that falls exactly in the middle of the interval of both dates. Although the Aztecs assigned totally new meanings to old mythology, they still took good care to justify the departures with strict adherence to the ancestral symbolism and cosmology of the Soconusco.

The review of Aztec festivals and rituals would not be complete without a mention of the ball game and the New Fire Ceremony. The ball game was originally devoted to the cult of the solar god and performed in the corresponding season, during the winter solstice. The ball game had been eclipsed from all of Teotihuacan civilization and reappeared, charged with new war-related meanings, with the later Toltecs of Tula. In an image of the Codex Magliabechiano we see four human skulls toward the corners of the court, and at the center three death-heads associated with the god Mictlantecuhtli. With the Aztecs as well as with the Toltecs before them, the game had lost the solar connotation. It was simply a sacrificial game. The ball game acquired a further use as a form of divination. Games would be called to predict the outcome of future events. Finally, the game was used for gambling. People would lose their entire fortunes at the game and even wager their freedom.[15]

Of all Aztec ceremonies, none had the solemnity and the multiple layers of meanings of the New Fire Ceremony. The kindling of the New Fire, also called the "Binding of the Years," indicated the rebirth of the sun and fire, the renewal of the calendar and of time itself. On that date all the fires were extinguished. A victim was sacrificed and her heart removed. The fire lit in the cavity of the chest served to re-light the fire throughout the territory. The New Fire Ceremony stood for the preservation of order in the midst of threatening chaos. Here is the counterpart of the galactic meaning of the Izapan ball game in Aztec ritual. The need for the New Fire Ceremony, a ritual associated with the notion of cyclical time, squarely contradicts the notions of eternity associated with the galactic astronomy of the ball game.

Sahagun has preserved information about the last New Fire Ceremony, which occurred in AD 1507 to the south of Tenochtitlan. He records that the New Fire Ceremony was determined by the seasonal appearance of the Pleiades. Their midnight transit happened that year on November 14.[16] However they could not serve for a calibration of the calendar because, due to the precession of the equinoxes, after every 52-year cycle their transits would shift by thirteen days. The corrections to the calendar were probably done on a more regular basis. Nevertheless, the New Fire Ceremony had an important religious meaning, and played a central part in Aztec cosmology.

Tenochtitlan and the Fifth Sun

The Templo Mayor of Tenochtitlan was discovered in 1968. It is situated in the very heart of Mexico City, close to the Zocalo—the main square and largest plaza of the city—and next to the cathedral. It is in fact mostly hidden from view until one reaches it. The excavations have left it in the middle of the surrounding structures, partly sunk under the level of the asphalt. The constructions, built with a dark lava rock, have an odd undulating gesture, resulting from years of tectonic movements in this place affected by earthquakes. The ruins offer the visitor a completely different feeling from Izapa and Teotihuacan. What catches the visitor's attention most is the double platform of the larger pyramid dedicated to Huitzilopochtli and Tlaloc, now sheltered by a corrugated aluminum roof. Right under the pyramid to the north is the house of the jaguars. There, one can reconstruct in the imagination what is known of the rituals that the Aztecs celebrated. It was a mix of historical interest and contradictory emotions that led me to visit the place where thousands of captive warriors marched in procession to reach the top of the platforms and be sacrificed by the priests. The sacrificial rock is still in place as well as the reproduction of a *chacmool*—a reclining human figure whose exact function is unknown—one of which adorned the Tlaloc shrine. Izapa, Teotihuacan, and Tenochtitlan: no three sacred precincts could better portray, in the shortest sequence, the whole evolution of the Mexican Mysteries.

Tenochtitlan! What is now the center of a large metropolis was once an island in the lake of Texcoco. Tenoch, a leader of the Aztec migration, had died in 1363, almost forty years after the foundation of the city. The Aztec migration myth tells us that on arriving at the island to which they had been exiled, the Aztecs found signs of the favor of their god Huitzilopochtli: a white juniper tree with two great rocks at its foot. From the rocks flowed a stream of two colors, one red, the other blue. That night the god promised them that they would see a further sign. This was the famous nopal cactus where the eagle had set a nest, which they found the next day. The cactus—Huitzilopochtli said—had sprouted in the place where had fallen the heart of Copil whom the man-god had slain. The first part of the myth, Eduardo M. Moctezuma indicates, is almost an exact repetition of the signs received by the Toltecs upon reaching what would become the future city of Cholula. In the Aztec myth, one day separates symbolically Toltec from Aztec history.[17]

Tenochtitlan became the center of Aztec cosmogony. An Aztec poem says, "Who could conquer Tenochtitlan, who could shake the foundation of heaven?"[18] According to the Cronica Mexicayotl, the city was built above two caves filled with water, one facing east, the other north. In those waters resided "the father and mother of gods," according to Sahagun.[19] This is a reference to historical precedents, such as the cave under the Pyramid of the Sun in the city of Teotihuacan. The Great Temple that encodes all of Aztec symbolism and cosmology is the heart of the sacred city. The two mythical caves reside in the underworld. The platform supporting the temple, with its representations of serpents, identifies the terrestrial level. The four tiers of the pyramid ascend to heaven, toward the double shrine of *Omeyoacan*, Place of Duality. The southern half, representing the patron god Huitchilopochtli, symbolizes the hill of Coatepec where the god defeated his opponents. Faithful to the legend, at the base of the pyramid lay the famous large, round stone bas-relief that represents the body of the dismembered Coyolxauhqui. Associated with the stone were the skulls of many decapitated females. The serpents on this side of the pyramid are feathered serpents. The northern side of the temple represents the "Hill of Sustenance," or *Tonancatepetl*, where Tlaloc was the deity. Serpents, goggle-eyed like Tlaloc, complete the allegorical setting. The sun rose behind Tlaloc during the wet season and behind Huitzilopochtli during the dry season, further reinforcing a symbolism that had remained unaltered for centuries.

Aztec Consciousness

We now have enough archaeological material to venture into a determination of the nature of the cults performed by the Aztecs at Tenochtitlan. The evolution that the mysteries underwent in Teotihuacan, Tula, and Chichen Itza reached a climax in Aztec civilization. Teotihuacan, at least initially, could be defined as a balance point between Izapa and Tenochtitlan. Teotihuacan struggled between the sun god of the Dawning and the fire god. With the advent of the Aztecs, a movement of evolution came to an end. Human sacrifice did not suffer the alternating fate of Toltec and Mayan civilizations. This was now the cornerstone of the new religion. Every ancient ritual was superseded with a new one involving human sacrifice. And even so, Aztec ideology claimed continuity with Toltec and Izapan cosmology. How can this be? Let us look at some of the claims of the Aztecs.

The Aztecs called themselves the civilization of the Fifth Sun. Both Chichimecs and Aztecs had very little to say about the preceding four ages, according to records collected by Motolinia and Gomara. The Aztecs started their chronology in the year AD 649; before that date they lacked history. Mayan chronology started in 3114 BC. However, better evidence of the Aztecs being in reality part of the consciousness of the Third Age is their clinging to the ceremony of the New Fire. The Fourth Age introduced the notion of eternity in the calendar. Dread of death and of the extinction of time is a trademark sign of the New Fire Ceremony and of the populations belonging to the consciousness of the Third Age as it survived in the Fourth and Fifth Ages.

Fear of death is accompanied in Nahua and Aztec civilizations with doubts and dread of the afterlife. Nahua and Aztec poets and sages doubted more and more of the afterlife. The sage Ayocuan, who lived in the second half of the fifteenth century, wrote: "What can my heart do? In vain have we come, have we blossomed forth on the earth. Thus alone will I have to go like the flowers that perish? Will nothing remain of my name? Nothing of my fame here on earth? At least my flowers, at least my songs! What can my heart do? In vain have we come, have we blossomed forth on the earth."[20] Another collection of the thoughts of the sages reiterates the theme in many different ways: "Where do we go, oh! Where do we go? Will there be existence again? Will the joy of the Giver of Life be there again?... For only on earth shall the fragrant flowers last and the songs that are our bliss. Enjoy them now!...I weep, I feel forlorn: I remember that we must leave flowers and songs. Let us enjoy ourselves now, let us sing now! For we go, we disappear."[21] Many other examples can be found in the literature. This inner despair was also stated in Aztec ritual, according to Sahagun. There the priest pronounces the following words: "Oh son, you have already endured the trials of this life; because we don't have a permanent dwelling on this earth...and now, the god, whose name is Mictlantecuhtli, has taken you...and the goddess called Mictacacihuatl has given you her seat, because all of us will go over there...and there will be no memory left of you...you have already gone to the darkest place that has no light and no windows, nor will you return or get out of there, nor do you have to pay attention and solicitude to your return."[22] We have quoted these passages at length because it is easy to dismiss thoughts of the end of the world associated with the New Fire Ceremony as allegories or figures of speech. There is nothing allegorical in the poems and ritual just quoted. They are a testimonial of the deep anguish of a consciousness representative of the Third Age, an anguish that reaches new heights with the advent of the Fifth Sun.

We have already found references to Mictlantecuhtli, first in relation to the ball game symbolism, and now in relation to the underworld, where he plays such a significant part. There is a very indicative passage taken from the Anales de Cuauhtitlan, where Quetzalcoatl descends to the underworld looking for the precious bones in possession of Mictlantecuhtli, in order to form with them the new humanity of the Fifth Sun. Upon obtaining the bones he extracts blood from his penis and says: "Now humanity is born and it will shed its blood over you the gods." Significantly, Quetzalcoatl carries the bones to Tamoanchan, the "place of our origin." The Aztecs take care to reconnect not only with Toltec but also with the earlier Izapan origin, just as we have seen in the instance of the birth of the Fifth Sun.[23] The image from the last myth provides a different perspective on the nature of the Fifth Sun. It also corresponds with much of the ceremonial life of the Aztecs that has been recently unearthed.

There seem to be in Aztec ritual two systems of reference: an outer one and an occult one; the two do not offer the same image. The twin temples are dedicated to Huitzilopochtli and Tlaloc. And yet the two deities don't play an obvious role at the deeper level of Aztec esotericism. No representations of the deity Huitzilopochtli have been found. E. M. Moctezuma hypothesizes that the god was represented by the symbol of the bow found on braziers. Chronicles tell us that his image was made of amaranth dough and seeds.[24] This would partly explain on an external level why nothing has survived of the god's representations, but would leave the observer puzzled as to the little recognition given to such an important being.

North of the Templo Mayor on the side of the deity Tlaloc is the House of the Eagle Knights, to whom the myth of the Fifth Sun ascribes higher courage than to the jaguar knights. The eagle was scorched by the fire; the jaguar only singed, hence its spotted skin. In the House of the Eagle Knights two life-sized statues of the god Mictlantecuhtli have been found. They have been set in a dark room of the museum of the Templo Mayor, with a recorded tape explaining the function and position of the statue in its context. The chilling appearance of the god and the recreation of the setting match the accounts of its rituals. The terra-cotta sculpture shows the god with grinning mouth and a bald head, perforated to the back of the hairline, ribs exposed with liver dangling from under the ribcage. The codices Tudela and Magliabecchiano show the god's attendants pouring blood over the same sculpture of the deity, in the area that corresponds to the perforated part of the head.[25] Elsewhere in the House of the Eagle Knights are friezes depicting scenes of blood-letting and penance, almost identical with the ones of Tula. Bones and thorns are shown as symbols of self-sacrifice.

Among the offerings most often found around the temple are the effigy representations that E. M. Moctezuma identifies as the Old Fire god. He is most commonly called Huehueteotl and is portrayed wearing a breechcloth in a sitting position. From the headdress rise two square projections, and two teeth protrude from his mouth.[26] Once again this is the old fire god that the Popol Vuh calls Tohil and also associates with Quetzalcoatl.

We have seen the evolution of Quetzalcoatl after the age of Teotihuacan. Quetzalcoatl, whom Steiner said did not take on a human form during the time of Christ, became for the Toltecs a warrior god. Their rulers identified themselves with the god. Quetzalcoatl, or more precisely the fire god taking his place, together with Mictlantecuhtli—god of the underworld—form a new alliance, aptly described by the myth of the inauguration of the Fifth Sun in the Anales of Cuauhtitlan, quoted above.

Steiner's research will help us to complete this tableau. The transition to the time of the Consciousness Soul that ushered in the advent of the scientific age in Europe was accompanied by the withdrawal of the Spirit of the Age, Michael, into the spiritual realms, where human beings could now follow him in freedom. Steiner adds this to the context given above: "While Michael above was teaching his hosts, there was founded in the realm immediately below the surface of the Earth, a kind of sub-earthly Ahrimanic school…there below are the Ahrimanic powers, sending their impulses with all the greater strength."[27] The Aztecs inaugurated the resurgence of the decadent Mexican Mysteries. Tenochtitlan was no doubt an important center in the preparation for the school of Ahriman on earth.

Quetzalcoatl—Fire God

The fire god Tohil/Quetzalcoatl has undergone a gradual evolution over fifteen centuries. It has come to be represented by the butterfly for example. In that symbol sun and fire are closely united. They are likewise linked in the symbol of the eagle, which the Aztecs associate with the sacrificial fire that set the sun in motion. The Popol Vuh identified the fire god with the original Quetzalcoatl. Progressively Quetzalcoatl acquired militaristic connotations after Teotihuacan.

In a next step we arrive at Tenochtitlan, where Quetzalcoatl is mentioned alternatively with the god Huitzilopochtli. Neither of them appears frequently in art. When Quetzalcoatl is represented it seems to be in homage of historic past and Teotihuacan tradition. The line of Quetzalcoatl/fire god is continued by Huehueteotl, the Old Fire God or Old God, and his representations clearly show a metamorphosis: no longer a feathered being but a human being. The word *Teotl* was used by the Aztecs with practically the same meaning as the word *Tau*. Thus it stood for everything in nature that was awe-inspiring or imbued with power, such as thunder and lightning. It stood likewise for all that represented the life force in animals, plants, and human beings. The two horns on the head of the god point to initiation and the clairvoyant vision of old atavistic faculties.

In Toltec-Chichimec history we find the following passage: "Mother of the Gods, Father of the Gods, the Old God, distended in the navel of the earth, engaged in the enclosure of turquoise. He who dwells in waters the color of the bluebird, He who dwells in the clouds, the Old God. *He who inhabits the shadows of the region of the dead, the Lord of fire and of the year*" (emphasis added).[28] Here we notice two elements that qualify the god. The first is the appellation of Old God, the second is the mention of the year god that here functions in a similar way to the year god in the Ancient and Semi-ancient Mysteries. This is another indication that Aztec tradition marks a returning to older traditions, to inspirations that guided past civilizations. However, now these correspond to a revival of old faculties out of time. Working hand in hand with this is the return of initiation procedures within caves—as in the caves situated under the pyramids of the Toltecs—or in the precincts of the Jaguar and Eagle Knights, underground at the base of the pyramids in the rituals performed in honor of Mictlantecuhtli. This too marks a return to the Ancient and Semi-ancient Mysteries. Final confirmation of the regressive gesture of all Aztec spirituality is the return to the celebration of the time of Atlantis through the myth of Aztlan that finds embodiment in the cosmology of Tenochtitlan, the city surrounded by the waters. The Aztec civilization was trying to recover Atlantean faculties but only through atavistic clairvoyance, at the time only possible through the blood and hence through human sacrifice.

In its original imagery, one still conveyed at present, Quetzalcoatl stood for the Lord of Wind and Water. This represented the original ability of Atlanteans and later Mesoamericans to manipulate the etheric forces of wind and water. Steiner says about these: "In Atlantean times the seminal forces in plant and animal were still at human command and could be drawn forth just as the forces of steam for propelling machines can be extracted from the mineral today. I have told you that when these forces are drawn forth they are connected in a mysterious way with the nature forces in wind, weather, and the like."[29] This was still true at the time of the pre-Mayan civilization—occurring a few millennia before the time of Christ—whose process of initiation was described by Grace Cooke in chapter 7. Cooke describes the candidates' initiation into the mysteries of the elements—particularly the weather—and their use for agricultural purposes. At that time the initiates had more power over the elements of nature and could influence them from within. Grace Cooke does in fact mention the being of Quetzalcoatl. Later on, sometime before the time of Christ, this deity acquired the traits of a regressive being as we know from Steiner. A further change occurred before the time of the Dawning with the advent of the fire god (Part III of the Popol Vuh).

Use of the element of fire, and the power to use it in conjunction with particular forces of the earth, had been a faculty of humanity during Lemurian times. This power could be recovered later in time through the use of black magic. In the same lecture quoted above Steiner refers to the time of the Persian civilization of post-Atlantean times. Something equivalent had happened in America. Huehueteotl, the Old God, now operated in the realm of the element of fire. Steiner characterizes this change as the transition from the use of Luciferic powers to the use of Ahrimanic powers: "Lucifer had brought humanity under the influence of the powers connected with air and water only; whereas it was Ahriman-Mephistopheles who has subjected him to the influence of far more deadly powers, and the civilizations directly to come will see the appearance of many things connected with Ahriman's influence."[30] Use of the Ahrimanic forces for the purpose of black magic is associated with the misuse of the forces of the physical body for the acquisition of occult knowledge. The forces of the physical body become the starting point of occult initiation.

The fire god is already known in the epic of Gilgamesh, whom the king and Eabani vehemently oppose. The epic says: "The cry of Humbaba is a hurricane, his mouth fire, his breath death." Humbaba, as a deity of fire and volcanoes, was known to the Babylonians. In his thorough research on the art of Mesoamerica and South America, von Wuthenau shows that numerous samples of masks of the fire god from Mexico, Colombia, and Ecuador resemble in all details the examples from Babylonia, Sparta, and Carthage.[31] This may be a further indication of possible links between the old Babylonian impulses and the New World, via the Phoenicians, that we explored in chapter 7. However a direct link is not the only explanation.

The similarity between Humbaba and fire god has in fact deeper roots. It comes from the old Atlantean Mysteries. The primeval Atlantean populations of the South were initiated into the Saturn Mysteries. Later the Mercury and Venus Mysteries added their effects. The influence of the Saturn Mysteries is clearly visible in Mesoamerican and Babylonian civilizations.

If Ahriman, or Ahrimanic beings, are the real spiritual beings behind the old fire god and Mictlantecuhtli, the particular features of Aztec mythology become much more understandable. Ahriman cannot produce imaginations of his own; he can only borrow them. The Aztecs therefore had to base the legitimacy of their power on historical and mythological precedent. Aztec myths are completely literal and practically no second reading is needed. It is not necessary to move to an imaginative level to understand the justification of human sacrifice. The myths explain that the gods sacrificed themselves and likewise should human beings. The gods expressly request the "most precious substance" of the human blood. In all degrees Aztec mythology is a return to the darkness of the Third Age or earlier. Even the Aztec claim of being the chosen race that will gather all the other scattered tribes—a further justification for empire—is based upon a return to the past, to the myth of Atlantis-Aztlan. The capital Tenoch-titlan—an island on the waters of the lake Texcoco—stood as a symbol of this continuity with Atlantean civilization. One could argue that Aztec rule too was a return to the older form of theocracy of the Third Age; witness the predominant role of the high priest, eclipsing that of the emperor. However, on other grounds, Aztec claim to being a Fifth Sun at the threshold of the fifth post-Atlantean epoch has some undeniable reality.

The response given to this change of consciousness by the Aztecs was the attempt to revive the old atavistic consciousness of communion with the gods through the practice of human sacrifice. Another Native American group gave America the possibility of a completely different response to the challenge of the times. There we can find the equivalent of a Fifth Age in keeping with the changed conditions of the times. Yet another response was brought forth by the Incas in Peru.

CHAPTER 3

THE IROQUOIS

THE IROQUOIS, as they were first called by the French, occupied the northern portion of present-day New York State in a territory extending roughly between the Genesee and Hudson Rivers. They were comprised of the five tribes of Seneca, Cayuga, Onondaga, Oneida, and Mohawk.

Iroquois links with Mayan culture go back to the pre-Maya stages of civilization. In North America we find these links with the first agricultural societies—the Adena and the Hopewell. The Adena, or Early Woodland, spread into the valleys of the Ohio and Mississippi rivers and their tributaries. They were followed by the Hopewell culture around 500 BC. At this stage the surrounding hunters/gatherers assimilated completely the culture and spirituality of the farming communities. This is revealed by the record of physical anthropology; the skeletons and skulls found show two marked ethnic differences. The Adena's and Hopewell's cultivars of maize, beans, and squashes come from the Mayan area—giving us an indication that this was their likely origin. The Hopewell also had earthen pyramid constructions very similar to the ones of the pre-Classic Maya, as for example those found around the Kaminaljuyu area of Guatemala.[1] The ceremonial sites of the Ohio and Illinois were abruptly abandoned in AD 100-200, a time in which we have seen that important spiritual battles and transitions were going on in America.

The Iroquois share many elements with the archaic Hopewell culture. They are the only group in the East that continued the pottery tradition of the Hopewell, and like them are excellent sculptors, often representing the same kind of maternity figures and preserving their funerary traditions. Finally, they built the same kind of towns surrounded by pentagonal enclosures. The Iroquois, or rather their ancestors, invaded from the south, taking over Algonquin territory and went as far north as the cultivation of maize allowed.

The Iroquois division between civil and religious authority is common to all agricultural nations of the continent. In the astronomical realm they base their observations on the Pleiades, Venus, and Milky Way, as did many societies at the level of consciousness of the Third Age, as well as Mayan pre-Classic culture. Their New Year falls in February as it does for the beginning of the Tzolkin, and it begins with the extinction of the old fire in the Longhouse. Their festival of the dead is also celebrated in November.[2] All of the above shows that the Iroquois share links with the Maya but only in the distant past. To the spiritual forces coming from the past the Iroquois added a completely original force of renewal.

The Legend of the White Roots of Peace: Deganawidah and Hiawatha

The Iroquois League of the Five Nations (later six, with the addition of the Tuscaroras) represents a radical departure from all previous models of government in North America. It is the first confederation of equal nations that does not depend on the idea of a monarch. The Five Nations' Confederacy traces its origin to the historical legend of the White Roots of Peace. The symbol of their legend, the tree of the white roots, stands for peace in the larger sense of the word, a peace that in their language corresponds with the sacred law.

In the past, the beginning of the Iroquois League was thought to have occurred in the fifteenth century.[3] More recent studies argue for an earlier beginning to the League, as far back as the eleventh to twelfth century. Seneca historians based their calculations upon the tallies of generations passed down in the oral record, which led to the date of 1090. Mann and Fields have ascertained the date of 1150 by going back to the record of the so-called "Condolence Canes."[4]

There are many versions of the historical legend of the founding of the league. Variations can be ascribed to the degree of thoroughness of the sources relating the events, the witnesses recording them, and the time of these recordings. Some versions are obviously shorter renderings, trimmed of any legendary connotation and made fit for the modem, rational ear. Of all the versions known, we will mainly refer to Paul Wallace's retelling, taken at the turn of the nineteenth century from three different sources.

Wallace is a thorough interpreter of Iroquois culture, and is completely immersed in their way of thinking. His legend is also more detailed than most. We will occasionally use other sources to amplify Wallace's version.[5] The following is an abbreviated rendering of Wallace's version.

> Deganawidah was born at a Huron settlement on the north shore of Lake Ontario. Before his birth, his grandmother received his name in a dream vision. The Great Spirit said to her, "It is the will of the Holder of the Heavens that your daughter, a virgin, shall bear a child. He will be called Deganawidah, the Master of Things, because he brings with him the Good News of Peace and Power. Care for him well, for he has a great task to perform in the world: to bring peace and life to the people on earth."
>
> When Deganawidah had become a man, one day he said to his mother and grandmother, "Now I will build my canoe, for it is time for me to set out on my mission to stop the shedding of blood among human beings. I will go toward the sunrise, seeking the council smoke of nations beyond this lake."
>
> Deganawidah crossed Lake Ontario in his canoe of white stone, and approached the land of the Iroquois. At that time the settlements were all back among the hills, whose steep sides offered protection to villages against their enemies. Those were evil days, for the five Iroquois peoples were all at war with one another, and made themselves an easy prey to the fierce Algonquin Adirondacks who came down on them from the northeast, and the Mohicans who assailed them from the east.
>
> As Deganawidah neared the land, he saw men running along the shore. Deganawidah swiftly beached the canoe and climbed the bank to stand before them. When the men told Deganawidah of the strife in their village, he said to them, "I am Deganawidah. Tell your chief that the Good News of Peace and Power has come, and that there will be no more strife in his village. If he asks where this peace will come from, say to him, 'It will come.'" The men were full of wonder when they saw that Deganawidah's canoe was made of white stone. The hunters swiftly went to their chief, and told him of the Good News of Peace and Power. When the chief asked them who had told them this, they replied, "He is called Deganawidah in the world. He came from the west and he goes toward the sunrise.

His canoe is made of white stone and it moves swiftly." And they told him of his message of peace. Then the chief replied, "Truly this is a wonderful thing. All will be glad and at peace in their minds to know that this thing will come to be, once men believe it."

After leaving the hunters, Deganawidah went to the house of a woman who lived by the warriors' path that passed between the east and the west. The woman placed food before him and, after he had eaten, asked him his message. "I carry the Mind of the Master of Life," he replied, "and my message will bring an end to the wars between east and west. All peoples will love one another and live together in peace. This message has three parts—Righteousness, Health, and Power (Gáiwoh, Skénon, and Gashasdénshaa)—and each part has two branches: Righteousness means justice between men and nations, and a desire to see justice prevail. Health means soundness of mind and body, and peace that comes when minds are sane and bodies cared for. Power means the authority of law and custom, backed by such force as is necessary to make justice prevail, and also the desire of the Holder of the Heavens and has his sanction."

"Your message is good," said the woman, "but a word is nothing until it is given form and set to work in the world. What form will this message take?" "It will take the form of the Longhouse," replied Deganawidah, "in which there are many fires, one for each family, yet all will live as one household under one chief mother. The five nations, each with its own council and fire, shall live together as one household in peace. They shall be the Kanonsiónni, the Longhouse. They shall have one mind and live under one law. Thinking shall replace killing, and there shall be one commonwealth." Deganawidah told the woman, "In that Longhouse the women shall possess the power to name the chiefs. That is because you, my mother, were the first to accept the Good News of Peace and Power. Henceforth you shall be called Jigónhsasee, New Face, for your countenance reveals the New Mind, and you shall be known as the Mother of Nations. Now I will take my message toward the sunrise." The woman told him that in the direction of the sunrise lived a man who eats humans. "That is my task," said Deganawidah, "to bring such evils to an end, so that all people may go from place to place without fear."

When Deganawidah came to the house of the "man who eats humans," he climbed to the roof and lay flat on his chest beside the smoke hole. When the man came home with a human body, which he put in his kettle on the fire, Deganawidah moved closer and looked straight down into the smoke hole. At that moment the man bent over the kettle and was amazed to see a face looking up at him. It was Deganawidah's face he saw reflected in the water, but the man thought it was his own. The face had such wisdom and strength as he had never seen before nor ever dreamed that he possessed. The man thought, "This is a most wonderful thing, which has never happened to me before. A great man looked at me out of the kettle. I did not know I was like that. I shall look again and make sure that what I have seen is true."

When the man looked into the kettle once more, there again was the face of a great man looking up at him. Then he believed it was true that he had wisdom and righteousness and strength. "Now I will no longer kill humans and eat their flesh," the man said. "But that is not enough. The mind is more difficult to change. I cannot forget the suffering I have caused, and I am miserable. Perhaps someone can tell me what I must do to make amends for all the human beings I have made to suffer."

Deganawidah climbed down from the roof and met the man. They entered and sat down across the fire from each other. The man told Deganawidah what had happened to him that day. Deganawidah replied, "Truly, a wonderful thing has happened today. The New Mind has come to you, bringing Righteousness and Health and Power. And you are miserable because the New Mind does not live at ease with old memories. You can heal your memories by working to make justice prevail, and bringing peace to those places where you have brought pain. You will work with me in advancing the Good News of Peace and Power."

Now nearby lived an Onondaga chief named Atotarho, who was a great and evil wizard. He had a twisted body and a twisted mind, and his hair was a mass of tangled snakes. Men feared to see him, and the sound of his voice sent terror through the land; but peace could not be completed without him.

"You will visit Atotarho," said Deganawidah, "for he is of your people, the Onondagas. He is ugly, but we need him. When he asks you for your message, say, 'It is Righteousness and Health, and when men take hold of it they will stop killing one another and live in peace.' He will not listen to you, but will drive you away. Yet you will come to him again and at last prevail. You will be called Hiawatha, He Who Combs, for you will comb the snakes out of Atotarho's hair."

Deganawidah visited Atotarho to prepare him for Hiawatha's message. "I have come to prepare your mind," said Deganawidah, "for the Good News of Peace and Power. When men accept it, they will stop killing, and bloodshed will cease from the land."

Atotarho said to Deganawidah, "When will this be?" and then he cried: "Hwe-do-né-e-e-e-eh!" It was the mocking cry of the doubter who killed men by destroying their faith.

"It will be," replied Deganawidah. "I shall come again, with Hiawatha, who will comb the snakes out of your hair."

Then Deganawidah took his course toward the sunrise, toward the land of the Mohawks. Deganawidah made camp by the Lower Falls of the Mohawk River, and in the evening sat beneath a tall tree and smoked his pipe. A Mohawk man passing by saw him and asked Deganawidah who he was. "I am Deganawidah," he replied. "The Great Creator sent me to establish the Great Peace among you." "There is no peace here," said the man. "But I will take you to my village, so that you can explain this message to the people."

So Deganawidah presented the Good News of Peace and Power, of Reason and Law, to the Mohawks in that place, and the people were glad, for they found it a good message.

But their chiefs were cautious and held back. The Chief Warrior would not believe Deganawidah's words were true without a sign. He decreed that Deganawidah should climb to the top of a tall tree by the falls, and then the tree would be cut down over the cliff. If by morning Deganawidah were still living, the Chief would accept his message.

Deganawidah climbed the tree to the topmost branch. Then the Mohawks cut the tree down so that it fell over the cliff into the water. The people watched to see if Deganawidah came up, but there was no sign of him.

Next morning, before sunrise, a man of the Mohawks came to the place by the falls where the tree had fallen, and saw at a little distance across the cornfields a column of smoke rising. Going toward it he saw a man seated by his fire. It was Deganawidah.

The people brought Deganawidah back to the place of council, and the Chief Warrior said, "Now I am in doubt no longer. This is a great man, who reveals to us the Mind of the Master of Life. Let us accept his message. Let us take hold of the Good News of Peace and Power." Thus the Mohawks were the first nation to take hold of the Great Peace. They were the founders of the League.

Meanwhile, Hiawatha could make no headway against Atotarho. Three times Hiawatha set out with the Onondagas to straighten Atotarho's twisted mind. But each time the wizard's evil power thwarted them. Some of the Onondagas were drowned in their canoes by the waves. Others were set fighting among themselves. Hiawatha was not injured in his body, but was wounded in his mind by the obstructions placed in his path.

One day he heard Atotarho's voice crying out, "Hiawatha-a-a-a-a-a-a!" and he was troubled, for he knew that mischief was hatching. Soon Hiawatha's three daughters were taken ill, and all died. Hiawatha's grief bowed him down. Seeing him thus depressed, the people arranged a game of lacrosse to comfort him. But when a mysterious bird dropped out of the sky, the crowd trampled Hiawatha's wife to death in pursuit of it, and his grief overcame him. He left the land of the Onondagas and traveled south.

Hiawatha soon came to the Tully Lakes. As he crossed one of them, at his request the ducks lifted the water for him to pass with dry moccasins. Picking up shells from the lake bottom, he threaded them on three strings of jointed rushes as a mark of his grief.

Every night when he made his fire, Hiawatha set up two crotched sticks with a third stick across them, and from this he hung the three strings of shells. Then he sat down and said, "If I found anyone burdened with grief as I am, I would take these shell strings in my hand and console them. The strings would become words and lift away the darkness covering them. Holding these in my hand, my words would be true."

For many days Hiawatha wandered through the forest without direction. When he came near settlements, the people saw the smoke from his fire at evening, but no one came to console him. The people knew that it was Hiawatha, for they had heard of his departure from the land of the Onondaga.In his loneliness, Hiawatha built himself a canoe and paddled down the Mohawk River until he came to the village by the Lower Falls, and there built his fire at the wood's edge.

That night Deganawidah went to Hiawatha's fire. As he approached, he heard Hiawatha saying, "If I found anyone burdened with grief as I am, I would take these shell strings in my hand and console them. The strings would become words and lift away the darkness covering them. Holding these in my hand, my words would be true." Then Deganawidah came to Hiawatha and taking the strings, he spoke the words of the Requickening Address, used for all generations since in the Iroquois Condolence Ceremony: "I wipe away the tears from your face using the white fawn-skin of pity...I make it daylight for you. I beautify the sky. Now your thoughts will be peaceful when your eyes rest on the sky, which the Perfector of our Faculties, the Master of All Things, intended to be a source of happiness to man." Thus Hiawatha's mind was cleared of its grief.

"Now," said Deganawidah, "Reason and judgment have returned to you. You are ready to advance the New Mind. Let us together make the laws of the Great Peace, which shall abolish war." So when the Great Law was completed, and a string or belt of wampum for each item was provided to enable them to remember it more easily, Hiawatha and Deganawidah carried the words of the Great Peace to the nations of the west: the Oneidas, Onondagas, Cayugas, and Senecas.

Accompanied by Mohawk chiefs, Deganawidah and Hiawatha approached the Oneidas and the Cayugas, who readily accepted the Great Peace. Now, with three nations at their back, Deganawidah and Hiawatha returned to the politically minded Onondagas, and were able to convince their chiefs (all but Atotarho) that it would be well to join. Then, accompanied by the chiefs of four nations— Mohawks, Oneidas, Onondagas, and Cayugas—they carried the Peace Hymn to Canandaigua Lake, where they persuaded the Senecas to end their rivalries and enter the Longhouse.

"Now," said Deganawidah, "we must go to Atotarho. He alone stands across our path. The twists in his mind and the seven crooks in his body must be straightened if the League is to endure." "Come," said Deganawidah to Hiawatha, "first you and I alone will go to the Great Wizard. I will sing the Peace Song and you will explain the

Words of the Law, holding the wampum in your hand. If we can straighten his mind, the Longhouse will be completed and our work accomplished."

As they neared the middle of the lake, they heard the voice of Atotarho: "Asonke-ne-e-e-e-eh? Is it not yet?" The wind blew and the waves struck angrily against the canoe, and again they heard Atotarho's cry rush out to meet them: "Asonke-ne-e-e-e-eh! It is not yet!" But Deganawidah put his strength into his paddle, and in a few moments they beached their canoe on the east shore of the lake, and stood before the wizard.

Holding the strings of wampum in his hand, Hiawatha said to Atotarho, "These are the words of the Great Law, on which we will build the House of Peace, the Longhouse with five fires that is yet one household. These are the words of Righteousness and Health and Power."

"What is this foolishness about houses and righteousness and health?" said Atotarho.

Then Deganawidah spoke his message: "The Words we bring constitute the New Mind, which is the will of the Holder of the Heavens. There shall be Righteousness when men desire justice, Health when men obey reason, Power when men accept the Great Law. These things shall be given form in the Longhouse, where five nations shall live in quiet as one family. At this very place, Atotarho, where the chiefs of five nations will assemble, I shall plant the Great Tree of Peace, and its root shall extend to far places of the earth so that all humankind may have the shelter of the Great Law."

"You yourself," said Deganawidah, "will tend the council fire of the Five Nations, the Fire That Never Dies. And the smoke of that fire shall reach the sky and be seen by all men. If you desire it, you will be the Head Chief of the Five Nations."

"Of course I desire it," said Atotarho, "if there be anything in it. But you are a dreamer—where is the power to bring it to pass? At that Hiawatha and Deganawidah returned across the lake to bring the chiefs to Atotarho. They heard the voice of Atotarho rush out to meet them, crying, "Asonke-ne-e-e-e-eh! It is not yet!" The wind lifted the waves against the canoes, but they put their strength into their paddles and, before the voice had died away, they stood before Atotarho.

"Behold!" said Deganawidah. "Here is the power of the Five Nations. Their strength is greater than your strength. But their voice shall be your voice when you speak in council, and all men shall hear you. This shall be your strength in the future: the will of a united people." Then the mind of Atotarho was made straight, and Hiawatha combed the snakes out of his hair. Deganawidah laid his hand on Atotarho's body and said, "The work is finished. You will now preside over the Council, and you will strive in all ways to make reason and the peaceful mind prevail." Then Deganawidah placed antlers on the heads of the chiefs as a sign of their authority, and gave them the Words of the Law.

Let us now look at the implications of this legend and the historical facts that ensued. In the language of the legend, the "New Mind" has to bring about a "New Form"; new ideas shape a new reality in the social world.

The Actors of the Drama

In most versions of the legend, Hiawatha and Deganawidah form a duality. Occasionally they merge into the single individuality of Hiawatha. The dynamic of the legend revolves around the two of them and Atotarho.

Deganawidah's biography is by far the most extraordinary of the three. He is conceived by a virgin, thus echoing the manner of birth of Ixbalamqué in the ancient Mexican Mysteries at the time of Christ. As we have abundantly illustrated, the virgin birth forms a link to Native American precedent and tradition rather than a concession to Christianity as some authors have argued. Deganawidah's mission is clearly defined by a messenger of the Great Spirit. In some versions of the legend, the messenger also prophesies that Deganawidah would indirectly bring the downfall of his people, the Hurons. The Grandmother tries to kill him by throwing him in the freezing waters and twice more in unspecified manners.

In Deganawidah we see an initiate who tries to introduce new spiritual principles. That he is an initiate or an exceptional individual is also indicated by the fact that he rides a white canoe made of stone, symbol that in another context is associated with Chebiabos, the guide who carries the souls to the land of the dead. This white canoe is also the one used by Glooskap, the equivalent of the initiate in the Algonquian Northeast. Glooskap too is a Guardian of the Threshold, awaiting the souls at their death.[6] In one version of the legend, once his mission is accomplished,

Deganawidah rows his canoe toward the setting sun, never to be seen again. In the version given by Horatio Hale it is also said that Deganawidah's name is the only one that cannot be used down the line of heredity, contrary to all the other names of chiefs present at the foundation of the League. This is because none can do what he has done.[7] The confusion between Manabozho and Hiawatha that Longfellow perpetuated becomes more understandable now, in the light of the fact that in some versions the Hiawatha character is in fact a blending of Hiawatha and Deganawidah, and appears therefore as the initiate.

Like Deganawidah, Atotarho (sometimes alternatively spelled Thadodaho) shares a mixture of human and superhuman attributes. His cry is "the mocking cry of the doubter who killed men by destroying their faith." The translation of the cry means, "When will this be?" This impatient attitude is typical of a being who wants to bring forth events before their time. The physical appearance of Atotarho—his crooked body, his head garlanded with snakes—denotes an unlawful penetration by earthly powers. It can be said that in him work the powers of Ahriman, which enable him to use magic and hurt enemies at a distance.

Between these two extremes stands Hiawatha. His flaw, cannibalism, is a major spiritual trespass that he has adopted as a cultural habit from society around him. Cannibalism stands at the center of the encounter between Hiawatha and Deganawidah. It is used like human sacrifice among the Aztecs, although on a minor scale, as a means to revive ancient atavistic inspirations. Because Hiawatha is in touch with his true humanity, he is able to recognize his lower self. His encounter with Deganawidah is a beautiful portrayal of the meeting with the Lower Guardian, showing the shortcomings of the lower self and submitting to the guidance of the higher self. The encounter brings about the recognition of the pain caused to others and the desire to redeem the lower self, made possible by Deganawidah's message.

Soon after, Hiawatha takes on the task of helping his people. This brings upon him the karma of his community, a pain that he has not karmically deserved but that he willingly embraces. The length of the process of grief is emphasized by the establishment of the Ritual of Condolence, the burdensome journey to the Mohawk nation, and the earnest desire to bring consolation to others. Only Deganawidah knows the depth of Hiawatha's sorrow; he can reach to the spiritual source that offers him peace and allows the perception of the truth that suffering has obscured.

The dynamic of development played by the two founders shows significant nuances not immediately perceptible. Hiawatha is as much a pupil of Deganawidah as he is a collaborator. While the prophet carries the vision, he is impaired by stuttering. He needs someone else with oratorical skills; that is Hiawatha's role. Although Deganawidah guides and inspires, it is Hiawatha who carries out the burden of the central confrontation with Atotarho. He cannot make use of supernatural powers as Deganawidah does in the instance of the test of the fallen tree. However, it is Hiawatha who establishes the Ritual of Condolence and who combs Atotarho's hair. The initiate has to find a willing companion before he can realize his mission. Hiawatha represents in the will what Deganawidah carries in the realm of ideas. His is a will imbued with heart forces. Atotarho embodies a ruthless will, devoid of morality. With the achievement of the League, Deganawidah's task of the spirit comes to an end; Hiawatha still has a political task to carry out.

The New Path to the Social Mysteries

We can now revisit the main events in the drama. Two pivotal points will underline the character of the mysteries inaugurated by Deganawidah with the help of his pupil Hiawatha. We have already pointed to the first event: the initial meeting of Hiawatha with Deganawidah. After seeing the reflection of the initiate's face in the water kettle, Hiawatha says: "It is my own face in which I see wisdom and righteousness and strength. But it is not the face of a man who eats humans. I see that it is not like me to do that." Thus the first stage of what we have defined as the meeting with the Lower Guardian of the Threshold is marked by the perception of one's shortcomings.

After emptying the kettle Hiawatha continues: "Now I have changed my habits. I no longer kill humans and eat their flesh. But that is not enough. The mind is more difficult to change. I cannot forget the suffering I have caused, and I am become miserable." At this stage Hiawatha truly meets the Guardian with the desire to take on a different direction in life. He wishes that somebody would tell him what to do next. This is when Deganawidah appears to him bringing the message of the White Roots of Peace. The initiate only speaks when the pupil has readied himself in soul and spirit. Deganawidah first confirms to Hiawatha what he has already understood, then shows him the way to redeem himself: "The New Mind has come to thee, namely Righteousness and Health and Power. And thou art miserable because the New Mind does not live at ease with old memories. Heal thy memories by working to make justice prevail. Bring peace to those places where thou hast done injury to man." These are the words that set Hiawatha on his new course. He then works to spread the word of the New Mind. The ensuing events bring him the grief of the deaths of his wife and daughters.

The later part of the narrative offers us further clues about Hiawatha's transformation. Two consequences follow the tragedies occurring in Hiawatha's life. Grief overcomes him to such a degree that he is unable to regain his place in society; he wanders off aimlessly. Implicit in his wandering is a renouncement of vengeance. Though he seeks consolation and everyone knows who he is, no one is able to offer consolation to the Onondaga chief. At this point an enigmatic imagination occurs. Hiawatha in his grief arrives at one of the Tully lakes. To ease his way the ducks lift the water to let him pass. From the bottom of the lake he picks up shells that he threads into three strings. With these, which he sets on a horizontal pole, he instates the Ritual of Condolence. A further change has occurred at this stage. Not only has Hiawatha given up all thought of vengeance, but he can now offer consolation to anyone else who grieves, just as he wishes to receive consolation himself. The narrative underlines that this is an important step. Hiawatha recognizes not only his personal grief but also the collective grief that the practices of cannibalism, warfare, and black magic have brought upon his people. The first experience of the wrong he had committed through cannibalism was an experience in the realm of thought. At this stage Hiawatha receives the full impact of it in the realm of his feelings and will. It is the kind of experience that overwhelms the life of feelings and that is usually avoided in every way—outwardly through revenge, inwardly with drugs or anything that can provide oblivion. Hiawatha is as if immobilized by the experience. All his activity is turned inward toward the experience of grief. He is as if absent to the outside world, but new powers are coming to birth in his soul.

Deganawidah arrives at the place where Hiawatha is staying in Mohawk territory. Approaching unbeknownst to the Onondaga chief, he hears him pronouncing the words of the "Requickening Address," used for the Ritual of Condolence. Then, and only then, does the initiate offer consolation to Hiawatha. Once again the initiate awaits indication of readiness on the part of his pupil. Hiawatha, cleared of his grief, can now work for the good of the whole Iroquois people. This crucial point in the narrative corresponds in effect to the meeting with the Christ, the Higher Guardian of the Threshold. Deganawidah has a role reminiscent of the hierophant, but now outside the precinct of the mysteries.

To the Lower Guardian, Hiawatha has expressed his desire to overcome his lower nature. He has set himself a positive task, an ideal that would curb his cannibalistic habit. He has taken on the task of transforming his double, who is his own creation. Once this transformation is completed Hiawatha meets the Higher Guardian of the threshold. This is how Steiner describes in imaginative terms the difference between the meetings with the Lesser and the Higher Guardians. "Hitherto you have sought only your own release, but now, having yourself become free, you can go forth as a liberator of your fellows. Until today you have striven as an individual, but now seek to coordinate yourself with the whole, so that you may bring into the supersensible world not yourself alone, but all things else existing in the world of the senses. You will someday be able to unite with me [Higher Guardian]"[8] Henceforth Hiawatha can in effect work to further the condition of his people and the Five Nations.

The roles of the initiate and his pupil should not hide the fact that the whole of society participates in the unfolding of the events. First, in a passive way, the tribes of the west accept the message of Deganawidah. It is still a very superficial acceptance as the narrative shows: "Deganawidah passed from settlement to settlement, finding that men desired peace and would practice it if they knew for a certainty that others would practice it too." When Hiawatha starts spreading the new message among the Onondagas, the black magician reacts by drowning some of his followers, or by setting them against each other. When Deganawidah wanders toward the east he reaches the Mohawk who take up his message actively. Later Deganawidah and Hiawatha proceed to meet the black magician only because they have the full support of the five tribes.

We now come closer to the understanding of the Mysteries inaugurated by Deganawidah and Hiawatha. These are mysteries that unfold in the social world itself, no longer in isolated Mystery centers. These Mysteries leading to the time of the Consciousness Soul tackle the matter of coming to terms with evil and its representatives. To Hiawatha the initiate says: "Thou shalt visit this man Atotarho, for he is of thy people, the Onondagas. He is ugly but we need him." Thus from the beginning the encounter with Atotarho is unavoidable. Atotarho is an essential protagonist in the unfolding of the story.

The importance of Atotarho appears in the outcome of the legend. He has a place as an important obstacle in the way and realistically he cannot be swept aside. The final meeting between Deganawidah and Atotarho has the appearance of a bargaining party. Atotarho wants to know why he should yield to the desire of the five tribes. When he is told that he himself will have an important political role, he willingly accepts. Evil cannot be transformed without the higher forces of trust. Deganawidah has to trust Atotarho by taking a calculated risk. This can be done because as the initiate says: "Their strength [Five Nations] is stronger than thy [Atotarho] strength." Without the black magician the five tribes would not have found their greater strength. Without the new power of the tribes Atotarho could not have been healed.

The Iroquois Mysteries can also be defined as "Social Mysteries," borrowing a term coined by Harry Salman.[9] Hiawatha's initiation occurs within the world, and to each of the transformations of his soul correspond outer events. Inner and outer are continuously intermeshed. The first meeting of the cannibal with Deganawidah marks the beginning of Hiawatha's social work. It sets in motion the first challenge to Atotarho's authority. The second meeting with the Higher Guardian sets in motion the goal of uniting the tribes. We could say that Hiawatha's soul transformation ushers in a new epoch. The New Mind has completely penetrated an individual other than the initiate, through the levels of thinking, feeling, and will. This is all that is needed for others to be able to follow. Finally, the healing of Atotarho's mind and body is simultaneous with the forming of the League. The outer transformation of a decadent social form is intimately connected with the healing of its most representative individual, the black magician.

From all of the above we see that it is a particular kind of meeting that Hiawatha has with the forces of the Christ. The path that Hiawatha treads is similar to the one followed by Johannes Thomasius in Steiner's *Mystery Dramas*. Thomasius experiences the pain he has caused to a young girl who loved him and whom he abandoned; he feels her pain as if it were his. Steiner in fact indicates that the pain Thomasius has caused to the young girl stands as a theatrical device for the whole of Thomasius' encounter with the Lower Guardian, an experience normally incurred after death in the state of kamaloca. It is accompanied in Thomasius by the painful recognition of the reality of his lower nature. It is expressed in the following words in Scene Two of the *Portal of Initiation*: "Yet how do I behold myself. My human form is lost; as raging dragon I see myself, begot of lust and greed. I clearly sense how an illusion's cloud has hid from me till now my own appalling form." We find this inner experience of Thomasius prolonged in the inability to continue exerting his life-task of painting, a sort of soul numbness comparable to Hiawatha's grieving. Yet it is through this trial that new forces emerge from Thomasius' soul. It is in fact the starting point of Thomasius' later experiences in the spiritual world and the recognition of the reality of his higher self.[10]

The Iroquois Mysteries play a counterpart to the Mysteries that the Cathars and Templars developed in Europe, both at least partly influenced by Mani's doctrines. The Mysteries have in common the emphasis on the cultivation of a way of life within new social structures. Cathars and Templars strove to create a social order that made manifest the essence of the Christ impulse and prefigured social impulses of the future. The Cathars and Albigensians especially held a truly Manichean attitude toward evil, based on the belief that it could only be opposed through gentleness and transformed by the good. The Templars attempted to establish a truly Christ-imbued social order in which the individual would be emancipated from both religious and worldly authority, as they expressed it in the motto: "May every man be his own Pope and King."

The Iroquois Mysteries are mysteries of education of the will through thinking, equivalent to what Prokofieff calls a "path of forgiveness."[11] The education of Hiawatha starts with remorse, leading to his encounter with the Lower Guardian. A conscious, retrospective review of one's life, corresponding to the experience of kamaloca after death, allows the development and cultivation of tolerance. Understanding our shortcomings allows us to develop tolerance for ourselves and others. A more precise word for tolerance may be empathy, as it denotes a mastery over the astral body in the overcoming of sympathy and antipathy. In empathy, we avoid either extremes of separation in antipathy and an unconscious identification with the experience in the other person's soul in sympathy.

Hiawatha moves the process of empathy a step further in the ability to offer forgiveness. The act of forgiveness is the elevation and potentization of empathy, since it requires more than simple understanding. It is a stage in which the soul experiences inner powerlessness. This is an experience of death of the lower ego, allowing the higher ego to assert its presence and influence. In effect we can only forgive through our Spirit Self. The process of forgetting the evil perpetrated against oneself sustained in forgiveness can only be achieved through repeated effort, in order to avoid the pitfalls of retaliation or renunciation, the Ahrimanic and Luciferic temptations. In Hiawatha's case forgiveness means passing through a long period of "soul-numbness" before the higher self can start sending down its rays into the soul.

Finally, the awakening of his Spirit Self redirects Hiawatha to the higher calling of his individuality, to the pre-birth resolution that he carried into incarnation. This is the intention to take on his people's karma, working at the redemption of an evil that has its roots beyond his personal karma. Hiawatha's determination leads to the formation of the League and the transformation of the Ahrimanic impulse in the person of Atotarho, leading to his healing. Here, we may surmise, it is the influence of the initiate Deganawidah that plays a pivotal role in such an exalted task.

The Message and the Form

The tree of the White Roots of Peace, with roots spreading in the four directions, is a reference to the Tree of Life in other Iroquois myths. The eagle is the embodiment of the God Hinum, the Storm God (7 Elohim/ Great Spirit) represented by the Thunderbird who brings the grace of the rain upon the earth. The cosmic tree is often represented standing on the back of a turtle. This animal—a symbol of the land surrounded by the world waters—fittingly portrays the lingering Atlantean consciousness of the Native American. All the elements of the symbol of the White Roots of Peace point to a law that brings harmony between heaven and the earth.

The legend has yet other implications on the social level. The Ritual of Condolence has a central place in Iroquois society, not immediately notice- able from the legend. Previous to the advent of the League, the strife between the tribes was perpetuated by cycles of war and revenge, cannibalism, and black magic. Overcoming grief occupies a central place in Iroquois cere- mony and worldview. The cornerstone of Iroquois society is the recogni- tion of the need for the process of grief and consolation to replace the cycle of violence. The Iroquois believed that grief is what renders a human being irrational, anti-social, and dangerous. "These people believe that sadness, anger, and all violent passions expel the rational soul from the body, which meanwhile is animated only with the sensitive soul that we have in common with the animals," wrote the French Jesuit, Jean de Quen, in the seventeenth century. The same principle pervaded their system of justice. In the case of murder, the Law of Atonement envisioned a system of symbolic and mate- rial compensation to help restore harmony. The offender had to humiliate himself in order to expunge the community and his own shame. He had to compensate the offended party by giving them twenty strings of wampum, ten of which went for the life of the victim and ten others for his own life, symbolically forfeited in the crime. Finally, an equivalent principle was at work in the idea of mitigating loss through adoption. The adopted person took the place of a deceased person. The practice was so widespread that Jesuit missionaries report that in some villages there were more adopted strangers than Iroquois themselves.[12]

The birth of this new "social ritualism" enshrines the recognition of the role of individual destiny in the social fabric. The Ritual of Condolence makes possible the harmonization of the aims of the community by allowing individuals to overcome their grief and align their destiny with the community's endeavor. Grief is seen as a veil coming over the senses and the heart. The Ritual of Condolence lifts this veil and makes explicit the second principle expressed by Deganawidah: health as harmony between spirit and body.

There is equally important outcome of the legend in the form of government that appears with the Iroquois League—the Haudenosaunee. The New Word is the message of justice, health, and power. The Iroquois know that a word is nothing without a form. They have embodied the word in the form of the Longhouse—the union of many fires—representing the idea of confederacy. For the first time nations stand as equals, no longer as vassals. Authority is shared by a complex hierarchy of power, built to ensure that no individual or single nation can at any time impose their will over the community. It is in fact a system of checks and balances, obliging the representatives of power to seek broad consensus in all their decisions. Hereditary titles within family lineages were conferred through decisions of the leading women; otherwise, especially at the time of the colonies, "pine-tree chiefs" were elected based on their merits and outside hereditary considerations. Any chief could be revoked if he had broken the provisions of the law. Additionally, each nation nominated a war chief who raised fighters in time of war. The system of clans was built in such a way to overlap the boundaries of the nations and build social cohesion within the league. More detail about the Iroquois form of government can be found in the fine analysis of Bruce Johansen.[13]

Iroquois spirituality cannot be properly understood if we do not perceive how intimately the new form of government is linked with what we could call the new Social Mysteries. A government structure alone does not define and hold a new social vision; society requires a new spirituality. The Iroquois have a true "social spirituality," naturally added to all previous sacred practices that continue to be carried on through centuries of tradition.

The Ritual of Condolence is a spiritual cornerstone of the Iroquois form of government, as are the Law of Atonement, the practice of Adoption, and other social practices. Through these relatively recent traditions the individuals can reach in stages a perception of their own karmic doubles, meet with the Lower Guardian of the Threshold, and eventually in the distant future, with the Higher Guardian of the Threshold. The new rituals give a dimension of sacredness to the cultivation and restoration of healthy relationships within the social body. In a sense they are the esoteric aspect of government, the inner aspect of the problem of governance. Left to themselves, the Iroquois forms of government are nothing more than beneficial but empty shells. The social rituals contain the life that sustains these forms.

In the Iroquois legend, one may perceive a continuation of the fight against the decadent Mexican Mysteries as they are reborn in a milder form in Northern America through the practices of cannibalism and black magic. For the first time in North America the structures of government respect personal individuality. Power has only a temporary and limited nature and can be transferred according to personal merit, not heredity alone. The Iroquois League also marks a remarkable departure from the idea of the old blood ties. Anyone who can accept the ideas of the legend of the White Roots of Peace can belong to the Iroquois society. In fact, adoption becomes a common principle, a practice extended to numerous European colonists in later centuries. Another major advance is that now evil can be at least partly redeemed, as is made clear in the figure of Atotarho. This is the important next step that the Iroquois Mysteries add to the Mexican Mysteries.

Conclusions

W e have seen that the Iroquois and Aztec legends echo the Mexican Mysteries at the time of Christ. What is the relation of these new mysteries with the Mexican Mysteries? After the vanquishing of the Mysteries of Taotl, at the time of Christ, Steiner indicates that:

> Nothing survived from these regions of what might have lived on if the mysteries of Taotl had borne fruit. The forces left over from the impulses that lived in these mysteries survived only in the etheric world. They still exist subsensibly, belonging to what would be seen if in the sphere of the spirit, one could light a paper over a solfatara.[1]

Later on in the same lecture cycle the thought is thus completed:

> Nevertheless, so much force remained that a further attack could have been made upon the fifth epoch, having as its aim so to mechanize the earth that the resulting culture would not only have culminated in a mass of purely mechanical contrivances, but would have made human beings themselves into such pure homunculi that their egos would have departed.[2]

Fifteen centuries later America arrived at another crucial crossroads: the transition into the fifth post-Atlantean age. It is sheer coincidence that the fifth post-Atlantean epoch corresponds in time with the Mesoamerican Fifth Age or Sun. This transition takes a different dimension in America than in Europe, where it brings forth the birth of the Consciousness Soul whose key signature is the development of modern science and the materialistic outlook on life, antedating the development of spiritual science and a new apprehension of spiritual reality. In America the changes did not manifest as clearly in the realm of consciousness, but rather in the development of new socio-political models, best exemplified by the Aztec Empire and the Iroquois League. These are two developments on the opposite ends of a continuum: a centralized, unified state on one end and a federal system on the other. In the language of the Popol Vuh, they are the forms of the Fire God and Hunahpu respectively. To anthroposophy, Aztec social forms are the manifestation of an Ahrimanic society; the Iroquois League offers the embodiment of a new Christ-centered society.

Aztecs and Iroquois: Two Different Views of the Human Heart

In the myths and legends of the two civilizations a set of central images contrasts each other: heart sacrifice and the Ritual of Condolence. Human sacrifice by heart removal is a second attempt to discourage the human soul from the further aims of Earth evolution. Aztec mythology is pervaded by a simple, dualistic thinking in which good and evil play very static roles. Human sacrifice is the means to fight against the evil that wants to stop the regular course of the sun. Aztec myth in its literalism bans the imagination from the human heart, and its simplistic dualism binds the human being to automatic reactions. Revenge follows attack, war follows war. The ultimate Aztec worldview makes the human being an automaton relinquishing all true humanity.

Against the dualistic Aztec picture stands the threefold nature of the Iroquois message. Three are its central participants: Deganawidah, Atotarho, and Hiawatha, and threefold is the central message of righteousness, health, and law. Its approach toward evil is not an either/or proposition. Evil is simply an element of a human soul life that is out of balance. The "evil person" needs to be understood in order to be healed. The Iroquois recognize that evil lives on two levels: on the outer level it corresponds to the practices of cannibalism, war, and black magic, and on the inner level it corresponds to the heart's unresolved grief and the resulting desire for revenge. The Ritual of Condolence offers a "re-quickening" of the heart and senses burdened by the weight of grief. The whole society turns its attention to the fate of the individual, knowing that the destinies of everyone else are affected by it. The Iroquois know that warfare and revenge have their roots in the human heart and soul. Hiawatha's and

Deganawidah's healing of Atotarho is the most spectacular instance of healing—a Ritual of Condolence practiced on the black magician's heart.

The difference of worldviews is reflected clearly in the Aztec and Iroquois power structures. The Aztecs started as a Triple Alliance, but there was nothing federal about it or about their later empire. It was in fact the most extreme form of centralized government. The Tlaotani held the reins of education and culture, political and administrative functions, the army, and the economy. Behind him, and invisible, stood the true power of the high priest. All of the tribute flowed from the farthest parts of the empire toward Tenochtitlan. With it followed the captive warriors that justified the existence of the bloodthirsty priesthood. A unitary, centralized state and human oppression, going hand in hand, characterized the deepest essence of Aztec domination.

An opposing image emerges from the Iroquois League. It is a true confederacy where each of the nations stands on a footing of true equality. The Longhouse is a complex and diversified form of government, whose main concern is to grant power at the level where it is functional. Each nation has autonomy over internal matters, and in common matters no nation or group of nations can prevail over the others. Seeking consensus is the mandatory outcome of the delicate balance of powers devised by the founders of the league. Religious power is separated from political power.

The two world-views call upon completely different social forms. The Iroquois achieve the first stages of realization of a true federalism based on decentralization and local autonomy. Whereas in the Aztec Empire the individual is a simple tool for the aims of the state, the Iroquois social form favors the freedom of the individual and allows her to offer her best contribution to the benefit of the whole.

The ultimate Aztec achievement is the subversion of moral codes. After fifteen centuries of preparation, Ahriman, the Fire God, has managed to bring forth a completely new moral code. Absolute dualism is central to the Aztec worldview, while revealed as a fallacy to a deeper observation of reality. It is only through such rudimentary dualism that complex problems can become trivial, and simplistic solutions offered in the name of the good. The outcome of Aztec rule is the numbing of the forces of the heart. To this was turned the effort that some historians have called "creative mythography." Aztec myth glorifies the worst evil—deliberate ritual murder—by elevating it to the level of the highest good. Ritual murder is equated with an act of co-creation, a sacred offering to the gods.

To the changes arising in the fifth post-Atlantean age the Iroquois responded not with external sacrifice or self-sacrifice (bloodletting), but with another faculty of the heart: inner sacrifice. Through his soul sacrifice Hiawatha can contribute to the healing of Atotarho and to the formation of the League. A careful reading of the legend shows that the two are achieved simultaneously. Hiawatha embodies the ideal of true inner self-sacrifice done for the good of all. This is the heart sensing that in the soul's grieving and its conscious inner recognition lies the ability to affect not only personal but also social destiny.

Heart and blood form links with heredity when looked at from the perspective of the past, and with the furthering of social evolution, when looked at from the perspective of the future. The Iroquois strengthen the individual by releasing the bonds of heredity. Their frequent use of adoption reflects the idea that to be Iroquois means accepting the idea of the White Roots of Peace, more than a matter of bloodline and inheritance. The Aztecs exalt the weight of heredity. Their claims of descent from the Toltecs and the mythical Aztlan are obvious untruths in the face of history, but necessary to their re-writing of history. The return to the past of Aztlan stands in clear contrast with the evolutionary possibilities of the "New Mind."

The heart plays a vital role in Aztec and Iroquois worldviews. The Aztecs stamped out the heart—ultimately, only in a physical way. Their code of ethics negated the reality of the value of human relationships. The Iroquois made the understanding of grief the very cornerstone of their worldview. Only a heart that can understand its own grief can accept, forgive, and return to positively integrate into society, contributing to its functioning.

We have followed some of the main events of American history from the time before our era to the time of European colonization. We have named those spiritual forces that animated the changes occurring over time, the Mexican Mysteries, according to the term first used by Rudolf Steiner. It can be a confusing term because, to those who have read him in this context, it may only evoke the image of human sacrifice. We have therefore specified that there were progressive and decadent Mexican Mysteries. At the time of the Consciousness Soul—roughly equivalent to the time of the Conquest—we should more properly speak of American Mysteries, since their centers are no longer exclusively associated with Mexico or Central America.

To unveil the deeper meaning of the American Mysteries and their relevance for modern times, we first have to deepen our understanding of the purpose of human sacrifice involving organ removal. Here, only spiritual scientific research will allow us to understand what science and history cannot penetrate—particularly Steiner's assertion that it was the stomach that was removed at the time of Christ, whereas it was the heart at the time of the Aztecs.

Stomach and Heart: From the Fourth to the Fifth Post-Atlantean Age

The wisdom to be taught to the initiate of the decadent mysteries could only be unveiled through the performance of particular human sacrifices. This is what Steiner has to say concerning these mysteries at the time of Christ and before:

> When the candidates to be initiated had matured on this path and had come to experience its inner meaning, they had learned the nature of the mutual interaction between the one who had been murdered and the one who had been initiated. Through the murder, the victim was to be prepared in his soul to strive upward to the Luciferic realm, whereas the candidate for initiation was to obtain the wisdom to mold his earthly world in such a way that souls would be driven out of it. Through the fact that a connection was formed between the murdered and the initiated— one cannot say "murderer," but "initiated"—it was made possible for the initiated to be taken with the other soul; that is, the initiated could himself forsake the earth at the right moment.[3]

What was the further purpose of these mysteries is again unfathomable to modern history. Once again we return to Steiner's research:

> If their impulses and workings had been victorious, these mysteries would have driven souls away from the earth. By this means the service performed by Ahriman, the squeezing out of the lemons, would have become effective. The earth would gradually have become desolate, having upon it only the forces of death, whereas any living souls would have departed to found another planet under the leadership of Lucifer and Ahriman.

In order to execute the Ahrimanic part of this task, it was necessary for the priests of these Ahrimanic Atlantean mysteries to acquire faculties possessing the highest degree of control and mastery over all the forces of death in earthly working. These forces would have made the earth together with physical man—for the souls were to depart—into a purely mechanistic realm, a great dead realm in which no ego could have a place. These faculties would have to be connected also with mastery of the mechanistic element in everything living, of the mechanistic element in all life.[4]

Steiner goes on to reiterate the way in which the practice of human sacrifice was performed.

For this reason these mysteries had to be instituted in a truly devilish form, because such forces as would have been needed for the powerful aims of Ahriman can only arise when initiations of a special kind are attained. Such were these initiations of the Ahrimanic post-Atlantean era in America. Everyone who was to attain a certain degree of knowledge was made to realize that this knowledge is acquired through certain faculties of perception that can only be engendered through an act of murder. Thus nobody who had not committed murder was admitted to a certain degree of this initiation. The murder was performed under special circumstances. Steps led up to a kind of catafalque, a scaffold-like structure. The one to be murdered was tied to this and his body bent in such a way that his stomach could be excised with a single cut. This operation, the excision of the stomach, had to be preformed with great dexterity. Certain experiences arose from the act of having cut into the living organism with such consummate skill, and under such special conditions. These experiences had to be acquired and through them a certain degree of knowledge concerning the mechanization of the earth could be attained. Every time higher stages of initiation were to be reached, further murders had to be committed.[5]

The above statements of Steiner allow us to understand what was at stake in the battle between Vitzliputzli/Ixbalamqué and the super-magician for the future of America. The Amuesha myth, quoted in Chapter 1 (given in full in Appendix 1), indicates a consequence of the Ahrimanic initiations with the phenomenon of women's sterility and the resulting threat to continued incarnation. The Popol Vuh knew of it as well. The sacred book is not concerned with issues of a simplistic moral nature. The whole attention of the Maya Quiché text turns away from the fate of kings and rulers, and focuses instead on the deeds of the gods and the responses of human beings to their calls. Hunahpu and Tohil/Fire God/Ahriman form the pivotal point of the sacred drama. Solar God and Fire God offer two different propositions to the human being, and the Popol Vuh follows and illustrates each one.

Steiner's assertion of the stomach being the object of excision rather than the heart before the time of Christ is impossible to prove historically. It must be found at a much deeper level, and this work can only provide partial answers on the subject. There is no doubt that Aztec priests removed the heart, but we must remember that there is a discontinuity of a millennium as far as human sacrifice with organ removal is concerned. Steiner's assertion that the knowledge of the sacrificing priesthood had been overcome for the whole of the fourth post-Atlantean period is confirmed historically to quite a degree. Human sacrifice continued with alternate phases during the following centuries. Teotihuacan from the second century, and the Maya starting from the end of the fourth century, practiced "exoteric forms" of human sacrifice (e.g., decapitation or arrow shooting). Sacrifice with heart removal was first practiced by the civilization of Chichen Itza in the eleventh century. However, it was the Aztecs who brought the practice of human sacrifice with heart removal to a new height. They not only reinstated it but also accompanied their practice with the first wholly coherent ideology. Furthermore, the scale of human sacrifice reached unprecedented dimensions.

What has been the process of evolution of the Mexican Mysteries? Why would human sacrifice concern first the stomach and then the heart? These are weighty questions to ask, and ultimately the answer can only be given through direct spiritual perception. Our exploration can only be tentative. I invite the reader to try to formulate the direction of an answer by entering into the central imaginative representations of the two turning points that this book has explored: the time of Christ in Izapa and Central Mexico, and the fifth post-Atlantean epoch among Aztecs and Iroquois. These were the two periods accompanied by the major changes of consciousness on the American continent. We will try to live in the qualities of the polarities that present themselves at these two historical turning points.

The first contrast is offered to us by the Popol Vuh in Parts II and III. It is given in the central image of the Dawning and the equivalent phenomenon that we have labeled the "anti-Dawning." Keep in mind that the second is simply a particular manifestation of the first. The Popol Vuh indicates that this is the exact moment of the transition between the Third and the Fourth Age. The central question of the Third Age was the problem of death. American humanity of the Third Age felt abandoned by the gods. The Ahpus left their abode in the heavens in order to penetrate the reality of earth and of death.

Let us look at the "anti-Dawning" first, the condition faced by the Toltecs. The Camé replaced the cult of the Ahpus with those of Taotl and Quetzalcoatl. The whole desire to reside on earth was threatened, and the Popol Vuh lingers long on this wrenching soul condition. Once the sun arises, the text says: "The sun rose and came up like a man. And its heat was unbearable. Certainly it was not the same sun that we see..." Human sacrifice with organ removal was nevertheless overcome and the priesthood had to hide. However, regrets, anxiety, and doubts were not quelled. The gift of fire could not compensate for the emptiness the soul felt, especially after the Dawning. The "anti-Dawning" experienced by the Toltecs was accompanied over many centuries by a progressive state of dependence upon Tohil/Ahriman.

On the other hand, in Izapa, while Hun Hunahpu's head hung on the World Tree and the tribes awaited the deeds of the Twins, another image emerges. We need to picture vividly the soul of the Native American for whom the outer world and inner reality formed an indivisible unity. The priests in Izapa prepared the American soul through the ritual cultivation of maize. In an allegorical manner they showed the immortality of the soul, compared to the grain of maize undergoing death and resurrection below the earth. This is a truly universal image that accompanies American humanity from north to south, wherever maize is cultivated.

The Dawning, accompanying the final deed of the initiate Ixbalamqué/Vitzliputzli, was the realization of the prophecy of immortality of the sacred calendar. It was a true resurrection for nature and for man. This is why it is equated with a new creation. Outwardly the sun, moon, and stars appeared in their full glory to the Atlantean-like consciousness of the Native American. The celestial bodies were fully experienced in a new physical dimension. The event was further reflected in the birth of the new galactic astronomy and the Long Count. Eternity was fathomed as the true essence of time and of man. Gone was the dread of the end of time. If the world had a future beyond the reality of death by not having succumbed to the attempts of the super-magician, then souls could continue to live on earth filled with renewed desire to further its evolution. Life goes through death and resurrection; this was the deeper answer brought by the deeds of Ixbalamqué. Steiner indicates that Vitzliputzli/Ixbalamqué killed the black magician because only through his death could evil be contained and banned until the fifth post-Atlantean epoch. The Popol Vuh refers to the death of the sevenfold Hun Camé/Vucub Camé, and mentions that evil would now operate only within restricted boundaries.

The second contrast is the one we have set forth in the previous chapter. In Tenochtitlan conquest is accompanied with literal rivers of blood. The sight of blood and skulls, the stench that accompanies decaying bodies, are an everyday scene in Aztec life, one that the imagination has difficulty grasping. Society is built upon the cardinal rule of suffering imposed on others or self-imposed through bloodletting. The supreme religious authorities see the human being in a continuous state of debt toward the gods. The sun that sheds his light for the good of the human beings is that very same sun that requires their lives in order to exist. Ultimately this proposition is a conundrum that cannot be resolved and denies even simple Aztec dualism. The Aztecs made evil supreme by devising a dualistic worldview and painting evil as the good to be attained. For this purpose they rewrote history and myth.

The Iroquois at their best offered a polar opposite image to that of the Aztecs. The grief of one is potentially the grief of all, because grief is the source of social unrest. It is the duty of each and every person to offer relief for the suffering of others. This duty is accompanied not by vague moral injunctions but by the powerful institution of the Ritual of Condolence and other social rituals, such as the Ritual of Adoption or the Law of Atonement. The gods want humanity to strive toward happiness and fulfillment. This happiness is not something that human beings can take for granted, but something they take a part in building. The social order that the Iroquois devised makes the human being a co-creator with the gods. Through the individual's willingness to perform the Ritual of Condolence, the miracle of true human encounter can occur ever and ever again, between two people or two groups. The rituals allow human beings to work at transforming their karmic double. Grief is a stage in the encounter with the Lower Guardian. Only by facilitating that meeting and transformation can true human encounter and social healing occur in society.

True encounter allows spiritual forces to add their strength to the cohesion of society. In every true encounter a certain amount of karmic order is restored, allowing the spiritual world to be present and active. The result can then be larger than the sum of the parts brought in by the two individuals or groups. Healing of grief acts therefore both at the individual and at the collective level.

The Iroquois have a reciprocal relation with the creator. By observing their threefold law they can receive the blessings of the Holder of the Heavens. They need not be enemies of evil. In their worldview, evil is a necessary step toward the accomplishment of a higher good, and can only be overcome with gentleness. Only in this way can true individuality blossom. Since evil is not the outer demon that the Aztecs portray but an inner constituent of the human soul, it cannot be simply stamped out without deadening the forces of the heart and soul at the same time. The inner aspect is accompanied and reflected outwardly by social forms that make true encounter possible. Social forms have a complementary role. They are so devised that they can hold the image of the higher self in front of the human being. The threefold law expresses this on one side in the desire for justice and the search for harmony between body and spirit. On the other hand, the lower self needs to be kept under check from possible excesses, in order to preserve society; this is specifically the role of the third part of the message, the one referred to as the "law backed up by force." Iroquois social structures are effective because they are accompanied by the rituals that sustain them and form their inner backbone. It would be impossible to envision an effective Iroquois political structure without the spirituality that accompanies the rituals. If one were divorced from the other, the forms would be emptied out.

Individuality and social compacts are two sides of a precarious balance. Society can foster or hinder the development of the Spirit Self in the individual. Every intermediate social form evolves by necessity over the long term toward either the Iroquois or the Aztec pole. Social forms that necessitate and promote true encounter have to reflect and be based upon the threefold nature of the human being. There could be no better examples than the extremes of the completely rigidly centralized Aztec State and the flexible set of forms of true federalism envisioned by the Iroquois.

Looking then at the two sets of contrasting images we can try to envision the nature of the changes that the Mexican Mysteries have undergone over fifteen centuries. Steiner succinctly characterizes the new condition facing humankind in the fifth post-Atlantean epoch in the following way:

> Today when Christ is destined to appear again in the etheric body, when a kind of Mystery of Golgotha is to be experienced anew, evil will have the significance akin to that of birth and death for the fourth post-Atlantean epoch! In the fourth epoch the Christ impulse was born out of the forces of death for the salvation of humankind. We can say that we owe the new impulse that permeated humankind to the event on Golgotha. Thus by a strange paradox humankind is led to a renewed experience of the Mystery of Golgotha in the fifth epoch through the forces of evil. Through the experience of evil it will be possible for the Christ to appear again, just as He appeared in the fourth post-Atlantean epoch through the experience of death.[6]

We have moved in time from the mysteries of life and death to the mysteries of good and evil at the onset of the fifth post-Atlantean epoch. This evolution lives behind the transformation of human sacrifice from removal of the stomach to removal of the heart. At the time of Christ the decadent mysteries were stamping out all desire of the soul to live in a world moving toward death, both at the microcosmic and the macrocosmic levels. The stomach represents this pure level of will in all the figurative ways we know of, in our own and many other languages. In the fifteenth century, the Aztecs were threatening all real understanding of good and evil and all human desire to try to grasp the difference. This is the realm of "knowledge of the heart," as is once again acknowledged by common language.

The Mexican and American Mysteries are in a higher sense "Mysteries of the Will." At the time of Christ this is made visible in the figure of the initiate, Ixbalamqué. His initiation is an initiation in the world. There were no precedents to his deeds, nor any Mystery School that could have taught a way to accomplish them. Ixbalamqué had to face ever anew completely different situations with the help of Christ and the spiritual world.

For the disciples of the mysteries the initiation took the form partly recorded in Izapa. Cosmology taught the disciple the path into the macrocosm. There he could learn of the fallacy of Polar God and Fire God in the new conditions of evolution. He was also taught all of the knowledge of the Popol Vuh concerning the past. The descent into the microcosm was accompanied by the trials of the soul in the Caves, where the powers of Xibalba could be known and overcome. The pupil had to experience the temptations of the Fire God and had to hold on to the memory of the deeds of the initiate Ixbalamqué and of the solar spirit Hunahpu.

At the beginning of the fifth post-Atlantean epoch these Mysteries of the Will attained a larger social dimension. Hiawatha is initiated in the will by Deganawidah. His path is the path of forgiveness that forms the prelude to the encounter with the Christ and the ability to carry the destiny of his people. The opposite gesture is carried in Aztec spirituality, where individuality is stamped out and where the initiate high priest personifies ruthless Ahrimanic will in the carrying out of human sacrifice. We have seen that this dichotomy is reflected in the social ordering of Iroquois and Aztec polities. The American Mysteries are first and foremost Social Mysteries. The same could be intuited about the revolution carried out by the Incas in Andean South America. They too introduced a completely new social form in the southern continent, close in time to the Aztec rise to power.

The contrasting Fire God/Hunahpu forms the central pivot of the Popol Vuh. Through it Mesoamerican and North American spirituality anticipate the themes of what we can call the modern Social Mysteries. These have manifested in two directions. On one side lies the centralized state in its most extreme forms: Bolshevik communism since 1917, and later fascism and Nazism. Over and against this context Steiner saw the urgency for humanity to apprehend the ideas of a threefold social order in which he articulated the separation and autonomy of cultural, political, and economic spheres of activity.

Mexican Mysteries, American Mysteries, and Modern Social Mysteries

The following is a thumbnail sketch of the relevance of the American Mysteries for the present time—no more than a general indication that should be further developed.

Steiner's threefold social order is an attempt to focus the social question in directions that move away from the abstract formulations that lived in the nineteenth and twentieth century (and at present), which could not and can no longer bring any social renewal. In the threefold social order, for the first time an initiate brought to humankind an impulse for social renewal, resting on a spiritual understanding of the membering of the human being in spirit, soul, and body, and its reflection in the articulation of the social body in cultural, political, and economic realms. Although it derives its foundations from spiritual knowledge, the application of three-folding at any level of social reality does not require anything more than an earnest desire to apprehend the practical applications deriving from it.

At present, all inherently political alternatives to cultural and social decay that we witness will fall short of their stated goal. Humanity is crossing the threshold of the spiritual world and new temptations face all human beings. Steiner puts it thus: "certain, shall we say, occult knowledge is forcing its way into the present-day development of humankind. Actually, this knowledge is forcing its way to the surface of its own accord as the result of human evolution, so that it is not necessary to make any extra effort to place it within the development of humankind."[7] This is the source of knowledge that is presently made available for the goals of occult brotherhoods, particularly the Western Lodges, laying the ground for the aims of political imperialism, as it was made historically apparent first in British and now in American imperialism. This is the temptation from which the fifth post-Atlantean epoch can barely escape: the use of esoteric knowledge, applied for the selfish benefit of national or super-national groups. "For in this fifth post-Atlantean period humankind has reached a stage in evolution at which it is very difficult for the individual to escape from his personal affairs. The individual is in danger of mixing up his personal instincts and passions with what is common with humankind as a whole."[8]

Steiner foresaw the danger that the above tendency embodied in the extreme in Anglo-American imperialism. "People today must be shown how the economic life, introduced by Anglo-American habits of thought, is creeping along the ground, and that it will only be able to climb its way upward if it works in harmony with those things which people in other spheres are capable of doing and for which they have talents. If this does not happen, world dominance by the economic life will be a catastrophe."[9]

There is no doubt then that the social future lies in what use will be made of the occult knowledge that reaches the surface of consciousness. Will this knowledge benefit small circles that keep it secret for the sake of the political, economic, and spiritual goals of the few or will this knowledge be made accessible to the uninitiated in ways that benefit the whole of society indistinctly? These are the terms of the dilemma that Steiner perceived with great clarity.

Seen under the light of the above considerations, the polarity between Aztec and Iroquois worldviews does in no way correspond to opposite political views. The Aztec social model reappears metamorphosed in the twentieth century in the extreme political forms of communism and fascism. These tendencies are presently latent in the unified state—even in the form of a democracy, wherever the social form tends to consolidate into the unified state, rather than articulate the autonomy of cultural, political, and economic spheres. Iroquois polity was introduced by an initiate for the good of people that had long been entrenched in fratricidal wars. It brought initiation knowledge for the purpose of social and individual renewal.

In modern terms the Iroquois/Aztec contrast was articulated by Steiner and emphasized over and again: "A great battle is taking place between the threefold social impulse that can come from spiritual science and that which throws itself against this threefoldness as the wave of Bolshevism, which would lead to great harm amongst humanity. And there is no third element other than these two."[10] For Steiner, the term Bolshevism is intended as something larger than what appeared on earth with the Russian Revolution. The Russian example is a first, tragic embodiment of a reality that will accompany humankind for a long time to come. It was followed by fascism and Nazism, and arguably at present with the forms of worldwide religious fanaticism.

Steiner characterizes Bolshevism thus: "[In Bolshevism] the animal, bristling with intelligence, seeks to work its way to the surface and to make all the Ahrimanic forces that have the aim of excluding the specifically human element, together with the cleverness of the animal kingdom... into forces that exert a formative influence upon humanity."[11] And he reminds us, "If things were to turn out the way they are developing in Russia at present, it would mean that the Earth would lose its task, would have its mission withdrawn, would be expelled from the universe and fall prey to Ahriman."[12] The consequences of Bolshevism closely remind us of what Steiner said about the Mexican Mysteries, both at the time of Christ and at the time of the Aztecs.

Steiner has offered us ample evidence of the Ahrimanic nature of the Bolshevik state and of the initiation undergone by its hierarchy. What appeared in North American history anticipates modern developments by four to five centuries. Future social forms in their most developed stages will correspond to either the Ahrimanic state and its corresponding initiation or the threefold social order with its grounding upon modern spiritual science. This set of alternatives underlines the necessity of the times to come to a conscious spiritual knowledge. Where that knowledge is absent or unconscious the void is filled by Ahriman, leading to the unified, centralized state. Where natural evolutionary tendencies want to acquire fuller consciousness of themselves, these will lead to the emergence of a newly independent cultural sphere and the development of new social forms along the lines of threefolding. The latter will ultimately be nourished by spiritual knowledge as it flows through the fountainhead of spiritual science. Every intermediate form, resting solely on political grounds, is ultimately unstable and will evolve in either direction toward the unified central state or toward threefolding.

The polarity of Aztec/Iroquois illustrates four to five centuries before our time the close link between social forms and their corresponding initiation paths. This is the little known and appreciated contribution of American spirituality to the world. The Aztec Empire rests upon the central occult practice of human sacrifice; the Iroquois League is supported through the message of power and peace and the social ritualism most clearly exemplified by the Ritual of Condolence. Human freedom and co-creation with the progressive gods or gradual enslavement to the powers of the Fire God: this is the core central message of the Popol Vuh and its relevance for modern humanity.

APPENDICES

Yompor Ror and Yachor Arrorr: the Origin of the Sun and the Moon

Amuesha myth from: *The Power of Love: The Moral Use of Knowledge Amongst the Amuesha of Central Peru* by Fernando Santos-Granero

In the old times when Yompor Rret, the ancient solar divinity, still illuminated this earth, the world almost came to an end. Women gave birth only to rotten wood, lizards, or beings that looked like co'ch, the woolly monkey. This happened because the people did not follow the words of Our Father.

One day a priest instructed his followers to select a pair of siblings—a boy and a girl—and to build a house where they could be brought up away from other people. Thus, brought up in isolation, the siblings became adults. One day they went out fishing. On their way to the river the girl found two beautiful flowers which she picked and kept on her bosom. It was thus that she became pregnant.

When she noticed that she was pregnant they went to see the priest. The priest asked them whether they had had sexual relations. They denied it. They were ordered to undress, and were found to be innocent. The priest then realized that it had been Yato' Yos, Our Grandfather Yos, the supreme divinity, who had sent the flowers by means of which the girl became pregnant, and ordered her brother to keep close watch on her from then onwards. But he disobeyed the priest, and one day she was killed by Patonell, the mother of the jaguars. The twins she was bearing jumped into the river, where they were suckled by Meshet, the armored catfish, and played day after day.

The priest wondered how they could recover the lost twins. He asked his followers which of them would be able to capture them. Sha'rep, the lizard, offered to seize them, but the people made fun of him, saying that nobody who was covered by scales would be able to get hold of them. Very much offended, Sha'rep left and went down-river.

The people attempted to capture the twins, without success. The priest then reprimanded them for not allowing Sha'rep to talk. He sent them to find him and bring him back, but Sha'rep would not come back. Five times they went to him before he agreed to capture the twins.

After several unsuccessful attempts Sha'rep finally captured the twins. The people rejoiced and decided to raise them. Two summers went by and the twins would not grow. The people became angry with them. One day the mother of the jaguars came by and asked who the children were. She did not recognize them as the children of the woman she had killed. The people told her that they were bringing them up, but that they would not grow. Patonell offered to bring them up herself, as she had lots of meat in her household. She took the children with her and fed them all sorts of wild game, but they still would not grow. They were constantly dirty with their own excrement. Patonell bathed them every morning and, before leaving for her garden, she left them some fermented manioc mash to eat, warning them not to touch her manioc beer with their dirty hands. Every day, when she came back, she would find them drunk. She asked them how they had become drunk and they would always answer that they were drunk from the fermented manioc mash she had left them. But this was not true; they got drunk on the beer prepared for them by their sister bee. They visited her every day, got drunk, and when Patonell was about to return from her garden they would go back to her house and become small and dirty again. They looked like children, but they were already adults.

One day the jaguars failed to bring back game, so they told their mother that were they to fail again she should cook the twins. One day they left and told her that they would be back in five days, and she should have the twins cooked by that time. When the day arrived Patonell told the twins to bring some water and boil it because she was going to cook them. Then she told them to pick out her lice so that she would remember them with affection. While they were doing so they belched, and Patonell asked them what they had been drinking that their belches smelt so strongly. They told her that they had prepared some beer and she should not be afraid, for they had washed their hands before doing so. So Patonell asked them if she could try it. She drank and drank until she fell asleep. Then the twins cut her into pieces and threw her into the pot of boiling water. They buried one of her back paws in her main garden, the other in her coca garden, and her front paws they buried where she always used to go to fetch water.

By then they could hear the jaguars returning from their hunting expedition, so they hid under the roof. The jaguars arrived at the house and called their mother. One of the buried back paws answered from her garden. One of the jaguars went there to tell their mother to come home. He went to the garden and called Patonell. This time she answered from her coca garden. Her son went there and called her again. This time she answered from the stream and said: 'I have already cooked the little ones. You can eat them. I do not want to see them because I am sad for them.'

So they started eating the meat that was in the pot. While they were doing so the twins sang from the roof: 'Piripi, they are eating Patonell with hot pepper.' Manor, the jungle's puma, had not eaten yet and he was sitting on the floor with Porren, the margay and Oshcoll, the ocelot. Those who had not yet eaten told the other: 'You are eating at ease and are not paying attention to that voice that is saying we are eating our mother.' So they stirred the contents of the pot and discovered Patonell's head. They realized that the twins had deceived them, but as they had already started eating they decided to finish.

When they had finished they decided to take revenge, so they set the house on fire. Whenever an insect jumped out they devoured it, in the hope that it would be one of the twins. When the house collapsed the twins flew and landed in a field covered with tall grass. The jaguars went after them. The twins crossed a lake, and with the woven ropes of their slings they formed a bridge. They then told the jaguars that if they wanted to avenge their dead mother they should cross the bridge. All of them started to cross it, but when they were halfway across the twins twisted their slings and all the jaguars fell into the boiling waters of the lake. Only a pregnant female jaguar escaped. Her offspring was a male. They bred, and that is why jaguars still exist today.

The twins became adults again. They had pretended all the time to be children to take revenge on the jaguars for the death of their mother. Afterward they went straight to heaven. There the man illuminated the heavens during the day, while the woman illuminated the heavens during the night. Before that this earth was illuminated by Yompor Rret. He was evil, and every five days he threw stones from above and killed many people. It was for this reason that they isolated and ritually brought up the two siblings. This is how the story of Yompor Ror, Our Father the Sun, and Yachor Arrorr, Our Mother the Moon, ends.

The Birth of Huitzilopochtli, Patron God of the Aztecs

(Taken from: *Florentine Codex, book 3, chapter 1*, translated by M. Leon-Portilla)

The Aztecs greatly revered Huitzilopochtli; they knew his origin, his beginning, was in this manner. In Coatepec, on the way to Tula, there was living, there dwelt a woman by the name of Coatlicue. She was mother of the four hundred gods of the south and their sister by name Coyolxauhqui.

And this Coatlicue did penance there, she swept, it was her task to sweep, thus she did penance in Coatepec, the Mountain of the Serpent. And one day, when Coatlicue was sweeping, there fell on her some plumage, a ball of fine feathers. Immediately Coatlicue picked them up and put them in her bosom. When she finished sweeping, she looked for the feathers she had put in her bosom, but she found nothing there. At that moment Coatlicue was with child.

The four hundred gods of the south, seeing their mother was with child, were very annoyed and said: "Who has done this to you? Who has made you with child? This insults us, dishonors us." And their sister Coyolxauhqui said to them: "My brothers, she has dishonored us, we must kill our mother, the wicked woman who is now with child. Who gave her what she carries in her womb?"

When Coatlicue learned of this, she was very frightened, she was very sad. But her son Huitzilopóchtli, in her womb, comforted her, said to her: "Do not be afraid, I know what I must do." Coatlicue, having heard the words of her son, was consoled, her heart was quiet, she felt at peace.

But meanwhile the four hundred gods of the south came together to take a decision, and together they decided to kill their mother, because she had disgraced them. They were very angry, they were very agitated, as if the heart had gone out of them. Coyolxauhqui incited them, she inflamed the anger of her brothers, so that they should kill her mother. And the four hundred gods made ready, they attired themselves as for war.

And those four hundred gods of the south were like captains; they twisted and bound up their hair as warriors arrange their long hair.

But one of them called Cuahuitlicac broke his word. What the four hundred said, he went immediately to tell, he went and revealed it to Huitzilopochtli. And Huitzilopochtli replied to him: "Take care, be watchful, my uncle, for I know well what I must do."

And when finally they came to an agreement, the four hundred gods were determined to kill, to do away with their mother; then they began to prepare, Coyolxauhqui directing them. They were very robust, well equipped, adorned as for war, they distributed among themselves their paper garb, the *anecuyotl* [the girdle], the nettles, the streamers of colored paper; they tied little bells on the calves of their legs, the bells called *oyobualli*. Their arrows had barbed points.

Then they began to move, they went in order, in line, in orderly squadrons, Coyolxauhqui led them. But Cuahuitlicac went immediately up onto the mountain, so as to speak from there to Huitzilopochtli; he said to him: "Now they are coming." Huitzilopochtli replied to him: "Look carefully which way they are coming." Then Cuahuitlicac said: "Now they are coming through Tzompantitlan." And again Huitzilopochtli said to him: "Where are they coming now?" Cuahuitlicac replied to him: "Now they are coming through Coaxalpan." And once more Huitzilopochtli asked Cuahuitlicac: "Look carefully which way they are coming." Immediately Cuahuitlicac answered him: "Now they are coming up the side of the mountain." And yet again Huitzilopochtli said to him: "Look carefully which way they are coming." Then Cuahuitlicac said to him: "Now they are on the top, they are here, Coyolxauhqui is leading them."

At that moment Huitzilopochtli was born, he put on his gear, his shield of eagle feathers, his darts, his blue dart-thrower. He painted his face with diagonal stripes, in the color called "child's paint." On his head he arranged fine plumage, he put on his earplugs. And on his left foot, which was withered, he wore a sandal covered with feathers, and his legs and his arms were painted blue.

And the so-called Tochancalqui set fire to the serpent of candlewood, the one called Xiuhcoatl that obeyed Huitzilopochtli. With the serpent of fire he struck Coyolxauhqui, he cut off her head, and left it lying there on the slope of Coatepetl. The body of Coyolxauhqui went rolling down the hill, it fell to pieces, in different places fell her hands, her legs, her body.

Then Huitzilopochtli was proud, he pursued the four hundred gods of the south, he chased them, drove them off the top of Coatepetl, the mountain of the snake. And when he followed them down to the foot of the mountain, he pursued them, he chased them like rabbits, all around the mountain. He made them run around it four times. In vain they tried to rally against him, in vain they turned to attack him, rattling their bells and clashing their shields. Nothing could they do, nothing could they gain, with nothing could they defend themselves. Huitzilopochtli chased them, he drove them away, he humbled them, he destroyed them, he annihilated them.

Even then he did not leave them, but continued to pursue them, and they begged him repeatedly, they said to him: "It is enough!"

But Huitzilopochtli was not satisfied, with force he pushed against them, he pursued them. Only a very few were able to escape him, escape from his reach. They went toward the south, and because they went toward the south, they are called gods of the south. And when Huitzilopochtli had killed them, when he had given vent to his wrath, he stripped off their gear, their ornaments, their *anecuyotl*; he put them on, he took possession of them, he introduced them into his destiny, he made them his own insignia.

And this Huitzilopochtli, as they say, was a prodigy, because only from fine plumage, which fell into the womb of his mother, Coatlicue, was he conceived, he never had any father. The Aztecs venerated him, they made sacrifices to him, honored and served him. And Huitzilopochtli rewarded those who did this. And his cult came from there, from Coatepec, the Mountain of the Serpent, as it was practiced from most ancient times.

NOTES AND BIBLIOGRAPHY

NOTES AND REFERENCES

INTRODUCTION

1) Rudolf Steiner, *Inner Impulses of Evolution: the Mexican Mysteries and the Knights Templar*, (Hudson,N.Y.: Anthroposophic Press, 1984).

PART I: AMERICAN PREHISTORY

CHAPTER 1: PROPHET LEGENDS ACROSS THE AMERICAS

1) L. T. Hansen, *He Walked the Americas* (Amherst, WI: Legend Press, 1963).
2) Longfellow writes: "Into this old tradition I have woven other curious legends, drawn chiefly from the various and valuable writings of Mr. Schoolcraft...." Taken from H. R. Schoolcraft, *Schoolcraft's Indian Legends from Algic Researches, The Myth of Hiawatha, Oneota, The Race in America, and Historical and Statistical Information Respecting...the Indian Tribes of the United States*, ed. P. P. Mason (1956; repr., East Lansing: Michigan State University Press, 1991), 313.
3) The following are excerpts from Longfellow's journal on the subject of the composition of "Hiawatha":
June 25, 1854: "I could not help this evening making a beginning of 'Manabozho', or whatever the poem is to be called."
June 28: "Work at 'Manabozho', or, as I think I shall call it, 'Hiawatha' that being another name for the same personage."
October 19: Hiawatha occupies and delights me." Schoolcraft, *Schoolcraft's Indian Legends*, 314.
4) Stith Thompson, *Tales of the North American Indians* (Cambridge, MA: Harvard University Press, 1929), 5-6.
5) Schoolcraft, *Schoolcraft's Indian Legends*, 297.
6) Hansen, *He Walked the Americas*.
7) Gerald Mc Dermott, *Arrow to the Sun* (New York: Viking Press, 1974).
8) G. M. Mullett, *Spider Woman Stories: Legends of the Hopi Indians* (Tuscon: The University of Arizona Press, 1979).
9) Some examples are the stories "Puukonhoya Wins a Bride," "The Youth Conquers Man-Eagle," and "The Youth and the Eagles." Mullet, *Spider Woman Stories: Legends of the Hopi Indians*.
10) "Suma y narracion de los Incas," Juan de Betanzos, from Cottie Burland, Irene Nicholson, and Harold Osborne, *Mythology of the Americas* (London: Hamlyn Publishing Group, 1970), 332.

11) "The Second Part of the Chronicle of Peru," chapters 4 and 5, Pedro de Cieza de Leon (1532-1550), Hakluyt Society, # 68, London, 1883, from Burland, Nicholson, and Osborne, *Mythology of the Americas*, 330.

12) Hansen, *He Walked the Americas*, 160-163.

13) Harold Osborne, *South American Mythology* (London: Chancellor Press,1968).

14) "Account of Antiquities of Peru," Juan de Santa Cruz Pachacuti Yamqui Salcamayhua, from Burland, Nicholson, and Osborne, *Mythology of the Americas*, 343.

15) The first legend has been preserved by H. H. Bancroft (*Antiquitie, Native Races, etc....*); the second one was communicated to L. T. Hansen by the archaeologist J. C. Tello. Both are found in Hansen, *He Walked the Americas*, 156-159, and 22-23.

16) Hansen, *He Walked the Americas*, 24-25.

17) Fernando Santos-Granero, *The Power of Love: the Moral Use of Knowledge amongst the Amuesha of Central Peru* (London: Athlone Press, 1991) 54-57.

18) Ibid., 71.

19) Alfred Metraux, "Twin Heroes in South American Mythology," *Journal of American Folklore* (American Folklore Society of Philadelphia) 1946.

20) Hansen, *He Walked the Americas*.

21) See: "The Priests of Ek-Balaam" and "The Bow String of Power" in Hansen, *He Walked the Americas*.

22) Ibid.

CHAPTER 2: POPOL VUH: THE COSMIC AGES

1) Rudolf Steiner, *The Gospel of Saint John and Its Relationship to the Other Gospels*, 14 lectures between June 24 and July 7, 1909, lecture of June 27, 1909 (Spring Valley,N.Y.: Anthroposophic Press, 1982).

2) Guenther Wachsmuth, *The Evolution of Mankind: Cosmic Evolution, Incarnations on the Earth, The Great Migrations, and Spiritual History* (Dornach, Switzerland: Philosophic-Anthroposophic Press, 1961), 19.

3) See Steiner, *Egyptian Myths and Mysteries*, lectures of Sept 10 and 11, 1908 (Hudson,N.Y.: Anthroposophic Press, 1997); and Steiner, *Wonders of the World, Ordeals of the Soul, Revelations of the Spirit*, lectures of August 25 and 26, 1911 (London: Rudolf Steiner Press, 1983).

4) Steiner, *The Apocalypse of Saint John*, lecture of June 23, 1908 (Hudson,N.Y.: Anthroposophic Press, 1993).

5) Rudolf Steiner, *Wonders of the World, Trials of the Soul and Revelations of the Spirit*, lecture of August 26, 1911 (London: Rudolf Steiner Press, 1983).

6) Steiner, *Gospel of Saint John in Relation to the Other Gospels*, lecture of July 1st, 1909.

7) Steiner, *Cosmic Memory*, 1904, chapter 4: "Transition of the Fourth into the Fifth Root-Race" (NY: SteinerBooks, 1987).

8)   Wachsmuth, *Evolution of Mankind*, 85-90.

9)   Steiner, *Gospel of Saint John in Relation to the Other Gospels*, lecture of July 2, 1909.

10) Ibid., lecture 12.

11) Ibid., chapter 4.

12) Steiner, *The Search for the New Isis, the Divine Sophia*, lecture of December 23, 1920 (Spring Valley,N.Y.: Mercury Press, 1983).

13) *The Mission of Teutonic Folk Souls in Relation to Teutonic Mythology*, Rudolf Steiner, lecture of June 14, 1910 (London: Rudolf Steiner Press, 1970).

14) Rudolf Steiner, *The Book of Revelation, and the Work of the Priest*, 18 lectures reconstructed from notes taken by the participants, lecture of September 5, 1924 (London: Rudolf Steiner Press, 1998).

15) Ibid.

16) *The Guardian of the Threshold*, Rudolf Steiner, 1912, in *Four Mystery* Plays (London: Rudolf Steiner Press, 1997) See Scene One, the speech of the Grand Master Hilary.

17) *The Book of Revelation, and the Work of the Priest*, lecture of September 6, 1924.

18) Steiner, *Man and the World of Stars: The Spiritual Communion of Mankind*, lectures of December 23 and 24, 1922 (New York: Anthroposophic Press, 1963).

19) Steiner, *The Archangel Michael: His Mission and Ours*, lecture of August 11, 1924 (Hudson,N.Y.: Anthroposophic Press, 1994).

20) Steiner, *The Spiritual Guidance of the Individual and of Humanity*, 1911, lectures 2 and 3 (Hudson,N.Y.: Anthroposophic Press, 1992).

21) Steiner, *From the History and Contents of the First Class of the Esoteric School*, 1904-1914, lecture of January 6, 1907 (MA: Anthroposophic Press, 1998).

22) Rafael Girard, *Los Chortis ante el problema Maya*, vol. 3 (Mexico, D.F.: Antigua Libreria Robledo, 1949), 865-867.

23) Doris Heyden, "From Teotihuacan to Tenochtitlan: City Planning, Caves, and Streams of Red and Blue Waters," in *Mesoamerica's Classic Heritage: from Teotihuacan to the Aztecs*, ed. David Carrasco, Lindsay Jones, and Scott Sessions (Boulder: University Press of Colorado, 2000), 166-7.

24) Ibid.

25) Adrian Recinos, trans., *Popol Vuh: las antiguas historias del Quiché* (Mexico: Fondo de Cultura Economica, 1947); D. Tedlock, trans., *Popol Vuh: The Definitive Edition of the Mayan Book of the Dawn of Life and the Glories of Gods and Kings* (New York: Touchstone Books/Simon and Schuster, 1985); and Recinos, *Popol Vuh: The Sacred Book of the Ancient Quiché Maya*, trans. Goetz and Morley (Norman: University of Oklahoma Press, 1950).

26) Throughout the Americas, lightning is not perceived as a homogenous phenomenon but in different forms. In South America for example, male lightning does not reach the ground, whereas female lightning is that which strikes objects or people. This is also the source of the distinction between the big lightning and small lightning, or what is called lightning and a flash.

27) Rafael Girard, *Esotericism of the Popol Vuh* (Pasadena, CA: Theosophical University Press, 1948).

28) Ibid., 239.

29) Frank Waters, "The Myths: Creation of the Four Worlds," in *The Book of the Hopi* (New York: Penguin Books, 1963).

30) Girard, *Historia de las civilizaciones antiguas de America*, vol. 3 (Madrid: Editorial Istmo S.A., 1976), 1692-1706.

CHAPTER 3: POPOL VUH: THE DEEDS OF THE GREAT SPIRIT

1) Nahum Megged, *El universo del Popol Vuh: analisis historico, psicologico y filosofico del mito quiche* (Mexico: Editorial Diana, 1991).

2) For a characterization of Mephistopheles see: Steiner, *The Deed of Christ and the Opposing Spiritual Powers*, lecture of January 1, 1909 and *Mephistopheles and Earthquakes*, lecture of March 22, 1909. Here Steiner basically equates Mephistopheles with Ahriman.

3) Rudolf Steiner, *Inner Impulses of Evolution: The Mexican Mysteries and the Knights Templar*, lecture 3 (NY: Anthroposophic Press).

4) Steiner, *The Mission of Folk-Souls in Connection with Germanic-Scandinavian Mythology*, lecture 6 (New York: Spiritual Research Editions/Garber Communications).

CHAPTER 4: THE THIRD AGE

1) Richard A. Diehl and Michael Coe, "Olmec Archaeology," in *The Olmec World: Ritual and Rulership* (Princeton, NJ: Princeton University Art Museum, distributed by Harry N. Abrams, 1996), 12.

2) Ibid., 12-13.

3) Vincent H. Malmström, *Cycles of the Sun, Mysteries of the Moon: The Calendar in Mesoamerican Civilization*, Austin: University of Texas, 1997, 17-18.

4) Ibid., see Table 1: Archaeological Chronology of Soconusco, 27.

5) Ibid., 44.

6) Jennifer Pinkowski, "A Place by the Sea: Early Urban Planning on Mexico's Pacific Coast," in *Archaeology*, Jan.-Feb. 2006: 48.

7) David Cheetham, "The America's First Colony: a Possible Olmec Outpost in Southern Mexico," in *Archaeology*, Jan.-Feb. 2006: 42-46.

8) Pinkowski, "Early Urban Planning," 46-49.

9) Malmström, *Cycles of the Sun*, 31-32.

10) Ibid., chapter 3: "Strange Attraction: The Mystery of Magnetism."

11) It is interesting to note that the right temple is associated with the perception of etheric forces in near-death experiences; the navel is the etheric link between mother and child.

12) Diehl and Coe, "Olmec Archaeology," 23-24.

13) Malmström, *Cycles of the Sun*, 66.
14) Ibid., 66-71.
15) Malmström, *Cycles of the Sun*, 88, 91.
16) Carolyn E. Tate, "Art in Olmec Culture," in *The Olmec World*, 65.
17) From *The Olmec World*: Diehl and Coe, "Olmec Archaeology," 12; F. Kent Reilly, III, "Art, Ritual and Rulership in the Olmec World," 39; and Karl A. Taube, "The Rainmakers: the Olmec and Their Contribution to Mesoamerican Belief and Ritual," 83, 89.
18) Beatriz de la Fuente, "Order and Nature in Olmec Art," in *Ancient Americas: Art from Sacred Landscapes*, ed. Richard Townsend (Munich: Prestel Verlag, for The Art Institute of Chicago, 1992), 132.
19) Neil Baldwin, *Legends of the Plumed Serpent* (New York, Public Affairs, 1992), 16.
20) From *The Olmec World*: Carolyn E. Tate, "Art in Olmec Culture," and Peter T. Furst, "Shamanism, Transformation and Olmec Art," 56, 79-80.
21) Carolyn E. Tate, "Art in Olmec Culture," 47-67.
22) Peter T. Furst, "Shamanism, Transformation and Olmec Art," 79.
23) Beatriz de la Fuente, "Order and Nature in Olmec Art," 121-133.
24) Karl A. Taube, "The Rainmakers," 100.
25) Richard L. Burger, *Chavin and the Origins of Andean Civilization* (New York: Thames and Hudson, 1992).
26) Peter T. Furst, "Shamanism, Transformation and Olmec Art," 71.
27) Carolyn E. Tate, "Art in Olmec Culture," 62-63.
28) Ibid, 74.
29) Karl A. Taube, "The Rainmakers," 83-103.
30) Ibid.
31) Rafael Girard, *Los Chortis ante el problema Maya*, vol. 3 (Mexico, D.F.: Antigua Libreria Robledo, 1949), 519.
32) A. G. Gilbert and M. M. Cotterell, *The Mayan Prophecies: Unlocking the Secrets of a Lost Civilization* (Rockport, MA: Element Books, 1995), 39.
33) Malmström, *Cycles of the Sun*, 77, 84-85, 89.
34) Ibid., 88, 91.
35) Marion Popenoe Hatch, "An Hypothesis on Olmec Astronomy, with Special Reference to the La Venta Site," in *Contributions of the University of California Archaeological Research Facility: Papers on Olmec and Maya Archaeology* (Berkeley, University of California, June 1971).
36) Ibid.
37) Milla Villena Carlos, *Genesis de la Cultura Andina*, (Lima, Peru: Colegio de Arquitectos del Peru, Fondo Editorial C. A. P., Coleccion Bienal, 1983).
38) Roman Piña Chan, *The Olmec, Mother Culture of Mesoamerica*, ed. Laura Laurencich Minelli (New York: Rizzoli, 1989), 132-3.
39) Rudolf Steiner, *The Spiritual Guidance of the Individual and of Humanity*, lectures 2 and 3, 1911 (Hudson, N.Y.: Anthroposophic Press).
40) Ibid., lecture 2.

41) For a further exploration of this matter see Emil Bock, "The World of the Canaanites," heading 3.4 in *Moses: From the Mysteries of Egypt to the Judges of Israel* (Rochester, VT: Inner Traditions International, 1986).

42) Karl A. Taube, "The Rainmakers."

43) Carolyn E. Tate, "Art in Olmec Culture," 61.

44) Ibid., 48.

CHAPTER 5: POPOL VUH: THE DEEDS OF THE TWINS

1) Vucub Caquix is identified by the numeral 7 indicating the seven stars of the Ursa Major constellation. For characterizations of Vucub Caquix, Chimalmat, and Zipacná see D. Tedlock, trans., *Popol Vuh: The Definitive Edition of the Mayan Book of the Dawn of Life and the Glories of Gods and Kings* (New York: Touchstone Books/Simon and Schuster, 1985), 330, 360 and 372.

2) Nahum Megged, *El universo del Popol Vuh: analisis historico, psicologico y filosofico del mito quiche* (Mexico: Editorial Diana, 1991), 61.

3) Rafael Girard, *Los Chortis ante el problema Maya*, vol. 4 (Mexico, D.F.: Antigua Libreria Robledo, 1949), 1330.

4) A. Mediz Bolio, trans. *Libro de Chilam Balam de Chumayel* (Mexico: Ediciones de la Universidad Nacional Autonoma, 1941), and R. L. Roys, *The Book of Chilam Balam of Chumayel* (Norman: University of Oklahoma Press, 1933).

5) See the following translations of the Mayan book of prophecy: Bolio, *Libro de Chilam Balam*, Book 9: Libro del Mes; and Roys, *Chilam Balam*, XIII: the Creation of the Uinal.

6) Rudolf Steiner, *The Fifth Gospel*, lecture of October 13, 1913 (London: Rudolf Steiner Press).

7) Ibid., lecture of December 18, 1913.

8) Steiner, *The Gospel of Saint Mark*, lecture of September 18, 1912 (New York: Anthroposophic Press).

9) The same use of the singular for the Camé had already appeared when the Ahpus descended to the underworld and arrived at the four paths: the red, the black, the white and the yellow. The black path told them: "I am the path you need to take, that will lead you to the Lord" (Popol Vuh, Part II, Chapter 2).

CHAPTER 6: THE FOURTH AGE

1) Rudolf Steiner, *True and False Paths in Spiritual Investigation*, lecture 2 of August 12 (London: Rudolf Steiner Press).

2) Cristobal de Molina, *Relacion de las fabulas y ritos de los Ingas*, vol. 5, 120. Quoted in Arthur A. Demarest, *Viracocha: The Nature and Antiquity of the Andean High God* (Cambridge, MA: Harvard University Press, Peabody Museum Press, 1981) number 6, 32.

2) Steiner, *The Fifth Gospel*, lecture of October 2, 1913 (London, Rudolf Steiner Press).

3) Steiner, *Mystery Centers,* lecture of December 9, 1923 (Blauvelt,N.Y.: Garber Communications, Spiritual Research Editions).

4) Steiner, *Man and the World of the Stars, The Spiritual Communion of Mankind,* lecture of Dec. 24, 1922 (NY: Anthroposophic Press, 1963).

5) Steiner, *The Fifth Gospel,* lecture of January 13, 1914.

6) Rafael Girard, *Los Chortis ante el problema Maya,* vol. 2 (Mexico, D.F.: Antigua Libreria Robledo, 1949). See chapter 13: "El culto estival y el calendario civil."

7) Girard, *People of the Chan* (Chino Valley, AZ: Continuum Foundation, 1966), 407-8. The tableau has been modified with additional information taken from Girard himself.

8) Girard, *Los Chortis,* vol. 2, 515.

9) R. L. Roys, "The Ritual of the Four World Quarters," in *The Book of Chilam Balam of Chumayel* (Norman: University of Oklahoma Press, 1933), heading 6: "Notes on the Calendar."

10) H. J. Spinden, "The Question of the Zodiac in America," *American Anthropologist* 18, 1916. See also *Maya Cosmos: Three Thousand Years on the Shaman's Path,* 101-103 (New York: W. Morrow, 1993).

11) Steiner, *At the Gates of Spiritual Science,* lecture of September 4, 1906 (London: Rudolf Steiner Press).

12) Girard, *Los Chortis,* vol. 3, 944-952.

13) Taken from: Girard, *People of the Chan,* 410-413 and Girard, *Los Chortis,* vol. 2, pp. 512-514. (Slightly modified to include the ball game of older times.)

14) Girard, *Los Chortis,* vol. 3, 933-935. Table modified with author's additions.

15) Ibid., vol. 2, see chapter 13: El culto estival y el calendario civil.

16) John Major Jenkins, *Maya Cosmogenesis 2012: The True Meaning of the Maya Calendar End-Date* (Santa Fe, NM: Bear & Co., 1998), 308. See also Maria Teresa Uriarte, "Practica y simbolos del iuego de pelota," *Arqueologia Mexicana* 44, no. 8 (Julio-Agosto 2000).

17) Jenkins, *Maya Cosmogenesis,* 138.

18) Richard A. Diehl and Michael Coe, "Olmec Archaeology," in *The Olmec World: Ritual and Rulership* (Princeton, NJ: Princeton University Art Museum, distributed by Harry N. Abrams, 1996), 23-24.

19) Eric Taladoire, "El juego de pelota Mesoamericano: origen y desarrollo," *Arqueologia Mexicana* 44, no. 8 (Julio-Agosto 2000).

20) Linda Schele and David Friedel, *A Forest of Kings: the Untold Story of the Ancient Maya* (NY: William Morrow and Company, 1990), 77 and 126.

21) Steiner, *Karmic Relationships,* vol. 3, lecture of August 3, 1924 (London: Rudolf Steiner Press).

22) D. Tedlock, trans., *Popol Vuh: The Definitive Edition of the Mayan Book of the Dawn of Life and the Glories of Gods and Kings* (New York: Touchstone Books/ Simon and Schuster, 1985), 348.

23) Vincent H. Malmström, *Cycles of the Sun, Mysteries of the Moon: The Calendar in Mesoamerican Civilization* (Austin: University of Texas,. 1997), 125-9.

24)   Johanna Broda, "Calendrics and Ritual Landscape at Teotihuacan: Themes of
      Continuity in Mesoamerican Cosmovision," in *Mesoamerica's Classic Heritage:
      from Teotihuacan to the Aztecs*, ed. David Carrasco, Lindsay Jones, and Scott
      Sessions (Boulder: University Press of Colorado, 2000), 418-419.
25)   Schele and Friedel, *Forest of Kings*, 97.
26)   Ibid., 94.
27)   Peabody Museum of Archaeology and Ethnology, "The Early Maya Murals at
      San Bartolo, Guatemala," <http://www.peabody.harvard.eduwww./SanBartolo.
      html>; see also Thomas H. Maugh II, "Mural Reveals Pre-Classic Maya as a
      Civilized Society," *Los Angeles Times*, December 14, 2005.
28)   Let us review in quick succession some of the most important findings of the
      recent years:

Olmec writing: The Cascajal Block:
A serpentine block was found in the site of Cascajal, State of Veracruz, that may
well be the oldest written document of the Americas. The block is 14 inches long
and 8 inches wide. Of the 62 glyphs carved in it, some are repeated, so that we
have 28 different characters. Not surprisingly, some of the glyphs, it is surmised,
have maize-related meaning. The other glyphs seem to reproduce insects,
animals, plants, and objects. Joel Skidmore concludes that the signs present all
the characters of glyphs, since they each have an autonomous and recognizable
expression; they appear in short, separate sequences within larger groupings of
variable length.

Two other objects—the Tlaltenco Celt and the Humboldt Celt—may also
display glyphs. This kind of writing could be what the specialists call "Shamanic
script," a system that was strictly reserved for use by religious specialists.

It is thought that this Olmec writing was introduced around 900 BC, which is
in keeping with the dating of the site of Cascajal as covering the Early Formative
(1200-900 BC). It seems that this kind of writing died out without leaving derived
forms of writing.

(References: "Early Olmec Writing? The Cascajal Block," <Archaeology.about.
com/od/olmeccivilization/a/cascajal_block.htm>, and Joel Skidmore, "Mesoweb
Reports: The Earliest Precolumbian Writing," <www.mesoweb.com/reports/
Cascajal.pdf>)

Isthmian Writing: Stela 1 of La Mojarra
This is a stela discovered buried under the river Acula in the State of Veracruz.
The monument had the image of a ruler and a total of 465 glyphs ordered in
21 columns. Other examples of this writing appear near the Tehuantepec Isth-
mus. They have been dated to periods ranging from 32-36 BC to AD 162 or later.
Scholars call this "Epi-Olmec" or "Isthmian script." It seems that in the area of
Oaxaca and in the isthmus of Tehuantepec, writing was firmly established by 400
BC and continued until the first century AD. (**) This writing has similarities
with Mayan in as much as it is logophonetic. Some signs have phonetic value; the

others, called "logograms" represent words or parts of a word, similar in effect to syllables, prefixes, or suffixes. In fact some of this writing has been found in pre-Maya sites. A particular case is that of San Bartolo, reviewed below. (References: "Ancient Mask Adds to Corpus of Isthmian Script: 100 BC to 500 AD?," <www. ancientscripts.com/epiolmec.html>, and Andrew Lawler, "Beyond the Family Feud: After Decades of Debate, Are Younger Scholars Finally Asking the Right Questions About the Olmec?," *Archaeology*, March/April 2007.)

Writing in San Bartolo (Guatemala)
The San Bartolo site contains the earliest paintings in which the Maize God is portrayed in a style closely reminiscent of later Maya. Here has also been found another instance of Isthmian writing, antedating later known Mayan writing by four to five centuries. Radio-carbon dating suggests that the text was painted between 300 and 200 BC. There are other examples of this kind of writing at El Mirador and El Porton, Guatemala. (Reference: William A. Saturno, David Stuart, and Boris Beltrán, "Early Maya Writing at San Bartolo, Guatemala," <www.sanbartolo.org/science.pdf>)

29) Peabody Museum of Archaeology and Ethnology, "The Early Maya Murals at San Bartolo, Guatemala," <http://www.peabody.harvard.edu>

30) Schele and Friedel, *Forest of Kings*, 59.

31) Ibid., 128

32) See R. Tom Zuidema, *La Civilisation Inca au Cuzco* (Collège de France, essays et conférences Presses Universitaires de France, 1986).

33) Schele and Friedel, *Forest of Kings*, 106.

34) Schele and Friedel, *Forest of Kings*, 52.

35) Linda Schele and Mary Ellen Miller, *The Blood of Kings: Dynasty and Ritual in Maya Art* (New York: George Braziller, 1986), 177.

36) Girard, *Historia de las civilizaciones antiguas de America*, vol. 3 (Madrid: Editorial Istmo S.A., 1976), 69.

37) Tedlock, *Popol Vuh*, 348.

38) Nahum Megged, *El universo del Popol Vuh: analisis historico, psicologico y filosofico del mito quiche* (Mexico: Editorial Diana, 1991), 224-225.

39) The Ah Tza and Ah Tukur are believed by Brasseur de Beaubourg to refer to the Itzae tribes and the tukures (magicians) of Tecolotlan, who inhabit Verapaz (Guatemalan Soconusco). Quoted in Adrian Recinos, *Popol Vuh: las Antiguas Historias del Quiché* (Fondo de Cultura Economica, 1947), 170 and 174.

40) Girard, *Los Chortis*, vol. 2, 539.

41) Gareth Lowe, Thomas A. Lee Jr., and Eduardo Martinez Espinosa, "Izapa: An Introduction to the Ruins and Monuments," *Papers of the New World Archaeological Foundation* (Provo, UT: Brigham Young University, 1982), 31.

42) Barba de Piña Chan, B., *Buscando Raices de Mitos y Leyendas Mayas* (Campeche, Mexico: Ediciones de la Universidad Autonoma del Sudeste, 1988).

43) Michael D. Coe, *The Maya* (New York: Thames and Hudson, 1994), 52.

44) Girard, *Los Chortis*, vol. 5, 1484-1488.

45)   *The Mexican Mysteries and Pre-Columbian Art: The Influence of the Deed of Vitzliputzli on Mesoamerican and Andean Culture (33-1492 AD)*, Williamson, Glen (unpublished paper, July 1999).

46)   Girard, *Los Chortis*, vol. 4, 1491-1492.

47)   Jenkins, *Maya Cosmogenesis*, 297.

CHAPTER 7: IXBALAMQUÉ: INITIATE OF THE AMERICAS

1)   Rudolf Steiner, *The East in the Light of the West*, 1922 (NY: Anthroposophic Press). See particularly chapters 5, 8, and 9.

2)   Ibid.

3)   Unless otherwise noted, most of the information about the Mexican Mysteries originates from the lecture cycle: Steiner, *Inner Impulses of Evolution: the Mexican Mysteries and the Knights Templar*, Dornach, September 1916 (NY: Anthroposophic Press). See particularly lecture 3 of September 18 and lecture 5 of September 24.

4)   "They were, then, Xiquiripat and Cuchumaquic lords of these names. They were the two who caused the shedding of the blood of men. Others were called Ahalpuh and Ahalgana, also lords. And their work was to make men swell and make pus gush forth from their legs and stain their faces yellow, what is called Chugana. Such was the work of Ahalpuh and Ahalgana. Others were Lord Chamiabac and Lord Chamiaholom...Others were called Lord Ahalmez and Lord Ahaltocob.... Immediately after them were other lords named Xic and Patan." Quoted from Adrian Recinos, *Popol Vuh: The Sacred Book of the Ancient Quiché Maya*, trans. Goetz and Morley (Norman: University of Oklahoma Press, 1950), Part II, Chapter 1.

5)   Steiner, *Karmic Relationships*, vol. 5, lecture 7 of May 25, 1924 (London, Rudolf Steiner Press).

6)   Stephen Clarke, Introductory notes to "Rudolf Steiner's Inner Impulses of Evolution's 'Mexican Mystery' lectures," *Southern Cross* 20 (Autumn 2002).

7)   Constance Irwin, *Fair Gods and Stone Faces* (New York: St. Martin's Press, 1963), 224.

8)   Among others we have Herodotus (480 BC), Theopompus (378 BC), Strabo (~100 BC), Seneca (~AD 30), Mela (~AD 44), Pausanias (~AD 150), Proclus (~AD 440). See Salvatore Michael Trento, *The Search for Lost America* (Chicago: Contemporary Books Inc., 1978), 12-13.

9)   Irwin, *Fair Gods*, 219-222.

10) David Allen Deal, *Discovery of Ancient America* (Irvine, CA: Kherem La Yah Press, 1984).

11) Barry Fell, *Saga America* (New York: Times Books, 1980), 75.

12) Irwin, *Fair Gods*, 241.

13) Ibid., 132-134 and 176-178.

14) Roll-seals are found all over Mesoamerica, going as far back as the Middle Pre-Classic period. These are similar to the ones used in the ancient Orient in the 1st and 2nd millennia BC: they are either round, oval, or cylindrical and bear images of animals, gods, persons, or simple geometrical patterns. The Phoeni-

cians sealed their bargains with such roll-out seals. Ceramic jugs found off the New England coast are identical with amphorae recovered from the Iberian Peninsula at Lagos and Evora, Portugal. "From North Salem, New Hampshire, came a piece of broken pottery which revealed, under an 'X-ray mineral-content analysis,' that the composition of the clay had a Mediterranean or Near-East geographical origin. Ceramic amphorae found in Castine Bay, Maine, have a composition and consistency of the jar's clay identical to ceramics excavated from Portugal and Spain." From Trento, *Search for Lost America*, 26 and 194.

15) See Fell, *Saga America*. The Carthaginians didn't have their own coinage. They copied coins from Syracuse but added their own coat of arms on the back: a horse's head and a palm tree. Base metal coinage or debased Carthaginian currency has been discovered in Connecticut, hence the hypothesis that it was used for trade with the natives who would have been unaware of the difference in quality. See pp. 55-59 and pp. 62-64. For the limestone horse head, see pp. 57 and 61. A gold zodiac with all the signs was discovered in the Cuenca area. It is lettered in the Paphian script of Cyprus in a language close to the Minoan-Hittite, and carelessly executed. Another two reproductions of Babylonian art represent a winged anthropomorphic being and an anthropomorphic horse that could be dated 800~600 BC. (See pp. 68-69 and 80-81 for more detail.)

16) Phoenician history and some other key dates:

1440~1415 BC: reign of the Egyptian Amenophis II, settlements of Phoenician merchants in Egypt, not colonies. Others spread toward the Aegean Islands.

1250 BC: Cretan trade controlled by the Phoenicians.

1112 BC: founding of Utica (Tunisia).

1104 BC: colony of Agadir (Gades) later Cadiz, in Spain.

981-947 BC: reign of King Hiram. Solomon requested the help of Hiram for the building of the Temple.

950 BC: Phoenician mariners sailed the Red Sea.

825 BC: founding of Carthage, only 15 miles away from Utica.

640 BC: Assyria weakened and Phoenicia slips away from the Empire's grasp.

605 BC: Phoenicia conquered (conquered?) again by Babylonia. A little later, Tyre revolted and was crushed after a siege of 13 years.

609-593 BC: reign of Necho of Egypt; Phoenician circumnavigation of Africa; Herodotus disbelieves the fact that they may have had the sun on the North (Southern Hemisphere), since it had never been reported before.

587~574 BC: mastery of the Mediterranean passed from Tyre to Carthage. In 587, Nebuchadnezzar began the 13-year siege of Tyre. The Carthaginians prevented all vessels from sailing into the Atlantic Ocean. The profit motive from the monopoly was a strong incentive for secrecy.

~360 BC: Aristotle confirms knowledge of the island in the Atlantic and informs us that Carthage had tried to discourage emigration by threatening the death penalty.

264-242 BC: First Punic War.

218-201 BC: Second Punic War. In 150 BC, after the two Punic wars, Carthage had 70,000 inhabitants. Overpopulation stimulated colonization.

149-146 BC: Third Punic War. Complete annihilation of Carthage and another incentive for emigration.

17) Fell, *Saga America*, 74-87.

18) The Phoenicians had an intimate acquaintance with the Deccan and the East Indian Peninsula and islands. They conducted this business as in many other places through intermediaries. For example, in England and the Baltic their business was conducted through the Celts. Their intermediaries in the Deccan were the Dedanites, who inhabited the islands in the Bay of Gerrha and controlled the navigation of the Persian Gulf and the Indian Ocean. This seems to be confirmed by 2 Chron 9:21. Vessels of considerable tonnage were used there according to 2 Chron 8:18. This development toward the East was the equivalent of what had happened toward the West with Gades and Tarshish, as bases of operation.

Things changed at the beginning of the 11th century BC when David became king of Israel. Phoenicia was dependent on Israel for its supplies of foodstuffs: wheat, barley, oil, and wine. Israel was dependent on Phoenicia for manufactured goods. King David soon became closely associated with King Hiram of Tyre according to 1 Kings 5:1; in fact Hiram built a palace for King David in Lebanon. The Syrian campaign of David reduced Damascus to a Hebrew dependency, and rendered Phoenician trade safe. In another campaign against the Edomites, David raised the embargo that the Edomites had placed on the navigation of the Red Sea toward Hebrew ports. David recovered the ports of Eloth and Eziongeber on the Gulf of Aelana. There the Phoenicians could build vessels for trade with the Persian Gulf. There, was also decided the construction of a double fleet of seven ships of the largest type, modeled after the large armed ships of Tarshish. David was instructed by God to entrust the building of the Temple to his son Solomon. An immense treasure had been set aside by King David: 100,000 talents of gold and 1,000,000 talents of silver, according to 1 Chron 22:14. Immediately after the accession to the throne of Solomon, Hiram sent his servants to the new king, according to 1 Kings 5:1. Possibly the two had met many times at the summer palace in Lebanon constructed for David by the Tyrian king (2 Sam. 5:11).

Seven years were spent in building the Great Temple (1 Kings 6:38) and thirteen years for the summer palace in Lebanon (1 Kings, 7:1). See Thomas Crawford Johnson, *Did the Phoenicians Discover America?* (London: James Nisbet & Co., 1913), 108-126.

19) All but five letters are recognizable as common forms of Paleo-Hebrew. Another three letters were common in Iberia. One is a variant of a letter used in Iberia and also found in the mound culture of the Americas. There seems to be some evidence pointing to Jews living in Spain at the time of the return of the Judahites to Judea from Babylonia; these were the so-called Sephardic Jews. The kind of writing quoted above became popular after the period of the great Babylonian conquest of Judea (which began in 608 BC and continued past the

destruction of Jerusalem in 586 BC). In 586 BC Nebuchadnezzar overwhelmed the House of Judah (the tribes of Judah, Benjamin, and Levi). This form of alphabet would most likely have been used between 500 and 100 BC. See Deal, *Discovery of Ancient America*, 2, 12-13, 26-29.

For evidence supporting the recognition of the solar eclipse, see: Deal, *Discovery of Ancient America*, 18-24.

20)   See: Deal, *Discovery of Ancient America*, chapter 1: "The Hidden Mountain Inscriptions," under heading "Ancient Americas Visited," 33-45. The Grave Creek Stone of Moundsville is called the Tablet of Tasach. It was excavated in 1838. See Barry Fell, *America B.C.: Ancient Settlers in the New World* (New York: Pocket Books, 1976), 158. The Braxton Tablet appears to be a poetic grave marker ending in an invocation to Baal. See Deal, *Discovery of Ancient America*, 39.

21)   Alexander von Wuthenau, *Unexpected Faces in Ancient America, 1500 BC-AD 1500: The Historical Testimony of Pre-Columbian Artists* (New York: Crown Publishers, 1975), 43, 46, 54.

22)   Nigel Davies, *The Ancient Kingdoms of Mexico: A Magnificent Re-creation of Their Art and Life* (London: Penguin Books, 1982), 26.

23)   *Unexpected Faces in Ancient America*, 130, 134.

24)   Von Wuthenau, *Unexpected Faces*, 34-37.

25)   Fell, *Saga America*, 58, 79.

26)   Johnson, *Did the Phoenicians Discover America?*, 116-117.

27)   Steiner, *Turning Points of Spiritual History*, 1911-1912. See: "Elijah," lecture of Dec. 14, 1911, Berlin, (MA: SteinerBooks, 2007).

28)   See evidence of cranial deformation in la Venta, in Irwin, *Fair Gods*, 168.

29)   Here are some of the Biblical references, from the Revised Standard Version:
Leviticus 18:3: "You shall not do as they do in the land of Canaan, to which I am bringing you. You shall not walk in their statutes."
Leviticus 19:26-28: "You shall not practice augury or witchcraft. You shall not round off the hair on your temples or mar the edges of your head. You shall not make any cuttings in your flesh on account of the dead or tattoo any marks upon you: I am the Lord."
Leviticus 19:31: "Do not turn to mediums or wizards: do not seek them out to be defiled by them...."
Leviticus 20:1-2: "The Lord said to Moses, 'Say to the people of Israel, any man of the people of Israel, or of the strangers that sojourn in Israel, who gives any of his children to Mo'lech shall be put to death....'"
Leviticus 21:5: "They (priests) shall not make tonsures upon their heads, nor shave off the edges of their beards, nor make any cuttings in their flesh."
Leviticus 21:10-11: "The priest who is chief among his brethren...shall not go into any dead body...."
Other Biblical quotes:
2 Kings 16:1-4: "In the seventeenth year of Pe'kah the son of Remali'ah, A'haz the son of Jo'tham, king of Judah, began to reign....He even burned his son as an offering, according to the abominable practices of the nations whom the

Lord drove out before the people of Israel."

2 Kings 17:1: "In the twelfth year of A'haz king of Judah, Hoshe'a the son of E'lah began to reign in Samaria over Israel, and he reigned nine years, and he did what was evil in the sight of the Lord..."

2 Kings 17: 16-17: "And they forsook all the commandments of the Lord their God, and made for themselves molten images of two calves; and they made an Ashe'rah, and worshipped all the host of heaven, and served Ba'al. And they burned their sons and daughters as offerings, and used divination and sorcery."

Judges 2:2: Angel of the Lord enjoining "[Y]ou shall make no covenant with the inhabitants of this land; you shall break down their altars."

Judges 2:11-12: "And the people of Israel did what was evil in the sight of the Lord and served the Ba'als; and they forsook the Lord, the God of their fathers...."

Judges 2:14: "They forsook the Lord, and served the Ba'als and the Ashtaroth."

30)   Quoted by Irwin, *Fair Gods*, 261.

31)   Ibid., 262. See also J. M. Arguedas and Pierre Duviols, trans., *Dioses y hombres de Huarochiri. narracion quechua recogida por Francisco de Avila* (1573-1647) (Lima, Peru: Museo Nacional de Historia y el Instituto de Estudios Peruanos, 1966). In this Native Quechua document the Spaniards are called Huiracochas, a more correct phonetic rendering of Viracocha.

40)   Steiner, *The Fifth Gospel*, lecture of October 2, 1913 (London: Rudolf Steiner Press).

41)   Ibid., lecture of Dec. 18, 1913.

42)   Patrick Dixon, "America: the Central Motif," *Shoreline* 4 (1991).

43)   Grace Cooke, *The Illumined Ones* (New Lands, U. K.: The White Eagle Publishing Trust, 1966), 51-53.

44)   Steiner, *World History and the Mysteries in the Light of Anthroposophy*, lecture 4 (London: Rudolf Steiner Press).

45)   Steiner, *Mystery Centers*, lectures 7 to 9 (Blauvelt,N.Y.: Garber Communications, Spiritual Research Editions).

46)   John Major Jenkins, *Maya Cosmogenesis 2012: The True Meaning of the Maya Calendar End-Date* (Santa Fe, NM: Bear & Co., 1998), chapters 21, 22, and 23.

47)   Ibid., pp. 277-279.

48)   V. G. Norman, "Izapa Sculpture, Part II: Text," in *Papers of the New World Archaeological Foundation* (Provo, Utah: Brigham Young University, 1976), 154-158.

PART II: FROM THE TIME OF CHRIST TO THE CONQUEST

CHAPTER 1: TEOTIHUACAN
AND TOLTEC INFLUENCE

1)   Although the text refers to the heart, we have argued that this may be knowledge derived from the later Mexican Mysteries. Steiner refers to human sacrifices with stomach excision. See chapter 7: *Spiritual Scientific Background to the Mexican Mysteries*. More about this will be said in the conclusion.

2) Steiner, *Cosmic Memory*, 1904, chapter 4: "Transition of the Fourth into the Fifth Root-Race" (MA: SteinerBooks, 1987).

3) John Major Jenkins, *Maya Cosmogenesis 2012: The True Meaning of the Maya Calendar End-Date* (Santa Fe, NM: Bear & Co., 1998), p. 92.

4) Eduardo Matos Moctezuma and Leonardo Lopez Lujan, "Teotihuacan and Its Mexican Legacy," in *Teotihuacan: Art from the City of the Gods*, Kathleen Berrin and Esther Pasztory, eds. (London: Thames and Hudson, 1993).

5) See for example J. Antonio Villacorta C. and Flavio Rodas N., *Manuscrito de Chichicastenango (Popol Buj)* (Guatemala: Sanchez and De Guise, 1927). See chapter 4: Los Toltecas.

6) Rafael Girard, *Los Chortis ante el problema Maya*, vols. 4 and 5 (Mexico, D.F.: Antigua Libreria Robledo, 1949), 1369-1371 and 1791.

7) Ibid., 1391.

8) Moctezuma and Lujan, "Teotihuacan and Its Mexican Legacy," 159.

9) Nigel Davies, *The Ancient Kingdoms of Mexico: A Magnificent Re-creation of Their Art and Life* (London: Penguin Books, 1982), 109-110.

10) Girard, *Historia de las civilizaciones antiguas de America*, vol. 3, (Madrid: Editorial Istmo S.A., 1976), 2269.

11) *Anales de Cuauhtitlan*, quoted in Miguel Leon Portilla, *Pre-Columbian Literatures of Mexico* (Norman: University of Oklahoma Press, 1969), 41.

12) "They say that when Quetzalcoatl lived there, often the wizards tried to trick him into offering human sacrifices, into sacrificing men. But he never did, because he loved his people who were the Toltecs," from *Anales de Cuauhtitlan*, 41.

13) Girard, *Los Chortis*, vol. 5, 1786.

14) Vincent H. Malmström, *Cycles of the Sun, Mysteries of the Moon: The Calendar in Mesoamerican Civilization* (Austin: University of Texas, 1997), 105.

15) To the 15° 30' orientation correspond the azimuths: 74° 30', 105° 30', 254° 30' and 285° 30'. This gives the following dates:
    - 105° 30': sunrise on Feb. 12 and October 30
    - 74° 30': sunrise on April 30 and Aug. 13
    - 285° 30': sunset on April 30 and August 13
    - 254° 30': sunset on Feb. 12 and October 30
    These four dates mark some of the most important calendrical events in Izapa and divide the year in sections of 260 and 105 days.

16) Saburo Sugiyama, *Human Sacrifice, Militarism and Rulership* (Cambridge: Cambridge University Press, 2005), 201-202.

17) Ibid., 224- 226.

18) Ibid., 229- 232.

19) S. Milbrath, "Astronomical Imagery in the Serpent Sequence of the Madrid Codex," in *Archaeoastronomy of the Americas*, R. A. Williamson, ed. (Los Altos, CA: Ballena Press/College Park, MD: University of Maryland Center for Archaeoastronomy, 1981).

20) Esther Pasztory, "The Iconography of the Teotihuacan Tlaloc," *Studies in Pre-Columbian Art and Archaeology* 15, (1974), Dumbarton Oaks, Washington D.C.

21) Johanna Broda, "Calendrics and Ritual Landscape at Teotihuacan: Themes of Continuity in Mesoamerican Cosmovision," in *Mesoamerica's Classic Heritage: From Teotihuacan to the Aztecs*, David Carrasco, Lindsay Jones, and Scott Sessions, eds. (Boulder: University Press of Colorado, 2000), 414-415.

22) Anthony F. Aveny, "Out of Teotihuacan: Origins of the Celestial Canon in Mesoamerica," in Carrasco, Jones, and Sessions, *Mesoamerica's Classic Heritage*, 257.

23) See studies by S. Iwaniszewski (1991) quoted in Broda, "Calendrics and Ritual Landscape at Teotihuacan: Themes of Continuity in Mesoamerican Cosmovision," 420. Broda offers corrected dates, matching the dates of the sacred calendar, resting on Iwaniszewski's admission that an error of up to six days on the dates he offers is possible, given the poor condition of the pecked crosses.

24) Chicomostoc is one of Mesoamerica's farthest northern sites, located near the headwaters of the Rio Juchilpa in the state of Zacatecas. It appears to date from the first centuries of the Christian era and was very likely a defense post against the nomadic warriors of the north. On the northern and western base of the hill that the city rests on is a series of caves, hence the indigenous name of Chicomostoc (seven caves).

25) Doris Heiden, "Una interpretacion en torno a Ia cueva que se encuentra debaio de Ia piramide del sol en Teotihuacan," 1975, *American Antiquity* 40, no. 2, 131-147.

26) H. B. Nicholson, "The Iconography of the Feathered Serpent in Late Postclassic Central Mexico, " in Carrasco, Jones, and Sessions, *Mesoamerica's Classic Heritage*, 146, 147.

27) Davies, *Ancient Kingdoms*, 138-139.

28) Ivan Sprajc, *Venus, lluvia y maiz: simbolismo y astronomia en la cosmovision mesoamericana* (Mexico: Instituto Nacional de Antropologia e Historia, Serie Antropologica, 1996), 94-97.

29) Ivan Sprajc, "The Venus-Rain-Maize Complex in the Mesoamerican World View: Part II," *Archaeoastronomy* 18 (1993), 34-37.

30) Sprajc, *Venus*.

31) Esther Pasztory, "The Iconography of the Teotihuacan Tlaloc," 1974, *Studies in Pre-Columbian Art and Archaeology* (Dumbarton Oaks, Washington DC), no. 15.

32) Geoffrey G. Mc Cafferty, "Tollan Cholollan and the Legacy of Legitimacy During the Classic-Postclassic Transition," p. 358 in *Mesoamerica's Classic Heritage: From Teotihuacan to the Aztecs*, edited by David Carrasco, Lindsay Jones, and Scott Sessions (Boulder: University Press of Colorado, 2000).

33) Julia Guernsey Kappelman, "Sacred Geography at Izapa and the Performance of Rulership," p 302 in *Landscape and Power in Ancient Mesoamerica*, Rex Koontz, Kathryn Reese-Taylor, and Annabeth Headrick (New York: Westview Press, 2001).

34) *Mountain of Heaven, Mountain of Earth: The Great Pyramid of Cholula as Sacred Landscape*, Geoffrey G. Mc Cafferty in *Mesoamerica's Classic Heritage: From Teotihuacan to the Aztecs*, edited by David Carrasco, Lindsay Jones, and Scott Sessions (Boulder, CO: University Press of Colorado, 2000), 289-291.

35) The legend of the Virgen de los Remedios speaks of a native man in the terri-
     tory of Tlacopan. He was a Christian cacique by the name of Juan. Every time
     he passed in front of his house he would have visions of the Virgin and he
     would recognize her. Once he went hunting, and when he got tired he set to
     rest on the summit of the pyramid. There he saw an image half covered by
     stones, and recognized it as the Virgin that he had seen so many times before.
     He took it with him and hid it in his house. When he left home the image
     left and went to the summit of the hill [where presumably he would see it].
     He tried to lock it under key but the image always returned to the hilltop.
     One day he decided to confide the story to the *mastrescuela* of the cathe-
     dral, Alvaro Tremiño. The latter helped ensure that an altar was built in the
     house of Juan. However the image continued to appear on the mountaintop.
     Therefore it was decided to move it to a nearby church, but still the image
     continued to appear on top of the old pyramid. Finally it was decided to build
     a chapel at the very spot on which Juan had found the image.

     Many miracles are credited to the image. Devout observers saw that angels
     appeared building the future church before the construction of the chapel.
     This occurred on the very significant day of August 13—the day the zenith
     Sun. (From: *Dos cultos fundantes: los Remedios y Guadalupe (1521–1649):
     Historia documental*, Francisco Miranda Gomez (Zamora, Mexico: El Colegio
     de Michoacan, 2001).

36) Linda Schele and David Friedel, *A Forest of Kings: the Untold Story of the
     Ancient Maya* (New York: William Morrow and Company Inc., 1990) 130, 159.

37) David Stuart, "The Arrival of Strangers: Teotihuacan and Tollan in Classic
     Maya History," in Carrasco, Jones, and Sessions, *Mesoamerica's Classic Heritage.*

38) Ibid. p. 485.

39) Schele and Friedel, *A Forest of Kings*, 161.

40) Aveny, "Out of Teotihuacan," 254-5.

41) Schele and Friedel, *A Forest of Kings*, 130-131.

42) Ibid., 163.

43) Schele and Friedel, *A Forest of Kings*, chapter 6: "The Children of the First
     Mother: Family and Dynasty at Palenque."

44) "The Terminal Classic in the Maya Lowlands: Assessing Collapses. Termina-
     tions and Transformations," Arthur A. Demarest, Prudence M. Rice, and Don
     S. Rice in *The Terminal Classic in Maya Lowlands: Collapse, Transition, and
     Transformation*, edited by Arthur A. Demarest, Prudence M. Rice, and Don S.
     Rice (Boulder. CO: University Press of Colorado, 2004).

45) Neil Arun, "Mass grave yields Mayan secrets," BBC News, November 21, 2005.
     <http://news.bbc.co.uk/2/hi/americas/4450528.stm>, and John Noble Wilford,
     "A 1,200-year-old Murder Mystery of Maya King in Guatemala Begins End of
     Maya Civilization," New York Times, November 17, 2005. <http://lamnews.
     com/1,200-year-old_murder_mystery_of_maya_king_in_guatemala_begins_
     end_of_maya_civilization.htm>.

46) Schele and Fridel, *A Forest of Kings*, 149.

47) Ibid., 356-357.

48) Ibid., 393.

49) The Inca Empire established its new forms under the reigns of the eighth and ninth kings, Viracocha and Pachakutik. The transition between the two rulers therefore marks an important milestone in Inca history. 1438 is the date commonly attributed to the inauguration of Pachakutik's reign. See for example: Victor Von Hagen, *Realm of the Incas* (New York: The New American Library, 1957). This may not be the precise date; it nevertheless gives us an idea of the timeframe in which the Inca Empire underwent its most fundamental transformations.

CHAPTER 2: THE AZTECS

1) Bernardino Sahagun quoted in R. H. Markman and P. T. Markman, *The Flayed God: the Mesoamerican Mythological Tradition: Sacred Texts and Images from the Pre-Columbian Mexico and Central America* (CA: Harper San Francisco, 1992), 388.

2) J. Broda, D. Carrasco, and E. Matos Moctezuma, *The Great Temple of Tenochtitlan: Center and Periphery in the Aztec World* (Berkeley: University of California Press, 1987), 80.

3) Another reference of the same tenor is the following: "There shall be no lack of men to inaugurate the temple when it is finished. I have considered what later is to be done. And what is to be done later, it is best to do now. Our god need not depend on the occasion of an affront to go to war. Rather, let a convenient market be sought where our god may go with his arms to buy victims and people to eat as if he were to go to a nearby place to buy tortillas...whenever he wishes or feels like it." Both references are taken from Diego de Duran, *Historia de las Indias de Nueva España y las Islas de Tierra Firme*, vol. 1, 241-242, quoted in Leon Portilla Miguel, *Aztec Thought and Culture*, trans. J. E. Davis (Norman: University of Oklahoma Press, 1978), 163-164.

4) G. W. Conrad and A. A. Demarest, *Religion and Empire: The Dynamics of Aztec and Inca Imperialism* (Cambridge: Cambridge University Press, 1984), 47.

5) The Aztec migration myth is here taken from Markman and Markman, *Flayed God*. The myth is divided in three segments. The first two appear in *Florentine Codex*; the last one in *Cronica Mexicayotl*.

6) Rafael Girard, *Los Chortis ante el problema Maya*, vol. 4 (Mexico, D.F.: Antigua Libreria Robledo, 1949), 1431.

7) Ibid., vol. 2, 748.

8) Carrasco and Moctezuma, *Great Temple of Tenochtitlan*, 72.

9) Girard, *Los Chortis*, vol. 3, 855 and 936.

10) Carrasco and Moctezuma, *Great Temple of Tenochtitlan*, 151.

11) From *Cantares Mexicanos*, fol. 9-r, quoted in Miguel Leon Portilla, *Pre-Columbian Literatures of Mexico* (Norman: University of Oklahoma Press, 1969), 87-88.

12) Carrasco and Moctezuma, *Great Temple of Tenochtitlan*, 152-3.

13) Douglas Gillette, *The Shaman's Secret: The Lost Resurrection Teachings of the Ancient Maya* (NY: Bantam Books, 1997), 189.

14) G. J. Trejo, "Solar Observations in Ancient Mexico: Malinalco," *Archaeoastronomy* 15 (1990).

15) Mercedes de la Garza, "El juego de pelota segun las fuentes escritas,"*Arqueologia Mexicana* 8, no. 44 (July-August 2000).

    E. C. Krupp, "The Binding of the Years, the Pleiades and the Nadir Sun," *Archaeoastronomy* 5, no. 1 (Jan-Mar 1982).

16) *The Great Temple of the Aztecs: Treasures of Tenochtitlan*, Eduardo Matos Moctezuma (London: Thames and Hudson, 1988), 43.

17) Carrasco and Moctezuma, *Great Temple of Tenochtitlan*, 130.

18) Ibid., 93.

19) Miguel Leon-Portilla, ed., "The Poems of Ayocuan," in *Native Mesoamerican Spirituality: Ancient Myths, Discourses, Stories, Doctrines, Hymns, Poems from the Aztec, Yucatec, Quiché-Maya and Other Sacred Doctrines* (NJ: Paulist Press, 1980), 257.

20) Ibid., "The Thoughts of the Sages," pp. 181-187. Other poems carrying the same theme can be found in Portilla, *Pre-Columbian Literatures of Mexico*. An example is the following: the poet Cuauhtencoztli doubts the reality of life on earth. He says: "I, Cuauhtencoztli, here I am suffering. What is perchance true? Will my song still be real tomorrow? Are men perhaps real? What is it that will survive? Here we live, here we stay, but we are destitute, oh my friends!" (p. 82). Another Nahuatl sacred poem echoes the same theme: "Do men have roots and are they real? No one can know completely what is Your [Giver of Life] richness, what are Your flowers, oh Inventor of Yourself We leave things unfinished. For this I weep, I lament" (p. 69). We will close with another poem agonizing over the question of life after death: "Given to our sadness we remain here on earth. Where is the road that leads to the region of the dead, the place of our landfall, the country of the fleshless? Is it true perhaps that one lives there, where we all go? Does your heart believe this?…I will have to go down there; nothing do I expect. They leave us, given over to sadness" (p. 85).

21) Sahagun, libro III. apendice, cap. I, Porrua, pp. 293-296, quoted in Nahum Megged, *El universo del Popol Vuh: analisis historico, psicologico y filosofico del mito quiche* (Mexico: Editorial Diana, 1991), 251 (translation of the author).

23) Girard, *Los Chortis*, 1433-1434.

24) Carrasco and Moctezuma, *Great Temple of Tenochtitlan*, 73 and 140.

25) Luis Barba, Luz Lazos, Karl F. Link, Agustin Ortiz and Leonardo Lopez Lujan, "Arqueometria en Ia Casa de Las Aguilas," *Arqueologia Mexicana* 6, (May-June 1998).

26) Carrasco and Moctezuma, *Great Temple of Tenochtitlan*, 92-94.

27) Steiner, *Karmic Relationships*, vol. VI, lecture of July 20th 1924 (London: Rudolf Steiner Press).

28) Miguel Leon-Portilla, *Pre-Columbian Literatures of Mexico* (Norman: University of Oklahoma, 1969), 63.

29)   Steiner, *Mephistopheles and Earthquakes*, January 1st 1909 (Vancouver, Canada: Steiner Books Center, Inc.).

30)   Ibid.

31)   Alexander von Wuthenau, *Unexpected Faces in Ancient America, 1500 BC-AD 1500: The Historical Testimony of Pre-Columbian Artists* (New York: Crown Publishers, 1975), chapter 7: "The Question of Semites and Semitic Symbolism." See different masks from all the places quoted, 34-37.

CHAPTER 3: THE IROQUOIS

1)   Rafael Girard, *Historia de las civilizaciones antiguas de America*, vol. 1 (Madrid: Editorial Istmo S.A., 1976), 745- 758.

2)   Ibid., vol. 1, chapter 12: "Culturas femininas en Norte America."

3)   See for example: Paul A. W. Wallace, *The White Roots of Peace* (Philadelphia: University of Pennsylvania Press, 1946).

4)   Charles C. Mann, 1491: *New Revelations of the Americas Before Columbus* (New York: Alfred A. Knopf, 2005), 332-333.

5)   Wallace, *White Roots of Peace*. Other useful retellings of the legend are the following:
     Horatio Hale, *The Iroquois Book of Rites* (New York: AMS Press, 1969).
     Arthur C. Parker, *Parker on the Iroquois* (Syracuse,N.Y.: Syracuse University Press. 1968).
     Thomas R. Henry, *Wilderness Messiah: the Story of Hiawatha and the Iroquois* (New York: Bonanza Books, 1955).
     Nancy Bonvillain, *Hiawatha Founder of the Iroquois Confederacy* (New York: Chelsea House Publishers, 1992).

6)   About Chebiabos see "The White Stone Canoe" in H. R. Schoolcraft, *Schoolcraft's Indian Legends from Algic Researches, The Myth of Hiawatha, Oneota, The Race in America, and Historical and Statistical Information Respecting...the Indian Tribes of the United States*, ed. P. P. Mason (1956; repr., East Lansing: Michigan State University Press, 1991). About Glooskap see Stith Thompson, *Tales of the North American Indians* (Cambridge, MA: Harvard University Press, 1929).

7)   Hale, *Iroquois Book of Rites*.

8)   Rudolf Steiner, *How to Know Higher Worlds* (Hudson,N.Y.: Anthroposophic Press, 1994), chapter 1, "Life and Death: The Great Guardian of the Threshold."

9)   Harry Salman, *The Social World as Mystery Center: The Social Vision of Anthroposophy* (Seattle, WA: Threefold Publishers, 1998).

10) Steiner, *The Portal of Initiation*, 1910 (New York, Steiner Books), and *Three Lectures on the Mystery Dramas*, Basel, Sept. 17, 1910; Berlin, Oct. 31, 1910; and Berlin, Dec. 19, 1911 (New York: Anthroposophic Press).

11) Sergei Prokofieff, *The Occult Significance of Forgiveness* (London: Temple Lodge Publishing, 1991). See chapter 5, "Forgiveness as an Essential Part of the Modern Path to Christ," and chapter 7, "The Nature of Forgiveness and the Sevenfold Manichean Initiation."

12) Matthew Dennis, *Cultivating a Landscape of Peace: Iroquois-European Encounters in Seventeenth Century America* (New York: Cornell University Press, 1993), 101.

13) Bruce E. Johansen, *Forgotten Founders: How the American Indians Helped Shape Democracy* (Boston: The Harvard Common Press, 1982).

CONCLUSIONS

1) Rudolf Steiner, *Inner Impulses of Evolution: The Mexican Mysteries and the Knights Templar*, lecture 3 (Hudson, N.Y.: Anthroposophic Press, 1984).

2) Ibid., lecture 5.

3) Ibid., lecture 3 of September 18, 1916.

4) Ibid.

5) Ibid, lecture 5 of September 24, 1916.

6) Lecture of October 25, 1918 in Dornach.

7) Rudolf Steiner, *The Karma of Untruthfulness*, vol. I, lecture of December 18, 1916 (Forest Row, UK: Rudolf Steiner Press, 2005).

8) Ibid., lecture of December 25, 1916.

9) Steiner, *Ideas for a New Europe: Crisis and Opportunity for the West*, lecture of December 15, 1919 (London: Rudolf Steiner Press).

10) Rudolf Steiner, *New Spirituality and the Christ Experience of the Twentieth Century*, lecture of Oct 17, 1920 (London: Rudolf Steiner Press, 1988). The same idea is reiterated in many other places, for example in Steiner, *Spiritual Science as a Foundation for Social Forms*, lecture of August 7, 1920 (Hudson, N.Y.: Anthroposophic Press, 1986) thus: "In regard to the immediate future, the so-called civilized world faces only two options: Bolshevism on one side, and the threefold social order on the other. He who does not recognize that only these two alternatives exist in the near future understands nothing of the course of events on the larger scale."

11) Rudolf Steiner, *Spiritual Science as a Foundation for Social Forms*, lecture of June 13, 1920 (Hudson, N.Y.: Anthroposophical Press, 1986).

12) Rudolf Steiner, *Practical Advice to Teachers*, lecture of August 22, 1919 (MA, SteinerBooks, 2000).

13) Sergei O. Prokofieff, *The Encounter with Evil and Its Overcoming through Spiritual Science* (London: Temple Lodge, 1999).

BIBLIOGRAPHY

BOOKS AND JOURNALS

Arguedas J. M. and Duviols, Pierre, trans. – *Dioses y hombres de Huarochiri. narracion quechua recogida por Francisco de Avila (1573-1647)* (Lima, Peru: Museo Nacional de Historia y el Instituto de Estudios Peruanos, 1966).

Baldwin, Neil – *Legends of the Plumed Serpent* (New York: Public Affairs, 1992).

Barba, Luis; Lazos, Luz; Link, Karl F.; Ortiz, Agustin and Lopez Lujan, Leonardo – "Arqueometria en la casa de las aguilas," in *Arqueologia Mexicana*, mayo-junio 1998.

Barba de Piña Chan, B. – *Buscando raices de mitos y leyendas Mayas* (Campeche, Mexico: Ediciones de la Universidad Autonoma del Sudeste, 1988).

Berrin, K. and Pasztory, E., editors – *Teotihuacan: Art from the City of the Gods* (New York: Thames and Hudson, 1993).

Bock, Emil – *Moses: From the Mysteries of Egypt to the Judges of Israel* (Rochester, VT: Inner Traditions International, 1986).

Bonvillain, Nancy – *Hiawatha Founder of the Iroquois Confederacy* (New York, Philadelphia: Chelsea House Publishers, 1992).

Broda, J.; Carrasco, D. and Matos Moctezuma, E. – *The Great Temple of Tenochtitlan: Center and Periphery in the Aztec World* (Berkeley, Los Angeles, London: University of California Press, 1987).

Burger, Richard L. – *Chavin and the Origins of Andean Civilization* (New York: Thames and Hudson, 1992).

Burland, Cottie; Nicholson, Irene and Osborne, Harold – *Mythology of the Americas* (London: Hamlyn Publishing Group, 1970).

Carrasco, David; Jones, Lindsay and Sessions, Scott – *Mesoamerica's Classic Heritage: from Teotihuacan to the Aztecs* (Boulder: University Press of Colorado, 2000).

Cheetham, David –"The America's First Colony: a Possible Olmec Outpost in Southern Mexico," in *Archaeology*, Jan.-Feb. 2006.

Clarke, Stephen – Introductory notes to "Rudolf Steiner's Inner Impulses of Evolution's 'Mexican Mystery' lectures," in *Southern Cross* 20 (Autumn 2002).

Coe, M. D. – *The Maya* (Fifth edition) (N. Y.: Thames and Hudson, 1993).

Coe, M. D.; Diehl, R. A.; Freidel, D. A.; Furst, P. T.; Reilly III, F. K.; Schele, L.; Tate, C. E. and Taube, K. A. – *The Olmec World: Ritual and Rulership* (Princeton, NJ: Princeton University Art Museum, 1996).

Conrad, G. W. and Demarest, A. A. – *Religion and Empire: the Dynamics of Aztec and Inca Imperialism* (New York : Cambridge University Press, 1984).

Cooke, Grace – *The Illumined Ones* (Cambridge, U. K.: The White Eagle Publishing Trust, 1966).

Davies, Nigel – *The Ancient Kingdoms of Mexico: A Magnificent Re-creation of Their Art and Life* (London: Penguin Books, 1982).

Deal, David Allen – *Discovery of Ancient America* (Irvine, CA: Kherem La Yah Press, 1984).

De la Garza, Mercedes – "El juego de pelota segun las fuentes escritas" in *Arqueologia Mexicana*, vol. 8, numero 44 (Julio-Agosto 2000).

Demarest, Arthur A. – *Viracocha: The Nature and Antiquity of the Andean High God* (Cambridge, MA: Harvard University Press, Peabody Museum Press, 1981).

Demarest, Arthur A., Rice, Prudence M. and Rice, editors Don S. – *The Terminal Classic in Maya Lowlands: Collapse, Transition, and Transformation* (Boulder, CO: University Press of Colorado, 2004).

Dennis, Matthew – *Cultivating a Landscape of Peace: Iroquois-European Encounters in Seventeenth Century America* (New York: Cornell University Press, 1993).

Dixon, Patrick – "America: the Central Motif," in *Shoreline* 4 (1991).

Fell, Barry – *Saga America* (New York: Times Books, 1980).

– *America B.C.: Ancient Settlers in the New World* (New York: Pocket Books, 1976).

Freidel, David; Schele, Linda and Parker, Joy – *Maya Cosmos: Three Thousand Years on the Shaman's Path* (New York: W. Morrow, 1993).

Gilbert, A. G. and Cotterell, M. M. – *The Mayan Prophecies: Unlocking the Secrets of a Lost Civilization* (Rockport, MA: Element Books, 1995).

Gillette, Douglas – *The Shaman's Secret: the Lost Resurrection Teachings of the Ancient Maya* (N. Y.: Bantam Books, 1997).

Girard, Rafael – *Los Chortis ante el problema Maya* (Mexico, D.F.: Antigua Libreria Robledo, 1949).

– *People of the Chan* (Chino Valley, AZ: Continuum Foundation, 1966).

– *Historia de las civilizaciones antiguas de America* (Madrid: Editorial Istmo S.A., 1976).

Goetz, Delia and Morley, Sylvanus G., trans. – *Popol Vuh: the Sacred Book of the Ancient Quiché-Maya*, from the translation of Adrian Recinos (Norman: University of Oklahoma Press, 1950).

Hale, Horatio – *The Iroquois Book of Rites* (New York: AMS Press, 1969).

Hansen, L. T. – *He Walked the Americas* (Amherst, WI: Legend Press, 1963).

Heiden, Doris – "Una interpretacion en torno a la cueva que se encuentra debajo de la piramide del sol en Teotihuacan" in *American Antiquity*, vol. 40, #2, 1975.

Henry, Thomas R. – *Wilderness Messiah: the Story of Hiawatha and the Iroquois* (New York: Bonanza Books, 1955).

Irwin, Constance H. – *Fair Gods and Stone Faces* (New York: St. Martin's Press, 1963).

Jenkins, John Major – *Maya Cosmogenesis 2012: The True Meaning of the Maya Calendar End-Date* (Santa Fe, NM: Bear & Co., 1998).

Johansen, Bruce E. – *Forgotten Founders: How the American Indians Helped Shape Democracy* (Harvard and Boston, MA.: The Harvard Common Press, 1982).

Johnson, Thomas Crawford – *Did the Phoenicians Discover America?* (London: James Nisbet & Co., 1913).

Koontz, Rex; Reese-Taylor, Kathryn and Headrick, Annabeth – *Landscape and Power in Ancient Mesoamerica* (Boulder, CO: Westview Press, 2001).

Krupp, E. C. – "The Binding of the Years, the Pleiades and the Nadir Sun" in *Archaeoastronomy*, Jan-Mar 1982.

Leon-Portilla, Miguel, translator, editor – *Pre-Columbian Literatures of Mexico* (Norman and London: University of Oklahoma Press, 1969).

– *Aztec Thought and Culture* (Norman and London: University of Oklahoma Press,1978).

– *Native Meso-amenican Spirituality: Ancient Myths, Discourses, Stories, Doctrines, Hymns, Poems from the Aztec, Yucatec, Quiché-Maya and Other Sacred Doctrines* (N.J.: Paulist Press, 1980).

Lowe, Gareth; Lee, Thomas A. Jr., and Martinez Espinosa, Eduardo – "Izapa: An Introduction to the Ruins and Monuments," in *Papers of the New World Archaeological Foundation* (Provo, UT: Brigham Young University, 1982).

Malmström, Vincent H. – *Cycles of the Sun, Mysteries of the Moon: The Calendar in Mesoamerican Civilization* (Austin, TX: University of Texas Press, 1997).

Mann, Charles C. – *1491: New Revelations of the Americas Before Columbus* (New York: Alfred A. Knopf, 2005).

Markman, R. H. and Markman, P. T. – *The Flayed God: the Mesoamerican Mythological Tradition: Sacred Texts and Images from the Pre-Columbian Mexico and Central America* (San Francisco: Harper San Francisco, 1992).

Mc Dermott, Gerald – *Arrow to the Sun* (New York: Viking Press, 1974).

Mediz Bolio, A. trans. – *Libro de Chilam Balam de Chumayel* (Mexico: Ediciones de la Universidad Nacional Autonoma, 1941).

Megged, Nahum – *El universo del Popol Vuh: analisis historico, psicologico y filosofico del mito quiché* (Mexico: Editorial Diana, 1991).

Metraux, Alfred – "Twin Heroes in South American Mythology" in *Journal of American Folklore* (American Folklore Society of Philadelphia) 1946.

Milla Villena, Carlos – *Genesis de la Cultura Andina* (Lima, Peru: Colegio de Arquitectos del Peru, Fondo Editorial C. A. P. , Coleccion Bienal, 1983).

Miranda Gomez, Francisco – *Dos cultos fundantes: los Remedios y Guadalupe (1521–1649): Historia documental* (Zamora, Mexico: El Colegio de Michoacan, 2001).

Mullett, G. M. – *Spider Woman Stories: Legends of the Hopi Indians* (Tucson: The University of Arizona Press, 1979).

Norman, V. G. – "Izapa Sculpture, Part II: Text," in *Papers of the New World Archaeological Foundation* (Provo, Utah: Brigham Young University, 1976).

Osborne, Harold – *South American Mythology* (London: Chancellor Press,1968).

Parker, Arthur C. – *Parker on the Iroquois* (Syracuse, N. Y.: Syracuse University Press, 1968).

Pasztory, Esther – "The Iconography of the Teotihuacan Tlaloc," in *Studies in Pre-Columbian Art and Archaeology*, # 15, 1974, Dumbarton Oaks, Washington D. C.

Piña Chan, Roman – *The Olmec, Mother Culture of Mesoamerica*, ed. Laura Laurencich Minelli (New York: Rizzoli, 1989).

Pinkowski, Jennifer – "A Place by the Sea: Early Urban Planning on Mexico's Pacific Coast," in *Archaeology*, Jan.-Feb. 2006.

Popenoe Hatch, Marion – "An Hypothesis on Olmec Astronomy, with Special Reference to the La Venta Site," in *Contributions of the University of California Archaeological Research Facility: Papers on Olmec and Maya Archaeology* (Berkeley: University of California, June 1971).

Prokofieff, Sergei O. – *The Occult Significance of Forgiveness* (London: Temple Lodge, 1991).

Recinos, Adrian – *Popol Vuh: las antiguas historias del Quiché* (Mexico D.F.: Fondo de Cultura Economica, 1947).

Roys, R. L. – *The Book of Chilam Balam of Chumayel* (Norman: University of Oklahoma Press, 1933).

Santos-Granero, Fernando – *The Power of Love: the Moral Use of Knowledge amongst the Amuesha of Central Peru* (London: Athlone Press, 1991).

Schele, Linda and Miller, Mary Ellen – *The Blood of Kings: Dynasty and Ritual in Maya Art* (New York: George Braziller, 1986).

Schele, Linda and Friedel, David – *A Forest of Kings: the Untold Story of the Ancient Maya* (New York: Morrow and Company, Inc., 1990).

Schoolcraft, H. R. – *Schoolcraft's Indian Legends from Algic Researches, The Myth of Hiawatha, Oneota, The Race in America, and Historical and Statistical Information Respecting...the Indian Tribes of the United States*, 1956, ed. Mentor L. Williams (East Lansing: Michigan State University Press, 1991).

Spinden, H. J. – "The Question of the Zodiac in America," in *American Anthropologist* 18, 1916.

Sprajc, Ivan – "The Venus-Rain-Maize Complex in the Mesoamerican World View: Part II," in *Archaeoastronomy* #18 of 1993.

–   *Venus, lluvia y maiz: simbolismo y astronomia en la cosmovision mesoamericana* (Mexico: Serie Antropologica, Instituto Nacional de Antropologia e Historia, 1996).

Steiner, Rudolf – *Inner Impulses of Evolution: the Mexican Mysteries and the Knights Templar*, 1916 (Hudson, N.Y.: Anthroposophic Press, 1984).

–   *The Deed of Christ and the Opposing Spiritual Powers*, 2 lectures, 1909 (Rudolf Steiner Publications, 1976).

–   *The Mission of Folk-Souls in Connection with Germanic-Scandinavian Mythology*, 1910 (Blauvelt, New York: Garber Communications).

–   *The Spiritual Guidance of the Individual and of Mankind*, 1911 (N.Y.: Anthroposophic Press, 1992).

–   *The Fifth Gospel*, 1913, (London: Rudolf Steiner Press, 1998).

–   *The Gospel of Saint Mark*, 1912 (Hudson, N.Y.: Anthroposophic Press, 1986).

–   *True and False Paths in Spiritual Investigation*, 1924 (London: Rudolf Steiner Press, 1985).

–   *Mystery Centers*, 1923 (Blauvelt, N.Y.: Garber Communications).

–   *Man and the World of the Stars: The Spiritual Communion of Mankind*, 1922 (N.Y.: Anthroposophic Press, 1963).

–   *Founding a Science of the Spirit*, 1906 (London: Rudolf Steiner Press, 1999).

–   *Karmic Relationships*, vols. 1, 3, 5, 6, 7 1924 (London: Rudolf Steiner Press, 1977).

– *The East in the Light of the West*, 1922 (N.Y.: Anthroposophic Press, 1940).
– *Turning Points of Spiritual History*, 1911-1912 (MA: SteinerBooks, 2007).
– *From Symptom to Reality in Modern History*, 1918 (N.Y.: Anthroposophic Press, 1976).
– *The Christ Impulse and the Development of Ego Consciousness*, 1910 (N.Y.: Anthroposophic Press, 1976).
– *The Book of Revelation and the Work of the Priest* (18 lectures and questions-and-answer sessions in Dornach from 5 to 22 September 1924) (London: Rudolf Steiner Press, 1998).
– *Ideas for a New Europe: Crisis and Opportunity for the West* (London: Rudolf Steiner Press).
– *Spiritual Science as a Foundation for Social Forms* (N.Y.: Anthroposophic Press, 1986).
– *Mephistopheles and Earthquakes*, 1909 (Steiner Books Center, Vancouver, Canada).
– *How to Know Higher Worlds*, 1904 (N.Y.: Anthroposophic Press, 1994).
– *The Portal of Initiation*, 1910 (NJ: Rudolf Steiner Publications, 1961).
– *Cosmic Memory*, 1904 (N.Y.: SteinerBooks, 1987).
– *Three Lectures on the Mystery Dramas*, Basel, 1910-1911 (N.Y.: Anthroposophic Press, 1983).
– *World History and the Mysteries in the Light of Anthroposophy*, 1923-24 (London: Rudolf Steiner Press, 1997).
– *Practical Advice to Teachers*, 1919 (MA: Anthroposophic Press, 2000).
Sugiyama, Saburo – *Human Sacrifice, Militarism and Rulership* (Cambridge: Cambridge University Press, 2005).
Taladoire, Eric – "El juego de pelota Mesoamericano: origen y desarrollo" in *Arqueologia Mexicana* 44, no. 8 (Julio-Agosto 2000).
Tedlock, Dennis, trans. – *Popol Vuh: The Definitive Edition of the Mayan Book of the Dawn of Life and the Glories of Gods and Kings* (New York: Touchstone Books/ Simon and Schuster, 1985).
Thompson, Stith – *Tales of the North American Indians* (Cambridge, MA: Harvard University Press, 1929).
Townsend, Richard, ed. – *Ancient Americas: Art from Sacred Landscapes*, The Art Institute of Chicago (Munich: Prestel Verlag, 1992).
Trejo, G. J. – "Solar observations in Ancient Mexico: Malinalco," in *Archaeoastronomy* # 15 of 1990.
Trento, Salvatore Michael – *The Search for Lost America* (Chicago: Contemporary Books Inc., 1978).
Uriarte, Maria Teresa – "Practica y simbolos del juego de pelota," in *Arqueologia Mexicana* 44, no. 8, Julio-Agosto 2000.
Villacorta J. Antonio C. and Rodas Flavio N. – *Manuscrito de Chichicastenango (Popol Buj)* (Guatemala: Sanchez and De Guise, 1927).
Von Hagen, Victor – *Realm of the Incas* (New York: The New American Library, 1957).
Von Wuthenau, Alexander – *Unexpected Faces in Ancient America, 1500 BC-AD 1500: The Historical Testimony of Pre-Columbian Artists* (New York: Crown Publishers, 1975).

Wallace, Paul A. W. – *The White Roots of Peace* (Philadelphia: University of Pennsylvania Press, 1946).

Williamson, Glen – *The Mexican Mysteries and Pre-Columbian Art: The Influence of the Deed of Vitzliputzli on Mesoamerican and Andean Culture (33- 1492 AD)* (unpublished paper, July 1999).

Williamson, R. A. – *Archaeoastronomy of the Americas* (Los Altos: Ballena Press, CA.; and College Park, MD.: Center for the Archaeoastronomy cooperative publication, University of Maryland, 1981).

Zuidema, R. Tom – *La Civilisation Inca au Cuzco*, Collège de France, essays et conferences (Paris: Presses Universitaires de France, 1986).

INTERNET AND NEWS SOURCES

About Mayan Murals of San Bartolo
Peabody Museum of Archaeology and Ethnology, "The Early Maya Murals at San Bartolo, Guatemala," <http://www.peabody.harvard.edu>

Thomas H. Maugh II, "Mural Reveals Pre-Classic Maya as a Civilized Society," *Los Angeles Times*, December 14, 2005.

About Early Olmec Writing
References: Early Olmec Writing? The Cascajal Block, <Archaeology.about.com/od/olmeccivilization/a/cascajal_block.htm>

Mesoweb Reports: the Earliest Precpolumbian Writing, Joel Skidmore (Precolumbia Mesoweb Press). <www.mesoweb.com/reports/Cascajal.pdf>

About Isthmian (Epi-Olmec) Writing
Ancient Mask Adds to Corpus of Isthmian Script: 100 BC to 500 AD?, <www.ancientscripts.com/epiolmec.html>

Beyond the Family Feud: After Decades of Debate, Are Younger Scholars Finally Asking the Right Questions About the Olmec?, Andrew Lawler, Archaeology, March/April 2007).

Early Maya Writing at San Bartolo, Guatemala, William A. Saturno, David Stuart, Boris Beltrán, <www.sanbartolo.org/science.pdf.>

About Massacres in the Ancient Maya City of Cancuen
Neil Arun, "Mass grave yields Mayan secrets," BBC News, November 21, 2005 at <http://news.bbc.co.uk/2/hi/americas/4450528.stm>

John Noble Wilford, "A 1,200-year-old Murder Mystery of Maya King in Guatemala Begins End of Maya Civilization," New York Times, November 17, 2005. <http://lamnews.com/1,200-year-old_murder_mystery_of_maya_king_in_guatemala_begins_end_of_maya_civilization.htm>.

www.ingramcontent.com/pod-product-compliance
Lightning Source LLC
Chambersburg PA
CBHW020656270326
41928CB00005B/145